North of Empire

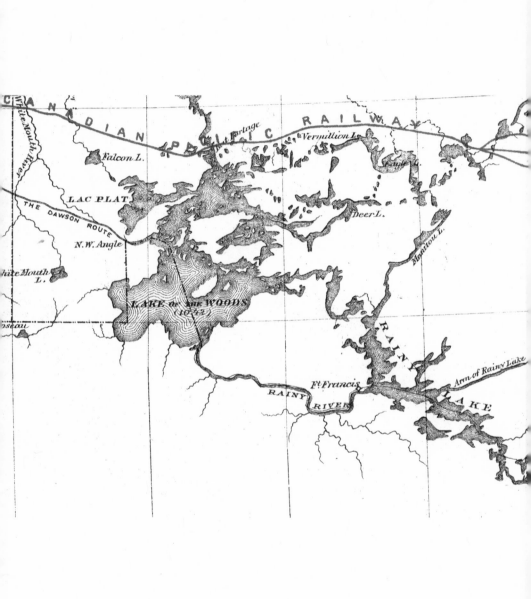

North of Empire

Essays on the
Cultural Technologies
of Space

Jody Berland

DUKE UNIVERSITY PRESS
Durham and London 2009

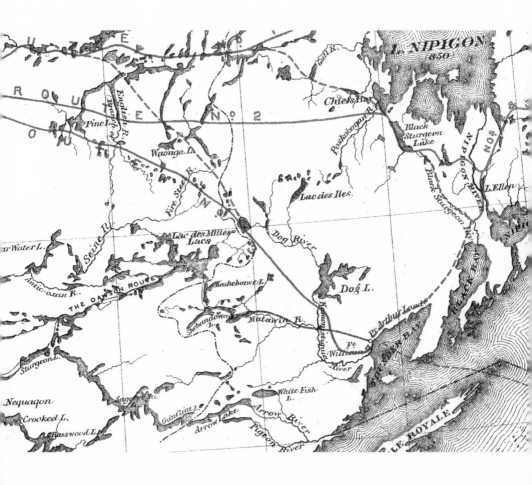

© 2009 Duke University Press. All rights reserved. Printed in the United States of America on acid-free paper. ∞ Designed by Jennifer Hill, typeset in Arno Pro by Achorn International. Library of Congress Cataloging-in-Publication Data appear on the last printed page of this book.

This book is dedicated to my dear parents,
Jayne and Alwyn Berland.

Nature and history seem to have agreed to designate us in Canada for a corporate, artistic role. As the U.S.A. becomes a world environment through its resources, technology, and enterprises, Canada takes on the function of making that world environment perceptible to those who occupy it. Any environment tends to be imperceptible to its users and occupants except to the degree that counter-environments are created by the artist.—MARSHALL MCLUHAN, *Canada: The Borderline Case*

The question of "speaking as" involves a distancing from oneself. The moment I have to think of the ways in which I will speak as an Indian, or as a feminist, the ways in which I will speak as a woman, what I am trying to do is trying to generalize myself, make myself a representative, trying to distance myself from some kind of inchoate speaking as such. There are many subject positions which one must inhabit; one is not just one thing. That is when a political consciousness comes in.—GYATRI SPIVAK, *The Postcolonial Critic*

My theorem that there is no philosophical "first thing" is coming back to haunt me. Much as I might be tempted, I cannot now proceed to construct a universe of reasoning in the usual orderly fashion. Instead I have to put together a whole from a series of partial complexes which are concentrically arranged and have the same weight and relevance. It is the constellation, not the succession one by one, of these partial complexes which has to make sense.—THEODOR ADORNO, correspondence, in *Aesthetic Theory*

Contents

There were times when the pleasant prospect of acknowledging my debts was the only thing that kept me interested in finishing this project. Every book is testimony to the generosity of the author's mentors, teachers, colleagues, friends, relatives, and editors, who make its completion possible and its pages intelligible. My parents, Jayne and Alwyn Berland, have been all of these. I also write in remembrance of Ioan Davies and Alex Wilson, who shared their gifts with so many of us, and of my mother, whose heart still beats.

This writing has benefited from the critical insight of Katey Anderson, Alwyn Berland, Marcus Breen, Rosemary Donegan, Zoe Druick, Greg Elmer, Len Findlay, Jean Franco, Simon Frith, Barbara Godard, Larry Grossberg, James Hay, Brenda Longfellow, Richard Maxwell, Scott McCracken, Richard Rathwell, Ned Rossiter, Robinder Kaur Sehdev, Ato Sekyi-Otu, Sarah Sharma, Jennifer Daryl Slack, Cheryl Sourkes, Will Straw, Susan Willis, Greg Wise, and Bob Wright. I am grateful to the book's anonymous reviewers for their kind and constructive insight, to Ken Wissoker and Courtney Berger at Duke University Press for their wisdom and patience, and to Mark Mastromarino for his thoughtful editing. They did their best with me.

I would also like to thank David McKie, Brian Shoesmith, the Department of Media Studies, Edith Cowan University; Ien Ang; Tony Bennett; the Social Sciences and Humanities Research Council of Canada; the Department of Communication Studies, Concordia University; Atkinson College, the Office of Research Administration, the Faculty of Graduate Studies, the Graduate Program in Culture and Communication, the Division of Humanities, and the Faculty of Arts, York University, for their academic support.

These chapters were written and rewritten over a period of time in which technological, political, and cultural changes have both clarified and deranged my thought. Editors are never unsung heroes in my world. Earlier versions appeared in the following publications.

"Writing on the Border," CR: The New Centennial Review 1, no. 2 (2001): 139–69. Published by Michigan State University Press.

"Space at the Margins: Colonial Spatiality and Critical Theory after Innis," TOPIA: Canadian Journal of Cultural Studies 1 (1997): 55–82; and in Harold Innis in the New Century: Reflections and Refractions, edited by Charles Acland and William Buxton (Montreal: McGill-Queens University Press, 2000). Used by permission of McGill-Queen's University Press.

"Spatial Narratives in the Canadian Imaginary," New Formations: A Journal of Culture/Theory Politics 57, theme issue The Spatial Imaginary (2005/2006). Used by permission of Lawrence and Wishart.

"Angels Dancing: Cultural Technologies and the Production of Space," in Cultural Studies, edited by Lawrence Grossberg, Cary Nelson, and Paula Treichler (New York: Routledge, 1991). Used by permission of Taylor & Francis Books.

"The Musicking Machine," in Residual Media, edited by Charles Acland. (Minneapolis: University of Minnesota Press, 2007).

"Locating Listening: Technological Space, Popular Music, Canadian Mediations," Cultural Studies 2, no. 3 (1988); and in The Place of Music, edited by Andrew Leyshon, David Matless, and George Revill (New York: Guilford Press, 1998). Used by permission of Guilford Press.

"Weathering the North: Climate, Colonialism, and the Mediated Body," Provincial Essays 8 (1989), theme issue Shifting Fields: Images of Colonialism and the Look of the Postcolonial; and in Relocating Cultural Studies, edited by Valda Blundell, John Shepherd, and Ian Taylor (London: Routledge, 1993). Used by permission of Taylor & Francis Books.

"Mapping Space: Imaging Technologies and the Planetary Body," *Found Object* 5 (spring 1995): 7–19, theme issue *TechnoScience/Cyberculture*; and in *Technoscience and Cyberculture*, edited by Stanley Aronowitz, Barbara Martinson, and Michael Menser (New York: Routledge, 1996). Used by permission of Taylor & Francis Books.

"Cultural Technologies and the 'Evolution' of Technological Cultures," in *Contemporary Cultural Theory and the World Wide Web*, edited by Andrew Herman and Thomas Swiss (New York: Routledge, 2001). Used by permission of Taylor & Francis Books.

There is nothing more wonderful than the exchange of ideas, and I hope the twenty-first century university will continue to offer a place for that to happen. I am grateful for the perspicacity and generosity of graduate students and research assistants over the years: Neil Balan, Natallia Barykina, Kelly Bronson, Yolande Daley, Murray Forman, Daniel Hadley, Mike Hunter, Rob Kerford, Jean Koo, Jess Malkin, Tanner Mirlees, Marcia Ostashewska, Robinder Kaur Sehdev, Sarah Sharma, Lyndon Way, and Lesley Williams. This book took a long time to complete as a consequence of illness. I thank Dr Alison Bested, many talented health workers, and Canada's health system for making it possible.

Special thanks to Bob Hanke, my sweetheart, critic, comrade, and culinary magician.

Mapping *North of Empire*

I want to begin with a quite central theoretical point which to me is at the heart of Cultural Studies but which has not always been remembered in it. And this is that you cannot understand an intellectual or artistic project without also understanding its formation; that the relation between a project and a formation is always decisive; and that the emphasis of Cultural Studies is precisely that it engages with *both*, rather than specializing itself to one or the other.—RAYMOND WILLIAMS, "The Future of Cultural Studies," *The Politics of Modernism*

Just as none of us is outside or beyond geography, none of us is completely free from the struggle over geography. That struggle is complex and interesting because it is not only about soldiers and cannons but also about ideas, about forms, about images and imaginings.—EDWARD SAID, *Culture and Empire*

The movie *American Dreamz* (Paul Weitz, 2006) opens with the delightful premise that the president of the United States wishes to catch up on his reading. The day after reelection to his second term, he decides to lie in bed and read the newspapers. As attention switches to the television Mr. President isn't watching, we discover that weeks have passed and he has disappeared from public view. There are rumors he has suffered a nervous breakdown. As we return to the presidential bedroom, the chief of staff, a perfect ringer for Dick Cheney, storms into the room and demands to know what the president, now surrounded by paper, is up to. "You want to be careful with that pile," the president cautions. "That is the Canadian Press." The chief of staff is dumbfounded. "Who outside of Canada gives a shit about the Canadian Press?" he wants to know. "They are our neighbor," Mr. President mumbles, "and . . ." Before you know it, he is on "happy pills" and wearing a ventriloquist's earpiece.

In recent years, there is no surer sign of satiric intent in American films and late night television than a reference to Canada. In *American Dreamz*, reading the Canadian press is prima facie evidence of mental instability in the Oval Office. In *South Park: The Movie* (Trey Parker, 1999), American parents panic about Canadian pornography creeping across the border and demand that the army wage war against the corruptors. "They're not even a real country," they warble in *South Park*'s Academy Award–winning song, "Blame Canada." In *Canadian Bacon* (Michael Moore, 1995), in which several concerned Americans charge the border and attack the enemy in Toronto, Jim Belushi jokes about the cities lined up on the Canadian border to forestall an American invasion.[1] In *The Daily Show*, reference to Canada signals a moment of political panic or gay fantasy detour before the performer takes a breath and returns to normal. "Canada" stands in here for both the absence of politics and despair about politics; the joke expresses a strongly ambivalent affect that can safely be discharged against the one group who will never demand retribution. It is easy to forget that the United States did in fact invent a war for electoral purposes (against the Philippines, in the late 1880s), that Belushi is not altogether mistaken about the cities built along the U.S. border, and that Canadian newspapers sometimes have, you know, different perspectives on world affairs. So what makes these jokes funny?

Aside from providing American entertainment with crucial natural resources—humor and talent—Canada appears in postwar transnational media culture in two distinct discursive contexts. In the first, Canada is a model international citizen responsible for founding the United Nations and initiating an international peacekeeping force that travels the world enforcing truces. Here Canada stands for political moderation, tolerance, multiculturalism, and sophisticated mediation skills personified by its writers and politicians, one of whom, former prime minister Lester Pearson, won a Nobel Peace Prize for his work for the UN. This image of exemplary cosmopolitanism has been refurbished since Canada legalized same-sex marriage and decriminalized marijuana, refused to join the war against Iraq, and salvaged the touring career of the Dixie Chicks. In the second discourse, Canada is a poignant instance of what happens when a country loses control of its media and natural resources. Here Canada is a colony that struggled to become a nation and disappeared back into a colony. Early researchers in the media imperialism school warned of the dangers of "Canadianization": the loss of sovereignty that arises when you see the world through another country's eyes. In a "tragic paradox" Canada built a cross-country public media infrastructure only to lose control of its contents.[2] In both of these simplified accounts, the country is characterized by fluid boundaries with either positive or negative effects. American political humor seems to bring these two meanings together. We could invade Canada, but it wouldn't matter, and anyway we already have. And yet, the subject keeps coming up. Evidently there is something about that border. . . .

This border is the subject of the first chapter of *North of Empire*. "Writing on the Border," proposes that Canadians experience a form of double consciousness similar to yet profoundly different from the "doubling" of black consciousness described by race theorists such as W. E. B. Du Bois, Frantz Fanon, and Paul Gilroy.[3] In this writing, the black person sees himself from the vantage point of both the other and himself, and experiences an irresolvable schism between the two perceptions. Rather than remaining invisible behind the veil of the raced body, the Canadian hides behind verisimilitude, "passing" as the other while recognizing the other as not oneself. This vantage point is double-reflected through a one-way mirror in which "America" does not see Canada at all. The nonknowing of the other is part of what the Canadian knows, and it shapes her scholarship and art. In the first epigraph to this book, Marshall McLuhan argues that the porous quality of Canada's borders provides Canada's thinkers with particular insights on the media age. "Nature and history seem to have agreed to designate us in Canada for a corporate, artistic role," he suggests. "As the U.S.A. becomes a world environment through its resources, technology, and enterprises, Canada takes on the function of making that world environment perceptible to those who occupy it. Any environment tends to be imperceptible to its users and occupants except to the degree that counter-environments are created by the artist."[4] Could it be this creative counterreflection that so compels Hollywood scriptwriters to joke about invading the country to their north? Only psychoanalysis can unravel the unconscious acts through which humor, revenge, power, and ambivalence reiterate their logic in the relationship between the two countries. Categorically, as everyone knows, "No one in 'America' loves an anti-American";[5] this causes difficulties for Canada, which is "in 'America'" and yet not. Under the circumstances, the best solution is to be "as Canadian as possible, under the circumstances."[6]

North of Empire addresses the politics of media culture in connection to a border that separates different approaches to the study of both media and space. On the northern side, scholarship has tended to understand culture in terms of a longstanding struggle around sovereignty and space, while to the south, a growing literature on culture and globalization holds the very premise of borders open to question. Canadian research foregrounds media technologies as agents in the production of space, knowledge, and power, while Anglo-American cultural studies considers the focus on media technology suspect or simplistic. Negotiating this double duality counteracts blind spots on both sides of the border. There are theoretically sophisticated authors who consider Canada too provincial to produce its own complex accounts and the United States too universal to require them. Some scholars "apply" contemporary theory to support the claim that Canada imposes a narrative of singular identity by the elementary fact of being a nation. They impose a universalizing narrative on a space whose history they forgot, while scholars on the other side of the border and the ocean forget the space and its history altogether. Hoping for a different kind of dialogue with these ideas, I explore both the concept of media space and the space in which this concept emerged in connection with the study of empire. I connect this inquiry to culture and power through an analysis of cultural technologies that mediate and shape our sense of ourselves and the places and times of everyday life. In this introduction, I review these methodological and political commitments and consider how they inform and trouble one another.

This book began as a collection of essays that traveled across (a decade of) time and (a country away of) space to find a publisher. Its vantage point from the margin or "counterenvironment" is in this context both actual and symbolic. My first prospective publisher in the United States determined that Canada was not part of the Americas after all, and returned the manuscript. My second and third attempts failed because the publishers were in Canada, a country whose cultural industries are over 90 percent foreign owned; with the smaller market, publishing an academic book, like producing a film or recording an album, requires government subvention. A manuscript like this one containing more than 30 percent previously published material is ineligible for such support. Formative (for me) essay collections by Harold Innis, Theodor Adorno, Walter Benjamin, Roland Barthes, Michel Foucault, James Carey, Stuart Hall, Gayatri Spivak, Homi Bhabha, Donna Haraway, Doreen Massey, Meaghan Morris, Larry Grossberg, Andrew Ross, or Rey Chow, for instance, would not be eligible for publication under this policy. Meanwhile, my colleagues and I are accustomed to receiving letters from American and British editors saying that our work might be of interest if references to Canada could be removed. This power/knowledge complex can be quite discouraging. Fortunately, Duke

University Press welcomes Canadian scholarship, and I have been able to revise this work for the press without abandoning its origins.

This story reiterates the trajectory of a capitalist Second World country which functions as both colonizer and colonized. This trajectory invites a translation of media analysis into postcolonial critique and vice versa through dialogue with cultural studies and Canadian communication theory. *North of Empire* explores the fragmented and globalized landscapes of "teletopographic" culture; that is to say, the technical, historical, and discursive shaping of cultural practices in which distance is simultaneously inscribed in and overcome by mediating technologies, and considers the role of such teletopographic practices in shaping (as they are shaped by) concepts of identity and justice. This project elaborates Innis's premise that empire is constituted through means of communication, a theme explored at length in "Space at the Margins" (chapter 2), and McLuhan's related premise that the media must be understood in relation to changing topographies of space, a theme that underscores this book as a whole. Like others informed by their work, I have learned to think about culture in the context of a complicated social and material process that reproduces and extends itself in space and time.[7]

In McLuhan's cartography, nations and neighborhoods have become equally irrelevant, the planet shrunk irrevocably to the space of a screen by the electronic pathways of contemporary media. In calling this new entity a "global village," McLuhan joins the influences of his Catholic faith with the assumption popular in the 1960s that television's real-time representation of suffering in one part of the world would inevitably produce empathy and action in another. "In a culture like ours, long accustomed to splitting and dividing all things as a means of control," begins *Understanding Media*, "it is sometimes a shock to be reminded that, in operational and practical fact, the medium is the message. This is merely to say that the personal and social consequences of any medium—that is, of any extension of ourselves—result from the new scale that is introduced into our affairs by each extension of ourselves, or by any new technology."[8] Anglo-American cultural studies scholars have largely sided with Raymond Williams's critique of McLuhan for overstating the consequences of the medium. As Williams argues, media technologies are agents in a complex and often unpredictable social process in which we are not passive entities.[9] McLuhan's claim that television creates a global village betrays the shortcomings of his media formalism. But his premise that each new medium reorganizes the communication system as a whole, alters social space and scale, and realigns the human senses is nonetheless incontrovertible. This premise is one of the pillars of Canadian communication theory, which posits that you can acknowledge the codeterminant forces of capitalist relations and geopolitical contexts while insisting that each medium has specific material properties which extend and alter the knowledge and perception of its users.

"We can perhaps assume," Innis ponders, "that the use of a medium of communication over a long period will to some extent determine the character of knowledge to be communicated and suggest that its pervasive influence will eventually create a civilization where life and flexibility will become exceedingly difficult to maintain."[10] A new medium can unleash creativity but if left unchecked can result in a monopoly of knowledge forms and inflexibility in the forms, relations, and spaces of communication. In Carey's summary of Innis's approach, changes in technologies of communication affect culture by altering the structure of interests (the things thought about), the character of symbols (the things thought with), and the nature of community (the arena in which thought developed).[11] Anticipating the idea that "all technology is biotechnology," these scholars subvert the dualism that separates idealist and materialist historiography because they "never consider human history as anything else than an *embodied history* inscribed upon the *communis sensus*. History is human history or *biotextual* because it alters our sensory and cognitive ratios but always in concert with the history of our land, its rivers and forests, its fish, fur and minerals."[12] This tradition locates communication as a material practice; distance, land, and proximity as conditions and outcomes of this practice; and eyes and ears as biosocial mediators of their own prosthetic histories.

This understanding of history reminds us of the dangers of measuring new technologies by what their users say about them. To rely on such accounts is to "remain divorced from a relation to subsequent production, which is the actual, *historically effective* measure of reception."[13] In "Angels Dancing" and the chapters that follow, I explore technological changes in culture in connection with this idea. While electronic communication makes space increasingly homogeneous and heterogeneous, the regulation of space is central, in ways that users may not recognize, to the practices of power. Part of the constitution of mediated or teletopographic geopolitical space is the growing distance between those who cannot discern these connections and those for whom such connections are fundamental. This difference is one meaning I have in mind when I use the term *culture*.

Reflections on Culture

A few hundred years ago, culture was peripheral to the philosophical exploration of meaning. With the rise of modern means of reproduction and academic disciplines, it now occupies the center of such inquiry. As Michel Foucault demonstrates in *History of Sexuality*, a proliferation of discourse suggests an underlying governmental project that is as important as any explicit purpose manifested in the texts. This idea has particular poignancy with respect to culture, for the more that media culture produces and circulates meanings, the less people seem to know or care about what "meaning" is. In part we can attribute this dilemma to the culture industry, through which the tangible, affective issues experienced in peoples' ordinary lives are condensed and crystallized into charismatic textual operations in increasingly large-scale spatial and economic contexts. In coining the term "culture industry," Theodor Adorno and Max Horkheimer also anticipated these Canadian critiques of modernity, arguing that "the technical contrast between the few production centers and the large number of widely dispersed consumption points" is simply evidence of the fact that "a technological rationale is the rationale of domination itself." As a consequence, "the gigantic fact that speech penetrates everywhere replaces its content."[14] In these accounts, modern culture is both where such effects are produced and the realm within which we learn to feel and assess such effects. Modernity thus produces a dazzling field of self-referentiality that these authors exemplify and sometimes misunderstand.

Thinking about culture in the context of these issues requires a double consciousness in which the thinker is—or I am—obliged to think about how (and where) I think when I think about culture. As Williams so famously noted, "Culture is ordinary";[15] it is the part of everyday life through which we understand and feel our solidarities and differences with others. But this observation may now disguise as much as it illuminates. We live with increasing proliferation of cultural experiences, affects, commodities, and mediations which face the challenge of supporting a mundane and often disappointing everyday life while simultaneously offering a virtual mode of transport out of it. Ordinariness shifts and doubles back on itself. Signs (brands, symbols, interfaces, digital tools) seem more alive than what they represent. Such liveliness can reconcile a listener with her afternoon or persuade her never to live that afternoon again. In the shadow of the modern and morphing spaces of empire, culture still produces diverse implications and effects.

My analysis of these issues draws on Canadian communication theory and critical theory as intellectual traditions posing powerful challenges to discourses of economic rationality and technological progress, and like them I link these aspects of modernity to conquest, colonization, and empire.[16] Both schools of thought deploy multiple analytical perspectives to probe these processes from a self-consciously decentered or marginal vantage point.[17] To do so they had to be "theorists against themselves";[18] they had to find ways to assess their own knowledge production reflexively in relation to the overwhelming technological bias, present-mindedness, and economic instrumentalism of Western capitalist modernity.

These ideas shape my thinking and challenge me at every step. If my knowledge of the world is shaped by technological mediation, how is it possible to rethink it? If Western culture is dominated by spatial perspectives and ambitions, what defines a critical politics of space? If culture is about belonging, and there is so much culture, why is belonging so fraught? If place is problematic, can I love and hate my own? And finally, who or what determines the answers to these questions? *Culture* is not an answer to these questions, but a term that has organized how Western intellectuals have posed them and what is thought to be at stake in doing so. To address such questions reflexively is to acknowledge the uses and the limits of culture as we generally understand it, and to reopen these interpretive and political debates.

McLuhan's concern is not symbolic culture but rather the heretofore invisible grammar of media such as print and television and their shaping of human perception. "The man in a literate and homogenized society ceases to be sensitive to the diverse and discontinuous life of forms. He acquires the illusion of the third dimension and the 'private point of view' as part of his Narcissus fixation, and is quite shut off from Blake's awareness or that of the Psalmist, that we become what we behold."[19] Even "after" print, we are subject to multiple forces that reproduce this privatized perspective. In "probing" intellectuals who consider themselves exempt from the perspectives they critique, McLuhan draws on Innis's recognition that

We must all be aware of the extraordinary, perhaps insuperable, difficulty of assessing the quality of a culture of which we are a part or of assessing the quality of a culture of which we are not a part. In using other cultures as mirrors in which we may see our own culture we are affected by the astigma of our own eyesight and the defects of the mirror, with the result that we are apt to see nothing in other cultures but the virtues of our own. I shall assume that cultural values, or the way in which or the reasons why people of a culture think about themselves, are part of the culture.[20]

Here culture is not just a symbolic system within a representational field; like Williams, McLuhan is concerned with a larger field of ontology and power/knowledge complex that shapes, and is shaped by, the properties of knowledge transmission. These ideas challenge us to think through, beyond, and against the systems of symbolic meaning and expression that dominate our study of the realm of culture. McLuhan foregrounds the sensory and ontological grammar of the media in order to emphasize its role in producing and disguising epochal changes in Western culture. Adorno evokes "culture" only to interrogate the fetish that cultural criticism makes of its forms and purposes.[21] Signifying "English Canada" follows an analogous logic; it asserts national identity but rejects the logic of identity through which the modern nation-state "others" the world. In *North of Empire* I take account of these three moves—the foregrounding of material media properties, the reflexive questioning of the discursive codes of cultural analysis, and the challenging of the logic of identity—as not just analogous, but also deeply interconnected. The book pursues this theme across a range of cultural forms and practices.

Canada's formative literature on culture joins the idea of culture to political goals of nation-building and political sovereignty, and, within these definite constraints, to the idea of justice and equity in difference. The energetic history of this literature inspired me to pay close attention to changing imbrications of culture and government. If culture is a mode of government within which identity and subjectivity are produced and regulated, where does utopian imagination or transformative solidarity arise? Where can it take us? Innis warned academics to resist the orientation toward management needs, as this would transform the university into "reserve pools of labour to supply political parties" (or more currently, telecommunication companies and creative industries). Overwhelmed by perceived parallels between culture administration and fascism (a less bizarre claim than it appeared to foundational thinkers in what we now call cultural studies), Adorno posits the negative dialectic as the only truly ethical response.[22] Wary of the elitism of mass-culture critique, Tony Bennett proposes a strategy of institutional research dedicated to the reform and administration of specific cultural technologies.[23] You might call these probes, prisms, and pragmatics long-term and short-term approaches to the problem of criticizing the culture of which one is a part. Each seeks to shed light, as Judith Stamps suggests, on "the interplay of the material and ideal forces that led to the eclipse of dialogue and dialectical processes in the West."[24]

The corporate transformation of the academy represents one such interplay in our contemporary environment. Another is the ever-increasing mobility of cultural commodities, texts, practices, values, and subjects as they flow across the existing borders of language, discipline, state, and global space. Such movement changes the nature of (but does not eliminate) borders and boundaries and the identities and discourses constituted by them. This process is generated within and without these borders. Underlying the problematic interplay of material and ideal forces is the continuous innovation of technologies that mediate our spaces and subjectivities. If technological environments remain opaque when we are accustomed to them, rapid technological change shocks our sense-making strategies and destabilizes our cultural, sensory, and collective modalities.

> The division of faculties which results from the technological dilation or externalization of one or another sense is so pervasive a feature of the past century that today we have become conscious, for the first time in history, of how these mutations of culture are initiated. Those who experience the first onset of a new technology, whether it be alphabet or radio, respond most emphatically because the new sense ratios set up at once by the technological dilation of eye or ear, present men with a surprising new world, which evokes a vigourous new "closure," or novel pattern of interplay, among all of the senses together. But the initial shock gradually dissipates as the entire community absorbs the new habit of perception into all of its areas of work and association.[25]

Despite McLuhan's prognosis of numb absorption, anxiety is the inescapable companion of information altered and transmitted at the speed of light.[26] Individuals must exert considerable effort and thought to persuade themselves that they are the agents of such change. In fact contemporary scholarship theorizes agency differently in the wake of such technological change. Social and cultural studies of technology concur that we share our human agency with keyboards, software, and implants (if less comfortably with the hands that assemble such technologies or recycle them as toxic trash). New technologies present compelling opportunities (for some) to revive their sense of agency and personal freedom. Through this process, as I show in "The Musicking Machine" (chapter 5) and "Weathering the North" (chapter 7), skill and agency are constantly redefined along with the processes through which we valorize and transmit them. The reflexivity offered by postcolonial theory, Canadian communication theory, and environmental politics shows that we are exercising a will to power whose satisfaction comes with a price. The dark side of modernity demands that we calculate the costs as clearly as the benefits so insistently paraded before us.

Reading Cultural Technologies

Rather than theorizing culture in the abstract, as part of a social or ideological totality, or as the arbitrary outcome of diverse techniques of identity and subject formation, *North of Empire* investigates the trajectory of specific cultural technologies as they mediate and alter relations between human bodies, technology, space, and empire. This gives "space" a substantial theoretical mandate which can only be met through connection with the other terms. I explore such connections through a range of practices: from nation-building to pianos, music recording, the television weather forecast, the Internet, and satellite-imaging technologies through which our global sensorium is extended ever upward and out.

The concept of cultural technology is commonly traced to Foucault's work on "governmentality," and signals the intent to address a wider field of interactions than the discussion of communication technology ordinarily invokes. Jim McGuigan understands the term "to reference the 'machinery' of institutional and organizational structures and processes that produce particular configurations of knowledge and power."[27] When Bennett approaches the museum as a "cultural technology" of history, he locates the museum as a governmental institution responsible for the regulation of knowledge and social conduct.[28] In *Technologies of Gender*, Teresa de

Lauretis points out that feminist film theorists were approaching cinema as a "social technology" or "cinematic apparatus" contemporaneously with but independently of Foucault's work; she emphasizes "not only how the representation of gender is constructed by the given technology, but also how it becomes absorbed subjectively by each individual whom that technology addresses." Thus, "the F next to the little box, which we marked in filling out the form, has stuck to us like a wet silk dress. . . . The construction of gender is the product and the process of both representation and self-representation."[29]

My use of the term draws on and elaborates these various senses of the term. It refers to the formal, phenomenological, and social properties of media technologies together with the machineries of knowledge and power through which they emerge and within which they work, and it acknowledges the subjects and subjectivities produced through interaction with these technologies along with their heterogeneity and ambivalence. The term *cultural technology* connects the various processes and practices that comprise culture: the materialities that produce it (radios, televisions, photographs, pianos, satellites, computers, networks, and books like this one); the geopolitical contexts within which such media emerge; the complex machineries of spatial dissemination through which their structures and materialities circulate and are put to use; the discourses and narratives through which such processes are made meaningful and familiar; the symbolic practices, disciplines, and forms of literacy and skill that arise in connection with them; the modes of political and corporate governmentality that define and order these contexts; the responsive subjectivities acting within them; and the fissures and spaces in which oppositions or alternatives are inspired and imagined. Addressing these processes and practices in relation to a critique of empire acknowledges that these technologies, machineries, practices, and subjectivities do not proliferate randomly or endlessly, but emerge within and are shaped by specific geopolitical regimes.

In *North of Empire*, the stories we tell, contest, and enact are important agents in the fabrication of ourselves and of the spaces we inhabit. Media technologies secure a working relationship with the practices, needs, and understandings of people who employ them. These interactions are shaped by narrative frameworks and technological forms. "Whatever human rationality consists in, it is certainly tied up with narrative structure and the question of narrative unity."[30] The search to reestablish narrative unity in the face of technological velocity is an important impulse in the "ordinary" production of culture. As I show, the ascendancy of neoliberalism has relied on a concerted mobilization of narratives: the frontier, progress, sovereignty, entertainment, convenience, mobility, globalization, evolution, freedom. Understanding these narratives as part of the assemblage of cultural technologies helps to contest the way they are being mobilized irrationally to promote so-called rational technological or other ends.

Heidegger famously argues that "the essence of technology is by no means anything technological. Thus we shall never experience our relationship to the essence of technology so long as we merely conceive and push forward the technological, put up with it, or evade it."[31] This insight can be usefully extended to a critique of the literature on globalization, which commonly attributes this process to the proliferating speed and scale of information and computing technologies. "Although communication technologies are absolutely central to the globalization process, their development is clearly not *identical* with cultural globalization." While technology is expanding instrumentally and symbolically through globalization, "the media form only part of the total process by which symbolic meaning construction proceeds and only one of the forms in which globalization is experienced culturally."[32] If globalization is taken up by Western scholars in terms of the expansion of media and electronic space, it is equally the product of corporate expansion and economic "re-structuring," political revision, transnational migration, and cultural practice. "*Just as there can be no cultural transmission without technological means,*" Regis Debray emphasizes, "*so there is no purely technological transmission.*"[33] Media may be inseparable from their technical properties, but media technologies succeed for reasons that are not purely technological. Similarly, it is possible to analyze specific national contexts without overdetermining the administrative agency of the nation-state.

As part of the modernization and postmodernization of society, cultural technologies are implicated in changing structurations of space and time in the forming and fragmentation of communities; the development and transformation of national communities; the transmission of collective values and memories; the spectacular translation of information to image; the exploitation and management of the physical environment; the administration of wealth, poverty, industry, and war; the social adoption of new information technologies; and the spatial and discursive contexts in and through which these activities and experiences take place. To emphasize the degree to which cultural technologies connect these domains is not to say that they pursue an entirely utilitarian logic. Like the idea of culture, the term has the potential to "face both ways," and to provide a critical ground for immanent critique.[34]

To historicize technological assemblages such as that among pianos, piano rolls, sheet music, and magazines or among satellites, image processing, digital graphics, prediction software, and television, is to engage with these issues. Building on the questions Williams brought to television as a cultural technology, they broaden our understanding of the media's dynamic capacities to organize historically significant social-technical assemblages.[35] What were their conditions of emergence? What institutions were involved, and how did they change? What narratives and desires fueled their emergence and dissemination, and how were they taken up by diverse interests? To what extent have these technologies shaped the modes of attention or structures of thought that contemplate their effects? To what extent are they shaped by their imbrication with one another? Can their analysis shed any light on relations of power or positive transformation?

Cultural Technologies of Space

The promise that technology will enhance freedom has repeatedly legitimated the extension of technological systems across and into private and public space. Because technology is such a powerful myth whether in the broader sense of organizing beliefs or in Barthes's particular sense of "de-historicizing speech,"[36] it is not possible to advance the cause of citizenship or justice without a critique of that myth. This requires rethinking of the relationship between technology, space, and discourse through which thought acquires its worldly dimensions. As Terry Eagleton writes, "The very word *culture* contains a tension between making and being made, rationality and spontaneity, which upbraids the disembodied intellect of the Enlightenment as much as it defies the cultural reductionism of so much contemporary thought": Like "culture" and "gender," "space" contains tensions between process and object, being and being made.[37]

A similar rethinking of process and object has changed our understanding of space. "Is space a social relationship?" Lefebvre asks.

Certainly—but one which is inherent to property relationships (especially the ownership of the earth, of land) and also closely bound up with the forces of production (which impose a form on that earth or land); here we see the polyvalence of social space, its "reality" at once formal and material. Though a product to be used, to be consumed, [space] is also a means of production; networks of exchange and flows of raw materials and energy fashion space and are determined by it. Thus this means of production, produced as such, cannot be separated either from the productive forces, including technology and knowledge, or from the social division of labour which shapes it, or from the state and the superstructures of society.

In capitalist space, nature's space is replaced by space-qua-product, to the degree that space becomes a central category for connecting matter and thought. "In this way, reflexive thought passes from produced space, from the space of production (the production of things in space) *to the production of space as such.*"[38]

North of Empire elaborates this idea by situating cultural technologies in the context of their role in forming the spaces of empire. Said defines imperialism as "the practice, the theory, and the attitudes of a dominant metropolitan center ruling a distant territory."[39] Such practices and attitudes are lived as complicated everyday realities. As Massey demonstrates, the time-space compression of the planet involves an unequal "power-geometry" through which people are placed and mobilized differently, often reinforcing power imbalances that were there already.[40] The growing multinationalism of capital production involves "the stretching out of different kinds of social relationships over space, [which] means also the stretching out over space of relations of power. . . . Along with the chaos and disorder which characterize the new relations there is also a new ordering of clear global-level hierarchies."[41] Extending this thought, Canada and the United States both exist because European settlers pillaged and foraged indigenous lands and populations. But Canada has been "ordered" as both subject and object of empire. Canada is now more closely tied to the American economy than is any other Western nation, and as its closest neighbor and largest trading partner has experienced greater vulnerability to American politics, finances, military investments, and cultural industries than any other country.[42] The sense of being marginal to a "dominant metropolitan center" and divided within its borders—the "split screen" described in "Locating Listening" (chapter 6)—is formative to its constitution.

My work on cultural technologies of space began with my interest in the electronic reproduction of music, and particularly the ways that it mediates listeners' relations with their surroundings.[43] The more media technologies alter space, my research suggested, the more they seem to speak to the question of where we "belong." Music's temporal preponderance in radio and subsequent media accentuates the importance of producing a sense of belonging through the changing triangulation of technology, artistry, and pace. Changes in the mediation of sound introduce changes in other media and in the practices of listening. Just as the automated piano finds a home in the domestic space it helps to create, as I argue in "The Musicking Machine" (chapter 5), so radio history arises from and helps to create the mediation of musical forms, publics, and social spaces, as I show in "Locating Listening" (chapter 6). "Radiophonic" space is not one thing: it emerges from a particular conjunction of music cultures, sound recording technologies, modes of dissemination, and techniques of administrative and demographic production which together with the spaces and feelings of everyday life constitute the cultural technologies of listening.

Like music, weather mediates connections between our bodies and our social and natural environments. As I show in chapters 7 and 8, this mediation is itself mediated by technocultural forms, practices, and desires. Playing or listening to music and watching the weather forecast both depend on communication media joining together diverse technologies and forms of knowledge in specific sites of convergence. These cultural technologies work in conjunction with one another to shape the world within a larger media ecology (in McLuhan's terms) or historical conjuncture (to use a familiar term in cultural studies). They play a significant role in shaping how we understand and experience our environments. Acknowledging the continuities and sometimes unpredictable discontinuities in their history provides a valuable counterpoint to the shadow of technological determinism that haunts medium theory.

I employ the concept of the topos to extend the question of technology to encompass and connect the materialities of communication, longstanding habits of expression and feeling, and meanings of place. Communication technology, colonial history, popular culture, and administrative knowledge are different knowledge systems that overlap and intersect to form the topos. What Belton describes as the "dialectic between the description of a place and its production as a space" overturns the idea that a space *precedes* its interaction with these knowledges and practices. Rather, the topos is formed by

> the interaction of a literary system of scientific, academic and novelistic narratives with global systemic capitalism. These interactions worked to produce and distribute knowledge about that system's periphery. The distribution of this knowledge—a process intimately associated with the extension of concepts of modernity and development—has over time produced an historically layered and sometimes contradictory archive of information. Narratives within this archive that refer to specific regions and places provide raw data that helps to form the *topos* (imaginary cultural image) of a place.[44]

Corporations and nation-states deploy powerful and sometimes competing cultural technologies to reconstitute the topos at various scales while seeming to responding to citizens' desire for community and belonging. To think about technology in its relationship to topos is to draw attention to the contradictory logic of the spatial imaginary.

This project has particular relevance for a "new world" which comes into representation through the mediation of modern communication systems. Margaret Turner describes the writing of this so-called new world as an "infinite rehearsal," through which "the simultaneous construction and representation of the culture results in a continual remaking of the discursive place, or recreation of cultural space in which, as Paul Carter puts it, places might eventually be found."[45] As her comment illustrates, Canada's discourse on space continuously elaborates ideas about place, ethics, history, and belonging, and explores their role in binding together inhabitants who lack a shared history. Writers suggest that such discussions mark Canada as the exemplar of the postmodern nation (see chapter 1, "Writing on the Border," and chapter 3, "Spatial Narratives in the Canadian Imaginary").[46] It is certainly the most teletopographic, given the degree to which it has been lived and archived in terms of the inscribed interdependency of technology and distance.

Technically, "teletopography" describes the practice of determining coordinates, altitudes and heights, distances, and "true (geographic, not magnetic) north for geographical azimuths."[47] Having resolved to unify a large land mass with regionally dispersed settler communities, Canada famously relied on space-conquering technologies to assemble a nation-state.[48] The connection between landscape and technique is continuously reaffirmed in the iconographic languages of Canadian nationalism. The technologies of valorizing and overcoming distance, and the ways these technologies produce the spaces they simultaneously represent, are a central part of the Canadian topos. Because explorers traversed, conquered, and mapped this vast landscape, because this teletopographic work was foundational to nation-building, and because imaging technologies are now enveloped in a continental apparatus, Canada occupies a secure niche in the military-industrial complex, wherein it specializes in optical technologies, continental aerospace surveillance, and outer space robotics (see chapter 8, "Mapping Space"). Technology thus represents both the precondition for social connection and the continuous geopolitical mobilization of power/knowledge that defers and diffuses such connection.

The connection between teletopography and the North offers irresistible ground for metaphorical play. The North appears in the cultural imaginary as a mythic topos in which distance is part of its representational vocabulary. Because we "have" the North, "we" are the north. There is an obvious disconnect between this imaginary of the North and the experience of those who live there. That said, it is possible to describe the country's "coordinates" as teletopographic in three respects: in terms of Canada's reliance on technology as a material solution to the settlement of a small colonial population over a large land mass; in terms of its status as a satellite of the United States, whose cultural products are widely disseminated and consumed via that same technology; and in terms of the complicated translation of these technomaterial realities into the discursive structures, symbolic landscapes, modes of knowing and speaking, and shared experience that constitute what we call culture. This translation inspires artists, philosophers, satirists, and communication theorists to return frequently to the narrative and technological inscription of space, as I show in "Writing on the Border" (chapter 1) and "Spatial Narratives in the Canadian Imaginary" (chapter 3).

Space, Foucault suggests, is a relation between sites.[49] Nowhere is this more salient than in Canada, a country formed by competing British and French imperial ambition which opened its doors to the United States in aid of sovereign economic development and then sought to develop multilateral political institutions to offset American influence. Not surprisingly, Canadians claim to feel as if they belong to more than one space, "more than one history and more than one group."[50] The country is comprised of at least three founding nations; the French and English, who are recalled daily in both official languages, and the First Nations, who are rising up to reclaim their stolen lands. In this topos, globalization is a powerful process within as well as outside the country's borders. If Canada and the United States are both colonial projects, their approaches to technology and space have followed different trajectories. For instance (although this is not an instance, but a central argument), the nineteenth-century idea of an endlessly receding horizon advanced by America's "Manifest Destiny" reappears in the twentieth-century vision of a new respatialized frontier in cyberspace, and fuels twenty-first century ideas about transformation through digital technologies. As I show in "Cultural Technologies and the 'Evolution' of Technological Cultures" (chapter 9), the frontier's geopolitical history is extended through cyberpolitics and the militarization of space. "America" is constituted by a longstanding preoccupation with frontiers and an optimistic view of technology as a solution to its manifest difficulties. English Canadian cultural theory resists both ideas by elaborating the connections between them.

North of Empire

For philosopher George Grant, writing in the 1960s, Canada's difference held out the possibility of living outside the technological consensus of capitalist liberalism. Here the question of culture is founded in the critique of technology which prizes open unacknowledged contradictions in liberal capitalism. "The frenzied drive to 'freedom through technique' is, in a word, the horizon of modern culture," he writes. "And as with any horizon which serves, after all, to envelop the human project in a coherent system of meaning, we can never be certain of our ability to think against and beyond the horizon of technical reason." In this horizon, reflexivity is a tragically lost opportunity. As Darin Barney writes,

> This symbiotic relationship between liberal politics and technology underscores the reality that liberalism is not, as many of its contemporary exponents would claim, a purely procedural constitutional order

devoid of substantive preferences and content. Liberalism is a politics of getting-out-of-the-way of technological mastery and the material progress it always promises and sometimes delivers. . . . The public good is equated with the economically rational, which, in any given instance, is defined by either individual accumulation or corporate efficiency [in which] legitimate public purposes are those that are amenable to technological solutions.[51]

In Grant's portrayal of American liberalism (a prescient description of university research policies today), technological "progress" and American imperialism are justified through the idea of a universal culture founded on an open market.[52] Since this universal culture stands in for and helps to advance a neoliberal model of progress and freedom, resistance to it seems inexplicable; it suggests failure to understand the relationship between capitalism and democracy which America so generously shares with the rest of us.

From the rise of the frontier mythology as an early narrative of American destiny,[53] to Michael Hardt's and Antonio Negri's *Empire* (2000), limits to America have been targeted as a function of the nature America was meant to conquer. Ian Angus argues that these texts share with the Monroe Doctrine the readiness to justify the transborder extension of the U.S. constitutional project by reference to the legacy of the frontier. "'The great open American spaces ran out,'" Hardt and Negri explain; "'the open terrain had been used up,' closing off the 'boundless frontier of freedom.'"[54] Hardt and Negri have acknowledged the controversy created by their claim that there is no outside to empire. "This Empire has no center and it has no outside," they explain in a 2001 interview. "(We do recognize, on the other hand, that US history does occupy a privileged position in the formation of Empire and that is where our analysis of the US role becomes more complex, but that is a somewhat different matter and allow us to set that aside for the moment.)"[55] But it is one thing to set aside the position of the United States parenthetically and another to reproduce its logic. This discussion perpetuates the idea of a limitless horizon of new technological capacities in which geography means everything and nothing. This strange dissemination has a long history. "The open space just ran out," Angus muses in his commentary on *Empire*:

> Not a geo-political or geo-cultural space, but a simply geographical space that is the only one that can "run out" or be "used up" in this way. The

politico-cultural discourse is brought to a decision-point because of an entirely non-political, non-cultural, geographical determinism. They do not consider that it might have been first opposed and then displaced— onto the space race as the "final frontier," for example—and still today be a constituent component of U.S. political culture.[56]

The rhetoric of natural ending displaces the contingencies of history and represses the recognition that this history unfolds into the present, where it is represented by the rhetoric of technology. A critical project that cannot confront its own legacy must fail to acknowledge the political subjects who enacted this original "decision-point" in the form of a border. The frontier remains a continuous "frontier of liberty" which (as Angus puts it) "the Yankees have been so kind as to export."[57]

Of course Canada had its own frontier (so to speak) and its own history of dispossession in the making of it, and the narrative logic of Canadian nation-building is also complicit with this history. Angus's point is that the American frontier ended at the 49th Parallel to the north and the Rio Grande to the south because of politics, not a predetermined geographical space. The denial of this outcome appears in the name the country gives itself, America; the frontier myth persists in the fact that America cannot offer an intelligible account of its borders, but projects across them the terror that insidiously threatens its freedom. This inscription of space differs markedly from that animated by the British Commonwealth, whose model of empire depended on the identification of others to whom progress and civilization could be brought.

Hardt and Negri draw on Gilles Deleuze's and Felix Guattari's analysis of deterritorialization and reterritorialization as the inevitable outcome of capitalism and view strategies of reterritorialization as mainly reactive, artificial, and perverted.[58] In this antiteleological teleology, there is little space for a positive politics of place. This idea has a larger circumference than their argument suggests. It is a convention in the literature on globalization from both the Left and the Right to argue that national borders have lost their relevance to the lives of people worldwide. Ulrich Beck presents the rhetorically familiar picture of an irreversibly globalized world:

> Globalization means that borders become markedly less relevant to everyday behaviour in the various dimensions of economics, information, ecology, technology, cross-cultural conflict and civil society. It points

to something not understood and hard to understand yet at the same time familiar, which is changing everyday life with considerable force and compelling everyone to adapt and respond in various ways. Money, technologies, commodities, information and toxins "cross" frontiers as if they did not exist.[59]

The question is not so much whether this is true, but what it means for thinking about the territories being crossed. For Beck, globalization presents an opportunity to confront the global challenges of environmental crisis without worrying about the demise of the nation-state. In other accounts global networks make nations obsolete, along with laws and governments which nonetheless participate in and reap the benefits from global networking technologies. In such accounts the concept of place is associated with "status and nostalgia, and with an enclosed security," Massey observes;[60] writers need to "face up to—rather than simply deny—people's need for attachment of some sort, whether through place or anything else."[61] It is no accident that this superior stance is so often linked to poststructuralist theory, with its tendency to "conflate the mobility or instability of the sign with existential freedom, and to confine the practice of critically nuanced thinking within specific ethnic parameters."[62] This paradigm infers that government and "public interest," are irrelevant, and that imperialism has no discernable geography. Like place, these concepts are relegated to the dusty bins of nostalgia and conservative regret.

Such dismissals reduce the role of government to the security state. In so doing they replicate the ambitions of transnational corporations while depriving activists of one axis of resistance to them. As Saskia Sassen argues, the transformation of the world economy does not displace national governments but transforms their functions. "Much of the writing on globalization has failed to recognize [the work of national legislatures and judiciaries, firms and markets, actors and processes] and has privileged outcomes that are self-evidently global."[63] In her analysis of the U.S. state since the 1980s, the processes identified with globalization—privatization, deregulation, marketization of public functions—actually "effected a significant shift of power to the executive . . . [and] an increased inequality in the power of different parts of the government."[64] Needless to say, the U.S. state apparatus has fought energetically to ensure that such administrative changes extend beyond its borders.

In any case, the paradigmatic experience of globalization for many people is not rapid mobility over long distances but displacement in one place.[65] The history of this process precedes modern means of communication, since the First Nations were violently conquered and to some extent demobilized by settlers fighting to bring the "New World" into being.[66] For Massey, "This point concerns not merely the issue of who moves and who doesn't, although that is an important element of it; it is also about power in relation *to* the flows and the movement."[67] Globalization doesn't implicate everyone equally; there are powerful and disempowered parts of the planet, and there are rich and poor, fast and slow classes within them. Canada's banks and oil and gas extraction industry are earning unprecedented billions in profits, while UNESCO scolds its government for the millions of children who live in poverty. For many people, government still matters. The places, rights, and resources that frame their lives matter, even or especially when they are being so visibly rewritten.

Or not so visibly. In a series of secret meetings initiated in Banff, Alberta, in 2006, "High-level politicians and business elite from Canada, the United States and Mexico discussed whether openness about their goals or continued secrecy called 'evolution by stealth' better suited their plans for strengthening border infrastructure."[68] Their social Darwinist narrative reinforces a topos of continental integration to advance corporate interests and the political agenda of the Right. Like the terrorism that defines America's monster, Canada's monster can no longer be projected outward to an external enemy. Globalization was here from the beginning, not something that came from elsewhere. The emphasis on "evolution" advanced in these proceedings shows how problematic the *post* in *postmodern* (if this is what Canada is) can be.

The Arguments

The encounter between Canadian communication theory and cultural studies offers an opportunity for reimagining the hermeneutic loop between place, culture, technology, and theory that so beguiles us north of the 49th. This imbrication arises from a history of struggles around culture where more than culture is at stake. The first three chapters address the paradoxical articulation of cultural technologies of space with the formation of

Canadian nationhood. The second group of chapters extends these ideas to music, sound technologies, and the production of space. The cultural technologies of music locate listeners in a diverse range of locations, contexts, and dispositions. Such technologies redefine *musicking* while contributing to and legitimizing their own spatial and discursive expansion. Echoing this theme, "Weathering the North" (chapter 7) and "Mapping Space" (chapter 8) explore technologies of mediation between nature and culture related to the weather forecast. "Cultural Technologies and the 'Evolution' of Technological Cultures" (chapter 9) connects these themes to the influential narrative of technological evolution. Extending the idea of the frontier through cyberspace and beyond, these final chapters draw our attention to where we must all learn to look: the increasingly militarized terrain of outer space.

These chapters advance three principal arguments concerning culture, space, and empire. The first is that electronic mediation is central to the constitution of social space, and that such mediation is pivotal to an anti-imperialist critique. To struggle against the ossification of centers and margins, it is necessary to reject a mimetic relationship between technological enhancement and future redemption (progress = progress, etc.), and to acknowledge that such enhancement disguises and impedes as well as precipitates social change. Forgetting this turns space into a metaphor, imperialism into a ghost, and culture into a lucrative pastime.

My second argument is that the continuity of this theme warrants a serious examination of narrative practices and their current efficacy. In Canadian writing and artistic practice, "space" functions metonymically (as it does more broadly in cultural studies after the "spatial turn") to describe connections between politics and culture. As a narrative moving across disciplines, genres, and media forms, this tradition encourages a reflexive and open-ended practice of storytelling, rather than a ritualistic reiteration of a fixed story already told. Stories matter. We inhabit them when we check the "F" box and when we see Canada represented as the snowy or feminine side of a continental system. There is a connection between how space is traversed, how it is narrated, and how it is used. I trace this principle at work in mapping (in the order in which they appear) the border, the margin, the landscape, the radio, the railway, the home, the weather, the sky, and cyberspace, as topos constituted by narrative and through the cultural technologies of space.

Like "sexuality," "technology," or "culture," space rehearses a powerful discourse of diverse meanings. Reflexivity aims to bring space down to earth and to the level of bodies that matter. The importance of feminist theory in bringing forward the interconnections of human and other bodies, forms of power, and the substance of representation, cannot be overstated. Feminist environmentalism builds on this legacy with its awareness of embodiment, the destruction of nature, and the lassitude of governments that sign away our futures. These are vital challenges, not all of them external to our endeavors as researchers in communication and culture. Cultural studies has been exceptionally slow to acknowledge the challenges posed by the physical environment.

My third argument thus concerns the spaces constituted by matter. David Harvey proposes that "all socio-political projects are ecological projects and vice versa"; thus "some conception of 'nature' and 'environment' is omnipresent in everything we say and do."[69] For Felix Guattari, "Without modifications to the social and material environment, there can be no change in mentalities. Here, we are in the presence of a circle that leads me to postulate the necessity of founding an 'ecosophy' that would link environmental ecology to social ecology and to mental ecology."[70] However placeless the world looks, however teletopogaphic the view, we still depend on water, air, and land. Communities can only partially be reconstituted through memories and stories. My computer will join millions of tons of toxic waste generated each year by communicating technologies. What we do in society, we do in the natural world that we inhabit and exploit. The natural world is also being speeded up, spectacularized, recommodified, damaged, poisoned, and forgotten. It too is perilously threatened by the neoliberal commodification of everything, including life. As computer and digital device manufacturers greedily plunder the world's natural resources and clutter up its landfill, our food and water poisons us, our weather confounds us, our future threatens us, and our animals break our hearts. We manipulate dualistic categories, but we cannot defend them.[71] We need better conceptual maps to cultivate and sustain the social and cultural diversities that are required to defeat nonsustainable ideas, technologies, and ways of life.[72] The desire to connect these matters owes something to the teletopographic subject. It knows how to inhabit several places at the same time, how to hold contradictory thoughts together in a single trope. This "amphibology" is the source of

Canada's popular internationalism,[73] its relative racial and sexual tolerance, its attractive sense of irony, and its hypocritical parading of progressive social values while millions of children starve.

Postscript on Method

We live in an invented state, but we don't agree on what is meant by "state," or by "nation," "globalization," or "culture." To counter this confusion, many academics use analytical terms as substantive terms: *globalization, postcolonialism, subject, hegemony.* These are complicated dynamic processes layered on one another, not concrete or discrete entities. The use of these terms to substitute for analysis is not so different from the obfuscation we critique in the Right: *terrorism, unnatural, taxpayer, national interest.* Every subject has a history; every history stores—even where it seeks to hide—traces of conflict. In the ahistorical cultures of the new world, it is easy to be dazzled by and to collaborate with the rhetorics of the new. To critique the compulsions of modernity (as I argue in the final chapter) is to abandon the rhetoric of inevitability. It takes time to think through histories and spaces and the relations between them.

To understand the present, I believe you need to listen. To listen, you need to talk.[74] I talk to people anywhere there is an opportunity. I try to remain alert to subjects and moods as they drift through the diverse situations of journalists, shopkeepers, taxi drivers, artists, hairdressers, activists, students, neighbors, transport workers, relatives, and the academy. I am interested in what makes people angry, hopeful, companionable, ambitious, indifferent. When Israel invaded Lebanon and the death toll mounted, I couldn't leave the house without losing half a day. The pet food salesman talked for half an hour; neighbors and salespeople could not contain their outrage. In being present to the world, there is no escaping it.

My Toronto neighborhood encompasses McLuhan's spacious family home and an economically and ethnically diverse part of Toronto recently nicknamed "the world."[75] The energies that connect and divide this neighborhood can point us toward a rethinking of the cultural technologies of space. Cultural studies is dedicated not only to the elaboration of meaning, but also to the exploration of the "resources of hope." In a late essay, Williams argues that "the habit of separating the different kinds of good from each other is entirely a consequence of a deformed social order." Identifying changes in the natural environment and the international economic order as decisive, Williams posits three critical challenges: a reuniting of politics, economics, and the environment that refuses to treat nature or people as raw material; a renewed sense of connection with reconstituted nature; and a move from "society as production" to society as a whole way of life.[76] Williams's essay, published in *Toward 2000*, cogently anticipates Guattari's "Three Ecologies," published in 2000, with its insistence on reconstellating social, mental, and environmental ecologies as the prerequisite to hope.

This approach does not ascribe hope to a particular medium, place, sense, or group of people. It insists rather on restoring balance to the relations among and between them. In that spirit, *North of Empire* invites readers to consider how researchers and citizens can engage with and contest the powerful processes of spatial abstraction and reification in which we are suspended, to subject the spectacles of empire to the challenges of reflexivity and transformative energy we seek to represent, and from these unsettled spaces to bring constellations of possible action and meaning into being.

one

Writing on the Border

Culture is always an idea of the Other (even when I reassume it for myself).
—FREDRIC JAMESON, "On Cultural Studies"

Those who only know one country know no country well.
—SEYMOUR LIPSET, "Pacific Divide"

Crossing the Border

I was twelve when I first crossed the border from the United States into Canada. My American classmates viewed my family's departure to that country with a combination of envy and alarm. Like them I would not have been surprised to find igloos in the towns with the streets full of dog sleds. My ignorance about my new home was astounding. But it was commonplace.

I was reminded of this memory by a storyline featured in the CBC satire show *This Hour Has 22 Minutes*, which ran through the late '90s and early 2000s. Each week featured an episode in which the comedian Rick Mercer interviewed Americans about Canada. Whether interviewing ordinary people on the street, Ivy League academics, political staffers, or a presidential candidate, Mercer's "Talking to Americans" segments turned his subjects' ignorance about their northern neighbor into ludicrous jokes. For several years, a growing audience witnessed friendly Americans congratulating Canada on the arrival of FM radio, personal fax machines, a second area code, and power steering. (Americans don't know that Canada houses the continent's largest automobile factories, generates significant innovations in communication technology, and remains their country's largest trading partner. But we do.) Interviewees sent cheery messages to "Canadian Prime Minister Tim Horton," congratulating him on his "double double" as though this was an appropriate prime ministerial accomplishment. (Tim Hortons, a popular doughnut shop chain named after a hockey star, was then running a TV ad campaign in which border officials distinguished returning Canadians from impostors by their knowledge of Tim Hortons. A "double double" is, of course, double sugar double cream. Subsequently purchased by Wendy's, Tim Hortons is no longer a Canadian company.) They begged the government not to close down Canada's last remaining university, Eaton's U. (Eaton's, a prominent, family-owned department store chain once identified with home catalogues, had just gone bankrupt. Universities are open for business.) They urged Canada to legalize VCRs (although a larger percentage of Canadians own VCRs, telephones, and computers than do their American counterpoints);[1] allow the introduction of a daily newspaper (though Toronto, where I live, produces five dailies in English, four in Chinese languages, and as many again in other languages); and change Canada's clocks, which interviewees were ready to believe ran on a twenty-hour cycle, to avoid disruption with American schedules. A parade of camera-ready Americans congratulated Canada for officially joining North America, and urged the mayor of Toronto not to restore the Toronto Polar Bear Hunt, which, they insisted, would be a "naive and uneducated" act. (There are no polar bears in this bioregion outside the zoo, which may soon provide their only habitable place of residence.) Amicably ignorant of the social safety net of which Canada has been most proud, they signed a petition, on camera, urging Canadians to stop putting their elderly out to die on icebergs.[2]

On the famous February 28, 2000, episode, Mercer interviewed the presidential candidate George W. Bush and the governor of Michigan (a border state), a key supporter of Bush's campaign. Pausing in the midst of a crowd of cameras and microphones, both men gracefully acknowledged the endorsement of Prime Minister Jean Poutine ("poutine" is the name of a popular Quebec dish of fries, gravy, and melted cheese curds) notwithstanding the fact that the then prime minister, Jean Chrétien, shares his surname with Canada's then ambassador to the United States, Raymond Chrétien, his nephew. By the time a compilation of the *Talking to Americans* segments was broadcast as a one-hour special in 2001, Mercer was Canada's most popular comedian.[3] *Talking to Americans* was an iconic event in Canadian pop culture and remains unequaled in television ratings. In a January

The comedian Rick Mercer interviews Americans at
Princeton University, 2000. Photograph by Bob Hanke.

Mercer informs George W. Bush of Prime Minister "Poutine's"
support for his presidential campaign, 2000. Photograph by
Bob Hanke.

2005 prime time broadcast, the fifth in less than four years on the public
network, it drew just under a million viewers, surpassing ratings for CBC's
regular audience grabber *Comedy Week* by almost 300 percent.[4] It is now the
most watched single hour in Canadian television history.

All this says something about Canada. After all, it was Canadians who
were watching, laughing, scripting the questions, and piling the cameras on
the planes to fly home to Halifax, Nova Scotia, where 22 *Minutes* is produced.
You don't have to be Canadian to get the joke, but you might not otherwise
understand its ironic complexity.[5] What made these interviews work so well

for their viewers was the shared implicit understanding that "getting it" did not require them to combat the invisibility so caustically mocked, except ironically, amongst themselves. Canadian comics are expected to be ironic, politically astute, and adept with play on televisual conventions. This formula depends on three essential assets: the ability to work collectively and individually in a small ensemble; a good working relationship with a video camera; and a sharp intellectual critique of contemporary media culture. Often associated with television programs like 22 *Minutes* and its famous forerunner, SCTV, these assets were first and perhaps most brilliantly joined by the three Toronto artists who exhibited, performed, and published together as General Idea (1969–94). Before elaborating on the subject of irony, however, we need to approach this much-publicized romp on a more obvious level. To represent or reflect on Canada is to write to, about, and across the border. Scholars claim that "Canada is unthinkable without its border with the USA,"[6] and they agree that its symbolic status has no parallel in American consciousness. This is the truism north of the 49th: Canadians live and write as though the border is everywhere, shadowing everything we contemplate and fear, while Americans live and act as though there is no border there at all. Americans visiting the country like to say that Canada is "just like home," congratulating their hosts for their apparent sameness on the basis of a day of ethnographic experience of hotels and airports. Their relief from anxiety about language or primitive conditions is palpable. This friendly gesture enables the visitor to seize control of his ignorance and offer it to his listeners. This behavior confirms his listeners' beliefs.

Dissimilar social constructions of the border pinpoint a fundamental difference between these countries which provokes us to think about narrative and power. History has produced diverse relationships to what borders themselves define: the social habitation of space and the self-delineation of collective subjects in relation to others. "The longest undefended border in the world" produces radically different meanings to the territories it divides. This border topos involves two protagonists, an attentive one and an inattentive one, which is not unusual in a close partnership between two unequal powers. "The beauty of being a ruler," comments Terry Eagleton, "is that one does not need to worry about who one is, since one deludedly believes that one already knows. It is other cultures which are different, while one's own form of life is the norm, and so scarcely a 'culture' at all."[7] This comment conveys the taken-for-grantedness of an imperial culture such as England, which assumes its right to bring its civilizing mission to distant parts of the globe. It assumes that it is the powerful who register, assess, and forgive the "difference" detected in the less powerful. But United States culture reverses the imperial gaze. Other cultures must pay attention, and Americans memorably fail to know back. Staunch exemplars of what Georg Lukács called "power-protected inwardness,"[8] or what Lipset describes as "American exceptionalism," they may glance; they may master expensive observational technologies to study and observe; but like Mercer's informants, incapable of imagining their listeners, they do not see.

The idea that relationships of unequal power involve a one-sided window surrounding the imperial center is brilliantly conveyed in Mercer's performance. His interviews interpellate Canadians as the more attentive and knowledgeable audience. They remind Canadians that we know more than we want to know about American politics, social problems, entertainment, and gossip, and that this knowledge gives us a special edge as we traverse invisibly through their midst. As the historian Kenneth McNaught wrote in 1976, "It is sometimes said that Americans are benevolently uninformed about Canada while Canadians are malevolently well-informed about the U.S."[9] The proliferation of media spaces has done little to counteract this pattern. "Talk-show hosts are the worst," one Toronto journalist exclaims:

> with everybody from Leno to Letterman to Kathie Lee and Regis displaying the utmost arrogance and ignorance about Canadian geography and history. When Céline Dion told Rosie O'Donnell she was from Canada, O'Donnell blurted out, "Canada! Do you know what I have to say to Canada? *Get a climate.*" This is ironic coming from a woman who lives in a country constantly buffeted by tornadoes, hurricanes and floods. Hey, Rosie, *get an atlas!*[10]

A 1994 survey found that 25 percent of Canadians agree: they object to the "superior attitude" of Americans, while Americans find nothing objectionable in their Canadian neighbors, who are characteristically more reticent with their opinions.[11]

Mercer's *Talking to Americans* breaks this silence and broadcasts the joke across the country. It plays with Canada's sense of superior knowledge and its underlying connection to an equally powerful sense of invisibility.

Invisibility is a concise term for describing a situation in which Americans see igloos, Mounties, cold fronts or wilderness, but certainly not Canadians, 80 percent of whom live in cities and over 98 percent of whom (at this point you have to laugh) have routine access to FM radio. Knowing observers are ready to be consternated and amused by Americans. Thus viewers and producers arrive at a delicious moment of strategic complicity. The mirror-wall they invoke together refracts two sides of the border, one gullible and myopic and the other wily and well versed. While critics remark on the smugness of this consensus, they overlook its cunning play on televisuality, and in particular its merciless unmasking of the average Americans' willingness to unburden themselves to anyone holding a television microphone. Sharp observation of American television culture has long been a central motif in Canadian satire. In the 1985 Genie Award–winning mock documentary *The Canadian Conspiracy*, coauthored by Mark Achbar (the coauthor of the films *Manufacturing Consent* [1992] and *The Corporation* [2003]), a terrified journalist (Eugene Levy), hiding in a motel room with the shades drawn, exposes a conspiracy of Canadians trained by state-owned institutions such as the CBC and the National Film Board (NFB) to infiltrate and take over the American entertainment industry undetected.[12] In this shadowy light, a parade of popular Canadian performers are revealed as secret saboteurs of the American way of life. Confronted by cameras, each suspect ostentatiously denies acquaintance with the other. "Never heard of him," Dave Thomas repeatedly insists from the back of his limousine when asked about fellow Canadian actors we know to be his creative collaboratos. Because their racially and ethnically unmarked bodies permit them to "pass" as Americans, their difference is invisible, but not (in this satire) insignificant. Their presence as undetected aliens is hazardous to the entertainment industry and to the political stability of the country as a whole.

The SCTV "mockumentary" "exposes" Canadians as saboteurs the way American fundamentalists have long sought to expose communists and terrorists. The portentous male voice-over, the black-and-white photography, the hands covering the face, the closed blinds, the denial of friendships and abruptly refused interviews, all echo true-crime and propaganda conventions of the Cold War, when Americans let their anxiety about hidden enemies run amok. In paying homage to this history, this satire is indebted to the actors' work in weekly SCTV parodies of American television and film produced in Toronto between 1976 and 1983. There is a harsher relevance behind this satire, for Americans were not always subtle in their suspicions of Canada's "socialist" leanings. Aggravated by terse policy negotiations between the two countries, officials in the United States have labeled Canadian films as "government propaganda," cultural policy as "government subsidy," and protectionist measures as "unfair trading practices." During the Cold War, U.S. government officials accused "Canuckistan" of being soft on communism and drove one high-ranking diplomat to suicide with their denunciations. Canada's Medicare system, foreign policy, gun legislation, former energy and agricultural policies, public broadcasters, and social policies smell like socialism to some American observers, whose strong patriotic rhetoric of differentiation and defense against the hidden enemy isolate ideas that in Canada have stood squarely in the mainstream.

The knowing play with invisibility reappeared in the summer of 2000 in an unprecedentedly popular television commercial for the beer brand Molson Canadian (the company subsequently merged with Coors).[13] In this commercial, "Joe," standing in front of a large screen projecting iconic images, emotionally proclaims the unrecognized virtues of being Canadian. "I don't know Jimmy, Sally or Suzy," he proclaims (addressing the strange but commonplace idea that Canadians all know one another), "though they are probably very nice people." We don't own igloos or dog sleds. We believe in peacekeeping, not war; "diversity, not assimilation"; our national animal is the beaver, a "noble animal"; in sum, Joe refuses to be or speak "American."[14] His crescendoing "Rant," supported by the exultant swell of Elgar's "Pomp and Circumstance," culminates with the heroic proclamation "I Am Canadian!" followed by a polite, apologetically mumbled, "thank you."

In the Rant "Joe" simultaneously performs a patriotic tirade and mocks the rhetoric of patriotic declamation. Critics who argue that no self-respecting identity defines itself in terms of what it is not seem to miss the affective undertow of the Rant, together with its playful continuity with a long history of Canadian prose. The Rant identifies patriotism with the declaration of the right to be recognized by the "other" against whom Canada struggles to define itself, but pairs this with an ironic distancing from such declarative acts. "Joe" speaks with increasing passion, but allows his words to be hijacked by ambivalence. Not surprisingly, the writer of this script had just returned to Canada after working in New York and was ready to unburden

"Joe's Rant" Molson Canadian commercial, 2000. "I can proudly sew my country's flag on my backpack. / I believe in peace keeping, not policing, / diversity, not assimilation, / and that the beaver is a truly proud and noble animal. / A toque is a hat, a chesterfield is a couch, / and it is pronounced 'zed' not 'zee,' 'zed' !!!!" Courtesy of Molson Canada.

himself of his experiences. Not surprisingly, he does so by saying several things at once. We must defend our identity with patriotic declarations; blustering patriotism is a characteristic of the "other" against which we must defend ourselves. I wish to make a heroic statement; modesty is preferable to dangerous heroism. I speak on behalf of all of us; all of us are already laughing.

This is the hyperconscious rhetoric of a "middle power" which, as Pierre Elliot Trudeau famously described it, is forced to sleep with an elephant. Following advertising trends of the time, the Rant interpellates viewers as being sophisticated and knowing what they are watching. By claiming to be more than a commercial, its script reharmonizes the glitches of previous corporate-sponsored nationalist events, in the course of which popular bands such as The Tragically Hip and Barenaked Ladies have simultaneously acknowledged and mocked the patriotism of their beer company sponsors.[15] Advertisements for Molson beer, Tim Hortons coffee, and Roots athletic gear brand their products with heartfelt nationalism in the wake of political devastations wrought by free trade. These ad campaigns profited companies that were subsequently acquired by or merged with corporations based in the United States. As Toby Miller observes, "The reaction to a loss of referentiality in the real is to heighten efforts to manufacture it."[16] The Rant sparked a temporarily volatile self-recognition for many Anglophone Canadians occupying the habitus of a space between, the space in the midst of a split screen (as I call it in "Locating Listening" [chapter 6]) where an observant partner can celebrate her resentment.

The commercial's effects reverberated for months. The actor performed the Rant live at several major league hockey games where sponsorship conflicts prohibited screening the commercial, and was met with an exorbitant response. Newspaper columnists could not get enough of it, suggesting that the actor should serve as Canada's next prime minister. Sheila Copps, then federal minister of heritage, screened the ad at a meeting of culture administrators in Boston to explain Canada's attitudes on culture. The Boston meeting was a prequel to the 2005 UNESCO conference on cultural diversity in which the United States stood alone with Israel in opposing national policies on cultural preservation. All this emotion disrupted ordinary divisions between diverse social and cultural spheres. The Rant was adapted and circulated in newspaper cartoons and Internet jokes, where it appeared as the self-differentiating proclamations of Italians, Pakistanis, Ukrainian-Canadians, and patriotic cats, among others, and it reappeared in parodistic form in *This Hour Has 22 Minutes*. People almost forgot the Rant was a beer commercial, judging from the crop of colloquialisms that rose in its wake. In 2001, the actor left for California to pursue a Hollywood career.

The sense of an aggrieved invisibility, anxiety about Canada's social policies, and the articulation of these with an ironic anti-Americanism momentarily reconnected the world of intellectuals to the popular domain. A sequel featured the "noble" beaver emerging from under a man's coat and attacking the throat of an American man who is belittling Canadians at a bar. The fact that the hard-working national animal has been usurped by industry that speaks in its name contributes to the poignancy of its patriotic role. Joe's refusal to merge with "America" aroused a passionate response in part because it was articulated with familiar political claims: the defense of Canada's disappearing social policies (peacekeeping, cultural diversity, non-violence) against the American military-entertainment complex, the desire to be (recognized as) different, and support for the rights of marginal peoples to fair and respectful representation. The performance thus provides an uncharacteristically flamboyant expression of ambivalent feelings about what Charles Taylor terms the "politics of recognition." Positing a dialogical relationship between how we see ourselves and how others see us, Taylor argues that "the projection of an inferior or demeaning image on another can actually distort and oppress."[17] Highlighting the problematic agency of this process, the Rant coalesced a frustrated response to the failure of a globalizing United States culture to challenge itself with otherness, while playing cat and mouse with conventions of self and other. The successful corporate mobilization of this trope confirms the popularity of these sentiments and the policies they support, even as such policies were being abandoned by a government elected to act on their behalf.

Rhetorics of Invisibility

The idea of living in the shadow of a myopic giant is a convention of English Canada, "a nation that dares not speak its name."[18] "We live with the exquisite fear that we are invisible people," notes Robert Kroetsch. "And yet we are reluctant to venture out of the silence and into the noise; out of the snow; into the technocracy. For in our very invisibility lies our chance for survival."[19] Like the polemical opposition between ignorance and knowledge, the trope of invisibility haunts English Canada's self-depiction and connects the disparate voices of its comics, writers, and philosophers. The theme of the invisible subject touched upon by Joe, an impassioned beer drinker, and Kroetsch, a novelist and literary critic, recurs in political philosophy, which maintains that "'English Canada' is nearly impossible to grasp. It tends to disappear downwards into the elements that make it up or upwards into the nation-state. We do not seem to have the necessary concept to grasp it for itself."[20] For the theorist Charles Levin, "everything about Canada is vague, ambiguous or unknown."[21] A recent anthology of Canadian historical documents was published under the title "A Country Nourished on Self-Doubt."[22]

Is this absence, this *lack*, a failure of collective mobilization or nostalgia for lost innocence? For Ian Angus, it is the manifestation of a positive abjection, a morally emancipating willingness to recognize the boundaries of self and the equivalent claims of others.[23] For Sherene Razack, on the other hand, it is the outcome of a history of denial through which white settler-colonists revise their history.[24] Canada is widely represented as a unique expression of the ideal of equality in difference. The multicultural ideal's lasting power, some critics suggest, lies in its unattainability. We may not achieve this equality but we can congratulate ourselves on having espoused it.[25] There is an obvious truth to this. Yet the ideal of equality in difference defines the country's founding narrative and unsettles the supposed uniformity of the colonizing powers. In 1840, for instance, Upper Canada's solicitor general, Robert Baldwin (Toronto) wrote a letter to his reformer counterpart in Lower Canada, Louis-Hippolyte LaFontaine (Montreal) about the history of tensions between English and French colonies and the need to form a new union independent from the founding powers and dedicated to responsible government. Baldwin wrote:

> I sincerely regret the [adversarial] position of parties . . . in Lower Canada, and am therefore more anxious for the proclamation of the union, as the first step towards changing it, and mitigating the evils which appear to me to have grown up under it. There is, and *must be no question of races*. It were madness on one side, and guilt, deep guilt on both to make such a question.[26]

Here Baldwin emphasizes that reformers of (English) Upper Canada wish to obtain for Lower Canada (Quebec) "justice *upon precisely the same footing in every particular as ourselves*."[27] Two years later Baldwin and LaFontaine were joint premiers of the new Province of Canada. By the 1850s, tensions between French and English Canadians caused Ontario and Quebec to split into two provinces under one Dominion. These tensions remain central to Canadian political and constitutional debates. Antagonism and equivalence form a single discursive framework through which the nation-state absorbs its subjects.

Can an ideal lack a subject? Northrop Frye argues that it can. "Perhaps the real Canada," he muses, "is an ideal with nobody in it. The Canada to which we really do owe loyalty is the Canada that we have failed to create."[28] The theme of ghosts recurs through Frye's writing and is taken up in various texts. In his analysis, as Kroetsch observes, "such politics arise from a realization of the close connection between identity and recognition. We have been told by various people that Canada lacks ghosts. Ha. We are our own ghosts."[29] These texts establish a canonic vocabulary on the existential status of the national subject (or nonsubject). They illustrate Katherine Fowkes's comment that "the ghost exhibits the fact that—as Jacques Lacan says—speech produces not presence, but absence. . . . Although ghosts attempt to use their voices and language to establish their presence, they inadvertently expose the lack on which their presence is based."[30]

The ambivalence of the Canadian subject finds its most frequent expression in irony. Canadian comics' expertise with unresolved dualities helps to explain the magnitude of their oft-noted success in both countries. Comic performers such as Eugene Levy, Marty Short, Dave Thomas, Catherine

O'Hara, Dan Aykroyd, John Candy, Rick Mercer, Paul Gross, Scott Thompson, Jim Carrey, Mike Myers, and Samantha Bee (to list a few) cast ironic light on American heroic conventions. Like Joe they stand poised with one foot inside and the other outside the subjectivity they portray, rhetorically refusing to fight for simple identification with a recognition from the imposing other. Addressing the film work of the actor, writer, and director Don McKellar, Andre Loiselle suggests that McKellar does not simply use irony but more complicatedly "*stands* for Canadian irony . . . as a canonized discourse framing Canadian culture as a whole."[31] The canonization process joins irony with other popular conventions: characters from diverse linguistic or ethnic groups, an embrace of realist traditions, a preoccupation with losers, a conviction that female characters carry greater strength and authenticity, a strong sense of alienation and identity crisis, and a sense of being outsiders, even in their own country.[32] These characteristics are parodied in McKellar's "emphatic understatement about Canada's civilized perversions or perverse civility," as Loiselle puts it.

The Canadian subject is simultaneously authenticated by realist conventions and erased by layers of irony folding in on one another until "the proverbial colourlessness of the Canadian protagonists is overexposed into oblivion."[33] Again the Canadian is represented as tactically invisible, hard to locate or pin down. "The fact that the country grew up from two peoples speaking different languages," notes Frye in his essay on ghosts—note the haunting absence of the people of the First Nations, who were presumably already grown up when these two peoples arrived—"meant that nobody could ever know what a 'hundred percent Canadian' was, and hence the population became less homogeneous."[34] The Canadian can be anything, and is therefore nothing. The contrast with the all-American athlete, commodity, or ideal is obvious.

"That's why I like it," counters Stephen Schecter in his commentary on Canada's postmodernism. "If nothing else, it's a reminder about the incomprehensible knot at the centre of things. . . . By flattening itself into a country that refuses to be one, it has also posed the paradox of our need for a country even as we would do without one."[35] If Canada is defined by the lack of an (acknowledged) subject or center, this lack is not a failure but a promise of tolerance and multiplicity for nations caught up in the political and ethnic battles of modern nationalism.[36] Indigenous peoples, having fought for and lost their own sovereignty to this supposedly diffident country, would not recognize the characterization of Canada as "a country that refuses to be one." But their perspectives are rarely taken into account in the discourse on diversity.

"Diversity, not assimilation," Joe proclaims. He could be quoting the philosopher John Ralston Saul, who admires the absence of the mythology found in other nation-states:

> This is described by most federalists and anti-federalists alike as the failure of Canada. The failure to become like the others. To regularize a monolithic mythology. Some weep before the ever-retreating mirage of the un-hyphenated Canadian. Others say its continued existence proves the country is not real and cannot exist. For me, this failure to conform is in fact our greatest success. A proof of originality which we refuse to grasp as positive.[37]

These cascading identity crises offer a narrative prophylactic against the virus of collective unself-consciousness. They form a one-way mirror image of two protagonists' rhetorical construction of their borders. This narrative derives its power from reading Canada dialogically against Europe or the United States, thereby displacing and projecting internal inequities outward in the name of resistance to external force. Such displacement is unworthy and unjust, but it is not a necessary element of postcolonial thought. In an influential essay, Stephen Slemon defines the "Second World" as a "neither/nor" grouping of invader-settler cultures grounded in "a confused, contradictory, and deeply ambivalent position within the circulations of colonialist power and anti-colonialist affect [which] present significant and enormously difficult problems for the field of postcolonial critical studies."[38] Both colonizers and subject to colonization, nations such as Australia, New Zealand, South Africa, and Canada, all former outposts of the British Empire, arise from the violent fusions of multiple identities. However strongly the landscape occupies the imaginary, Canada is "never homogeneous, never 'pure,' but constructed by First Nations peoples, Francophones, other European groups (from Russians to Italians), Asians (Chinese, Japanese and Indian), and yes, Africans (primarily African American and West Indian)."[39] The ambiguity of this composite identity prevents the contributions of Second World countries from registering in First World postcolonial writing, with its fundamentally binary model of "the West and the Rest." For Slemon, the Second World writer recognizes her complicity in colonialism's territorial appropriation of land, voice, and agency in the very act of voicing opposition to colonial power. For this reason, the mediated, conditional, radically compromised literatures of this Second World have something to teach postcolonial theory about the nature of resistance.

The 49th Parallel

The colloquial use of this term to reference the border recalls the memory of the only war the United States ever lost—before Vietnam, that is. Only when Niagara Falls was established in battle as "the site of the prime test of the integrity of the border" were Americans forced to confront the limit of the American Dream.[40] The border identifies the place where Manifest Destiny met its end.

"In the nineteenth century," notes historian Ramsay Cook, "the famous undefended frontier had yet to be discovered. The very existence of Canada, most nineteenth-century Canadians realized, was an anti-American fact."[41] Between 1790 and 1870, the west coast population of the United States increased from 4 to almost 40 million. Over 60 percent of the original forests in the United States were destroyed, first for export and then, after the 1848 gold rush, for settlement of the west. By the end of the century, the country's natural resources were so depleted that legislators were forced to intervene to try to reverse the popular association between patriotism and the destruction of nature. To the north, residents of British North America opposed forming a Dominion state throughout the late nineteenth century, championing Canada's continuing membership in the British Empire as "a vital bulwark against what they perceived as catastrophic Yankee annexationism."[42] The American side of Niagara Falls degenerated into an unattractive semi-industrial wasteland, a symbolic backyard for the American dream, in stark contrast to the lustrous landscaping on the Canadian side.[43] American uneasiness about their northern border was not limited to symbolic expression. Ongoing disputes about softwood lumber, agricultural subsidies, water, environmental regulation, military strategy, and communications provide tangible continuity with these earlier times.

Today southern Ontario extends almost a thousand kilometers south of the 49th Parallel, forming a peninsula amidst the Great Lakes that draws the border into a south-tending squiggle. As Canada's largest city, Toronto is roughly the same distance from the equator as Marseille, Budapest, or northern California. More than 3 million trucks cross the Ambassador Bridge between Windsor and Detroit every year, making it the world's busiest commercial crossing. More than $2 billion in commercial goods moves between Canada and the United States every day, 65 percent of this on Ontario roads.

Historians suggest that the border, 55 percent of which crosses water, followed the trail of early canoe routes. "The border with the United States is not an arbitrary line," Daniel Francis explains; "the watersheds flow away from it north and east. Following these waterways, the canoe created Canada." Innis was not alone in his emphasis on this space-binding technology. "If I were asked the question, 'What did most to pave the way for the development of the Dominion of Canada?' remarked John Murray Gibbon, "I should feel inclined to answer, 'The Canoe.'"[44] It is not surprising that Gibbon, a writer and publicist for the Canadian Pacific Railway (CPR), would emphasize transport, and that Innis would pursue this theme in his research. They are not suggesting that the border is defined by nature. The Loyalists who fought against the Revolutionaries and won the War of 1812 to establish Canada's border at Queenston Heights were not ethnically different from their opponents on the American side. Both countries were founded by European settler-societies who vanquished indigenous peoples and stole their lands. Both sides marshaled indigenous allies. But their border represented and constituted different relations to the spaces they circumscribed. The border's location is the outcome of history and politics, as well as water routes, and its status and meaning continue to be marked by them. Those who live on the northern side know that history and politics can also engineer its disappearance.

One such alteration occurred with the Hay-Herbert Treaty of 1903, a settlement of a longstanding border dispute between Alaska and the Yukon in which England ceded what is now Alaska to the United States. The area had been settled as a Russian and English colony, but its status changed dramatically, first when the Russians began to disallow foreign trading ships in its ports in the 1850s, and then again during the spectacularly successful (for some) gold rush in the late 1900s, when many Americans and Canadians moved to the area and staked their claims.[45] Canadians were confident that the British would defend their interest in this territory bordering the Yukon and were astounded when the British granted so much of the northern land mass to the United States. This concession dampened Canada's attachment

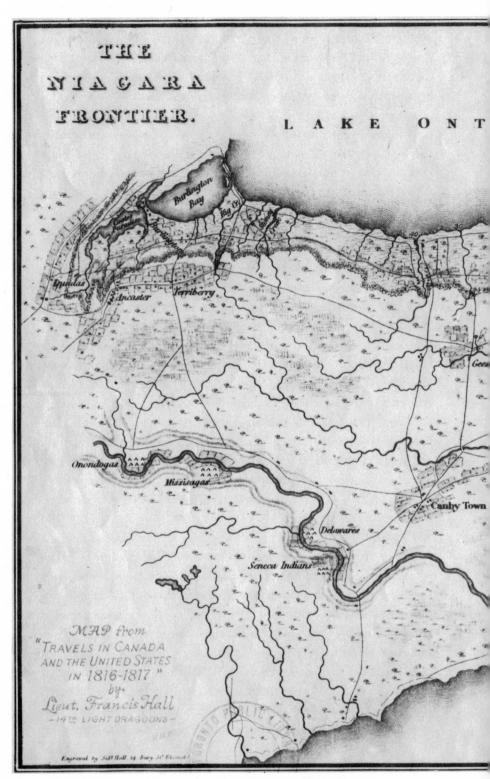

"Travels in Canada and the United States, 1816–17." Map by Lieutenant Francis Hall,
14th Light Dragoons, #2284. Courtesy of Metro Reference Library, Toronto, pp. 62–64.

Missisaga F.
Newark
Ft. Niagara
a mile Creek

Lewiston

O · I · O

Queenston
Fort Drummond

St Davids
Black swamp
Limestone Heights
Falls 150 ft

Falls of
Stamford
Chippewa
Navy Is.d
Tonawanta Creek

Beaver Drains
Bridgewater
GRAND ISLAND

Lundys Lane
Wiscmans Rock
Strawberry Is.d

Melling House
Black Creek
Conjockquaddy Creek

Browns Bridge
Lyons Creek
Ferry Black Rock
Scarrick

Fort Erie
Snake Hill
Buffaloe
Manuttel

CANBY MARSH
5 Mile Point

Point Abino

Sugar-loaf Point

P.t Industry

L · A · K · E   E · R · I · E

British Miles.

5   10   15   20   25

London Published by Longman Hurst, Rees, Orme & Brown, Paternoster Row May 30.th 1818.

West Canada. *The Illustrated Atlas and Modern History of the World,* R. Montgomery Martin, 1853. Courtesy of Metro Reference Library, Toronto.

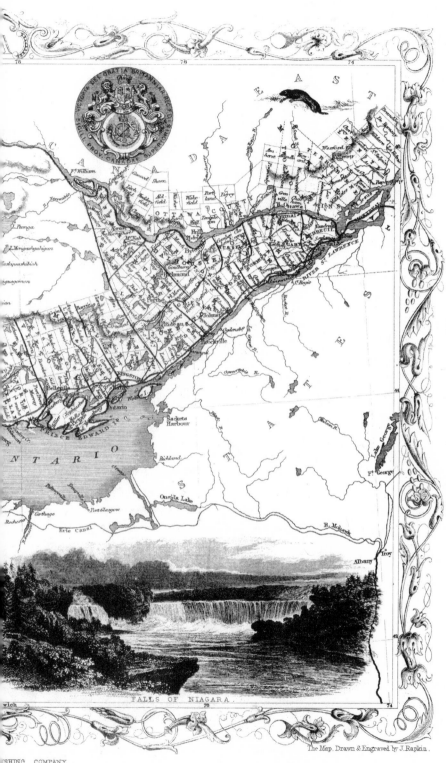

FALLS OF NIAGARA.

The Map, Drawn & Engraved by J. Rapkin.

Still of Ambassador Bridge, from the film *Great Lakes Transit*, directed by Tim Schwab (2007). Courtesy of the artist.

to the British Commonwealth, and strengthened their resolve to develop as a North American Dominion. Some politicians began to advocate a continental English-speaking political alliance to gain greater independence from British and French colonial authorities, especially after the bloodbaths of the First World War. However, the emergent shape of this continental economy fueled another swell of opposition to the "industrial invasion" of Canada.[46] After 1940 Canada, determined to affirm its North American identity, "found itself alone in North America alongside a gigantic American partner which was about to assume the role of policeman in a world passing rapidly from hot to cold war."[47] In this depiction Canada is both partner to its neighbor and alone on the continent, a schizoid location that reiterates the northerners' sense of invisibility. The ambivalence of this connection was intensified by Canada's disapproval of American actions in Korea and the Cold War, and then again in Iraq, when Canada was simultaneously called upon as military ally and repudiated as a moralistic sister because of its more pacifist views.[48]

Another border struggle concerns the rights of indigenous peoples to travel freely across bridges spanning the Niagara River. The United States Johnson-Reed Act of 1924 barred indigenous peoples from freely entering the United States from Canada, and the Indian Citizenship Act of the same year patriated, or granted U.S. citizenship to, indigenous peoples south of the border. During the same period, Canada's Department of Indian Affairs dismantled the Six Nations' independent governance at Grand River, north of the Niagara River, and subjected them to Canadian governance. The Indian Defense League, formed in 1926, fought for and won the right for native peoples to cross into the United States without restriction. For Robinder Sehdev, "The very real threat that colonial law would subsume Indigenous law and its citizens through coercive belonging meant that crossing and not crossing were equally fraught." The annual July Border Crossing Ceremony, held to protest imposed citizenship and border restrictions on the northern side and to commemorate American recognition of its treaty obligations, may be "the oldest continuous Native protest movement in northern America."[49]

Constituted by military actions and border skirmishes, deals and deliberations, and intense symbolic transmission, the border is now being quietly rewritten by the "natural" flow of corporate acquisitions, trade agreements, information flow, and military arrangements. Many online forms now list the provinces along with states as alphabetical options for my home address. Is Canada becoming a simulation of a nation rather than a modern nation-state? A "virtual" country? A "ghost" of itself, in other words? The humor of the parodistic war in the film *South Park* depends on the idea that "Canada is not a real country anyway." In contrast to "The Canadian Conspiracy," Canadians *look* different in this film, animatedly speaking, for their faces are cleft horizontally at the jaw, and they are clearly recognizable as hostile forces. "Blame Canada" was the Oscar-nominated theme song from *South Park*.[50] Viewers from the northern side might reasonably wonder whether the writers are mocking our country, or theirs. The determination of the United States to build stronger walls against drugs, terrorists, and unwanted aliens entering from the north has reinforced the impression of Canada not as a place but as a conduit for things—wood, comics, cold, terrorists. Demands that Canada improve the policing of the border are fueled by the fallacious claim that terrorists enter the United States from the north. A Canadian passport no longer guarantees the safety of (nonwhite) Canadians traveling in the United States, and some Canadians now refuse to travel there. Our government cooperates fully with Homeland Security because so much depends on unimpeded movements of goods between the two countries. The control of immigration and refugee movements between countries is another component of national sovereignty whose salience is increasing with the growing so-called fluidity of borders under globalization.[51] Canada admits the largest per capita quota of immigrants and refugees worldwide. Since early 2005, however, refugees seeking to enter Canada from the United States face stern procedures. Given the perceived need to protect American citizens from refugees and terrorists, "Canada is keen to shift the discussion away from increased border controls and toward an examination of perimeter security."[52] This pressure forced former prime minister Paul Martin to reopen talks with former president Bush about the unpopular "Star Wars" space defense initiative (see chapter 8, "Mapping Space"), and there has been a significant expansion of R & D in surveillance and communication technologies funded by the Canadian military.

Commentators have long justified the idea of a permeable border by observing that North America runs naturally north and south rather than east and west.[53] For neoliberal economists, the border is an unnatural entity which should not exist according to the "natural" laws of economic flow and continental trade. This is not the only context in which nature is evoked as an alibi for economic and social policies (see chapter 9, "Cultural Technologies and the 'Evolution' of Technological Cultures"). But the conceit doesn't bear scrutiny. Advocates of continental flow imagine the north-south flow to emanate south from Canada's cities, but not north; neither Ottawa nor Washington shows much interest in the far north except as an ostensibly empty space suitable for military testing and resource extraction, especially oil and natural gas.[54] Inhabitants of northern Canada are doubly marginalized by the metropolitan areas clustered at the border, whose inhabitants are encouraged to ignore the plight of northern and especially native communities. As Saul observes, "It is as if what those obsessed by natural free-market flows—the neo-conservatives [such as] the Business Council on National Issues—actually mean is that we are the north and our interest should therefore be to the south, even if it means turning our backs on the reality of our own northernness."[55] In this context the challenge of "moving forward" in the global marketplace contains geographical implications even more definite than the phrase would suggest. "Forward" means south: it entails releasing the north-south flow of goods and information (but not immigrants, lumber, or movies) into a comprehensive continental merger, with a military security system posted around the perimeters to protect Americans from missiles and aliens.

In an alternative writing of this history, the north-south pull is not a consequence of natural geography but an outcome of the growth of American and British investment in Canada in the early part of the twentieth century.

Canada became a resource-based economy, a provider of "staples" such as fur, lumber, and minerals, as a result of economically dependent trade relationships rather than as a consequence of natural destiny. That "nature" by which Canada is so often identified, not least by the beaver and the maple leaf, is the product of geopolitics, not the reverse. As cross-border corporate acquisitions in the years following FTA's and NAFTA's implementation reach record levels, newspapers today echo accounts of a century ago, reporting that capital is "flowing south" as if capital were a stream ineluctably drawn toward the natural pull of gravity. Or as if a wind, flowing like Canada's arctic air into the televised weather charts of a nation that erases the northern half of the continent; or as if blood, leaving a wounded body; or as if data, seeking to be free. However the "flow" resonates, it is endowed with the inevitability of nature that is presumed to determine the body politic. This discourse facilitates the flow of money and information, the intangible airborne particles of power, if not the free transnational movement of various peoples. South of the border, on the other hand, the "flow" is mapped east-west across the continent, with the Mississippi the crucial divider, just as it was in the nineteenth century. The east-west flow defines American travel, adventure, literature, weather forecasts, ecological studies, and political analysis. It directs eyes westward across the continent, and then, like the great Spaceship Enterprise, upward to new frontiers. American maps always end just north of the 49th Parallel, where the land appears unmarked, just visible enough to establish the territory metonymically by its border.

The Postmodern Parallel

How the border is written has consequences north of the 49th. The consciousness of the border's arbitrary location is one reason critics call Canada the world's first postmodern country.[56] Drawing on Lyotard's definition of postmodernism as "incredulity toward meta-narratives," Kroetsch posits that

> Canada is supremely a country of margins, beginning from the literal way in which almost every city borders on a wilderness. The centeredness of the high modern period [the first half of the twentieth century] made us almost irrelevant to history. In a high modern world, with its privileged stories, Canada was invisible. Lyotard attributes the decentring

to developments in science. I feel that the movement away from the European-centered empires to the current domination by America and the USSR has had an equal impact. In fact, I suspect that those two empires, in attempting to assert or reassert their meta-narratives, turn all other societies into postmodern societies.[57]

In other words, the struggle of multiple agents to possess and locate a territory makes colonies more reflexive about space and transforms utopia into a "heterotopia." As Katherine Hayles explains in another context, "Reflexivity is the movement whereby that which has been used to generate a system is made, through a changed perspective, to become part of the system it generates." Thus "an attribute previously considered to have emerged from a set of preexisting conditions is in fact used to generate the conditions."[58] These descriptions connect Canada's history to its representation by writers and artists in their frequent foregrounding of the border as a narrative device.

Canada has produced a topographic imaginary that defines itself in terms of the absence of a unifying subjectivity. To embrace this absence, the literature of postmodernism suggests, is to leave behind the Hegelian or universal logic of history. This difference or indifference is expressed not through binary opposition (though that is what a border is) but in the recognition of multiple decentered perspectives, together with a fascination with dualisms that cannot and should not resolve, and an identification with marginal, hybrid, and feminized perspectives. For Kroetsch, "All the reality of the story, the speech against the silence, is on the circumference. The margin. We live a life of shifting edges, around an unspoken or unspeakable question. Or, at best, in asking who we are, we are who we are."[59] For Frye, the question is "not who are we, but where is here?"[60] For McLuhan, Canada is "a land of multiple borderlines, psychic, social and geographic."[61] For these thinkers, the country registers the prospect of reconciliation among multiple identities, "in process" rather than complete; "in between" rather than whole; a "contrapuntal" form rather than a singular narrative.[62] Such borderlines are important within as well as outside of the country, perpetuating the sense of plurality founded in diverse languages, ethnicities, and regional cultures. "Tradition is usually thought of as linear," Frye suggests, "and as forming a series of conventions which continually go out of date. But in Canada tradition has become, in the last generation or so at least, a much more simultaneous and kaleidoscopic affair."[63]

These narratives constitute what Edward Said and Benjamin Belton call the colonial archive—a cumulative layering of diverse voices, time periods, and perspectives in a spatially defined, cross-disciplinary assemblage. The archive "becomes a repository of images about the region and the *topos* becomes the cultural site of those images when they are projected onto geographical space."[64] Belton understands the topos as the product of local narratives and actions circulating within the cultural sphere of capital development. "Using different sets of elements, different *topoi* may be constructed around a place, and form different 'filters' for how that place is projected and perceived. The *topos* becomes, in Jameson's formulation, the narrativization of that imaginary geography in the political unconscious."[65] Thus the topos layers diverse narratives over a topography that shapes and is shaped by them.

Canada's topos is shaped by the chronic questioning of its own possibility. "Ours is a history written in terms of 'colonial status,' 'imperial connection' and 'continentalism,' rather than 'Canadian Revolution,' 'self-determination' and 'national independence,'" Wallace Gagne wrote in 1976. As a consequence, "we must be open to the nature of technique and what it implies for man."[66] For Gagne, as for Grant, the "nature of technique" is connected to space through the concept of empire. As these terms circle one another, they are repeatedly rearticulated and reassembled. Tracing the effects of this staging of "heterotopos" reminds us that these races, ethnicities, and regions are more equal in theory than in practice. At the same time, it matters that the homogeneous identity referenced by European nation-building is rejected in these narratives. Writing on Canada's ongoing constitutional crisis, Schecter claims that "Canada is the answer to its own question, which in the end is its great trump card. . . . Imagine Canada: the first postmodern state willing to do something about post-modernity. Imagine Canada: a country willing in part to be the imaginary country it actually is."[67] The statement implies hindsight and a certain element of denial; it optimistically reverses Frye's idea, noted earlier, that Canada had failed to become the country it imagined. In accounts, multiple voices denaturalize homogenizing forces and posit a radical form of becoming. Apparently "becoming" is a matter of will catching up with the imaginary. But Canada can't make up its mind, and—is it for this reason?—enacts too little in the way of collective will. For what Schecter describes as "the most politically correct version of any constitution extant in a Western democracy" was rejected by popular referendum.[68]

There is an almost delirious nominalism in Schecter's description—an assumption that if something is named, if it is imagined, then it actually exists. Schecter is not alone in this imaginary fusing of the virtual and the actual; it is a mainstay of English Canadian writing that "the world can be spoken into existence by will and whim, or can unravel into absence and silence; the ways in which human life has been made possible in the new world are never stable or secure, and cannot be taken for granted."[69] Like the border, the subject of this narrative is described as the ambiguous outcome of concentrated effort and as vulnerable to revocation. Place and subject are created through discourse, and therefore subject to reappropriation. This idea can be distinguished from dependency theory, which focuses on the colonization of Canada's culture and regional economies and emphasizes national disempowerment as the crux of Canadian experience. In this account, Canada's economy is founded on and shaped by the export of raw materials and the import of manufactured goods, for example (as Innis showed) the export of wood pulp and the import of newspapers, or the export of talent and the import of films and television programs. Canada is an economically peripheral country characterized by excessive vulnerability to market fluctuations outside its borders, severe regional disparities, inadequate industrialization, a heavy emphasis on staples export, and the provision of financial services oriented toward continuing foreign investment. Extending this perspective, Canadian media studies research emphasizes highly centralized, predominantly foreign ownership structures, and builds on strong methodological bonds between political economy, media studies, and government research.[70] Such research depicts an economically disempowered and culturally uncertain national culture juxtaposed against the all-too-certain economic structures and strategies of foreign-owned corporate media culture.

Another reading of this topos, this layering of discourse and history, recalls that European settler-colonials appropriated, robbed, and poisoned the indigenous peoples of the First Nations, and that the narratives summarized above repress the memory of Canada's origin as a colonial conquest of someone else's land. The idea of a "Second World" colonial society is powerful because it builds on the simultaneity of these diverse accounts. Literary and postmodern discourse does not deny this colonial history, but emphasizes Canadian subjectivity as a reflexive response to the experience of being at the margin, and encourages readers to seek connection and empowerment through such reflexivity. The dependency account acknowledges the imperializing technologies of media forms and practices within the space and embrace of imperial power. Like the debate between cultural studies and political economy addressed in other contexts, one can make too much of this dichotomy. More problematic is the fact that the literary and dependency narratives collude in the disappearance of the memory of Canada as a colonial nation-state.

Diffident in the face of such uncertainty, Canadians are inclined to believe and radically disbelieve at the same time.[71] Viewers of *Talking to Americans* don't care if Mercer's interviewees are "really" as dumb as they appear to be, because the truth works at another level. Even if some interviewees are performing their roles as provincial *naifs* (though there is no evidence for this), or more knowledgeable Americans have been edited out (though experience belies this), we know that Mercer knows that we know what they don't; in the performance of this truth it "really" doesn't matter. Linda Hutcheon, following Roland Barthes, calls this fondness for ambiguity "amphibology: the opposite of the situation where context forces us to choose one of two meanings and forget the other."[72] With such epistemological laxity, binary oppositions don't work; they produce discomfort or disbelief (as charismatic heroes do, north of the border), rather than a sense of safety or power. English Canadian literary studies identify the absence of heroic male protagonists as evidence of a culture that is uncomfortable with charismatic solutions. Men don't need to die to be ghosts, for they are antiheroes, ghosts of themselves, already. Performers mock male heroism with a saucy ambience, making cross-dressing a mainstay of Canadian comic and dramatic performance by all sexes.[73] Once again General Idea can be said to be progenitor of this practice, for their work presented a series of memorable guerilla tactics against the conventional boundaries within which art and performance were still contained: boundaries between art and media, gallery and city, individual subject and collective author, and the underlying tenets of masculinity upon which such conventions relied. They mocked the "artist as rebel and hero" persona, brought AIDs into the forefront of contemporary art and design, and sat back and waited to see if anyone would take up their dance with gender. Canadian television's most conventional hero, Constable Fraser of the Royal Canadian Mounted Police (Paul Gross in the police series *Due South*, written by Paul Haggis and set in Chicago) occasionally assumed female disguise with relish, and his adroit management of highbrow cultural capital is not the target of the implicitly homophobic humor we see in *Frasier*, a contemporaneous television series about articulate men. Gross's Mountie performance is simultaneously a stereotypical confirmation of well-behaved citizenship, and an ironic commentary on such stereotypical conventions. These artists share a preference for play rather than heroic action; reticence about conventionally gendered power roles animates the tensions between "two sets of values, two ways of seeing, two worlds."[74]

Kathleen Morrison associates Canadian literature with "a dearth of heroes and a strong sense of place" and compares this tradition with the "frontier ideal" of the United States with its aggressive sense of manifest destiny.[75] In the latter, victims of poverty and violence earn their fate; heroes are men, and women are frightened or at least polite; and action heroes are the indispensable ingredient for every tale. Indeed the ascendancy of neo-liberalism has intensified the saliency of the gender metaphor, upholding an economic doctrine in which "caring" institutions such as Medicare are too soft for progress in the global era. With the trend toward privatization, women must "naturally" take on greater care for children and for elderly, disabled, or ill relatives. In *Politics on the Margin*, Janine Brodie notes that "the disappearance of the Keynesian welfare state and the radical redrawing of the boundaries between the public sphere, the market, and the home are eroding the very political identities and public spaces that empowered postwar Canadian feminism and distinguished it from its turn-of-the-century counterpart." In particular, Brodie's research suggests that "although restructuring discourse attempts to draw women into the public either as non-citizens with special needs or as genderless citizens, the restructuring process is, needless to say, neither gender- nor class- nor race-neutral. Indeed, its effects are already painfully obvious in the everyday lives of most Canadian women." This is because "the discourse around health care is changing, putting greater emphasis on a woman's private responsibilities for her own health and for caring for the needs of family members. . . . It has become increasingly apparent that the new neoliberal state marks a distinct shift in shared understandings of what it means to be a Canadian citizen and what the citizen can legitimately ask of the state."[76] Mounting pressure on women's time, income, and access to work are the controversial result of an expanding political culture of renewed masculinist or patriarchal attitudes in which marriage, divorce, cohabitation, abortion, homosexuality, and family relations are defined as appropriate matters for supervision and legislation. At the same time, a large proportion of English Canada's prominent writers and musicians are women. Women have led the NDP, Canada's national so-cial democratic party; its largest public-sector union; and its largest citizens' group, the Council of Canadians, which lobbies for global justice and whose membership outnumbers that of any political party. Masculinity remains an ambivalent property in a culture so proximate to the hypermasculinist performances of American politicians, movie stars, soldiers, border guards, and other representatives of the nation's destiny. Men in uniforms were, at least before Canada went to war in Afghanistan, the subject of parody, not pride; when a would-be writer dons a police uniform to develop material for a story in "The Big Slick," chaos ensues; when the hero of I Love a Man in Uniform "borrows" a police costume to roam the dark urban streets, the results are disastrous. In this daring depiction, "American popular culture is represented not as something external or foreign but as a deeply internal-ized facet of our national psyche.[77]

Using gender metaphors to represent national identity in this way is enticing, and resonates emotionally with many writers and readers, but it demands further reflection. The gender metaphor helps to reinforce the di-chotomy between "inner" and "outer" by means of which Canada asserts its position as "other," defined as the particular against the general, and in power terms, as margin.[78] This organization of difference as opposition rep-licates dependency theory in the cultural imaginary and limits the efficacy of a genuinely feminist topography. I return to this in "Space at the Margins" (chapter 1) and "Spatial Narratives in the Canadian Imaginary" (chapter 3). Across genres, the subjects of each identification forego or defer the idea that pleasure can arise from the conquest of a hostile force. It is as though there is no point to claiming power facing south (where the people and army are perilously large) or north (where nature cannot readily be made the subject of anyone's conquest) from this borderland. If the political other claims authority on the basis of strong categorical distinctions, it also evokes a mocking resentment of such certitude. Whether we see this as an abject dissembling of power or a powerful critique of it (a decision that depends on both context and conviction), this deferral of binary oppositions organiz-ing nation, sex, and identity has been signally important to Canadian writ-ers, performers, and artists. Obviously the regulation of territory is not the same as (or the inevitable outcome of) the cultural circulation of implicit understandings. Otherwise years of creative genius and citizens' consensus would be reflected in state policy, and equitable immigration policies, universal Medicare, and public control over natural resources, culture, media, and education would be enshrined in perpetuity. As an instrument for the elaboration of difference from difference, this sophisticated ambivalence encounters its own aporia.

Policing the Border

Throughout the history of negotiations between the two governments, "culture" has been a central point of dispute. "Few matters seemed to galvanize Canadian public opinion more in the postwar period, one of overwhelming American influence across the board, than that of culture."[79] The same globalization marks the federal election of 2008, a consequence of the incumbent prime minister's cut to arts funding with the rationale that the arts are a "niche" issue. When the logic of culture is translated from government to marketplace, the stakes move from rights and traditions to the competitive pursuit of consumers who freely choose their place in the orbit of commodity exchange. *Choice* is the magic word for privatization lobbyists in fields as diverse as movies, hamburgers, and medical care—ironic, given simultaneous ascendancy of antichoice politics in the realm of women's rights.

Policy analysts Steven McBride and John Shields argue that "Choosing a more independent economic course for Canada has always meant not only emphasizing trade links outside North America and government strategies to diversify the economy beyond resource exports, but also embracing communitarian values to partially offset those of the predominantly economic liberalism."[80] When Canadians criticize social or fiscal policies for moving to the Right, they speak of the "Americanization" of Canadian society. When politicians seek to assure voters of their honorable intents, they speak in favor of "Canadian values." When edgy neopunk twenty-somethings broadcast their thoughts to CITY TV's "Speaker's Corner" to protest high entry costs to local museums, they demand better public subsidy, lest we become moronic "like Americans." The projection of neoconservative values onto the United States—onto the dangerous and necessary "other"—remains a vital feature of Canadian political discourse and functions as a central meaning of the border. The idea of annexation between the countries is thus ideologically linked (positively or negatively) to the neoconservative agenda.[81]

Shortly before renouncing his Canadian citizenship, Conrad Black, the disgraced conservative ideologue and media *oligopolist*, denounced Canada as a pathetic place where money is redistributed from people who have earned it to the poor, who have not. In a *Globe and Mail* opinion piece entitled "Time for American Takeover," Black attacks Canada's "extravagant welfare system and [higher] tax rates" and proclaims his envy of the United States economy and political culture, where real debates occur, in contrast to Canada's, where "the right is fragmented and intimidated."[82] Given his eagerness to reverse Canada's pathetic money distribution practices in private as well as public, it is ironic that he has to serve his prison time south of the border.

The former prime minister Chrétien, on the other hand, urged voters to avoid the Americanization of health care and other social policies. A front-page headline reporting on the 2000 election reads, "PM vows to fight for poor, Medicare: Chrétien attacks 'Americanization' of country, and hints of fall vote."[83] "Americanization" is part of an enlarged subtitle, in quote marks. Like the Rant, this headline hazards a patriotic statement and disavows it at the same time. According to one pollster, Germans point to their machines, the French to their food and wine, Americans to their entertainment, and Canadians to their Medicare, as "their most potent symbols of national identity."[84] Health care and income support programs "represent and symbolize Canadians' sense of themselves as members of a community where solidarity and mutual responsibility are fundamental social norms," according to the Ontario Ministry of Intergovernmental Affairs in 1991.[85] These ideas form a popular consensus that few politicians dare openly contest. But social programs are increasingly vulnerable to privatization. The prospective collapse of the system to which Chrétien refers is a consequence of his own government's deficit-cutting policies and the "equalization" of social programs precipitated by the Free Trade Agreement (see "Angels Dancing," chapter 4) and newer trade agreements. In a recent sleight-of-hand, Prime Minister Stephen Harper's conservative government, which supports the development of public-private partnerships in health coverage, quietly dropped health care from its "Five Priorities" and replaced it with "security."

McBride and Shields maintain that "neo-conservatism remains fundamentally incompatible with the basic principles of the Canadian polity—particularly the well-established traditions of public enterprise and collective social provision."[86] (Black was making the same point, from the opposite point of view.) In the neoliberal climate, however, Keynesian liberalism, social democracy, and communism are condemned as variations of the same contemptible mistake. Such policies are portrayed as disincentives to economic growth (although comparative economic theory casts strong doubt on this assumption) and entrepreneurial freedom.[87] The ideal of the unfettered market is a distortion of economic history, with now-evident disastrous consequences, but that is another matter. Canada's difference is that its political culture has historically dissociated neoliberalism from national objectives and traditions. When food banks appeared in Canada in the 1980s, they were described as a temporary measure for difficult times. In 1995, the Province of Ontario rolled back welfare benefits by 20 percent; since then, rents in the city have climbed 10 percent to 12 percent annually. The food banks, serving an ever-expanding impoverished class, depend on donations from private and corporate sponsors. The public safety net is being transferred to the private sector and redefined as charity.

Whose Border?

It is a nice coincidence that the eruption of nationalist emotion constellated in the Rant was followed closely by a Canadian edition of *Time Magazine* published with the cover story "What Border?" This carefree capitalist caprice predates (but is not disproved by) the destructive events of 2001. The story describes the rise of cross-border regional economies and new levels of political cooperation between governments in these regions, and argues that the increasing consolidation of business interests in the Maritimes, southern Ontario, and the west proves that commerce and technology can efficaciously "leave behind" the political fiction of the border. *Time* claims that "Ottawa and Washington, which still dictate the formalities between two sovereign nations, have less and less to do with the way that Canadians and Americans actually relate to each other on issues that matter the most."[88]

Time's cover story highlights a dispute in which New Brunswick was persuaded to provide health insurance to workers living in Maine and thus to dispense benefits that are part of the political enfranchisement of Canadians to noncitizens. Maine residents employed by specific New Brunswick meat-processing companies can pay United States income taxes but receive Canadian health benefits. It is unclear who is supposed to pay for this windfall, but what seems certain is that it will not be the plant or the government of Maine. The report does not mention the fact that almost 45 percent of what the United States buys from Canada involves trade between branches of the same company. In this case, corporate lobbyists persuaded New Brunswick to subsidize personnel costs with Canadian public money in order to keep their residents employed. The University of Maryland business professor who produced this last statistic warns against any move that "would undermine the advantages of free trade," arguing that "a larger, more efficient integrated market enhances the worldwide competitiveness of U.S. companies." *Time* does not consider this prospect to be controversial.[89]

Readers with longer memories may recall similar statements, such as that of a former U.S. under secretary of state , George Ball, who in 1968 opined that

> Sooner or later, commercial imperatives will bring about the free movement of all goods back and forth across our long border. When that occurs, or even before it does, it will become unmistakably clear that countries with economies inextricably intertwined must also have free movement of the other vital factors of production—capital, services, labour. The result will inevitably be substantial economic integration, which will require for its full realization a progressively expanding area of common political decision.[90]

This statement bluntly acknowledges the leveling of social policy sought by the larger power. It is not only movements between countries but also policies within them that are subject to surveillance. Accordingly, Canadian pesticide regulation is being relaxed to "harmonize" with United States policies; soon, journalists speculate, the U.S. Federal Drug Administration will be the determining body for all Canadian drug and food administration and we will have lost the ability to set our own standards.[91] At the same time, Canadians are being warned of harsh penalties if they are caught downloading American television programs via the Internet.

In this context, how should we interpret these eruptions of nationalist emotions in Canadian popular culture? Is this a sentimental, corporately managed reiteration of values that no longer "really" matter, what John

Convenience store, Tobermory, Ontario, 2006. Photograph by the author.

Tomlinson calls a "simulacrum of anthropological place?"[92] With Canadians appearing in iconic scenarios, such as playing street hockey, struggling with blizzards, or fighting cross-border cultural misunderstandings, is national identity simply a convenient motif for slick Toronto advertising executives and corporate brand promotions? Is the nation an optional brand in a marketplace of identities?

Scott Lash and Celia Lury maintain that the brand has replaced the commodity in the global cultural industry. "The commodity is produced. The brand is a source of production. . . . Commodities work through a mechanistic principle of identity, brands through the animated production of difference."[93] You cannot go to a store and buy a brand; you can only purchase shares in a capital market that anticipates (as do current security measures) the expected future. This is an important change, because it marks a fusion of base and superstructure to a degree that was unimaginable in earlier critiques of the cultural industry. Lash and Lury reject categorical distinctions between the local and the global. But they do not consider what happens when the branding exercise refers to and informs a geopolitical entity such as a nation-state. "The brand experience is a feeling, though not a concrete perception," they note.[94]

Whether the symbolic projection of neoliberalism onto our southern neighbor is an accurate portrayal of difference or an irrational denial of forces at work within our own polity, the evocation of the border has important implications and effects that incorporate and exceed the symbolic. The resilience of these debates accentuates the degree to which popular defense of the border can be articulated to important political choices, consciously and pleasurably (if not always effectively) defiant of classical approaches to global economies and nation-states. The mobilization of citizen activism in the name of a sovereign culture was pivotal to the attainment of progressive social legislation: public broadcasting in 1936, national unemployment insurance in 1940, a family allowance in 1945, universal Medicare in 1966, the refusal to go to war in Korea and Iraq. These policies laminated the border between the two countries and provided substance to the symbolic work of cultural producers. The persistence of cultural traditions and narratives does not guarantee the safety of such policies, but political struggles cannot be won without them. There are consequences, not always as positive as these, when the eruption of public affect disrupts the boundaries between social and cultural critique.

Postscript

On September 1, 2006, the U.S. government announced, not for the first time, its determination to bolster its defenses at its northern border. Describing Canada as "a potential conduit for bioterrorism, pests and disease," the U.S. Department of Agriculture is increasing its search powers and charging travelers the costs through entry fees. These new inspection powers affect entry by air, sea, truck, or railway. Describing the Canada–U.S. border as the "longest undefended border in the world," the U.S. government bemoans its current "dearth of inspection activity at that border [which] could potentially leave the United States vulnerable to bioterrorism."[95]

It is impossible to chronicle the series of declared, threatened, and actual changes to border policy following September 11, 2001. A brief analysis of this report must suffice to summarize the effects of that event on the governing of the border between Canada and the United States. The idea of "the longest undefended border in the world" has been so transformed that the phrase no longer means success, but rather failure. The prominence of cross-border travel issues in news stories and political debates demonstrates significant divisions between and within the two governments. If one branch of U.S. government wants tighter policing of the border, another is concerned that billions of dollars will be lost by impeding commercial travel. If one branch of Canadian government wants to placate the United States at any cost, others lament commercial damage and still others object to the militarization of a historically peaceful national border. For Canada's minister of international trade, anything that is "trade disruptive" is a major concern; meanwhile Prime Minister Harper spends over $100 million on arming Canadian border officers. Meetings of NAFTA leaders have failed to resolve this contradiction.

Note that the dangers emanating from the north are identified as "potential" dangers, making the United States "potentially" vulnerable to bioterrorism. American plans for policing its borders are in this respect consistent with America's political trajectory. As Michel Foucault and Brian Massumi have shown, neoliberalism constantly reconnects with security through the evocation of a culture of danger.[96] The objects in question in this flurry of press releases are plants, animals, fruits, and vegetables. Such pronouncements invite us to reimagine their flight over the border as a possible act of hostility, and thus to be emotionally complicit with their redefinition as potential biohazards unleashed by future acts. They are not biohazards because they are being polluted every day by ecocriminals governing contemporary agribusiness, but because someday, somehow, imaginary terrorists may find ways of making them dangerous. The prospect of the imagined future imperializing the present anticipates my argument in "Cultural Technologies and the 'Evolution' of Technological Cultures" (chapter 9), where the oft-noted domination of time by space is implosively reversed. With this move the ideal of sovereignty is rededicated to security, without which all other rights of Canadians (according to current pronouncements) are simply theoretical.

two

Space at the Margins

COLONIAL SPATIALITY AND
CRITICAL THEORY AFTER INNIS

It is in space, on a worldwide scale, that each idea of "value" acquires or loses its distinctiveness through confrontation with the other values and ideas that it encounters there. Moreover—and more importantly—groups, classes, or fractions of classes cannot constitute themselves, or recognize one another, as "subjects" unless they generate (or produce) a space. Ideas, representations or values which do not succeed in making their mark on space, and thus generating (or producing) an appropriate morphology, will lose all pith and become mere signs, resolve themselves into abstract descriptions, or mutate into fantasies.—HENRI LEFEBVRE, *The Production of Space*

Branch plants of American industries were built in Canada in order to take advantage of the Canadian-European system and British imperialism. As part of her east-west program, Canada had built up a series of imperial preferential arrangements in which Great Britain had felt compelled to acquiesce and which proved enormously advantageous to American branch plants. Paradoxically, the stoutest defenders of the Canadian tariff against the United States were the representatives of American capital investors. Canadian nationalism was systematically encouraged and exploited by American capital. Canada moved from colony to nation to colony.—HAROLD INNIS, "Great Britain, the United States, and Canada"

The 1994 centenary of the birth of Harold Innis stimulated scholars from various regions and disciplines to enter into dialogue with his work and with one another. The work of this economic historian and communication theorist has been revisited by a number of Canadian cultural studies scholars interested in how Innis's work can inform newer issues and debates in cultural studies.[1] Innis's centenary assumed particular significance in relation to the "spatial turn" in cultural studies, which encouraged a shift away from the analysis of representation in texts toward an analysis of communication as a technological and spatial process with its own meanings in specific locales. I took this event as an opportunity to explore Innis's research on technology, space, and empire in relation to this later literature in terms of its approach to the cultural and spatial strategies of European colonization and globalization.

Significant works that appeared during the "spatial turn" included Edward Soja's *Postmodern Geographies*, Edward Said's *Orientalism*, Neil Smith's *Uneven Development*, Doreen Massey's *Spatial Divisions of Labour*, Timothy Mitchell's *Colonizing Egypt*, David Harvey's *The Condition of Postmodernity*, the English translation of Henri Lefebvre's *The Production of Space*, Mike Featherstone's *Global Cultures*, Rob Shields's *Places at the Margins*, Said's *Culture and Imperialism*, Anthony King's *Culture, Globalization and the World System*, Michael Keith's and Steve Pile's *Place/Culture/Representation: Place and the Politics of Identity*, Derek Gregory's *Geographical Imaginations*, Scott Lash's and John Urry's *Economies of Signs and Space*, Homi Bhabha's *Nation in Narration*, and related work by Fredric Jameson, James Clifford, Arjun Appadurai, Néstor García Canclini, and Meaghan Morris. None of these studies refers to Innis's ideas or influence. Reflecting on Innis's legacy, I wondered about the significance of this absence. My suspicions were confirmed when I heard a reputable scholar assert at a conference on "Postcolonial Geographies and Changing Sites of Subjectivity" that what was lacking in the literature was a materialist analysis of colonial space. "Excuse me," I said, "but Innis initiated such an analysis, and scholars have been elaborating it for some half a century—how do you account for its absence in the current discussion?" "Oh," he said in the casually helpful manner of a British academic teaching at a prestigious American university; "You have to understand about intellectual capital."

Happily I was able to go home and share this anecdote with colleagues who could recognize its ironic implications. The differential production of "intellectual capital" (as Pierre Bourdieu terms it) is a cornerstone of the machinery at work in the constitution of modern and contemporary relations between center and margin. Innis's principal contribution to the history of culture is his insistence on the crucial role of communication and transportation technologies in forming such spatial configurations of power. Shaped in turn by commercial and geopolitical contexts, these technologies facilitate the ongoing production of centers and margins; that is to say, spatially differentiated hierarchies of political-economic power. Placing technology and space at the center of his research enabled Innis and researchers influenced by him to establish a reflexively marginal approach to the strategic imbrications of technology, culture, knowledge, and power which have shaped Western imperialism.

My search of book indexes suggested that Innis's approach was incompatible with the paradigms framing culture and politics in international academia, which focused on the construction of subjects and identities, and assumed the material circulation of knowledge as a transparent frame for thought. Furthermore, white Anglophone Canadian scholars (especially political economists of any description) are not sufficiently charismatic models for the struggle against colonization as this struggle has been defined by subaltern scholarship in the United States. Canadians occupy neither the center nor the margin, and they possess insufficient intellectual capital because they are not perceived as "other" in the dominant terms through which culture and identity are construed. These are two different explanations, but they are connected.

This absence opens a convenient pathway to an exploration of the "margin" as a geophysical, cultural, and political entity. Given the rapid globalization of communication, the radical decentering claims made on behalf of network technologies, and recent attempts to disconnect empire from geography, this remains an important critical task. Marginality is now largely a metaphorical rather than spatial term. Fredric Jameson includes a feeling of being on the periphery amongst his seven features of postmodernity;[2] Michel de Certeau claims that "marginality is becoming universal";[3] and Shields suggests that modern liberalism is reconstituting itself by calling for "the incorporation of the 'marginal' into a de-politicising framework that co-opts it."[4] In such accounts, marginality is everywhere and nowhere. Tony Bennett argues that cultural studies was generatively structured by a discursive rule through which critics established the legitimacy of their position not via theoretical or methodological terms but rather on the grounds of marginality. This rule "offers an ethical-cum-political compensation for [cultural studies'] theoretical and methodological indeterminacy in construing social marginality as an experiential route which allows those who travel it to achieve an integrative kind of intellectual wholeness which stands in for theoretical and methodological criteria in furnishing cultural studies with its epistemological protocols."[5]

My purpose here is not to appraise such protocols for cultural studies but more modestly to consider what Innis's work contributes to the notion of the "margin"; what research on the production of space teaches us about this concept; and whether marginality still describes a spatial relationship in the contemporary global order of things.

Trains and Boats and Planes

Innis's analysis of colonial relations between center and margin preceded his research on communications and shaped its parameters. His notion of the margin relies on a notion of a center and a dialectically productive relationship between the two. As James Carey explains Innis's challenge to American history: "Every frontier, in short, has a back tier."[6] American historians identified the experience of conquering the frontier as the foundation of "manifest destiny." "Big spatial ideas," wrote Ellen Churchill Semple in 1911, "born of . . . ceaseless regular wandering, outgrow the land that bred them and bear their legitimate fruit in wide imperial conquests."[7] This popular view suggests that it was contact with the land that gave rise to the culture of conquest, and that it was the end of the expanse of the land that ended manifest destiny. (I explore this theme in my introduction, "Mapping *North of Empire*.") These attempts to represent land as both site and cause of colonial history invite a most skeptical response.

Innis's critique of the frontier hypothesis originated with his research on the fur trade, which led him to focus on the development of the canoe, boat, and rail routes that transported European commerce to the New World. European explorers entered into the fur trade in order to trade profitable goods in exchange for imported goods conducive to the continuation of their way of life in the new country. "The importance of metropolitan centres in which luxury goods were in most demand was crucial to the development of colonial North America. In these centres goods were manufactured for the consumption of colonials and in these centres goods produced in the colonies were sold at the highest price."[8] Two crucial and thoroughly imbricated historical patterns emerged from this trade: the development of increasingly rapid transport routes across the Canadian shield and eventually through to the Pacific coast; and the emergence of a mercantile policy dedicated to the export of natural resources, or "staples," for external markets. The combination of natural, economic, and administrative forces enabling the fur and fish trades contributed to the subordination of "agriculture, industry, transportation, trade, finance, and governmental activities . . . to the production of the staple for a more highly specialized manufacturing community."[9] This manufacturing community, or "back tier," was of course Europe. Later the United States assumed both roles.

Innis showed that patterns of transportation and trade in Canada were shaped by the ongoing imposition of European administrative and commercial imperatives onto indigenous landscape and culture, first through trade routes which traced and swallowed up traditional hunting and travel routes, then in the administrative patterns of governance, industry, and finance that created Canada as a colonial nation-state. Europeans followed the water transportation and riverside travel routes used by First Nations such as the Huron and the Algonkians, drawing on their knowledge and resources as well as their territory. The transformation from settlement to colony (and later to nation, and then, as Innis's famous phrase reminds us, back to colony) was accomplished through the strategic construction of transport and communication technologies along these same routes, enabling European colonizers to appropriate the land, the natural resources, and the cultures of the "New World." Hunters, navigators, and explorers relied on the knowledge and cooperation of the indigenous peoples, who in the early years of exploration derived power from their knowledge of the land and their usefulness to the explorers.[10] Before long, however, their access to land, traditions, and forms of knowledge collapsed before the pecuniary and technical advantages of the European explorers, and the land, along with its use, was profoundly altered. Treaties introduced radically new forms of property, distribution, and land use, and divided hunting and fishing "rights" from ownership of the land.[11]

In emphasizing the material practices through which Europe produced this geography of colonial space, Innis anticipates postcolonial geography by some fifty years. He describes a materially and ontologically based relationship between space and time which requires a fundamental reconceptualization of space itself. He conceives topographical space as produced space, and shows that the production of space and the production of social life form one process. Space is neither an uninhabited frontier nor a backdrop for history, but the very subject and matter of historical change. Communication technologies mediate the social relations of a particular society by setting the limits and boundaries within which power and knowledge operate.[12] While natural resources play a role in the emergence of geopolitical margins, colonial space is the product not of nature but of social practice.

"Country between Red River Settlement and the Rocky Mountains" (detail).
Map by Captain John Palliser, British North America Exploring Expedition, 1859.
Courtesy of Metro Reference Library, Toronto.

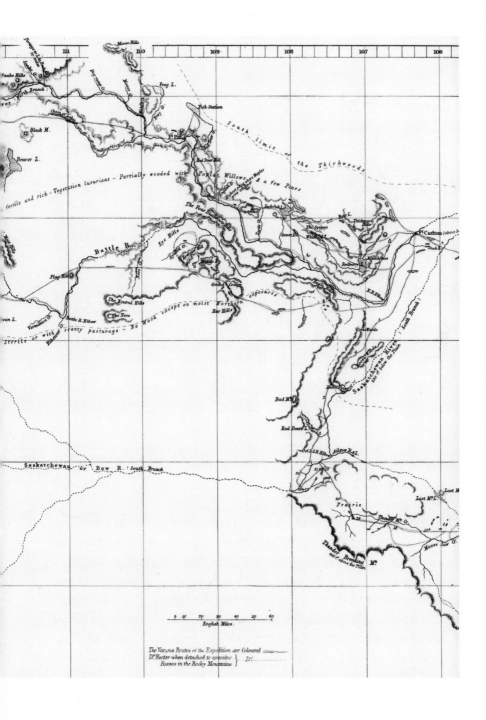

English Miles.

The Various Routes of the Expedition are Coloured ⸺
Dr Hector when detached to examine
Passes in the Rocky Mountains } Dr ⸺

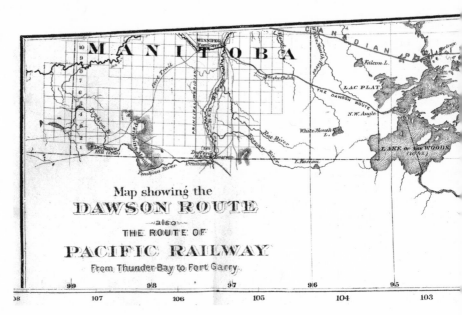

Dawson Railway Route. *New Standard Atlas*, 1875. Courtesy of Metro Reference Library, Toronto.

Central to Innis's understanding of this process is the proposition that communication technologies build societies through a dynamic interdependency between time and space. The tendency to enhance communication across space or across time at the relative expense of the other is part of a process through which rulers of a society constitute monopolies of knowledge. Transportation and communication media draw populations into the axis of imperial power across space or time, and political distortion arises when one grows in proportion to the diminishing of the other. Such bias ensures the foundation but also (since the loss of balance ensures collapse) the downfall of every empire.[13] In modern Western culture, space-biased communications such as telegraphs, trains, paper, and electronic networks enable the acquisition, transmission, and control of information over an ever-expanding geographic space. Because what is communicated is light, easily reproduced and disseminated, and quickly replaced, it is not amenable to preservation in time. Power is obtained through development of the most technically advanced, farthest reaching, and most quickly dissemi-

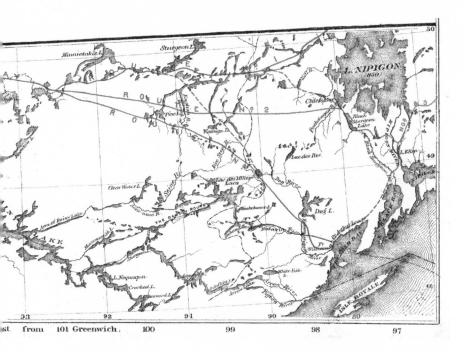

nated technologies. How people relate across distance and history—space
and time—is redefined through such mediation. Power over this process is
one definition of empire.

In analyzing political administration in terms of the balance of and control over space and time, Innis's framework is arguably more subtle than
many space theorists who posit, as Doreen Massey has cogently argued,
a variety of binary oppositions between space and time. Space has been
conceived as a passive entity that registers response to change in opposition
to time, which is dynamic and active. It is no coincidence, then, that both
"space and the feminine are frequently defined in terms of dichotomies in
which each of them is most commonly defined as not-A."[14] In this paradigm
space is a wheat field and time is a train shooting across it. Physics offers
an alternative critical vantage point on the basis of its insistence that "definitions of both space and time in themselves must be constructed as the
result of interrelations." Massey references the transformation of physics by
Albert Einstein and Hermann Minkowski, who reject "the evolution of a

CP Rail freight train passing through the small prairie town of Pilot Butte, Saskatchewan, in the winter of 1977. "The wheat cannot be understood separately from the train." Photograph by Hank Suderman.

three-dimensional experience" in favor of a four-dimensional physical reality. "Henceforth space by itself and time by itself, are doomed to fade away into mere shadows, and only a kind of union of the two will preserve an independent reality."[15] Innis's emphasis on interaction between space and time does not add any direct insight to relations between space and gender, but it does identify material processes through which time and space achieve their specific configurations and relations. The space of western Canada is both sought and produced by the building of the railway. The wheat cannot be understood separately from the train, and vice versa.

Like more recent theorists, Innis viewed colonial space as traversed space; not the empty landscape of a wilderness, or geometrical, abstractly quantifiable space, but space that has been mapped and shaped by specific imperial forms of knowledge and administration. Thus the fur trade routes, the Canadian Pacific Railway (CPR), the rise of American newspaper monopolies in interdependency with Canada's pulp and paper industry (and, later, cars, television, data processing, and satellites) are part of a fundamentally political apparatus through which colonial space is produced. Such technologies mediate ontologically between power and knowledge and spatially between center and periphery. Modern space-binding communications facilitate both the spread of empire and the reorganization of cultures within its reach.

Steven Kern notes that "by 1900 . . . all nations assumed that growth was good, and none questioned the wisdom of trying to achieve it." National cultures across Europe shared the conviction that "big is good," along with the "implied political imperatives—to expand for greatness or fall into mediocrity."[16] Innis's critique of these space-binding imperatives arose from his own experience as a Canadian returning from a devastating war and undertaking a historical study of empire while witnessing the rapid rise of the new one to the south.[17] If European officers bullied and humiliated Canadian soldiers on the basis of their own assumed cultural superiority, democracy seemed unlikely to fare any better under new forms of monopoly accompanying what Innis called "the change from British imperialism to American imperialism."[18] Postwar expansionism in American commerce and media seemed to reiterate Europe's imperial traditions and the imperial strategies of Greece and Rome, from which Innis derived his model of communication and empire. The rapid "mechanization of knowledge" and the flinging of media commodities across the continent had to be understood as the basis for a new mode of imperial expansion dedicated to conquest through technological forms and values.

Like Oswald Spengler, whose *Decline of the West* is mentioned in Innis's essays, and George Grant, whose writing appeared after his death, Innis sees modernity as the expression of a Faustian obsession with spatial expansion and conquest.[19] Innis expresses his dismay at the political effects of this obsession, specifically the vulnerability to an unstable body politic in which—as Spengler wrote in 1923—"moments seemed of overwhelming insignificance."[20] Writing after the First World War, Spengler contends that the modern era possesses "an unsurpassably intense Will to the future," wherein all meaning is embodied.[21] Responding both to the devastating effects of the First World War and the acceleration and expansion of electronic communications following the Second World War, Innis's critique is directed to the political and epistemological consequences of the accelerating mechanization of knowledge. He writes: "What Spengler has called the Faustian West is a result of living mentally and historically and is in contrast with other important civilizations which are 'ahistoric.'"[22] What Innis calls "the modern obsession with present-mindedness" is a consequence of space-biased communication and a crucial strategy of modern industrialism.[23] This obsession transforms all domains of knowledge production: journalism creates newsworthiness separate from ethics, place, or community; science accumulates knowledge by "continually liquidating its past"; academia suffers from overspecialization and the bureaucratic fragmentation and transience of knowledge, and (to extrapolate once again) modernist aesthetics elaborates the will to release perception from memory.

Innis's later essays are haunted by anxiety about the growth of a monopolistic mass media fueled by marketing and sensationalism, the ideological ascendancy of economic rationality and technological progress, Canada's distinctive but disempowered skepticism about the marketplace as the fountainhead of democracy, the increasing power of metropolitan centers, growing political instability, and social atomization. As with many interwar intellectuals, his combined military experience, education, and disposition encouraged a pessimistic view of mass media and popular culture. In his resistance to these developments, Innis represents, as Charles Acland suggests, a "historical bridge between an [Matthew] Arnoldian vision of culture and an epistemological critique of power."[24] Innis erects this bridge with a critique of new communication technologies and the way they contributed to monopolies of knowledge, and provides a countering evocation of oral culture, whose capacity for dialogue and creativity offers an antidote to the monopolization of thought in the new regime. Oral culture is then redefined as a mode of practice through which the "margins" resist the center's expansionary monopolies of knowledge with their dangerous lack of dialogue and reflexivity. As Stamps explains,

> These theorists not only spoke about marginalized realities; they consciously represented them. Innis saw his version of history as both a theory about margins and an instance of them. McLuhan wrote about marginal counter-environments as antidotes to rigid institutions and, at the same time, represented such an antidote. Adorno and Benjamin spoke about negative dialectic and tried in some sense to be that dialectic . . . by definition, its creators if they were to represent a positive theory of margins and still avoid developing a new super-positive.[25]

Spatial Strategies

For Innis, the conflict between technological expansion and the residual practices and continuities or discontinuities of oral culture is a central feature of modern history. Control of information technology shapes the parameters of communication, knowledge, and memory, and determines the proximity to and nature of power itself. A "margin" is a space which is drawn into the axes of imperial economy, administration, and information but which remains "behind" (to put it in temporal terms) or "outside" (spatially speaking) in terms of economic and political power. Communication technologies facilitate the simultaneous integration and extrusion of colonized territories. The margin is a spatial concept, but colonial space is the product, not the predecessor, of colonizing practices. Colonial space is not simply acquired; it is not an object. Its usable topographies are shaped, in dialectical interaction with its own agents and resources, to serve the requirements of empire.

We hear echoes of this idea in Lefebvre's insistence that (social) space is a (social) product.[26]

> The state and each of its constituent institutions call for spaces—but spaces which they can then organize according to their specific requirements; so there is no sense in which space can be treated solely as an a priori condition of these institutions and the state which presides over them. Is space a social relationship? Certainly—but one which is inherent to property relationships (especially the ownership of the earth, of land) and also closely bound up with the forces of production (which impose a form on that earth or land); here we see the polyvalence of social space, its 'reality' at once formal and material. Though a product to be consumed, it is also a means of production; networks of exchange and flows of raw materials fashion space and are determined by it. Thus this means of production, produced as such, cannot be separated either from the productive forces, including technology and knowledge, or from the social division of labour which shapes it, or from the state and the superstructures of society.[27]

Innis's ideas are not just complementary to this discussion but are crucial for understanding empire in its contemporary form. The materials and relations of communication are productive forces mediating the social transformation of space. The spatial and social organization of knowledge, in which media technologies play a central role, is part of the "means of production" whereby natural space is transformed into productive space, creating the social spaces of contemporary capitalism.

Taking Lefebvre's analysis as his own point of departure, Derek Gregory points to postcolonial scholarship as a project emphasizing "the dispossession that the West visited upon colonial societies through a series of intrinsically spatial strategies."[28] Gregory connects this project to de Certeau's notion of strategy, which describes "the means through which a constellation of power is inscribed in its own—its proper-place." Such strategies are

> actions which, thanks to the establishment of a place of power (the property of a proper), elaborate theoretical places (systems and totalizing discourses) capable of articulating an ensemble of physical places in which forces are distributed. They combine these three types of place and seek to master each by means of the others. They thus privilege spatial relationships. At the very least they attempt to reduce temporal relations to spatial ones through the analytical attribution of a proper place to each particular element.[29]

Gregory concludes that these strategies "mark the triumph of space over time (the production of a 'proper place') . . . the mastery of places through sight . . . and the power to 'transform the uncertainties of history into readable spaces.'"[30] Of course the securing of a "proper place" is never complete; as Harvey emphasizes in his research on urban form, the places of capitalism must be constantly recommodified and redefined, built and rebuilt. The triumph of space over time in this reading is contingent and temporary. Secured space must be continuously reproduced, its meanings reconsolidated through new strategies, new technologies, and new modes of negotiation and resistance.

Like other colonial historians, Innis understands colonial power as the right and capability to determine the principle strategies or technologies through which imperial forces seek to master and develop social space. Rather than emphasizing representations *of* space, Innis contextualizes representational spaces within the dynamics of space versus time, visuality versus orality, hierarchy versus community, and center versus periphery, through which technical developments in transport and communication take shape. This reorganization of space and time structures the material forms and limits of knowledge, as well as our relationships with place and with one another. This point reveals the limits to analyzing power in terms of representation. If visuality emerged as a preferred vehicle for colonizing strategies of representation, as postcolonial and critical visual theory contends, this is because visual media promote specific modes of perception and understanding which contribute to the organization of the society and culture in which they circulate. "Communication based on the eye in terms of printing and photography had developed a monopoly which threatened to destroy Western civilization first in war and then in peace," Innis writes in "A Plea for Time." "This monopoly emphasized individualism and in turn instability and created illusions in catchwords such as democracy, freedom of the press, and freedom of speech. . . . As modern developments in communication have made for greater realism they have made for greater possibilities of delusion."[31]

Innis refers here to his theory that the doctrine of freedom of the press was a key instrument in the formation of press monopolies which relied on (and worked to maintain) Canada as the industrially underdeveloped source of raw materials for American manufacture. He does not set out to analyze what is in the newspapers. Instead he analyzes the production of newspapers as a mediation of the materials, technologies, and "systems and totalizing discourses" (in de Certeau's words) which are imbricated by them. His analysis of newspapers focuses on their importance in the production of centers—which produce and disseminate such materials and technologies—and margins—which provide the raw material for newsprint together with local skepticism about the knowledge thereby disseminated. Newspapers, together with the transport technologies that produce and disseminate them, facilitated a centralization, or geographic "bundling," of news writing. The assembled technologies which gave rise to the news enabled publishers to gather it from a variety of places and juxtapose it on a single page, with the effect that place was emphasized in the expansion of technological capabilities but deemphasized in the editorial process.[32] Newspapers facilitated the center's power over the margins through productive relationships (wherein manufactured goods could be exchanged for raw materials), through the dissemination and influence of a particular mode of knowledge, and through the monopolizing ideology of the freedom of the press.

Innis's analysis of the press emphasizes the idea that the production of American industry (the center) cannot be separated from the production of a staples-based economy in Canada (the margin); the dialectical relationship which produces them is economic, technological, spatial, and cultural at the same time. The process of spatial transformation exemplified by the newspaper can be deciphered in all subsequent technologies.

Technologies of the Margin

"What is a margin?" I asked a friend. "You know what a margin is," she replied, "It's outside the body of the text. It's what holds the page together." "Also," she added, "it's where you write your notes." By pointing to the metaphor's roots in the spatiovisual configuration of the printed word, this description raises useful questions for interrogating the heterogeneous nature of marginal space. How does it hold the page together? What text is it outside of, and how is it kept there? To what extent is the margin's shape determined by the text? Is the determination unilateral, or fragmented, dynamic, and contradictory? To what extent does the determination go the other way? Isn't a text shaped by its margin? And does this occluded margin wish to be included in the central body which it stands apart from and observes?

As we have seen, Innis defines a margin as a dependent pole in a spatially administered dynamic hierarchy of political and economic power mediated by technologies and modes of communication. His research describes the formation of monopolies that control the circulation of knowledge and information, and the simultaneous emergence of territorial dependencies whose effect is to centralize and decentralize such knowledge and information. He also describes marginal uses of technology as potentially innovative and capable of destabilizing the control of information. Their efficacy is limited by the complex nature of communication technology itself, which (here Innis differs from McLuhan) comprises a set of relationships shaped by economic, legal, and cultural constraints as well as by technological capacities in the pure sense. In the center's attempt to maintain control through copyright, ownership and distribution, economies of scale, narratives of development, technical standards, technical obsolescence, tariffs and duties, and other government regulation, it seeks to maintain power over communicative space.

Relations between center and margin are the product of social, technical, and ontological imbalances of time and space, whose symptoms include an acceleration of speed in technological and cultural change; a constant displacement of oral culture and of collective memory; and an increasing instrumentalization of space as central to the practices of power. Historically, Innis argues, print media gave rise to the democratization of knowledge and the achievements of humanistic culture. Yet the spread of space-biased communication technology also led to the accelerating marginalization of oral cultures, the rationalization of knowledge, and the erosion of difference, reflexivity, and duration. The American empire's predilection for conquering space through media technology thus represents both a continuation of Western culture and a movement toward its destruction. Continuity with Western culture is expressed in the extension of the modernizing, visualizing, and rationalizing space-bias of paper and print, but this bias ultimately exceeds the possibility of spatial or ontological balance, marginalizing or obliterating sites of memory, tradition, spirituality, dialogue, and other aspects of oral culture that have been appropriated and transformed through the production of technological space.

Unlike other postwar intellectuals hostile to the perceived degradation of humanistic culture, Innis characterizes this threat not in terms of meanings or values, but rather in terms of the material processes through which knowledge is disseminated and through which such meanings and values are shaped. These material processes structure and normalize the ratios of reason and emotion, technique and memory, power and location, space and time. His is not a history of ideologies, states, classes, or representations, but a history of rivers, railways, radios, and rationalizations. Each represents a changing mediation between imperial power and its proximate and distant subjects. His approach is strongly materialist, but not Marxist; aside from his disinterest in class he focuses, as Daniel Drache has observed, on relations of trade—and thus the production of space—rather than on production itself.[33] Still, there are striking correspondences between Innis and Karl Marx in their treatment of time and space. In *Grundrisse*, Marx notes:

> Capital by its nature drives beyond every spatial barrier. Thus the creation of the physical conditions of exchange—of the means of communication and transport—the annihilation of space by time—becomes an extraordinary necessity for it. . . . Thus, while capital must on one side strive to tear down every spatial barrier to intercourse, i.e. to exchange, and conquer the whole world for its market, it strives on the other side to annihilate this space with time, i.e. to reduce to a minimum the time spent in motion from one place to another.[34]

For Innis, as for Marx, time succumbs to space in response to the technological changes orchestrated to expand international commerce and trade. His emphasis on this point, and his study of ancient and modern history through the conceptual lens of technology and media bias, reminds us how much the emergent imperialism of the modern age was based on covert economic and technological strategies for colonizing space. The classic imperialistic practices of the European "Age of Empire" reached a state of crisis in the early part of the twentieth century. Imperialism did not disappear, but it was transformed before Innis's eyes with the changing shape of global politics. If European officers ruled their battlefields with arrogance, Europe's claim to the superiority of an advanced civilization lay in bloody tatters in those same battlefields. A survivor of that catastrophic slaughter, Innis was alert to the replacement of one economy of power by a new type, predicated on the colonization of time by space and characterized, as Said puts it, by "the privileged role of culture in the modern imperial experience."[35]

Obviously this is imperialism of a new sort. The twentieth-century newspaper or network television does not replicate the contemptuous arrogance of a European who assumes that imperial privilege and cultural superiority are one and the same. However, both sets of practices convey the assumption of a local value made universal; the first concerning truth and beauty, the other fun and freedom. Stuart Hall describes this shift as

> [the emergence of a] new type of globalization [which] is not English, it is American. In cultural terms, the new kind of globalization has to do with a new form of global mass culture, very different from that associated with English identity, and the cultural identities associated with the nation-state in an earlier phase. Global mass culture is dominated by the modern means of cultural production, dominated by the image which crosses and re-crosses linguistic frontiers much more rapidly and more easily, and which speaks across languages in a much more immediate way. . . . One might think of satellite television as the prime example. Not because it is the only example but because you could not understand satellite television without understanding its grounding in a particular advanced national economy and culture and yet its whole purpose is precisely that it cannot be limited any longer by national boundaries.[36]

This passage helps to actualize the understanding of globalization already cited: "the process by which a grown local condition or entity succeeds in extending its reach over the globe and, by doing so, develops the capacity to designate a rival social condition or entity as local."[37] Hall avoids the terminology of empire. If his description otherwise echoes Innis's thoughts on newspapers and the mass media, this simply emphasizes how much Innis recognized and anticipated these globalization strategies. By 1900, commentators on new communication technologies were already predicting the rapid elimination of distance, cultural difference, and national boundaries. Electrified by telegraphs and telephones, these commentators tended to forefront the technologies rather than the political or economic contexts in which they emerged.[38] Innis insists on making explicit the connection between these forces. His comparison of European and American imperialism has less to do with culture as the term is conventionally defined than with the centrality of communication technologies to the administration of power and knowledge, and their cumulative effects in the reorganization of social space.

Like Kern, Innis and Carey identify the emergence of this new era with the telegraph. This innovation enables information to be separated from human bodies, so that henceforth it is possible to traverse and therefore control a range of sites by exporting messages—telegraphs, airwaves, databases, satellite beams, and so on—rather than armies.[39] Like paper and books, these new carriers extend the reach and potential impact of controlled knowledge over broader expanses of space. Unlike paper and books, such technologies are generally impervious to linguistic or national borders, a capacity that is increasingly part of their mandate and design. The capitalization of space thus takes a new form. Rather than setting out to conquer unclaimed or autonomous spaces around the globe, empires begin to expand their domain through the recolonization of already produced spaces by means of the recommodification of services, spaces (urban renewal), bodies (pharmaceutical, biogenetic, and space research), information (continuous software updating), everyday life (the influx of new entertainment and cultural technologies), and work (the dispersion of labor across the globe). An important effect of this shift is that American political leaders and citizens view themselves not as members of an imperial or advanced civilization, as their European predecessors had, but rather, to cite Said once again, as "righter of wrongs around the world, in pursuit of tyranny, in defence of freedom no matter the place or cost."[40] It is not hard to conjure up the pleasures and compulsions of writing on the margin of that text. On the other hand, it is more difficult to locate what or where the margin is.

Aporias of Uneven Development

The history of modern imperialism has been narrated here as the history of time colonized by space. In this narrative, local cultures and knowledge forms are uprooted, fragmented, and replaced by the space-leveling, distance-abolishing, rapidly changing dissemination of increasingly immaterial information via electronic media. Yet contemporary empire also involves a different, albeit related, process in which space succumbs to the continuous recommodification of time. The ongoing differentiation of space already associated with imperialism coexists with the growing equalization of space more recently associated with globalization. As Neil Smith argues, both processes are a necessary part of uneven development whereby different regions of the world (and within these regions, different social groups and cultural economies) are differentially empowered by global trade.[41]

The continuing differentiation of space is both the foundation and the geopolitical result of the global division of labor, wherein some regions provide natural resources (or, more contemporaneously, technical resources such as telecommunications hardware or silicon chips) to other regions whose more-advanced production capabilities thereby reproduce their relative advantages in wealth and power. This differentiation is what Innis had in mind when he placed the production of staples at the heart of Canadian economic history. While globalization (or, less euphemistically, transnational capitalism) continues to produce inequitable difference, there is also an unending, always incomplete process of capitalization which works to make regions interchangeable through what Smith calls the equalization of space.[42] This process "equalizes" spaces by subjecting local markets, industrial processes and commodities, patterns of urban growth, sciences and technologies, narratives and fantasies, forests and food, and so on, to competitive processes of innovation and exploitation defined and disseminated by powerful corporate oligopolies. This does not mean that every nation, region, or city (not to mention gender, class, or ethnicity) will—or can—achieve equitable levels of wealth and autonomy. Nor does it mean that difference among nations or regions disappears. It means that subjects on the margin experience both processes simultaneously: one which compels the palpable commodifiable differentiation of space, and one which compels its functional equalization with other spaces across the globe. This is a spatial configuration of what Arjun Appadurai calls the central tension of global culture: that between cultural homogenization and cultural heterogenization, with all their singular complexities.[43] Chatterjee locates this dynamic at the heart of colonial societies and analyzes it under the rubric of the "rule of colonial difference."[44] Nation-states seek to emphasize the cultural differences between the colonizer and the colonized, Chatterjee argues, so as to be able to declare sovereignty over the "inner domain of national life." At the same time, in the "outer" domains of economy, administration, and law, colonial nationalism fights to "erase the marks of colonial difference."[45] As these processes are interdependent, conflict is embedded in the body of the culture as well as the economy.[46]

Throughout the last century, communication has been the site of both difference-making and difference-abolishing policies and instruments. Government and corporate interests have employed strategies that variously encourage and sabotage cultural difference and heterogeneity. Such strategies are inextricably bound to emergent technologies and their paradoxical effects. A government apparatus which once evoked national difference to justify the spatial expansion of broadcasting technologies, later evokes the inexorable drive of the global information revolution to further the same end.[47] The often disruptive process of negotiation between these conflicting dynamics forms what Massey calls the "power-geometry" of contemporary globalization, whereby space becomes a "complex web of relations of domination and subordination, of solidarity and cooperation."[48]

The complex duality of this process finds a parallel in the technologies which materialize it. Like the social trajectories that frame them, communication technologies simultaneously produce and abolish difference in their subjects. Innis's historiography thus depicts technology as part of a complex and powerful apparatus that both generates and withholds power. Since communication media influence the forms of social organization that are possible, "competition for new means of communication [is] a principal axis of the competitive struggle."[49] Marginal groups both resist and depend upon the cultural technologies that create their awareness of themselves as margins. For spatially defined margins, whether a country or its peripheries, meanings of place are inevitably articulated to this ambivalent awareness.

Natural Differences

The concept of "equalization of spaces" has an easy set of visual referents: McDonald's golden arches, Hollywood, Sony, automated bank machines, cars, software that travels anywhere. This process depends on the technical ability to disembed the profitable capacities of a place from its physical or geographic specificities. Differentiation, on the other hand, involves learning new ways to derive profit from spatial and geographic difference. Again images spring readily to mind: sparkling lakes and snowy mountains, canopies of trees, sandy beaches or even monuments, so long as they appear ancient and unchanged, like mountains, in various parts of the world.

As we are so often reminded, wealth now depends less on sovereignty over natural resources (except in the tourist zones just described), than on access to information technologies. In traditional modernization theory, regional disparities are potentially abolished by the process of technological change. Any countries can have microchips, if they manage development properly, and so any country can join the First World, or at least the Second World. The flawed logic here stems from the supposition that it is the possession of natural resources (fish, lumber, ivory, beaches) that produced a marginal economy in the first place, forcing the country or region in question to depend upon them to the exclusion of other activities. If geography and nature account for the marginal status of peripheral countries, then technological development—the transcendence of nature—will, it is thought, transform that status. In fact, the possession of such natural resources properly makes a country rich, not poor. We need to demolish both propositions in this hypothesis—not only because Innis is (wrongly, I think) accused of being a geographical determinist, but more importantly, because this demolition has implications for thinking about nature and technology as these are articulated to marginal spaces.

Neither the "discovery" of natural resources, nor the arrival of the colonist explorers and settlers who discovered them, were fortuitous events. The "age of discovery" betrayed its residual medieval origins by endowing far-off places with extraordinary cosmological powers. Travelers' encounters with the New World were shaped by their readiness to find a natural paradise suffused with abundant riches and savage wilderness. As Mary Helms writes, "A form of paradise already held Western connotations prior to the discoveries, but the attribution of wilderness and its qualities to the West was new and clearly part of the effort to create and identify a new cosmological locale."[50] By the eighteenth century, when Jesuits and entrepreneurs were traveling up the St. Lawrence and setting out across the Canadian Shield—a story to which we return in "Weathering the North" (chapter 7)—the magical qualities projected onto the land and inhabitants of these newly discovered worlds were being appropriated and assigned to the travelers themselves. Eighteenth-century explorers began to view themselves as "'second creators' of distant worlds which for them were newly established and newly regarded not only with fear and fantasy, but also with the confident superiority of men, who, now God-like as much as God-fearing, having conquered the ocean with their bravery, skills, and intelligence, believed they could conquer whatever else they encountered."[51] The association between exploration and conquest, together with its "intimations of immortality," was reinforced by more worldly incentives. In 1817, frustrated with the material failure of previous expeditions, the British Admiralty offered 20,000 pounds to the discoverer of the Northwest Passage. Successive expeditions did much to popularize the vision of the Canadian north as a rich but dangerous place requiring great heroism and perspicacity to conquer.[52]

This history of associations between nature and power encouraged travelers to project onto their destination an emergent modern identification between temporal and spatial settings. The explorers possessed the powers of modernity, distance, and science, while aboriginal populations were disempowered materially and symbolically because they were traditional stationary societies. Commenting on the inability of Europeans to respond more constructively to the indigenous peoples, Georges Sioui emphasizes the perceived temporal distance between the two groups. Europeans were "ahead" of the indigenous people they "discovered." He attributes this to two ideas: first, "the theory of social evolution, which puts forward, as a truth, the principle that those peoples who possess the most 'advanced' technology and the 'capacity of writing' are in the vanguard of the process of 'evolution,' and thus have the right, inherent to their culture, and the responsibility, to bring about the 'development' of the 'less advanced.'" The second idea following from this is what Sioui calls the "inevitable disappearance of the Native."[53] The "Native" does not seek to control nature, a theme to which we return in "Weathering the North" (chapter 7), and thus is simply incapable of advancing. The colonizer does not wish her to advance. In *Inventing the Indian*, Thomas King describes the double bind this way:

Most writers who deal with Indian culture insist that, in order to maintain its purity and power, Indian culture must remain unchanged. Any deviations in the ceremonies or rituals are not signs of growth but signs of decay. Since it is impossible for a culture to stand still, the two options which writers give Indian culture are both untenable. If the culture remains static or if it changes, it is seen as being in the process of dying.[54]

This act of purification separating "traditional" (nature) from "modern" (culture) was fundamental to the genesis of the modern and to the identification of its others. As Bruno Latour shows in *We Have Never Been Modern*, it was also central to the triumphant collusion of science and society as two ostensibly autonomous forces. This "mechanism" was the paradoxical foundation of the practice of science that relied on the narrative of the "discovery" of nature to explain and disseminate its power. "Native Americans were not mistaken," Latour remarks, "when they accused the Whites of having forked tongues. . . . Century after century, colonial empire after colonial empire, the poor premodern collectives were accused of making a horrible mishmash of things and humans, of objects and signs, while their accusers finally separated them totally—to remix them at once on a scale unknown until now."[55]

Unlike Christopher Columbus, early explorers to Canada did not send Indians back to European sponsors as specimens of nature. Rather, they sent fish (mainly cod), fur (mainly beaver), lumber, and, briefly, gold. They exported these in exchange for manufactured goods which enabled settlers (Innis uses the less romantic term, *migrants*) to maintain "the cultural traits of a civilization . . . [with] the least possible depreciation."[56] Such goods provided material protection against cultural reversion in their own, more "advanced" civilization, as we see in the case of the piano (chapter 5). This pattern of trade came to dominate the economic, spatial, and administrative shape of Canada as a "staple economy."

This concept now requires our closer attention. In the same text, Innis writes:

The economic history of Canada has been dominated by the discrepancy between the centre and the margin of western civilization. Energy has been directed toward the exploitation of staple products and the tendency has been cumulative. The raw material supplied to the mother country stimulated manufacturers of the finished product and also of the products which were in demand in the colony. Large-scale production of raw materials was encouraged by improvement of technique of production, of marketing, and of transport as well as by improvement in the manufacture of the finished product. As a consequence, energy in the colony was drawn into the production of the staple commodity both directly and indirectly. . . . Agriculture, industry, transportation, trade, finance and governmental activities tend to become subordinate to the production of the staple for a more highly specialized manufacturing community.[57]

Innis's staples theory has engendered a lengthy debate about the place of natural resources in Canadian economic history. This theory has been criticized for two types of determinism: geographical determinism, which posits that land and natural resources determine trade and economic patterns; and economic determinism, which posits that such economic patterns determine politics. If staples theory is viewed as a marriage of these two types of determinism, it warrants critique as a reductionist and pessimistic view of Canada's history, politics, and potential future. To the extent that colonial exploitation is naturalized through reference to nature ("as though every cod holds the seeds of its own commodity and labour market,"[58]), Canada's resources become one with its marginal economic status.

But this is not Innis's argument. Criticizing it on this ground amplifies the role of nature while detouring both Innis's more complex argument and nature's more complex agency. In passages like the following, Innis provides a subtle analysis of the relationship between geographical, administrative, economic, and political factors:

The fur trade left a framework for the later Dominion. . . . Into the moulds of the commercial period, set by successive heavier and cheaper commodities, and determined by geographic factors, such as the St. Lawrence River and the Precambrian formation; by cultural considerations, such as the English and French languages; by technology, such as the canoe and the raft; by business organizations, such as the Northwest Company and Liverpool timber firms; and by political institutions peculiar to France and England, were poured the rivers of iron and steel in the form of steamships and railways which hardened into modern capitalism.[59]

Nature and geography are not absent here, but they are mediated by economic, political, and technological forces such as boats and trains. Nature, like any human biological trait, exists in a social context that determines its meanings and effects. Wilderness does not produce indigenous traditions, or prevent them from changing. Trees don't cause colonialism, but how trees are traded. Of course trees can be traded in many ways. Representations of landscape have also contributed to the premise of Canada's marginality. In the tree-filled, uninhabited landscapes dominating its paintings and postcards, Canada appears as a wilderness whose pristine nature counters a civilization that is elsewhere. In these representations, economic and technological factors are transformed into what Rob Shields terms an "imaginary geography" through which mountains, lakes, and beavers (along with Indians in ceremonial costumes) are identified with national history, values, and sentiments.[60] Historians, writers, artists, and the tourism industry have colluded with this trope by disseminating images of Canada as a wilderness, variously welcome, rich, and forbidding, but always "other"; its destiny defined by—and perhaps limited to—its beauty, wildness, and natural wealth.[61] The beauty of the wilderness veils the violence through which it came to be represented as uninhabited, and obscures the diverse people who confront one another within it.

In this topos, as with Chatterjee's topography of difference and equalization, economic development is either the sacrilegious plundering or the inevitable outcome of what nature has to offer. Either way, Canada's economic development is determined by its role as provider of natural resources. With this logic, the problem arises not from patterns of relative economic or political power but from the anticipated limits of nature itself. Canadian policy advisors acknowledge that the shift from resource to technology exporter poses challenges to their country's economy. Their research demolishes the second flawed proposition in the modernization hypothesis: that technological innovation will eliminate the dependency caused by nature. According to this proposition, the expansion of "high technology sectors" will resolve anticipated crises in the export of natural resources, Canada's major source of wealth.[62] There is a problem with this scenario, because Canada devotes proportionately smaller funds to research and development than any other nation in the G-7 group of Western nations, and carefully organizes its R&D in resources and technologies to be complementary to United States interests, as we see in "Mapping Space" (chapter 8). "Assuming that

Canadian industrial R&D is affected by the country's economic structure," one study observes, "the heavy reliance on resource-based industries seems to be the major reason for Canadian industry's apparent lack of propensity to perform R&D."[63] In other words, Canada's position as a deindustrialized space shapes its move into high technology in such a way that its dependent economic status is perpetuated. While government celebrates Canadian achievements in telecommunications and aerospace optical technologies, they do little to alter Canada's deindustrialized economy or its submission to the geopolitics of transnational capital.[64] As soon as high-tech enterprises reach the $1 million mark, as business analysts observe, they are sold to American companies. The country may produce technically "advanced" sectors, but it remains a strategically underdeveloped economy in relation to the technologies of empire. Like less-developed nations, it cannot consume what it produces or produce what it consumes.

Policy studies present these portraits of technological innovation and economic growth as matters of concern for the territorial space of the nation-state. Yet that space is being fractured and fissured by worldwide, increasingly interdependent changes in finance, communication systems, and industrial growth. There is no such thing as an autonomous national economy. Given new patterns of "postindustrial" marginalization, is marginality still a valid spatial concept?

Time and Space Revisited

We are witnessing a dramatic restructuring of social space in which the meaning of space is ever more thoroughly intertwined with its geopolitical context. Globalizing technology advances technical integration among nations and industries, and within their technology and science. This process leads to a radical destabilization of place (Innis would call this the displacement of time by space-biased technologies), leading to the rise of supranational formations ranging from Sony to Greenpeace; new patterns of colonization; and shifting strategies of representation identified with particular locales. Many observers believe that global communications and information technologies have effectively abolished relationships between center and margin, if not geopolitical difference in general.

The idea that new media abolish relations between center and margin was enthusiastically advanced by McLuhan in the 1960s. "Departmental sovereignties have melted away as rapidly as national sovereignties under conditions of electric speed," he maintains in *Understanding Media*. "Obsession with the older patterns of mechanical, one-way expansion from centres to margins is no longer relevant to our electric world."[65] While print and roads centralize, electronic media decentralize. "It is like the difference between a railway system and an electric grid system: the one requires railheads and big urban centres. Electric power, equally available in the farmhouse and the Executive Suite, permits any place to be a centre, and does not require large aggregations."[66] Through this decentralization of systems, margins are eliminated and everyone shares equally in the wealth of the global village.

> The wheel and the road are centralizers because they accelerate up to a point that ships cannot. But acceleration beyond a certain point, when it occurs by means of the automobile and the plane, creates decentralism in the midst of the older centralism. This is the origin of the urban chaos of our time. The wheel, pushed beyond a certain intensity of movement, no longer centralizes. All electric forms whatsoever have a decentralizing effect, cutting across the older mechanical patterns like a bagpipe in a symphony.[67]

Notice how speed figures here as an agent of spatial transformation. For McLuhan the rapidity of electronic communication abolishes distance and flattens the hierarchical relations once necessary to the administration of distant places. Every place is the center of the universe. His argument on the growing autonomy of places bears some similarity to audience research of the 1980s—which maintained that every audience makes its own meanings, employs their television sets as instruments of independence or resistance, and retains control over semantic and political space—and to Internet studies of the 1990s, which imagines endlessly self-determining virtual communities. In his initial comparison of McLuhan and Innis, James Carey speculates as follows. "If in fact the spatial bias of contemporary media does lead to a progressive reduction of regional variation within nations and transnational variations between nations," he says, "one must not assume the differences between groups are being obliterated as some mass society theorists characterize the process of homogenization. . . . I am suggesting that the axis of diversity shifts from a spatial or structural dimension to a temporal or generational dimension."[68] Undertaking this comparison in the late 1960s, Carey saw this "axis of diversity" manifested in generational conflict. Today the generation gap seems quaint, so drastically has it been compressed by speedy innovation and differentiation in technical knowledge, use, vocabulary, and psychic investments. Time is no longer measured in relation to biological or historical categories. To newer generations, Ursula Franklin observes, these changed relationships between individuals, groups, cities, and nations and across the globe seem normal and inevitable. Unless they are incited to remember the constellations of place and identity that preceded them, and to understand how the restructuring of time and space arises from agencies of power and control, no one questions the inevitability of their reordering.[69]

Innis's research suggests that empires collapse when their rulers' struggle for dominance overreaches itself, destroying the balance in space, time, and power that makes society viable. The conquest of time or space ultimately sabotages the ruling groups who seek to master them. Their dominance is undermined by emergent groups struggling for autonomous power through the use of countering technologies and means of communication. In his analysis, modern society arose when space-biased authority overruled time-biased authority with the rise of the printing press and the birth of modern capitalism. These developments led to the collapse of the church and ruling aristocracy and the rise of the nation-state. Whether or not this overturning held out the balance of a new order, the new empire's technological mastery of space destroys balance between space and time, and defeats the polity's capacity to maintain control over cultures within its reach. Writing on the telegraph, Carey observes that its dynamic expansionism created a tension "between the capability to expand and the capacity to rule."[70] The now-dominant space bias has overreached its own effectiveness and is being subsumed in a new paradigm: speed.

As Paul Virilio delights in reminding us, temporal acceleration permeates society at every level. "Today we are beginning to realize that systems of telecommunication do not merely confine extension, but that, in the transmission of messages and images, they also eradicate duration or delay."[71] Like the Canadian school, Virilio is describing the colonization of time by space. He adds:

After the crisis of 'integral' spatial dimensions, which gave increased importance to 'fractional' dimensions, we might be witnessing, in short, the crisis of the temporal dimension of the present moment. . . . The speed of exposure of time-light should allow us to reinterpret the 'present' or this 'real instant' that is (lest we forget) the space-time of a real action facilitated by electronic machines.[72]

Here the dual fragmenting-integrating production of space meets its limits; capital logic is not abandoned but subsumed by the escalating recommodification of time and space. Virilio envisages the crisis of space-time as a qualitatively new event rather than as an exacerbated ordering of spatiotemporal resources. Margins and centers are reconstituting themselves in a shifting, mobile, unstable process of electronically mediated flux.

Have the hierarchical production and differentiation of space been abolished then? What about space at the margins? "Throughout history," Lefebvre reminds us,

centralities have always eventually disappeared—some displaced, some exploded, some subverted. They have perished sometimes on account of their excesses—through "saturation"—and sometimes on account of their shortcomings, the chief among which, the tendency to expel dissident elements, has a backlash effect. . . . The interplay between centre and periphery is thus highly complex. It mobilizes both logic and dialectics, and is hence doubly determined. . . . This must emphatically not be taken as implying that contradictions and conflicts *in* space (deriving from time) have disappeared. They are still present, along with what they imply, along with the strategies and tactics to which they give rise, and along, in particular, with the class conflicts that flow from them. The contradictions of space, however, envelop historical contradictions, presuppose them, superimpose themselves upon them, carry them to a higher level, and amplify them in the process of reproducing them. Once this displacement has been effected, the new contradictions may tend to attract all the attention, diverting interest to themselves and seeming to crowd out or even absorb the old conflicts. The impression is false, however. . . . The production of things in space has not disappeared—and neither have the questions it raises . . . in the face of the production of space.[73]

I take this to mean that however much new technologies appear to efface spatial differences in favor of a more efficient mobilization of time, we find the latter inscribed onto and constrained by the history of the former. The modern has not "purified" either time or space. Sassen notes that global cities serve as "points of control and centers of finance of the great transnational economic empires; but they are also localities . . . [that] connect remote points of production, consumption, and finance."[74] Why, she asks, when the transnational system of production and consumption has become so diffuse, is management and finance still so concentrated? The answer concerns exactly those forces said to decentralize power along with space: technology and mobility. Global cities have access to networks of fiber optic and cable, to cheap service workers, to accounting and other professionals, to computer chips and migrant workers. Technologies don't just decentralize; they are at the heart of geographically and economically concentrated corporate power.

At the same time, we should not underestimate the capacity of technology to undermine and destabilize entrenched modes of authority and power. Nation-states are refashioned by global corporations; corporate structures are undermined by speculation, mergers, and fraud (if not as yet by home offices or the Internet); conventional bodies of knowledge are undermined by speed, uncertainty, and the threat of imminent displacement. Centers shift; margins create their own peripheries. Marginality becomes increasingly contingent, involving temporal as well as spatial relations. The race for technological supremacy paradoxically undermines the authority of every rule. The United States accumulates cutting-edge military capacities and hurtles toward bankruptcy. Yet margins have not disappeared, any more than power does. When we find that conjecture receiving too much attention, it is useful to recall that less than half of the world's population owns telephones and those regions most reliant on digital devices rarely have to live with their remains.

I conclude with a summary of the implications of Innis's work for such discussions. His emphasis on the mechanization of knowledge reminds us that colonization is a dispossession of history, of time, and of the resources of memory and knowledge, as well as of space in the traditional territorial sense. The drive to expand and conquer space leads to the hyperfragmentation of time, to what Innis calls the obsessive present-mindedness of contemporary culture. Many forms of knowledge become marginal: history, myth, and oral tradition, "nonrational" forms of knowledge, or even, as my introductory comments suggest, critical political economy, which

Pow-Wow, Croker Reserve, 2006. Photograph by the author.

challenges scholars to reflect on their complicity in the colonization of knowledge.

Strangely Innis, unlike McLuhan, failed to include the cultures of First Nations in his discussion of oral tradition. While contemporary scholars see oral tradition as an important source of memory and resistance among colonized peoples, Innis overlooks these and indeed all local cultures or practices in his account. Innis theorizes place as a spatial, temporal, and economic entity but takes into account no living place in particular. The technologies that produce his centers and margins never encounter the everyday lives, the complexly mediated power dynamics, the lively vestiges of myth and memory, the diverse imaginative activities of real men and women. It is this omission, not his attention to technology and space in the history and practice of empire, that makes Innis vulnerable to the charge of determinism.

Nevertheless, Innis's work offers useful insights for cultural theory and practice. His resistance to the industrialization of knowledge and the "penetrative powers" of capital, and his synthesis of anti-imperialism, technological materialism, and the history of communication, offer powerful tools to cultural critique. The analysis of communication technology as mediator between culture and power points to the need to defend a plurality of communication technologies enabling heterogeneous networks that can work together as vehicles for memory, dialogue, technological diversity, and the capacity for reflective critique—all endangered species in the new imperium. In this picture, no single technology can achieve democracy or ontological balance. Rather than celebrating or condemning the capacities of specific cutting-edge technologies, Innis suggests we seek better balance among space- and time-biased technologies and knowledge forms. This endeavor calls for a more nuanced understanding of how media work in combination with one another and with other forces. By struggling to defend the material resources for reflection, dialogue, and difference, we lay the foundation for resistance to all monopolies of knowledge and power.

This suggests we define the "margin" as any site which requires and enables communities to employ cultural technologies as counterhegemonic tools. Such spaces are currently subject to vicious assault; as I argue in "Angels Dancing" (chapter 4), the intense recommodification of information and experience, the erosion of noncommercial spaces, and the triumph of reactionary mercantile politics are part of the ongoing production of space which implicates communities at every scale. David Harvey argues that power derives from the ability to turn space into place. Following Foucault, he sees space as a "metaphor for a site or container of power which usually constrains but sometimes liberates processes of *becoming*."[75] Cultural technologies play an important role in this dialectic of constraint and enablement. They shape the material communicative practices which order and enable the production of space—of people, meanings, and things in space—as a repository of social meaning and possibility. To extrapolate from Innis's thought, our hope for democracy lies in a multiplicity of communication sites: the relative autonomy of these sites from commercial and political imperatives; the freedom to be slow and introspective, even dark and sentimental, as well as fast, canny, and pragmatic; and finally, the preservation of reflection, dialogue, memory, and the inconvenience of diverse oral cultures against continuous technocratic appropriation and the consequent ontological dispossession of both space and time. This remains the legacy of marginal thought in the contested politics of becoming.

three

Spatial Narratives in the Canadian Imaginary

Culture is ordinary; that is where we must start. To grow up in that country was to see the shape of a culture, and its modes of change. I could stand on the mountains and look north to the farms and the cathedral, or south to the smoke and the flare of the blast furnace making a second sunset. . . . The making of a society is the finding of common meanings and directions, and its growth is an active debate and amendment under the pressures of experience, contact, and discovery, writing themselves into the land.—RAYMOND WILLIAMS, "Culture Is Ordinary"

YOU ARE HERE
  The labyrinth holds me,
  Turning me around . . . a spiral . . .

—MARGARET ATWOOD,
"A Night at the Royal Ontario Museum"

If you read side by side the canonical twentieth-century texts in Canadian fiction and poetry, literary theory, art history, geography, and communication studies, you quickly realize how important space is in these otherwise varied discussions. In visual art, the Canadian subject is said to emerge with the collective invention of a landscape in which no one appears. In this literature, Canada finds itself addressed with Northrop Frye's famous aphorism, "The question is not who are we, but where is here?"[1] This emphasis on space has important implications for the practice of storytelling and for the understanding of communication in general. "Communication loves to tell stories about itself," Peter van Wyck observes in a review essay on Ian Angus's writing, anticipating this chapter.[2] What is significant about so many of these narratives is that they do not place speech at the center of their understanding of communicative practice—even their own practices—but rather, the spaces of and between speech, traversed by media or acts of communication through which people and situations are joined. By medium I do not mean an instance of pure materiality (paper, ether, code) but rather, as van Wyck and Angus emphasize, "both the transmission of a certain content, and more importantly, as the primal scene instituting social relations."[3]

Communication mediates social relations by materializing them across time or space. "Space," Angus explains, "exists only insofar as it is traversed in some manner, and time exists only through the means of transmission between generations. Communication media thus constitute, through human labour, the limits of what is experienceable, and the *manner* in which it is experienced, in a social formation."[4] Just as a medium is not reducible to its form, discourse is not meaningful solely in relation to the reality it conveys, truthfully or otherwise. Both are instrumental in the complex enactment of social, spatial, and ethical relations.

This literature's propensity to multispatial thinking—experiencing communication as a form of practice defining "here" in relation to "there"—is also evident in Innis's reference to the "difficulty of assessing the quality of a culture of which we are a part." This reflexive troubling of experience can be compared to the double consciousness described by W. E. B. Du Bois, Frantz Fanon, and Paul Gilroy in their discussions of race and the colonization of the self. In Canadian writing, the ontological split is theorized not so much in terms of the experience of race (although race is neither absent nor unimportant) but through unresolved contradictions in the production of space through which relations are formed, experience is understood, and stories are told.

These themes are taken up by Canadian novelists and poets, critics, political theorists, filmmakers, journalists, public commentators, writers of letters to newspapers, and countless others. Hearing the textual and thematic resonances in their words generates a unique hermeneutic pleasure that travels from texts to readers and back to texts. Echoing Innis's injunction, I cannot claim to comment on these texts from a position of intellectual autonomy. I *am* the "F" in the box, the photograph on the passport, the body standing on the border. These moments carry affective weight because of their relation to the *archive* I describe in chapter 1: the cumulative layering of diverse voices, media, and perspectives onto a space. To undertake a "reading" of this archive is also to reflect on my role in disseminating it. What are appropriate aims for such engagement in the context of international cultural studies? While the meanings of these texts resonate and change around as well as within me, they have not flown so far as to sever altogether the relations between history, action, and meaning. I check the box, I show the passport, I write the *we* to describe a country in which (like so many others) I was not born. Social change, Angus suggests, "does not occur by rejecting out of hand, in an [Louis] Althusserian fashion, the national identity in which the passions of the people are expressed. It occurs through accepting the feeling component and entering a struggle over its formation and destiny."[5] I acknowledge the "feeling component" here and the way it informs my engagement with this archive and the retelling of it. Witnessing my compatriots' extensive dance with "self-understanding" has indelibly shaped my writing.

This encounter is also shaped by the ways I am not a part of this culture and by my experience as a participant in a transnational dialogue on globalization and culture which frequently calls such identification with nations and places into question. In pointing to this debate, intellectual and political history justify a certain caution in the use of the term *transnational*. This term often functions as an alibi for multinational processes in which dominant American perspectives define all others as "local" understandings. American scholarship is shaped by its environment like any other, but its practitioners seem reluctant to reflect on the assumptions or conditions that organize their thoughts. When a conference, journal, or anthology summarizes a field without reference to its geopolitical origin, we know whence it springs. Eagleton remarks that the colonization of a country forces us to spend our time thinking about things that in the grand scheme of things mean very little.[6] The subject of space makes the truth of this insight indeterminate.

Social identity is rooted in place as well as discourse. Place is composed of a constellation of resources, habits, memories, narratives, choices, power relations, transit systems, landscapes, shared communicative understandings, and events. As Lefebvre shows in *The Production of Space*, spatial practice is shaped by representations and conceptions of space, and vice versa.[7] His trenchant model for the production of space has appealed to many Canadian writers because it demonstrates that space is not an object but a fundamental part of a complex social process. Spatial practice is thoroughly imbricated with politics, as Levebvre shows so well and as critics of colonization have illustrated with particular acuity. All space is co-constituted by narrative, regardless of its scale; all place, however local, is mediated by complex materialities such as transnational trade and economic development, travel and migration, the establishment of colonies, bioregional conditions, communication technologies, urbanization, and the regulation of peoples, all of which shape space in accord with their various logics.

Canadian writing relies on and yet further complicates this formula, for in reflecting on its own relation to space it lends a peculiar visibility to the narrative and technological apparatus in which such inquiry appears. This endeavor is concerned less with discrete identities than with the ways that such identities have been forcibly juxtaposed, mediated, and redefined as part of the ongoing formation and administration of space and place. To be a Canadian, Gerald Friesen remarks,

> is not a matter of birthplace, race, language, ethnicity, religious affilia-tion, genealogy, or some combination of these characteristics. To be a Canadian is to accept certain relations with others, to adopt a specific, historically moulded vocabulary . . . to orient oneself to the past accord-ing to community choices made during the previous centuries . . . to adjust to the inevitable contingency of the nation itself . . . a matter of circumstances that have been summarized as "relational, cultural, histori-cal, and contingent."[8]

Friesen emphasizes the importance of communication and citizenship in generating the adaptations and adjustments through which cultural identi-ties have changed within the territorial embrace of the nation-state. Post-colonial theory would describe this process somewhat differently. Homi Bhabha writes that

> Hybrid hyphenizations emphasize the incommensurable elements—the stubborn chunks—as the basis of cultural identifications. What is at is-sue is the performative nature of differential identities: the regulation and negotiation of those spaces that are continually, *contingently,* "open-ing out, remaking the boundaries, exposing the limits of any claim to a singular or autonomous sign of difference—be it class, gender or race."[9]

Both Friesen and Bhabha highlight the contextual reflexivity and performa-tivity of the colonial situation, and the degree to which the colonial project involves fraught encounters between different identities. They differ in that Bhabha's discussion foregrounds identity even in the act of contesting it, while Friesen's discussion foregrounds the space and time within which such identities are performed and changed. Despite this illustrative dif-ference, their shared emphasis on reflexivity confirms the degree to which the process of producing this space (to return to Lefebvre's model) inter-acts with the production of knowledge about that space. Building on this premise, Belton argues the archive becomes "a repository of images about the region and the *topos* becomes the cultural site of those images when they are projected onto geographical space."[10] Belton defines the *topos* as the product of local narratives and images circulating within the cultural sphere of capital development. "Using different sets of elements, different *topoi* may be constructed around a place, and form different 'filters' for how that place is projected and perceived. The *topos*, abstract and imaginary, becomes, in Jameson's formulation, the narrativization of that imaginary geography in the political unconscious."[11] This topos emerges from the layering of diverse identities and narratives over a topography that (as I show in "Weathering the North" [chapter 7]) shapes and is shaped by them.

The topos of (English) Canada is shaped by chronic questioning of the grounds of its own possibility. "Ours is a history written in terms of 'colonial status,' 'imperial connection' and 'continentalism,' rather than 'Canadian Revolution,' 'self-determination' and 'national independence,'" Wallace Gagne wrote in 1976. As a consequence, "we must be open to the nature of technique and what it implies for man."[12] For Gagne, as for many writers in this tradition, the "nature of technique" is connected to the history of space through the concept of empire. As these terms circle one another, they are repeatedly rearticulated and reassembled. Is this compulsion a "structural allegory" of postcolonial space, as Jameson suggests in his discussion of Third World literature?[13] Does it enunciate a speaking position that perpetuates colonization through its own narrative desires? Canadian writing echoes yet again complicates this understanding, for the topos I have described represents not a Third World people struggling for empowerment through their authors' ascendance to literature, but rather the ambivalent space of the Second World, the world of settler societies whose unequal, multiraced subjects are both subjects and objects of colonial power.

If an archive is produced by the layering of stories atop one another, telling stories offers an interesting archaeological entry to this topos. This is my starting point for understanding the political subjectivities formed in this middle ground of colonial (or postcolonial) space.

Telling Stories

History is a representation of the past; it is information transformed into story. Sometimes these stories are told as narratives; sometimes they are embedded in symbols or in art or in specific sites. The stories we tell about the past produce the

images that we use to describe ourselves as a community. If we are not telling ourselves the right stories, then we cannot imagine ourselves acting together to resolve
our problems. Nations *are* narrations.—DANIEL FRANCIS, *National Dreams: Myth,
Memory, and Canadian History*

I am sitting in the car listening to the radio, in the winter of 2002. It is 23
degrees below zero Celsius, the coldest March day since 1868, and I have
reached my destination, but I am listening to Cedric Smith reading a story
by Leon Rooke, *The Last Shot*, on the CBC. This story rehearses a familiar
narrative about a young girl with tough demeanor and heart of gold whose
life borders country and town at the edge of civility and convention. I am
compelled by the telling of the story and by the possessive fondness I feel
for this girl, her indomitable spirit, her ability to stand for a century of storytelling by hitting her brother and hitchhiking down to the corner store to
weasel some groceries. A harsh environment, authority figure, or institution
pushes this orphan toward the wild zone, past civility, and potentially beyond salvation. An alternative figure—perceptive, compassionate, friendly
with authority but indifferent to its routines—pulls her toward connection
and finally toward some complicated fulfillment of herself. In this narrative
topography of living at the borderline between wilderness and power, no
simple resolution will be possible. Judging from how often her story recurs,
she performs an iconic function for Canada.

This narrative routine can be traced back to the publication of Susannah
Moodie's canonical *Roughing It in the Bush* (1852), but it enters a wider
popular sphere with the appearance of Lucy Maud Montgomery's *Anne of
Green Gables* (1908), a novel, which turned into a series, about an orphan
who enters a farm family on Prince Edward Island and stirs up the neighborhood. Anne is by far "the best known fictional character in Canadian history . . . [and is] read by more people than any other Canadian book"; the
Anne stories are also a major cultural export embraced and "domesticated"
in national cultures worldwide.[14] Thousands of tourists visit PEI every year
to visit "the land of Anne."[15] Anne's adoptive parents expect a boy, but they
adapt and learn to love their daughter, a rebellious girl who triumphs over
adversity, making a useful and happy life without sacrificing her insistent
self. Her story reconciles prewar communal rural values with the modern individual aspirations of a young woman from town, an achievement
which appears to be particularly endearing to Japanese tourists. Through
her story oppositions of country and city, wilderness and civilization,

tradition and progress are revisited and repaired. Many instances of the female adventurer's homecoming can be retrieved from the archives of fiction, film, and television, often with ambivalent endings. Even the feisty Anne cannot escape the shadow cast by these struggles, for so fraught is the struggle for copyright income arising from her story that new legislation had to be passed just for her.

In this episode, sitting in the car, I am focused on the voice of the reader, Cedric Smith. I first heard him singing with the 1970s band The Perth County Conspiracy. Like the writing of Milton Acorn (Canada's "people's poet"), whose writing adorns their live album cover and provides lyrics for some of their songs, the Conspiracy's music enacted and commemorated the magic of storytelling in ordinary locations.[16] In the 1970s, such writing was being "pointedly located in a Canadian cultural, political, historical, and geographical landscape, sometimes presumably in response to the teaching of colonial models."[17] During this time, "the local" was acquiring a charismatic aura across the global musical marketplace. In this formative moment of global-local spatiality, music and storytelling brought local landscapes to life and inscribed our memories of them. In his storytelling, as in his singing, Smith's voice occupies each character as though it were a familiar place of residence. He gives each subject dignity and temerity; whatever the age or gender, he knows it, he has been there, and he is moving right in and taking us with him. At the same time, his voice tells us, we can't be sure what is going to happen. There is some uncertainty in this growing up. The voice, the girl, the uncertainty, and the comfort of being read to, together form a familiar sense of place. The voice is replete with storytelling pleasures and the sonic signature of the CBC; it is radio, and I am in the car, where my first thoughts about radio arose some twenty years ago.

These mythic echoes remind me that the earliest mobilization of a national imaginary—not just my own, but according to public records, Canada's—was already mediated by and made meaningful in terms of technology; the canoe, the railway, and then the radio carried it westward across the country. In 1924 R. G. MacBeth wrote that "the country and the railway must stand or fall together." In his telling of this story, Daniel Francis points out that the myth of the railway as creator of the nation is as old as the railway itself, "which is not surprising given that it was the railway itself which created the myth."[18] The country's vast geography, regionalized settlement, ethnic diversity, and vulnerability to United States expansionism were already being invoked as challenges by policy makers concerned with nation-building. As MacBeth issued his declaration, commercial American radio was assiduously enhancing north-south connections counter to the east-west solidarity the railway was intended to create. Radio complicates our relationship with space, tying it together and creating a shared sonic landscape in real time. Whatever space is made, sound promises to exceed it.[19] This ability to create new sonic spaces held different implications for the two sides of the border. The United States apparatus was designed to transcend its boundaries, while Canada's was designed to substantiate its border by connecting its citizens within the imaginary community of the nation-state.

The first trans-Canada radio transmission, broadcast from Ottawa in celebration of Canada's 1927 Diamond Jubilee, opened with a rendition of "O Canada" played on the Peace Tower's carillon. The performance was carried by the Canadian National Railroad (CNR) and its "shadow stations" for railway passengers and local residents. Writes a CBC historian, Sandy Stewart: "Loyal listeners at home were thrilled by the miracle of radio almost as much as the CNR passengers hurtling across the country."[20] One could travel by imagination almost as easily as by train, and along the same route. The simultaneity of these images—the loyal listeners at home, the CNR moving westward, the radio joining these spaces with music and news—is decisive for the establishment of the topos known as Canada. For the first time, dispersed residents of the Dominion were the subject of common rhetorical address in shared temporal space: addressed, celebrated, and circumscribed or, in more contemporary terms, constituted as national subject.

Records of the time are replete with evidence of rural listeners, train conductors, local orchestras, adult education cooperatives, activist women's associations, amateur inventers, radio league activists, journalists, and politicians celebrating the train-radio as a triumph of collective will as it chugged and fiddled across the country. Citizenship was thus born from the imbrication of space and hardware, locked in an indissoluble embrace. Radio established a new topos whose participants could transcend their regional isolation and join in the realization of a political ideal, making explicit the technical process of their own geopolitical construction. This origin myth sidesteps the tales of frontier and conquest (not always with salutary effect, for conquest is not best forgotten) in favor of an inclusive space-binding magic.

CNR Radio Poster, 1930s. Courtesy of CBC Still Photo Archives.

Insofar as this narrative is transmitted through pictorial histories, school textbooks, cultural policy documents, public broadcasting archives, travel agents, and fiction, the story of radio participates in the formation of the nation's archive.[21] It emphasizes the autogenetic character of the country, the way Canada was brought into being when inhabitants heard themselves in the aural mirror of the radio. Rather than promoting an ethnic lineage, these origin stories emphasize a performative, technologically mediated identity (if this is the right word) that must be continuously renewed through the reiteration of social policies and media practices. The railway tracks, the radio broadcasts, the pictures taken from the train, the recordings, the physical archives, and the values and memories attached to them are part of a concrete assemblage in which the interaction of space, medium, and narrative plays a principle role. Postwar programming and cultural policy furthered the idea that it is not identity that produces national culture, but rather cultural and political activity that engender—or conversely, threaten to disassemble—the nation. This formulation reverses the customary logic through which European thought has addressed nation-building. With this reversal the social processes of conceiving, ordering, and living space are more ambiguous and more transparent.

Where Is Here?

The preoccupation with space was crystallized by two postwar thinkers whose work indelibly shaped twentieth-century Canadian thought. In the 1940s Innis extended his research on the resource-intensive economy of dependent economies (the staples theory) to the field of technology and history. He argued that media's material properties encouraged space and time biases that were central to the formation of monopolies of knowledge, centers and peripheries, and the rise and fall of empires. In this process Canada changed from colony to nation and back to colony; it shifted from an outpost of the British Empire to an economically dependent colony of the new American empire, which was extending its reach by space-binding media designed to conquer space at the expense of time, memory, and continuity.[22]

In his 1965 essay on Canadian literature, Frye famously noted that the Canadian sensibility is "less perplexed by the question, 'Who am I?' than by the riddle 'Where is here?'"[23] Commenting on Frye and the "geografictional" imperative in Canadian writing, Barbara Godard suggests that "Where is here?" and its continuing elaboration in fiction and poetry should be read as "the consequences of specific colonial relations of power instantiating Canadian economic and cultural dependency."[24] For Richard Cavell, on the other hand, Frye's contention that "Canadian space is a space without place" corresponds to the colonial appropriation of indigenous cultures and the symbolic association of them with a natural environment from which they have been forcibly disconnected.[25] In both instances the emphasis on space and landscape provides an ordering principle for national narrative in the context of a colonial history that locates the nation, as Frye puts it, in "next year country."[26] The political scientist Abraham Rotstein diagnoses this pre-occupation as "mappism," "a conflation of national identity with territory," which "reacts viscerally whenever territorial integrity appears threatened and at other times seems entirely dormant."[27]

The focus on locality summed up in the iconographic question "Where is here?" functions as both symptom of and cure for Canada's inability to organize a national culture as traditionally understood: the coherent "natural" expression of history, tradition, cultural heritage, military prowess, and political will.

To the extent that Canada succeeds as a nation-state, a question which taunts so many representations of it, the presence of diverse peoples offers a central foundation for its legitimacy. The official motto of Toronto, Canada's largest city, is "Diversity is our Strength."[28] The discourse of multiculturalism encourages residents of the country to embrace an ethnicized identity, but it also provides a ground from which to challenge ethnicity as the foundation of identity.[29] Within the perimeters established by this discourse, citizens debate whether ethnicity should provide a foundation for identity, who defines and polices it, and who decides its limits and meanings or its implications for law and individual rights. Such debates remind us that the spaces of nationality are not simply products of geography or government; they are part of the topos in which the transmission of culture occurs. As Francis writes:

> Because Canadians lack a common religion, language or ethnicity, because we are spread out so sparsely across such a huge piece of real estate, Canadians depend on this habit of "consensual hallucination" more than any other people. We have a civic ideology, a framework of ideas and

aspirations which expresses itself in allegiance to certain public policies and institutions. The CBC, the social safety net, universal health care, hockey—these are just some of the components of our civic ideology. But unlike religion, language or skin colour, a civic ideology is not something we come by naturally. It has to be continually recreated and reinforced.[30]

Like McLuhan, Francis situates representations within the machineries of meaning-making and dissemination which mediate such images. This tactic reverses the naturalizing process familiar across Europe and some of its former colonies through which culture is the privileged index of the nation-state. Imperial powers such as the British Commonwealth are being supplanted by corporate trade in cultural commodities, communication networks, and data flow. Since Canada has been shaped by adaptation to three major imperial powers (France, England, the United States) and at least that many internal nationalities fighting one another in various strategic alliances, English Canadian writing and performance enact an understanding of culture that emphasizes not what it is, but what it does.

Just as empire produced Canada, so opposition, ambivalence, and resentment toward empire has been pivotal to the constitution of its collective imaginary. John O'Neill defines empire in terms of its "practices of violation whenever its imperial interests are at stake."[31] Said writes that "empire lingers where it has always been, in a kind of general cultural sphere as well as in specific political, ideological, economic and social practices."[32] Ties between citizenship, politics, place, and belonging are as complex as they are contingent. The emphasis on land and space can expedite or resist the forces of colonial power, and has done both throughout the country's history.

It is precisely this ambivalence that characterizes literature of the Second World, according to Stephen Slemon. In an influential essay,[33] Slemon defines the "Second World" as a "neither/nor" grouping of invader-settler cultures grounded in "a confused, contradictory, and deeply ambivalent position within the circulations of colonialist power and anti-colonialist affect [which] present significant and enormously difficult problems for the field of postcolonial critical studies."[34] Both colonizers and subject to colonization, these entities cannot draw on aesthetic or cultural traditions to articulate their dilemma. Nations such as Australia, New Zealand, South Africa, and Canada—all former outposts of the British Empire—arise from the violent fusions of multiple identities. However strongly the land-scape occupies the imaginary, Canada is "never homogeneous, never 'pure,' but constructed by First Nations peoples, Francophones, other European groups (from Russians to Italians), Asians (Chinese, Japanese and Indian), and yes, Africans (primarily African American and West Indian)."[35] The ambiguity of this composite identity prevents the contributions of Second World countries from registering in First World postcolonial writing, with its fundamentally binary model of the "West and the Rest." The Second World writer recognizes her complicity in colonialism's territorial appro-priation of land, voice, and agency in the very act of voicing opposition to colonial power. Ambivalent emplacement is the condition of possibility for this subject and has been so from the beginning. For this reason, Slemon suggests, the mediated, conditional, radically compromised literatures of this Second World have something to teach postcolonial theory about the nature of resistance.[36]

Thematizing space in this context requires the writer to internalize the perspective of the other while recognizing that otherness cannot be assimi-lated into a transcendent narrative. This pursuit distinguishes Canadian writing from American literary history, which, by contrast, overcomes the challenges of alterity through the myth of America, "which thus becomes indistinguishable itself from forms of transcendence."[37] Canadian texts on the other hand "possess more than one vanishing point" and "seem to offer an alternative to any single, totalizing story of globalization."[38] The recog-nition of internal alterity produces a strong sense of indeterminacy and a reluctance to be known in universalized terms of recognition and same-ness: "The right to opaqueness would be today the most evident sign of non-barbarism."[39]

Like a soliloquy on late-night radio, this discussion has traveled far afield but is still on the air. Opacity was not what the government had in mind when they constituted a national broadcasting program through which Canadi-ans might tell their stories. "In a country of the vast geographical dimen-sions of Canada," wrote Canada's 1932 Royal Commission on Broadcasting, "broadcasting will undoubtedly become a great force in fostering a national spirit and interpreting national citizenship"[40] American radio stations were broadcasting via transmission towers that were built to reach the towns and cities along the border, but no farther; extending beyond the cities was not profitable. Canada's broadcasting plan emphasized geographical inclusiveness; government promised to reach all citizens, and accrued substantial political legitimacy from fulfilling this mission. This privileging of dissemination across space has carried its contradictions forward into the present. Each successive medium, built with public funds and disseminated in the name of national interest, has become the vehicle for aggressive, primarily American commercial expansion with its famous "dumping" policies and its voracious economies of scale.

The conjuncture of space, identity, and technique established a lasting theme in Canadian society, a construct best envisioned as a semiotic square connecting space and time, citizenship and justice. A semiotic square shows that each term in each binary set achieves meaning only in relation to the other set of terms. Broadcasting's important role in the emerging discourse of citizenship was based on and helped to constitute the view that justice derives from a balance of space and time, while citizenship rights determine and are determined by how equitably time and space are mapped. Too vast a space is imploded by too fast a tempo; memory, continuity, democracy, and justice are ballast thrown overboard to hasten progress. This trope topples the identity question in favor of a critique of communication technologies as centralizing and decentralizing mediators of space and culture. This reformulation continues to matter in the struggle to eradicate colonialism from our social fabric.

The convergence of railway, radio, and citizenship; the girl navigating wilderness and metropolis; popular skepticism toward the "reactionary utopia" of globalization—each contributes to the archive as an exploration of the spatial imaginary and the politics of space. This topos is woven from a voluntarist myth of origin which evacuates the memory of those who do not conform to its logic. Let us look more closely at the history of the railway. In 1871 British Columbia agreed to join the Canadian Confederation on condition that the Dominion government would build a railway linking the western province with eastern Canada. Beginning in 1880, 17,000 Chinese workers arrived from China and California to build the CPR through the Rockies to the Pacific Ocean. At least 1,500 of them died in the process. These workers lived in tents that were vulnerable to falling rocks and were paid one dollar a day while white workers earned five or six times that amount. If the railway was the project that built the nation, as authors as diverse as E. J. Pratt and Pierre Berton so rhapsodically claim, it was the

Chinese that built the railway, and thereby created the nation.[41] The Chinese
laborers were subject to "absurd laws like tax on rice; special taxes on laun-
dries; Chinese restaurants could not employ white women; segregation of
schools; Chinese were denied welfare during the Depression; and in Vancouver, a by-law was passed to forbid the selling of vegetables brought into
the city by a shoulder pole with two baskets hanging on either end."[42] The
Head Tax and the Chinese Exclusion Act was combined with other racist
regulation to contain the Chinese community and to exclude its memories
of nation-building from the archive.[43]

   "Our community's history is entwined with Canadian history in more
ways than one," states the historian Ging Wee Dere. "We all know about the
Chinese railway workers. What else is written in the history books about
Chinese Canadians? Do we know any of the names of the Chinese railway
workers, the Chinese shipbuilders who settled on Vancouver Island, or the
names of the Chinese farmers who applied their peasant skills in the interior
of BC?"[44] The writer draws our attention to the conventional mapping of
this history, much as I first related it: a long, lonely railway across the land
north of the border; communities of settlers strung across the landscape; a
city at the end with markets and shipbuilders. This map does not recall the
land through which the train was built; nor does it commemorate the tribes
whose lands were stolen and livelihoods, languages, and stories destroyed.
The story does not relate the tales of chiefs who sold tribal land in exchange
for lifetime railway passes, the towns bypassed by the railway conniving
to induce businesses and children to return, the homeless hobos railcar-
hopping across the country. Such memories require a kinetic mobilization
of a map petrified by myth, and acknowledgment that communities defeated by history are conquered again and again through the telling of it.

   We need new ways of telling these stories, that might function as a counterpoint of simultaneous voices, unsettling the homogenizing narratives
while permitting "a combination of simultaneous voices (each significant
in itself) [to] result in a complex, but nevertheless coherent, structure."[45]
Ajay Hable finds a model for this counterpoint in the radiophonic fugues
composed by Glenn Gould under the title *The Idea of North*. It is not surprising that a postcolonial solution for writing Canada should be modeled
on a composition for radio. Gould's "contrapuntal radio" suggests a dehi-
erarchization of voices "akin to the process of cultural listening" which is
"predicated on our ability to recognize and understand the role that mul-

Chinese work gang on the CPR, Glacier Park, British Colombia, 1889. View-2117. Courtesy of Notman Photographic Archives, McCord Museum, Montreal.

tiple voices ('speaking simultaneously') have played in the construction of Canada."[46] The art of radio thus provides us inspiration for new models of literary criticism, even as such composition is being rendered marginal in a radio soundscape squeezed by economic and discursive monopolies. How much can change before this spatial imaginary collapses altogether, and another rises to ascendancy?

The National Question (continued)

Canadians do not share a common birthplace and cannot easily be identified by sight or sound. Canada never fought a revolution, does not employ a single official language or religion, and despite its relative wealth has never seemed to take hold of itself as an autonomous entity. Before the First World War, many English-speaking Canadians believed that the destiny of the country lay in a closer connection with the British Empire. Early twentieth-century school textbooks encouraged the view that "Canada's destiny was to be a member of the imperial flock, not a solitary bird flying alone."[47] In this manner, "Canada could participate in the great mission of spreading justice, freedom, and prosperity around the world, and incidentally find support for its independence from the U.S."[48] A century later, the British Commonwealth celebrated in this hymn to imperial solidarity is an indifferent power in world affairs. However, the Commonwealth's failure to supply a bulwark against the new empire did not abolish international awareness as an important value for the country's inhabitants.

Like participants in UNESCO's 2005 convention on cultural diversity, Canada's culture-producing communities have fought strenuously for interventionist initiatives in the cultural domain. Culture has been an important political and juridical term not just for symbolic producers but for governments like Canada's to legislate national policies and practices in various areas. For Laura Mulvey, writing in the 1980s, "The question of Canadian national identity is political in the most direct sense of the word, and it brings the political together with the cultural and ideological issues immediately and inevitably."[49] Activists seeking public intervention in the cultural domain have won broad support from diverse social groups on this basis.

When Canada erupted in controversy in the mid-1980s over the proposed Free Trade Agreement (FTA) between Canada and the United States, cultural policies were already changing. Canada represented a test case for a corporate lobby anxious to "liberalize" the national policies of its major trade partners. The agreement represented an entrenchment of neoliberal fiscal policies that were already undermining public institutions and policies. The Reagan administration found a ready ear in Mulroney's Conservative government, catalyzing renewed opposition between leftist nationalists and the Right.[50] These controversies brought face to face not just different economic and political interests, but different understandings of culture. For American negotiators, culture was a commodity, and other countries' attempts to institute cultural policies in the public sector were thinly disguised protectionist measures advancing unfairly subsidized competitive production.

The progressive coalition against free trade resolved to exempt culture from the 1989 agreement. This meant that tax shelters for film production, for instance, would not be countered with commercial retribution in shoes or refrigerators. United States interests might want a higher return on trade, the thinking went, but we get to keep our culture and political sovereignty. One problem with this idea was that it was above all trade in cultural and information commodities that inspired the United States to liberalize trade (i.e., to extinguish national protectionist policies in other countries) in the first place. If the modern conception of "culture" as an expressive activity in a politically autonomous realm helped to legitimize the nation-state, the administrative rationalization and commodification of culture has played an equally important role in the transition from nationalist to postnationalist policy and rhetoric.[51] The pecuniary fascination with the "creative" industries, the mobilization of the "knowledge economy," and the strategic transformation of academic research are all part of this transition.

Cultural policy is now the object of concerted attacks from corporate lobbies, the World Trade Organization, and various multinational trade agreements. The affective center of gravity has traveled defensively from *culture* to *values*, a term that articulates powerful emotive connections to diverse political trajectories in the struggle to define the terms of the national popular.[52] The right is determined to seize control over the agenda of this debate through attacks on multiculturalism, peacekeeping, social policy, academic and cultural exchange, and protectionism. The results are definitive. Since 2000, billions of dollars worth of corporate property has been sold to transnational corporations with head offices in other countries. Excited by the opportunity for solidarity with the Bush government, the Conservative Prime Minister Steven Harper (elected 2006) eliminated funding for Fulbright, Commonwealth, and other exchange scholarships and programs and for all Canadian Studies programs abroad, while expanding the military budget to ensure that Canada maintains a lucrative defense industry. It is impossible to predict how successful this strategy will be. But it is important to reflect on political resources that might support an effective opposition to them.

Communication and Dependency

Canada is profoundly shaped by its history as a colony, first as the old kind of colony within the British Commonwealth and later as the new kind appropriate to the geopolitics of the United States. Innis's research emphasized the degree to which global trade was built on extracting and exporting natural resources from the peripheral territory (Canada) to the homeland, from the "frontier to the back tier." As I outline in the previous chapter, this pattern served to perpetuate economic and political power for the countries who purchased the resources, manufactured the products, and sold them back to Canada. The imperial countries built industrial empires; Canada dug, plowed, chopped, and transported. This account of the "staples" economy forms the basis of dependency theory in Canada.

Dependency theory has held a powerful influence over Canada's academic and symbolic culture. Its descriptive capabilities are affirmed daily by statistics on ownership patterns in the cultural and resource industries, and by our encounters with recently logged, mined, paved, or excavated terrain. This paradigm depicts an economically disempowered, culturally indefinite nation juxtaposed against the all-too-definite economic structures and political strategies of transnational corporate capitalism. At the center of this dilemma stands the problem of the nation-state. In the trajectory of this intellectual history, the state is both central and absent. It is not hard to discover the logic of this ghostly presence. If Canada cannot be described as an identifiable *nation*, as eighteenth-century political theorists defined it—made one by common history, language, ethnicity, or religion—there was a *state* that advanced itself as speaking on behalf of a territory that would be a nation. With the state dedicated to defending a country that had yet to come into being, and given the tentative logic of a country embedded in and fighting against its role as service provider to an always already transnational capitalism, the problem of the state is implicit when culture and identity appear on the agenda.

What comes from this ambiguous bond between cultural trajectories and the state which appears to speak on their behalf? When "the state" speaks, whose voices are heard? Is this state best understood as a weak vessel for the expansion of subjectless, nationless capital, as a strategic margin of the American empire, or as a notable player in global capitalism? Is it primarily an agent of class domination, or an instrument of national self-governance? This debate accumulates and turns back on itself, proliferating across politics and political economy, literature and music, the cultural industries and the arts. Policy analysts influenced by Nicos Poulantzas have analyzed the state as a semiautonomous, internally conflicted structure mediating between contradictory aims. This approach envisions government as a site for continuous but unequal negotiation between legitimation (whereby the state secures public loyalty by protecting its citizens against the excesses of the market) and appropriation (whereby the state facilitates the ever-expanding stranglehold of transnational corporations as a way of securing the accumulation of capital). As Toby Miller writes, "The state's legitimacy is often drawn from its capacity to speak for its citizens, to be their vocalizing agent. This is achieved, depending on the type of society, at least in part through the doctrine of nations, the concept of particular space defined by the state itself but informed effectively by a sense of cultural belonging."[53] Canada's history offers itself easily to such a reading.[54] There are many countries in which citizens draw inspiration from performative hostility to the powers and symbols of the nation-state in general. Aside from satire, English Canada has not been one of them.

Foucault's rewriting of governmentality encouraged critics to view government policies more skeptically as part of a broader field, according to Gordon, of "specific, bounded rationalities inscribed in culturally particular 'technologies of the subject'." From this perspective, "The aim of the modern art of government [is] to develop those elements of individual lives in such a way that their development also fosters the strength of the state."[55] In the course of their work or in campaigning against imperial power, activists and writers enact a rationalized form of subjectivity—the "citizen," the "artist"—that inadvertently reinforces the strength of the colonial (or postcolonial) state. At the same time, so much of the archive reflects directly on the ambiguous political implications and effects of the technologies of culture. This reflexivity is not simply (or necessarily) the complacent reflexivity of a universal (European) bourgeois culture elevating itself above the crudeness of the people. It does not straightforwardly reproduce the important modern distinction between a bourgeois culture able to separate itself from affect, and a common culture subsumed by it. These tropes deflect critical engagement with the administration and commodification (or recommodification) of culture and its media (or mediated) technologies, encouraging metaphysical possession rather than political critique of the media.

In seeking to constitute the nation-state, cultural technologies are motivated practices which oscillate, sometimes explicitly, between opposing terms: citizenship and consumption, national and international, colonizer and colonized. Poulantzas's model helps to explain how such opposition is materialized in state organization, but it cannot show, as clearly as Foucault does, how this oscillation establishes itself in the core of citizen, consumer, and local subjectivities. Canada's divided location in this field of combat *is* its culture. It is the ambiguous culture of a Second World power constituted by settler populations and suffused with unequal power relations internal and external to the nation-state. It is an assemblage of ethnicities, languages, regions, nation-binding technologies, symbols, affinities, agencies, and corporate and social policies which together form the population of a national space. Foucault's ideas invite us to identify these modes of experience as the product of transformative governmentalities within broadly conceived and apparently seamless state regimes. But Foucault dissuades us from seeking any essential theory of states in general, and if read properly permits us to retain our ambivalent feelings of love and horror toward our own state in particular.

Needless to say, there are political as well as narrative and aesthetic consequences to how one addresses these questions. What if the state and its broad tapestry of social policies and public values is all Canada can claim as the specificity of its culture? Does "Culture" actually matter in the constitution of space, or is it, as the former Conservative prime minister Brian Mulroney mused while speculating on how to sell free trade, maple sugar icing on the cake? (Interesting that Mulroney would have imagined post-FTA capitalist accumulation as a piece of cake.) In other words, how necessary is the concept of culture to the nation (or postnation) we inhabit as difference? As continental agreements, regressive budgets, and changing cultural technologies erode this tapestry, does anything last aside from a multitude of differences? What are the ramifications of this process for any theory of the nation-state? Is a post–nation-state fundamentally different from a nation-state, or was the nation-state always an unstable construct? Has the Canadian state seemed relatively benign with respect to the common good because of its popular mandate, or because of its marginality to the country that stands adjacent? Is the struggle to retain sovereign powers and human rights, in this context, nationalism? Whose is this state, anyway?

More Stories

Such questions continue to play out in the spatial imaginary. You would hardly know, looking at Canada's canonical written and visual works, that nearly 80 percent of the population lives in cities. Students read the pio-

neering stories of Susannah Moodie and Catherine Parr Traill, the tender
small-town stories of Alice Munro, and the acerbic urban wilderness tales
of Margaret Laurence and Margaret Atwood. Theirs is a countryside that
bites. Caught parentless and compass-free between wilderness and civilization, the heroine looks for home. She has more knowledge than power, she
is displaced from her origins, she thrives on the edge of the community, and
she is naughty. She and Canada's symbolic imaginary are caught in a longstanding embrace. The figure moves more or less effortlessly across genres,
inciting readers and viewers to embrace this heroine so many times that
she remains a symbol of the space called Canada long after Queen Victoria,
much of the countryside, and their associated ways of life have disappeared
from the scene.

This narrative structure is constituted within the framework of a slightly
distanced, more reflexive perspective. The narrator relates a story of personal struggle from the vantage point of someone more knowing. As listeners we are located within an implied borderland space between the vantage
point of the young girl and the vantage point of the reader. What does this
narrator know? It appears to be something about absence. The listener is absent from her radiophonic interlocutor; the girl is absent from her parents;
the center of things is absent from us. Absence is popular in the Canadian
imaginary, and it too is a spatial idea—it implies that the desired object is
somewhere, just not here, like the girl's mother in *The Last Shot*, for she is off
somewhere having her last shot at love, and thus the title character never appears. The narrative frame evokes a sense of absence from a center. This trace
of colonial history points our attention to the legacy of colonial discourse as
a whole. The colonies gave rise to a textual archive comprised of "countless
self-aggrandizing and self-centred narratives of settlement, exploration, conquest and other kinds of imperial service," Gillian Whitlock suggests; these
were "produced within discourses of exploration, law, administration, religion, and science."[56] In her discussion of early Canadian writing, Whitlock
contrasts the "structural instability" of women's "life writing" to the assured
("white, male, heterosexual") writing of colonial administration. The narrative spaces of women and other "others" were "most unlikely to enter the
records as an imperial subject."[57] Whitlock offers as evidence of this "other"
space the autobiographies of Mary Prince (the first black British woman to
escape from slavery and publish a record of her experiences) and Susannah

Toronto women commentators of the 1950s: "Top Radio Personalities."
(Left to right) Kate Aitken, June Dennis, Jane Weston, Wendy Paige, Mona Gould.
Courtesy of CBC Still Photo Archives.

Moodie, the literary transcriber of Prince's account (1831) and later, having emigrated to Canada, author of the canonical autobiography *Roughing It in the Bush* (1852).

By the time Moodie wrote *Roughing It*, the role of gentlewoman elaborated for colonial wives by earlier writers was no longer available to her. Moodie's voice is fallible, self-doubting, satirical; her sketches "have all the marks of colonial counter-discourse, where the unsuitability of received systems of meaning, subjectivity and value are openly found wanting." Misao Dean also observes a "pattern of self-effacement" in Moodie's narrative form and describes "the narrator's continual denials of her authority to speak on almost any subject." For Dean, "This retreat into the stereotype of feminine self-effacement allows the narrator to implement the strategies of subversive communication developed by women to circumvent limitations of femininity."[58] *Roughing It*, Whitlock concludes, is "at one and the same time a site

Cover of Allan Gould's *Anne of Green Gables vs. G.I. Joe*, 2003. "Canada has a mouth, the U.S. has armor." With permission of the ECW Press.

of containment, cooperation and resistance."[59] The tactic of building self-effacing and yet subversive narrative strategies to connect to others occupying parallel "non-space" appears again and again in Canadian writing and performance. Literary theorists commonly point to irony as the dominant mode for conveying Canadian experience.[60] But the continuing transmission of the unironic "Anne" story can also be revisited as a contemporary strategy of "containment, cooperation and resistance," one which has become useful to the commodification of local culture in a global market. Like Moodie, Anne resists the class snobbery and misogyny of her neighbors. Her youthful subversion, together with the shrinking of wilderness and empire to the pastoral confines of PEI, allows her story to be embraced across the modern world as a parable of entrepreneurial femininity.

These texts participate in (if they also contest) the popular space-gender imaginary that has for 150 years depicted the United States as a severe Uncle Sam and Canada as a gushing or wily girl. Why is Canada always Anne, and the United States always GI Joe, as the title of a recent bestselling book suggests?[61] Why is the feminine national subject so often featured in canonic Canadian cinema?[62] How did this figure come to be such an important part of the archive? How much is it an outcome of narrative genealogy; how much a marketable convention with the sensibility and shape to please arts councils, commercial publishers, film producers, and funding agencies; how much a representation of the lived experience of arriving in a new, "open" territory and feeling compelled to re-create their cultures and known forms of life? Since it is surely all of these, we can understand it as an instance of Lefebvre's trilogy: perceived, conceived, and lived space. Through a complex of creative, political, commercial, and imaginative strategies, the feminine heroine is intractably embedded in the ways that readers inhabit the space called Canada.

Obviously narratives of hardy, independent, democratically minded women speak to the experience of some portion of the population. But this does not account for the lasting narrative identification between the female gender and the space of the nation. For William New,

> The characterization of land as female, of Canada as the Empire's child, as wilderness as savage, of utility and domesticity as the only acceptable measures of the beautiful: such judgements, however questionable and in whatever measure repudiated, remain influential. These metaphors encode attitudes and expectations; they tell of what some people take to be true, whether they are or not, and hence they reveal the unstable ground of social norms.[63]

"Woman" is associated here with "land" as a way of rationalizing the admiring exploitation of both. As Brodie argues, dependency in women did not carry any negative connotation in pre-industrial society, because "for women dependence on the male breadwinner was judged to be natural and proper [whereas] in the current period welfare dependency, as with drug addiction, is seen to be an individual shortcoming—one which is both blameworthy and avoidable. . . . The dependency metaphor also suggests certain policy responses and not others. It raises the spectre of the pathological and dysfunctional and thus invites surgical or technical intervention."[64] Being transformed from inside out by the politics of neoliberalism, the state ceases to benefit from its symbolic association with the tenderhearted sex and sets out to restructure the vocabulary so that the (feminine) dependent stands in for failure. Such restructuring has to contend with the real forces of feminism that are, so history suggests, more powerful than the dependency metaphor would suggest. This projection of passivity sits uneasily with the narrative landscapes with which we are concerned. Doesn't Anne break a slate writing board across Gilbert's head? American politicians and journalists have often berated Canada for its uncooperative character in the military arena. During the debate about Korea in the early 1950s, "Ottawa had serious concerns both about the way the war was directed from Washington, rather than from the United Nations in New York" (Norman Hillmer and J. L. Granatstein write prophetically), "and about the war aims that shaped the direction of the American-led United Nations effort. . . . Was the role of the United Nations to free South Korea of the invaders from the North or to conquer North Korea?"[65] Wishing to prevent an escalation and expansion of the war, Canadian legislators and diplomats were assiduous in pursuing a ceasefire through "the diplomacy of constraint." Americans resented what they called Canada's "preaching, which applied the superior morality of the relatively weak and powerless against them." Secretary of State Dean Acheson characterized Canada as " 'the Stern Daughter of the Voice of God,' an unflattering reference to the tendency of its government to act as if it alone always knew best."[66] Then as now, diplomacy was far less thrilling than war. Responding to these policy disputes over Korea and the Cold War, Prime Minister Pearson announced that the age of " 'easy and automatic relations' with the United States had ended."[67]

Whether Acheson's gender analogy or his theological inference is the more annoying, the insistence on introducing "morality" (or principles of self-governance for other nations) into military strategy was (and is) understood by American leaders to be fundamentally inappropriate. I find something both comforting and compelling in this perceived misdemeanor. Stern daughters perhaps, but Canadians rarely invoke God in their political rhetoric or military endeavors. As Gould, the author of *Anne of Green Gables vs. G.I. Joe*, observes, "Few if any politicians—federal, provincial or even municipal—would even think of saying that God should bless Canada, knowing that if he/she/it had ever done so the country would have far better weather. Most Canadians aren't even sure that God is on our side, much less on this side of the forty-ninth parallel."[68] In fact the myth of "women's moral superiority" is far more widespread in American than in Canadian culture, a facet of that country's "glorification of masculinity. . . . [and] the perception of English society as effeminate." This idea of an association between morality and the weaker sex played an important role in the vigorous struggle against miscegenation in the American South.[69] "There were no lack of women writers on both sides of the border," Morrison observes, "but in the United States they were more inclined to do what was expected of ladies: they wrote sentimental romances. . . . In contrast, Canadian women writers have always held their own with the nation's male writers."[70] Both the invocation of God to defend the country and the association of elevated morality with women were aspects of American political culture projected onto Canada.

The gender metaphor has also been mobilized to communicate national character north of the border. The gendering of nationality "means" differently even when the two countries share their binary cartography. The analogy draws a parallel between Canada's marginal yet intimate relations with the centers of power and the dominant figuration of male and female. The woman dedicates herself to challenging or circumventing men's power and authority; by doing so she helps to inaugurate a more equitable space for women, children, and foreigners, her natural allies. Thus the devout attachment expressed by Canadian women to Princess Diana, whose tragedy so captured the world's imagination. Diana was perceived from this benign distance as a compassionate outsider challenging aristocratic conventions, a lover of foreigners, a people's princess whose empathic femininity transcends race and class. Her rebelliousness and compassion endeared Diana to Canadian fans, one critic suggests, because Diana's life mirrors the sense of exclusion from the corridors of power.[71] Her image remaps this marginalization by imagining empathy and femininity at the center of political power.

How well the gender metaphor works at empowering Canadian or other women as national subjects depends, in part, on how successfully gender itself is contested and revalorized in our mapping strategies. Feminist theory reminds us that the figure of "woman" is used as an instrument for the manipulation of diverse figures and agendas independent of the speaking of real women. Insofar as Canada is figuratively "woman," it remains "other" to a more powerful entity. Presumably this is part of the trope's attraction. Its structured imaginary remains true to everyday experience while affirming centuries of local and colonial history. It is also a discourse of exoneration and exclusion. Not all techniques and disseminators of power are external to the nation-state, and not all the nation's subjects are made one by nature. If Woman can be conceived as a constellation of selves, possessed with the capacity to incorporate, struggle against, or even commit evil against the other, as Margaret Atwood so compellingly suggests in her novels, so the discourse of Canadianness must recognize the complexity of a subject still rehearsing the grammars of collective life.

I am interested in the continuity of these motifs in the face of changes so widely described as inevitable. This continuity can be further understood in terms of Regis Debray's distinction between "communication" and "transmission."[72] "Transmission" resembles what Belton describes as an "archive"; Debray uses the term to refer to what happens when motifs, narratives, or ideas are transmitted over time, from one generation to another, rather than simply disseminated or communicated through current media channels. Transmission occurs when a theme or image resonates with social experience and reinforces a shared understanding of history and space. Of course, the cultural apparatus selects and constrains the narratives transmitted across these times and spaces. The spatial imaginary transmitted through these texts maps Canada as a separate marginal territory, more interesting for being so equivocal in its understanding of itself. Authors and readers continuously reinvest in the viability of a topography wherein Canada provides a middle space between border and wilderness, autonomy and assimilation, capitalism and justice.

Such narratives have spatial as well as metaphoric effectiveness. Drawing on Lefebvre, William H. writes that "spatial metaphors—in particular, in the language of land—function in literature as part of the process of constructing, questioning, and confirming assumptions about social reality."[73] This middle ground produces a "self-effacing" narrative subject who confirms Slemon's depiction of the literature of the Second World. This narrative space actualizes a weak nation with a strong sense of internal plurality. Angus makes this link explicit, linking English Canada's willingness to coexist somewhere between multiculturalism and nationalism to its weak national identity. "Respect is derived not from positive knowledge of all cultures . . . but from a reflexive sense of one's own limitation. From this position, one can turn outward to encountering other cultures in a way that is genuinely expanding of one's horizon."[74] This encounter with others can be contrasted to stereotyping, a practice theorized astutely by Rey Chow as a compacted representation mobilized when one group encounters, at a distance and on the surface, an ethnically distinct group of others.[75] Rather, these encounters arise through routine interactions between multiple *individual* others within shared spaces: kindergarten and school, dating and romance, work, commerce, the street, social services, and causes neighbors and friends; and through proximate encounters with collective others gathered for religious events, street festivals, sports, or music. This is not to exonerate Canada for its racism, which people encounter every day. But the everydayness of urban multiculturalism offers a different space for conceptualizing relationships between self and other. Neither a solution nor an obstacle to racism, multiculturalism is a political contract within which such work continuously occurs.

A Petition

There are other sites for the performance of Canada's spatial imaginary. Consider Canada's self-nomination through the mantra of place names. I remember cold mornings en route to school when the car was warming up, listening to the radio announcer intoning temperatures from distant Canadian towns with exotic names. Medicine Hat. Moose Jaw. Sault Ste. Marie. Whitehorse. Kapuskasing. Thirty minutes later in Newfoundland and Labrador. My memory of adolescence is saturated with the names of strange places and the charismatic empathy of cold. Radio loves place names in part because they establish radio in the multimedia marketplace as a local medium, as I discuss in "Locating Listening" (chapter 6).[76] On the other hand, place names are discouraged in the lyrics of songs, whose producers seek a larger marketplace. An interesting side effect of this contradiction is the implicit popular awareness of the xenophobia of the continental music market. Using Canadian place names in their music, as The Tragically Hip did with their song "Bobcaygeon," represents deliberate "repatriation" and invites (if not intentionally) nationalist modes of fan appreciation.[77] When place names appear they carry forward a mediated legacy through which time and memory are attached to a broader sense of place. The same effect is achieved by showing snow on television, as I explain in "Weathering the North" (chapter 7).

This legacy is founded in the railway, the radio, and the print cultures of journalism, history, and literature, but it lives on in the newer medium of the Internet. In an electronic petition urging federal action on behalf of the 2002 Romanow Report on public health care—the largest electronic petition ever to circulate across Canada—each signature is accompanied by a place name with appended commentary.[78] Many believe that it is universal access to health care that most persuasively defines the Canadian body politic. In the petition defending this right against privatization, the place names attached to each signature confer the status of citizenship, while the commentaries announce what this citizenship means. The website functions as a bit-based mapping of what diverse Canadians think about the meaning of nationality. Is it just I who enjoys the pleasurable complicity of reading the entries? As a collective text, the petition explicitly aligns Canada with a compassionate and equitable social agenda. More than 66 percent of the signatures are women's.

"Privatization of health care brings a lot of problems because all the good facilities will go to the people who CAN AFFORD THEM . . . is that really fair??" queries Mariam Adega of Saskatoon (signature no. 42560). "Our public health care system is a vital Canadian value. Please uphold what Canadians value so dearly!" writes Rev. Neil Elford from St. Albert, Alberta (no. 42247). "Without at least health care we are just a more northerly US," warns Liam Rees Spear from Peterborough, Ontario (no. 42217). "Save our medicare system, no to private for profit healthcare, this is Canada, not the US!" writes Timothy Kenny of Vancouver (no. 33787). "I couldn't agree more. Canadian healthcare is the one thing that truly separates us from our US neighbours, our identity," says Kenneth Graham of Smith Falls, Ontario (no. 33773). "Thank you everyone that posted comments here. I needed a reminder as to why I MOVED TO THE US! I would love to move back home, just LOWER taxes and allow a two-tier system that includes PRIVATE, FOR PROFIT healthcare," says "Moved to the US." "Medicare is our national identity, please support it!" writes Frances Fry from Wabush, Newfoundland and Labrador (no. 42535). "Privatization would mean the 'survival of the fittest and richest'—truly uncivilized in a modern society," argues Olubasayo Ekunboyejo of Scarborough, Ontario (no. 42487). "Free public universal healthcare is the right of all Canadians. Let us all work together to improve our system not just for our sake but for the sake of future generations to come," writes Matthew Ng of Brampton, Ontario (no. 43263). "Public medicare is our Sacred Trust," maintains Bill MacLellan of Glovertown, Newfoundland (no. 10161). "Our public medicare system is what *binds us together* as a nation," writes Mary-Ruth MacLellan of Glace Bay, Nova Scotia (emphasis added). Parviz Marbaghi of Toronto (no. 43729) says flatly, "Undermining medicare should be regarded as treason."

The health care petition mobilizes the archive to reconnect the struggle for equality to the claims of citizenship. It asserts the power to draw boundaries by naming what is in them. As a representational space it shows what is wished for. For its signatories, national identity is useful to the extent that it serves to mobilize compassionate justice on behalf of its subjects. These archives and inventions comprise the topos of the region, and together with other resources can be mobilized for progressive ends.

National and Postnational Space

The nation-state's attachment to social-democrat values is nonetheless as contingent as other aspects of its history. While Canada's last government won wide popular support for refusing to fight in Iraq and for rejecting Bush's continental defense system, its stance did not extend to armaments contracts. While economic integration between Canada and the United States has increased since the 1989 signing of the Free Trade Agreement, the values expressed by residents of the two countries have ostensibly grown farther apart. A prominent researcher found Americans more tolerant of violence, consumption, social risk, religious fundamentalism, and ecological damage, but less committed to introspection, empathy, social intimacy, and global consciousness. Canada moved in the opposite direction.[79] This affective solidarity may be misleading, for Canada's current government supports military neoliberalism and humiliatingly parades its loyalty to Bush's White House. Such is the ambiguous fate of the national imaginary in a political sphere that is nonconducive to the rights of citizenship.

Still, such petitions affirm Michael Adams's finding (and Joe's Rant; see "Writing on the Border," chapter 1 in this volume) that Canadians see themselves as supporters of tolerance over aggression, common welfare over private self-interest, multiculturalism over identity. The agency of this "imaginary" Canadian interacts unpredictably with the political processes summarized in the term *globalization*.

As Angus reminds us,

> *All* social identities are constructed within the field of social power, and thus no social identity could ever be immune to manipulative and dominating uses. The issue is then not to defend or attack national identity or even nationalism in a general fashion from some vantage point that is

assumed to be unassailable. It is to investigate the specific conjuncture under which a formation of national identity brings into being a collective sense of belonging and a political project that can resonate with, and perhaps fuse together, other critiques of the social order.[80]

In the process of dismantling this conjuncture, globalization works like "a dream: more concretely we might qualify it as the name given to the 'reactionary utopia'—Samir Amin's term—which neo-liberal discourse is today inclined to project as an historical actuality." The projection of this reactionary utopia onto contemporary policy "helps to constitute and regulate social space through its pretence to *have resolved* what cannot in fact *be resolved* in terms of the market."[81] Sustainable citizenship can be constituted only by contesting this "reactionary utopia," and imagining an alternative topos, a turning spiral that by writing itself into the land inscribes its subjects in renewed articulations of culture and difference, space and time, citizenship and justice.

four

Angels Dancing

CULTURAL TECHNOLOGIES AND
THE PRODUCTION OF SPACE

For geography matters. The fact that processes take place over space, the facts of distance or closeness, of geographical variation between areas, of the individual character and meaning of specific places and regions—all these are essential to the operation of social processes themselves. Just as there are no purely spatial processes, neither are there any non-spatial processes. Nothing much happens, bar angels dancing, on the head of a pin.—DOREEN MASSEY, *Space, Place, and Gender*

Capitalism perpetually strives, therefore, to create a social and physical landscape in its own image and requisite to its own needs at a particular point in time, only just as certainly to undermine, disrupt and even destroy that landscape at a latter point in time. The inner contradictions of capitalism are expressed through the restless formation and reformation of geographical landscapes. This is the tune to which the historical geography of capitalism must dance without cease. —DAVID HARVEY, "The Geopolitics of Capitalism"

Angelology has been a popular framework for understanding and reenchanting contemporary entities that connect and communicate across space. As messengers, angels represent the conversion between the visible and the invisible. This process involves "an intermediary stage, a place where something is at once real and unreal."[1] Mechanical and digital reproduction have encouraged artists and inventors to explore changing relations between physical space and the human imagination. Recorded music combines the magic of automation—sounds appear, but you cannot see the source of their power; and the automation of magic—voices come like spirits from beyond, but beyond is nothing special. In his book on angels, Michel Serres writes that the world is becoming one pulsating network of mobile interconnecting messages, with each local area moved to defend its distinctive local identity.[2] Serres invites us to reflect on the possibilities and dangers deriving from the telematic assimilation of information and space. This invitation takes us some distance from the arcane theological differences that inspired the phrase "angels dancing on the head of a pin."

The phrase mocks angels for their failure to occupy space while mocking the idea of spacelessness itself. What an absurd cosmology, how ridiculous to *think yourself outside of space*. And yet, there they are, those angels, being evoked, taking up space on the page. They are still delivering messages, just as they did when they were real. Just so, this restless landscape finds a way to make us listen.

The Production of Culture
and the Production of Space

In a study of activity in a French recording studio, Antoine Hennion describes how producers, authors, musicians, and technicians are united by "the permanent and organized quest for what holds meaning for the public." The successful assimilation of this knowledge into the collective creative process is the basis for what he calls the "art of pleasing." Under the direction of the producer, the artists learn to "preserve and develop artistic methods that act as veritable mediators of public taste."[3] It is the producer who "must try to 'draw out' of the singer what the public wants and conversely to pave the way for the special emotional ties that bind the singer to his public, by himself embodying for the singer an audience that is as yet only potential."[4] None of the elements of the song are above negotiation, Hennion finds. What we should look for in trying to understand a song's success is not simply its musical form, but how such form realizes the self-consumption of "real audiences, in the form of consumers."

This account of the "art of pleasing" addresses a longstanding dilemma in the sociology of cultural production concerning the nature of the popular as an economic or aesthetic construction. I wish to approach this question from a different perspective: that of the constitution of space. Nowhere is this function more salient than in the world of music. For the "real audience"—which is from the singer's, DJ's, or director's point of view, "only potential"—has become more and more spatially dispersed, yet more and more spatially defined. The changing technologies of musical reproduction pursue listeners into heterogeneous spaces that are constituted by these same technologies. Music recording is engineered to maximize the sonic potential of particular media in particular spaces: mechanical pianos, car radios, Sony walkmans, dance clubs, CDs, download sites, and iPods all mediate listening in explicit connection with the anticipated spaces in which listening will occur. The process that produces audiences for different types of contemporary music is indissoluble from the process that produces the spaces they inhabit.

In theoretical terms, we need to situate cultural forms within the production and reproduction of capitalist spatiality. How does one produce the other: the song, the studio, the radio station, the road, the car, the radio, the town, the listener? What does it mean to conceive of producing a listening audience this way, to imagine it as mainly not temporal, or subjective, or the expression of something called taste? Why is the criticism of pop music so often empty of cars, not to mention elevators, offices, shopping malls, hotels, sidewalks, airplanes, buses, urban landscapes, small towns, northern settlements, or satellite broadcasts? Music is now heard mainly in technologically communicated form, and its circulation through these spaces (in connection with the movement of listeners) is part of the elaboration of its forms and meanings.[5] Music is a spatial, not just time-based, event. We need to consider music in relation to the changing production of spaces for listeners, and thus as an extension of the changing technologies that follow or draw their subjects into these spaces.

The bias toward the temporal is clearly audible in pop music, with its many techniques for marking the present and differentiating years and decades by distinct sounds, textures, samples, and styles. It is also evident in music criticism, which tends to emphasize precedence and antecedence in its teleology of aesthetic forms. Recognizing the spatiotemporal dimensions of media reminds us that the production of texts cannot be conceived outside of the production of diverse and exacting spaces. We are not simply listeners to sound, or watchers of images, but occupants of spaces for listening and watching who, by being *there*, help to produce definite meanings and effects. These "spaces for listening" proliferate and fragment continuously with the development of new audio technologies. Technological and social changes combine to make them more diverse, more mobile, and more omnipresent. Such changes represent complex negotiations between corporations, consumers, producers, desires, and everyday life. They challenge us to take into account the complexity of these relationships while recognizing the modes of power at work in them.

The mediation between these processes—producing texts, producing spaces, producing listeners—is emphasized by the term *cultural technologies*. The term points beyond understanding musical or audiovisual communication as event, whether in terms of text or expression, even one that has already absorbed, in order to be absorbed by, its listener. Rather, it draws our attention to the ways that popular culture articulates technologies, economies, spaces, and listeners, and mediates their paradoxical dynamics. Whether we are considering fiction, music, television, or the Internet, conditions of power and location are materialized not only in the reception of these stories, songs, instruments, or websites, but in their production. In each case the spaces of circulation and consumption are decisive factors in the form and mode of address. Looking back to earlier mediations, the appearance of Dickens's novels in serial production and the popular practice of reading them aloud as they appeared were instrumental in creating the rhythms of the novels. Their pacing alternately enthralls and meanders. Their prolonged publication schedule is materialized in the elaboration of minor characters' psychology, language, and strange deportment; in the simultaneous occurrence of differently located plots that gradually merge; in the narrator's editorial interruptions, through which the author lectures his reader-listeners on wealth, morals, and the English Poor Laws; and finally, in the long-delayed triumph of good over evil. While readers might know that honesty and virtue will triumph, the story would lack the power to mesmerize them over long periods without the deplorable antics of its wicked characters, who meet with punishment or redemption as family and property are returned to their rightful place.

As these early serializations demonstrate, reading and other modes of reception are not independent of the strategies of publishers and producers. The market for sheet music in the second half of the nineteenth century also contributed to the aesthetic improvement and deportment of the middle-class home, a subject to which I return in "The Musicking Machine" (chapter 6). Constituted in relation to these events, the reader and listener (the father) and the listener and pianist (the daughter) is each, as de Lauretis says of gender, "both the product and the process of its representation."[6]

Marketing Culture

The insertion of a targeted public into the heart of the production of popular culture marks the beginning of the industrial revolution within the realm of culture, and was a central dynamic in the rise of the cultural industries. From the early industrialization of popular entertainment in the 1800s, the profitable dissemination of entertainment commodities has relied on the ability of producers to make reception part of the productive apparatus by requiring more refined knowledge of audiences' situation and location as well as their taste and interpretive response. Adorno comments on this development in classical music in his essay on mediation.

> For the first time composers [of the mid-eighteenth century] were confronted with the anonymous marketplace. Without the protection of a guild or of a prince's favour they had to sense a demand instead of following transparent orders. They had to turn themselves, their very core, into organs of the market; this was what placed the desideratis of the market at the heart of their production. The levelling that resulted—in comparison with Bach, for instance—is unmistakable. Not unmistakable, although just as true: that by virtue of such internalization the need for entertainment turned into one for diversity in the compositions, and distinct from the relatively unbroken unity of what is falsely called the musical Baroque.... It was the source of a way to pose musical problems that has survived to this day. The customary invectives against commercial mischief in music are superficial. They delude regarding the extent to which phenomena that presuppose commerce, the appeal to an audience already viewed as customers, can turn into compositorial qualities unleashing and enhancing a composer's productive force.[7]

Adorno clearly understands the embrace between creator and market as both a leveling and a creative force in musical cultures. While Adorno limited his diagnosis to music, cultural technologies can be understood as versions of this same productive pursuit. As this process is entrenched within the culture industries, the search for listeners leads to increasingly rationalized methods for identifying their situations and subjectivities, and for formulating specific modes of address to please them. Finely tuned demographic categories can be inferred across the culture industries: differences in age, class, race, and other demographic indicators are reflected in and monitored by the producers of television, radio, advertising, Internet sites, and special media events. Cultural consumption is thus intertwined with the production of demographic data.[8]

In the space of electronic media, the audience is collectively both absent and present. As a vehicle for its potential audience's realization, its "self-consumption," as Hennion terms it, radio offers listeners the pleasure of hearing their music in the third space of electronic media. Methods for gaining information about audiences or users have grown ever more sophisticated, with the aim of being able to catalogue and measure the effects of every communicative act. It is not only content consumption that is subjected to such research. The interaction of audience research, creative design, and marketing can also be seen in the development of media technologies. As Paul du Gay and Stuart Hall demonstrate, the Sony Walkman evolved through a combination of accident, demographic research, and careful industrial design. Knowledge that informed its development included not only the technical expertise required to miniaturize the headphones, but also the demographic expertise that suggested that a music technology for teens would sell if it was under $100, but not over $200, that mothers supervised purchases for children until they reached the crucial marker of $100, at which time fathers became involved, and that earphones that could be deftly inserted into the ear were less likely to invite disapproval than earphones that were visible on the head. These findings were instrumental in the development of new mobile listening technologies and the collapse of commonplace categories of public and private space.[9] Today, premarketing research is even more detailed. Focus groups help Web page designers determine what cultural symbols might incite consumers to purchase gas from one company rather than another, what would successfully "Canadianize" a transnational book-marketing website, or what current colors can persuade buyers to replace their possessions.

This escalation of observational science has challenged the distinction between production and consumption in the making of culture. While neither determines the other—industry folklore is replete with stories of heavily researched projects that fail, or undermarketed projects that meet with wild popular success—we cannot understand the circulation of cultural commodities without analyzing the mutual interaction of production and consumption in their institutional and geopolitical contexts. Audience measurement in television is part of a history which has made studio production more expensive, more dependent on the integration and concentration of production and distribution, more hierarchical in internal production relationships, more international in concept and distribution, and faster in its forms and aesthetics. The structural integration of continuously refined audience observation with serial production was what enabled American dramatic television to assume its role as "telegenic entertainment incarnate" in many countries.[10] At the same time, the proliferation of programs in television, as in radio, contributed to deepening instability in program finances and resources.

Though technological duplication is commonly held to increase choice in the audiovisual marketplace, audience measurement technologies, digital selection programs and satellite dissemination have contributed more to the rationalization of radio programming than to the range of musical choices available to listeners.[11] In Canada, the effect of these mechanisms has been to develop lucrative local audiences for imported music and to encourage distribution and airplay for Canadian music that is deemed exportable, thus producing the patterns of "uneven development" of marginalized economies described in "Mapping Space" (chapter 8). The continuous seeking out and economic and symbolic rationalization of viewers and listeners is a necessary feature of producing entertainment through what Innis calls space-biased media, favoring dissemination across space over continuity in time. Space bias enhances the spatial extension and hierarchical differentiation of media, the centralization of its economic structure, and the wide and rapid dissemination of its supply. This has consequences beyond limiting the availability of local or marginal commodities, a grievance which would seem to call only for a better distribution system, as though distribution were not, in a sense, the determinant process. Space bias advances the interest of a particular mode of administration, in this instance the price system, which transfers control from the user to the price system.[12] As noted in "Space at the Margins" (chapter 2), Innis emphasizes this process's role in the continuous and expansionary structuration (or restructuration) of centers and margins. The expanding dissemination of commodities helps to build ever more encompassing cross-media monopolies, whose symbolic and economic practices perpetuate and legitimate bureaucratic relations of production and extend their economic and political territory in a continuous process of "pervasive recentralization."[13] Each new form of media changes the configuration of space. Cultural technologies work to set the terms, possibilities, and effects of their negotiation.

Since McLuhan, communication research has tended to emphasize the influence of technological change in processes of dissemination and centralization. However, the dual process of discursive rationalization and spatial dissemination was instrumental in drawing popular entertainment into the commodity market well before the rise of the electronic media. In the concerts, exhibitions, and music halls of the nineteenth century, "the crowd were as much producers as consumers of a form of social drama."[14] The sense of making the scene drew people to these sites and made them meaningful as spaces and as events. Through the evolution of such spaces, commercial entertainment emerged both as an industry and as a focal site for the expression and policing of urban popular culture. It was the music halls, prototype of nineteenth-century popular culture, that made it an industrial practice to "reconcile an invitation to indulgence with the newer norms of orderly consumption."[15] Previously, the largest entertainment institutions were traveling fairs, complete with melodramas, menageries, tricksters, ballad hawkers, and peddlers of food and drink. As the film Les Enfants du Paradis (1945) depicts so beautifully, such events were occasions for social and sexual transgression, for dramatic lapses of the taboos of everyday life. By the mid-1850s, fairs were perceived as out of date: "too rowdy," Briggs observes, "for the respectable mid-Victorians."[16] The 1851 Crystal Palace Exhibition in London signaled a new impetus toward moral improvement, accomplished through the increasing commercialization and regulation of music, sport, publishing, and spectacle in general.

The music halls' reconciliation of order and indulgence was indissoluble from their changing production of entertainment as a social space. The emergence of music halls took place through the differentiation of specific types of entertainment territories (new licensing regulations of the 1860s were introduced to distinguish pubs from theaters, thereby disallowing paid entertainment in pubs, not to mention drinking in theaters), the commercialization of their operation, the professionalization of their labor force, the standardization of types of entertainment offered, the fixing and stratification of the physical and social position of audiences (seats were gradually fixed to face the stage, and the architecture was renovated to permit clearer stratification between the pits and the boxes), and the integration of ownership structures. The commercial music halls were then able to spread to suburbs and provincial towns whose own entertainments fell into decline as a consequence of these same innovations. With this process in place, cinema was introduced; the new medium both appropriated and displaced the earlier structures as a means to extend the logic of their production.[17]

Throughout this transformation, the noisy dynamics of music hall "reception" remained a crucial element, both semantically and organizationally, in the production and style of performance. A sensitivity to the situation and disposition of audiences (who started as crowds, and ended—due to these architectural, economic, and regulatory actions—as audiences) made music hall performers successful, but in the end it made them obsolete. The concept of "cultural technology" helps us to understand this process. As part of a spatial production that is both determinant and problematic, shaped by both disciplinary and antidisciplinary practices, cultural technologies encompass simultaneously the articulated discourses of professionalization, territoriality, and diversion. These are the necessary three-dimensional facets of analysis of a popular culture produced in the shadow of American imperialism.

In locating their "audiences" in an increasingly diverse range of locations, contexts, and dispositions, contemporary cultural technologies contribute to and seek to legitimate their own spatial and discursive expansion. New types of listeners or listening contexts are produced through the creation of new mediated spaces for musical reception. This is another way of saying that the production of texts cannot be conceived outside of the production of spaces. Whether or not one conceives of the expansion of such spaces as a form of colonialism remains to be seen. The question is central, however, to arriving at an understanding of entertainment that locates its practices in spatial terms.

The Space of Entertainment
and the Colonization of Space

The political conditions surrounding this question justify my challenge to what Lefebvre called "the propagandist character, superficial and artificial, of optimism (socialist or American)" that dominated Anglo-American cultural studies in the 1980s and '90s.[18] Such optimism emphasizes culture as a site of popular empowerment and as a locus for questions of agency and practice, mainly with reference to collective and expressive difference. As the production of meaning is increasingly located in the activities and agencies of audience-consumers, so the topography of consumption is increasingly identified as (and thus expanded to stand in for) the map of the social. This reproduces in theory what is occurring in practice: just as the spaces of reception expand in proportion to the number of texts or textual types in circulation, so the time accorded to reception expands in proportion to (and through appropriation of) other modes of interaction. The increasing social, symbolic, economic, and physiological territory occupied by technologies of consumption needs therefore to be investigated in terms of the dynamics of spatial production within which such audience activity is situated, and by which it is constituted, and not only in terms of the linguistic or semantic renegotiation of representational meanings.

By situating the production of audiences in the context of these developments, Canadian communication theory differs from Anglo-American communications research, which has tended to approach the audience as an aggregate of individual dispositions, identities, and investments. To situate audience activity in spatial and geopolitical context is to confront other questions about the interaction between production and reception in the constitution of symbolic texts, for instance, to anticipate a later section in this chapter (see "Theses on Entertainment: A Polemic"), the importance of entertainment as a central discourse in contemporary neoliberalism. Foucault's definition of discourse as a regime of truth suggests the methodological limits of isolating and privileging reception as creative agency. To focus analysis on the moment of a work's reception, and to privilege interpretive activity as the determinant source of meaning, is as problematic as its analytic converse: the deterministic overemphasis on something called "production," which reifies economic relations and assumes that meanings are produced by abstract corporate machinery without agency of any type. We need to investigate cultural technologies of reception and production within the larger "mediasphere," and explore how they produce specific types of texts and textual experiences that together accomplish the combined ends of policing, profit, and pleasure.

For McLuhan, according to Daniel Czitrom, "It is the formal characteristics of the medium, recurring in a variety of material situations, and not in any particular 'message,' which constitutes the efficacy of its historical action."[19] That is, media produce not only individual texts and individual textual receptions, but also a continuous sensory and spatial reorganization of social life. In this quasi-materialist approach, each technical innovation produces new social and spatial relationships. In Lefebvre's terms, such innovation has continuously "produced a space" to be filled by capital exchange.[20] Just as print contributed to the emergence of literate nation-states, unifying language, territory, and routine chronicles of shared experience—the foundation of the "imagined community" described by Benedict Anderson[21]—so each subsequent communication technology has altered relations between individuals, communities, and social space. Thus consumption practices produce more than "meaning," just as media technologies produce more than "messages" in linear time or two-dimensional space. Media consumption partakes in tangible processes of economic and political transformation which make problematic the concept of consumption as social empowerment outside of the circumscribed parameters of consumer choice, upon whose privileging they rely. If pleasure is a determinative process, it is necessary to determine what exactly is being produced by the "art of pleasing," in the social sphere as well as in the life of the individual, outside the realm of entertainment as well as within its own morphologies. The particular sociopolitical conditions surrounding this question are variously inscribed in the movement between the space of entertainment and the colonization of space.

The capacities of new media for occupying and producing space were readily recognized by early mass marketers; by 1900 the marketing for mechanized instruments addressed the need to transform the home to a place of leisure, as I show in "The Musicking Machine" (chapter 5). Radio broadcasting introduced advertising into that same home; by the 1920s, advertisers understood radio as an ideal extension of their trade with "extraordinary power to carry them into the intimate circle of family life at home." The chairman of Westinghouse claimed that "Broadcast advertising is modernity's medium of business expression. It made industry articulate."[22] We can trace the domestic diffusion, technical integration, and economic concentration of radio through the 1920s; the advent of television; its subsequent demographic, spatial, and economic fragmentation; television's program proliferation and audience fragmentation; teen radio listeners who simultaneously abandoned the familial domestic scene for the physically dispersed teen cultures of the 1960s and after—all as elaborations of this prognosis. Once a market was saturated, new technologies were ready to mobilize the shifting social topography of postwar culture. Both the rise of television and its subsequent "obsolescence" in the wake of transistor radio, VCRs, DVDs, video games, walkmans, and the Internet advanced the goal of making "industry articulate."

McLuhan contends that each new medium adopts the "content" of its predecessor and thereby disguises its real historical efficacy.[23] Another way

GE ad "From receiver": In the 1950s the television simultaneously constituted and stood for the American family. Courtesy of the Museum of Modern Art.

of putting this is that cultural hardware precedes the software that will constitute its content. As Bertolt Brecht said of radio, it finds a market, and then looks for a reason to exist. "In our society," Brecht writes,

> one can invent and perfect discoveries that still have to conquer their market and justify their existence; in other words discoveries that have not been called for. Thus, there was a moment that technology was advanced enough to produce the radio and society was not yet advanced enough to accept it. The radio was then in its first phase of being a substitute: a substitute for theatre, opera, concerts, lectures, cafe music, local newspapers and so forth. This was the patients' period of halcyon youth. I am not sure if it is finished yet, but if so then this stripling who needed no certificate of competence to be born will have to start looking retrospectively for an object in life.[24]

Langdon Winner develops this idea in his concept of "reverse adaptation," in which, as I show in "Mapping Space" (chapter 8), a technological system is put in place and then searches for applications.[25] Bringing the study of technological history to the analysis of cultural technologies confirms this insight. In entertainment, as in the space industry, hardware is initially financed through the advertising of "software" appealing to a targeted market on the basis of established tastes and needs. Early gramophone records, for instance, were mainly recordings of opera and classical music; it was the middle class who could afford the gramophones, and classical music made gramophones respectable.[26] Early CDs were either new recordings of classical music or rereleases from the 1960s, which warranted the purchase of new playback technology that would then displace existing collections. Similarly, early satellites carried weather monitors that could transmit telegenic digital images back to earth and elicit revenue from television broadcasters who could display satellite images in their weather forecasts. As the hardware becomes more affordable and more widely available to consumers, new software (piano rolls, digital graphics, DVDs, home weather monitoring) is released for more diverse markets. By the time the market for one playback technology is saturated, there is a more "advanced" device on the horizon, and the established one has become old and defunct, with increasingly evident environmental consequences.

This dynamic changes everything but preserves two structural components: constant technical innovation and obsolescence as well as the social stratification of access to technologies available at any given time. The combined propulsion of technical innovation and recommodification has spatial consequences that include and exceed the mounting detritus of toxic trash. Just as music halls initially combined pub and theater, but gradually introduced new styles of professional variety performance, thereby facilitating the creation of a newly capitalized and centralized entertainment industry and the birth of cinema, so television began by offering live variety and film, and consolidated the dramatic series once the industry had been thoroughly capitalized through the purchase of sets. The dramatic series benefited from and helped to support television's highly integrated structure of financing. Their high-profile actors, costly production values, and addictive storylines reinforced the international popularity of American programs and productive relations. With the decline of the networks and the proliferation of channels, television turned to the cheaper formulas and casts of reality television whose texts and values proliferate across the Internet.

The intensification of international competition and institutional privatization, together with the increasing dominance of entertainment programming, has ensured that successful international formulas tend to be reproduced nationally in many countries.[27] Throughout the 1940s and 1950s, cinemas worldwide projected American movies while local cinema production was narrowed and displaced. In Canadian communities, one went to the cinema to see American big-budget entertainment; but one went to community centers, church halls, repertory theaters, and school classrooms to see Canadian films, often NFB documentaries on agriculture, war, or the lives of women.[28] Different production formulas were realized not only in terms of finance and ideology but also spatially, in the venues of reception, creating a pattern that resembled music reception, with its clubs and concert halls, rather than popular cinema attendance in standard accounts. Such films can currently be seen on the specialty channels of cable TV.

Today, reality programming and talent competitions provide the most cost-effective and exportable formulas for television networks. Like earlier dramatic series, these programs obey the discursive injunctions of mediated or teletopographic space by bringing the world into the home. But it is not the same home. To watch *Canadian Idol*, you need to have your home computer handy to vote for your favorite contender. To keep up to speed in gossip or public affairs, you need to follow the news through YouTube or other websites. As these forms evolve, they redefine personal and domestic space. Raymond Williams described the twentieth-century emphasis on domesticity as a trend toward "mobile privatization," technically distinguishable from the more public orientation of nineteenth-century innovations such as the railroad, the streetlamp, and, I might add, the music hall. The displacement of earlier systems within the entertainment apparatus is tied inextricably to a technological process that reforms the body politic. With television, one learned to join the community by staying home. With mobile digital devices, one is released from home and can connect from any location. This process has other material implications. "Monster" homes expand to accommodate the needs of children who stay in; vehicles expand to accommodate their growing bodies; and the public transit, roads, and public spaces of the cities deteriorate. The speedup in the turnover of mobile devices adds a final nail to the coffin of common space.

Did people choose to stay home and find themselves followed there by technological invention, or was this preference formed in more direct or more complex response to the force of technological imperatives? The complexity of the contemporary mobilization and privatization process recalls Nicos Poulantzas's incisive description of capitalist spatiality: "Social atomization and splintering . . . separation and division in order to unify . . . atomization in order to encompass; segmentation in order to totalize; individualization in order to obliterate differences and otherness."[29] How complicated such effects can be is evident with the transistorization of radio after the advent of television. This development, which coincided with the saturation of the North American home market with televisions, was formative in the creation of urban youth subcultures. Car radios were an important means of temporary escape from the claustrophobic performance of family life as it refracted endlessly between the living room and the screen. Cars and radios were available to and constitutive of the new species known as teenagers, a clear contrast to old family sitcoms whose audience, in the film *Pleasantville* (1998), morphs into reruns while an involuntary time traveler transforms the televisual politics of 1950s family life. Tracing such changes shows that social change is both product and cause of new cultural technologies such as the transistor radio. The symbiotic relation between technological innovation and social space can be disruptive as well as conservative, a realization that is beginning to de-center the emphasis on hegemony and social stability in critical media studies. For this reason the analysis of cultural technologies challenges the duality of stability versus subversion as a cognitive paradigm for the analysis of texts, as de Lauretis observed in connection with debates about postmodernism.[30]

Network television was the articulation of a particular historic conjuncture of family and economic-urban structuration. It has been transformed again by the proliferation of different kinds of families and residential units, by the exponential increase of working women, by new information technologies, by the so-called flexible worker of postindustrial capitalism, and by the transformation of urban landscapes ("reseparation in order to re-unify") in the wake of transnational movements of people and capital. And is this even a controversial claim? Capitalist modernity is founded in the necessity of dismembering what capital processes have already produced. As Harvey emphasizes,

> Capitalist development has therefore to negotiate a knife-edge path between preserving the exchange values of past capital investments in the built environment and destroying the value of these investments in order

to open up fresh room for accumulation. Under capitalism, there is then a perpetual struggle in which capital builds a physical landscape appropriate to its own condition at a particular moment in time, only to have to destroy it, usually in the course of crises, at a subsequent point in time. The temporal and geographical ebb and flow of investment in the built environment can be understood only in terms of such a process.[31]

This graphically elaborates the "pervasive and problem filled spatialization process" described by Lefebvre and warns us against a depiction of any media technology that endows space with the static quality once attributed to ideology.[32]

There is no lasting homogeneity in the production of social spaces into which we are so efficiently pursued. Cars no longer transport families to drive-ins for their weekend entertainment. Nuclear families are no longer the dominant family form, and women at home are no longer the broadcaster's primary consumption unit. Television and film are absorbed by VCRs, satellite disks, music and other specialty channels, videotapes, instructional and other software, video games, pay-per-view services, websites, and legal or other downloads. Viewers might be in pubs, bus stations, corner stores, dance clubs, or cafes (especially in towns in the United States, where the TV screen seems inescapable), or watching multiple screens in their bedrooms at home. Youth cultures hanging out in live clubs are no longer the primary (though they remain the elite) consumers of popular music, which is disseminated through radio, video, and the Internet in homes, cars, classrooms, walkmans, telephones, and watches; in television advertising, film soundtracks, websites, and an explosion of musical soundtracks in stores and offices. Television doesn't "mean" the hegemony of the nuclear family any more than popular music "means" or works to reproduce oppositional youth cultures erupting against the nuclear family, although both television and music texts still represent their audiences in terms of these mythic narratives, supporting perhaps their viewers' fantasies of reenactment. Television and music-based media are driven by semiotic reference to their spatial origins, the gendered architecture of family life on the one hand, so powerfully evoked with the woman at the piano in an earlier time (see "The Musicking Machine, chapter 6) or the quasi-defiant collectively defined hangouts of youth culture on the other. Displaced from the center of innovation and marketing, television and radio are remediated with aura and made newly desirable as content for newer technologies. Thus cable services offer television series reruns; *I Love Lucy* and *The Sopranos* are available on DVD; CD shelves are filled with rereleases; mixers channel the Beatles; cell phones carry pet photographs; and teenagers watch talk shows on their computer screens. We are subjects and carriers of a wide dissemination of consumer technologies that change in accord with the same economic and discursive rationality and disruptive social logic as the contents they convey. Their power to convey their own affect is confirmed by their ability to conquer and inflect the spatiotemporal practices of individual everyday life, whether in the home or at work, en route or at play among these spaces.

These consumer technologies function as distribution systems for an increasingly global entertainment and information industry that is continuously recapitalized. Such technologies are increasingly refined in their ability to adapt to individuated users, parts of the body, parts of the home, and parts of the city, and to separate and reunite users in differentiated spaces. Their physiological precision offers another expression of entertainment's mode of address, a kind of liberating fabulosity, a hint of possible excess superimposed upon the disciplines of everyday life. Yet the global circulation of cultural commodities reproduces and even intensifies hierarchies of access to information. The speed and expense of updating communications networks in eastern Europe, China, and the Third World, has brought with it a wave of deregulation and privatization. Investment by multinational communications corporations is "likely to follow the logic of the market rather than socially determined need," Featherstone and Lash conclude, because national governments lack the capacity to regulate multinational corporations and the flows of capital across global markets.[33]

But what governments want to do so? Canada has been a preferred testing ground for the cross-border dissemination of media and for the creation of bilateral and multinational trade agreements allowing corporations in the entertainment business and military-industrial complex to override national policies. The visibility of this process has encouraged scholars to question the dominance of content analysis and audience ethnography, whose practitioners are so adept at rendering assurance that power rests with the viewer. Such skepticism encourages a different mode of inquiry that investigates culture in the context of the technological proliferation, cumulative privatization, and spatial expansion of global cultural technologies.

Theses on Entertainment: A Polemic

The constellation of meanings associated with "entertainment" dates from the late nineteenth century and combines a number of opposing meanings. Entertainment provided the space in which people needn't "keep their place"; its conventional modes of address, originating in variety and vaudeville performance styles, worked to elaborate a pact with audiences whose feelings ran against the social order. The perceived need to "improve" such entertainment in the interest of civility was later extended to panic among the respectable about popular enthusiasm for cinema, pop music, and video games. The history of entertainment also traces the move from social spaces with a particular purpose—the music hall or theater club—to nonparticular spaces: shopping malls, cars, bedrooms. Entertainment has been transformed by technological mediation from "medium of the special" to "medium of the everyday."[34] Yet its value still lies in its claim to release audiences from the constraints of work, politics, discipline, boredom, history, and the "normal" confines of everyday life, of which it remains, in fact, an integral part.

As Brecht wrote with prescient insight in 1930:

> People say, this or that is a good work; and they mean (but do not say) good for the apparatus. Yet this apparatus is conditioned by the society of the day and only accepts what can keep it going in that society. We are free to discuss any innovation which doesn't threaten its social function—that of providing an evening's entertainment.... The more unreal and unclear [that] the music can make the reality—though there is of course a third, highly complex and in itself quite real element which can have quite real effects but is utterly remote from the reality of which it treats—the more pleasurable the whole process becomes; the pleasure grows in proportion to the degree of unreality.... It is a purely hedonistic approach.[35]

Could one ask for a better description of the experience of Hollywood epics or action movies? With the postwar saturation of electronic media, entertainment value expands its horizon with the alibi of restoring "real" pleasure to the banality of everyday life. To "entertain" means "to 'divert attention' or to 'keep steady, busy, or amused.'" Its purpose, Richard Dyer suggests, is to provide escape: "Show business operates in full awareness of the unpleasantness of most people's lives: it is built into its definition of its job that it must provide an alternative to the world of work and of general drudgery and depression."[36] "Show business" doesn't say this; it says it wants you to have a good time and make lots of money for its producers. The rhetorical embrace of pecuniary goals is part of its discursive routine. The transparently commercial context of performance brings credibility and implausibility together and cements the viability of entertainment as a discursive occupation. "Entertainment" is excess superimposed on the normal, in such a way that the normal itself—the breakfast hour news update, the upbeat shopping-hours soundtrack, the four-to-six afternoon drive home, the weeknight dinner hour slumped in front of the TV, Saturday night at the movies—is reconfirmed, naturalized, and enjoyed as the inevitable trajectory of ordinary life. The success of this pragmatic authority depends on an agile combination of narrative naïveté and technological sophistication. No one believes the products of this alliance, but watching entails succumbing pleasurably to the premises of its performance. We are cathartically released from the compulsion to draw conclusions, a release that in the case of television and film intensifies their ritual dimensions. The chief accomplishment of television and of Hollywood is not credibility, but the dispersion of other claims to our attention, including its own.

Rhetorically this discourse conflates two concepts: pleasure and democracy. Fun is fun, and has nothing to do with power (or, in an interesting twist, is power's sole and adequate source). Women are familiar with this formulation, for we sadly lack a sense of humor. The complement of this discursive separation of fun and power is that good entertainment is "what people want," which means if you don't like it, you aren't people. This rhetoric suggests that entertainment value arises from a classless, genderless, raceless popular desire, rather than as part of a productive process that seeks to produce such desire in its own image and thus to universalize its space. This makes a critique of entertainment values a critique of popular rights, an assault on the progressive ubiquity of pleasure in terms of which "the popular" is understood. The consequences of this discursive rule play out with disturbing violence.

The exclusion of other goals from the purview of entertainment echoes the modernist teleology of the purification of form. If painting is the outcome of the encounter between painter and paint, "entertainment" fulfills its promise through a similar exclusion. "The question posed by language analysis of some discursive fact or other is always: according to what rules has a particular statement been made, and consequently according to what rules could other similar statements be made? The description of the events of discourse poses a quite different question: how is it that one particular statement appeared rather than another?"[37] The statement "this is good entertainment" follows characteristically modern rules of exclusion and inference. It restores nominal autonomy to the busy spaces of leisure, and imposes a moralizing constraint on audiences who want more. It avoids all implication beyond the finite and excluding referent, the quality of being entertaining; it defers social meaning on behalf of this same quality, which thereby stands in for democracy. This discourse on entertainment has roots in the early modern industrialization of culture, and shapes its institutional and aesthetic practices. It valorizes at the same time the high production values arising from the professionalization of cultural production, and a performative indifference to established morals, authorities, or obligations, which helps to guarantee their popular success. In the current period it represents an important mechanism whereby populist discourse is appropriated by the Right. The conflation of pleasure and democracy under the rubric of entertainment constitutes, among other things, a central instrument in the neoconservative appropriation of democracy.

Notwithstanding the popular construction of "just entertainment," entertainment encompasses and contains (in both senses of the term) constant reference to social issues. Sexism, racism, feminism, violence, homelessness, poverty, homophobia, and American foreign policy are intelligibly and intelligently referenced across the terrain of North American popular culture. Part of the pleasure of seeing these issues taken up derives from the energy released by encountering subjects that are avoided in the daily news. The key aspect of such narrative is not the exclusion of issues, but rather their ritual containment.[38] Car chases, shootouts, exotic landscapes, natural disasters, romantic sex, happy endings, celebrity gossip, miraculous survivals, murder, special digital effects, and the graphic depiction of death are common means by which entertainment value is confirmed across genres. Through such containment, pleasure asserts its dominance over politics. This discursive maneuver can be seen in texts ranging from *War Games* (1983), in which a boy's troubled encounter with military aggression (an accident of online exploration) is semiotically overwhelmed by the captivating visuals of the military control room, to *The Devil Wears Prada* (2006), in which a young woman moralistically rejects the world of high fashion while visually transporting her viewers through a dazzling exhibition of its finest products.[39] While these narratives captivate us with affecting dilemmas and encourage us to land on the right side of them, their filmic rhetoric supersedes moral considerations. Through narrative inversion, private pleasure is posited as the greatest good. These rituals of representation sustain the privileging of pleasure as American society's special offer. Surely part of the pleasure of watching reality television is its aggressive reversal of such narrative conventions. In contrast to the hyperrealist representational conventions of conventional film and television, these situations are obviously simulations. No one is going to starve or drown. Viewers get to watch participants struggle in the safely volatile process of being brought to account.

Such structures and conventions are the site of continuous negotiation and contestation. The wish to reattach social meanings to performance is alive, active, and unpredictable. Participants in local music scenes, independent cinema and video, and Internet projects all purposively distinguish their activities from the mechanisms of the culture industries. The utopian moment arises when such performance takes us through and beyond the familiar zones of irony and boredom, and resonates against our habits as moments of wild, impossible yet strangely familiar "fabulation."

Entertainment and the New Rhetoric of International Trade

The discourse of entertainment has provided the central rationale for the socioeconomic structure and expansion of American culture industries. The broadcast industry's rejection of public interest in favor of the rhetoric of consumer choice has been closely allied to its deep integration with electronics manufacturing and its infamous affection for massive economies of scale. Media consumption constitutes a privileged source and signifier of social competence, forming the raw material of our "common culture" while disguising its global implications.[40] The idea of consumer choice, closely articulated to the idea of "free flow of information," has functioned as a crucial vehicle for the introduction of new economic and industrial policies in Western and "developing" countries. Building on the effectiveness of "free trade" in the nineteenth-century colonization of developing countries, the United States has pursued free trade and the "free flow of information" irrespective of other countries' cultures, socioeconomic conditions, or position within the world system.[41] What advertises itself as an open space for productive desire is part of a political-economic complex that advances "an open society bound by the total commitment of its worker/consumers in exchange for pleasure while its political system has donned the mantle of imperialism to control alien threats to American pleasure at home and abroad."[42] In *Culture and Imperialism,* Said revisits the nineteenth-century English novel as a genre that both veils and valorizes the distant conquests of British imperialism. Similarly, twentieth- and twenty-first-century technologies of entertainment have emerged in close conjunction with the disciplinary objectives of American social policy, which link together the production values of the entertainment industry and the political values of American foreign policy. Its effectiveness is demonstrated by the ability to represent entertainment as the product of democratic demand and thus as an essential and irreducible motivation for a foreign policy which is antidemocratic and even imperialist in its actions.

These ideals were employed by early radio broadcasters wanting to justify their antiregulatory stance. For their ideologists, "The democratic [i.e., commercial] control of programs . . . possesses all the strengths and weaknesses of democracy operating in the social and political fields. Democratic control of programs implies control by the listening majority," as an American professor named Hettinger wrote in 1935. When Hettinger concludes that "It is only to be expected that the majority of listeners would rather be entertained than edified," he is reiterating the central rationale for United States culture industries while outlining the rhetorical strategies that would propel their transnational expansion. This passage is cited negatively by the authors of the 1951 Massey Commission Report to support their defense of public broadcasting in the context of television's arrival in Canada.

> It was [the private broadcasters'] view, the Massey Report said, that radio was primarily a means of entertainment, a by-product of the advertising business. The United States, according to the Massey Commission, follows the view that radio broadcasting is primarily an industry; there radio has been treated primarily as a means of entertainment open to

commercial exploitation, limited only by the public controls found in all countries.[43]

In 1935, when Hettinger committed his thoughts to print, there were already sharp conflicts between Canada and the United States over control of the airwaves. As witnesses to and subjects of this growing entertainment apparatus, Canadian critics recognized its importance to the "mutation in political sovereignty without boundaries that ends up in the new world constitution of Empire."[44] These antagonisms were reinvigorated in negotiations for the Free Trade Agreement signed by Canada and the United States in 1989, when American representatives threatened a "scorched earth policy" should measures be taken to reclaim control of Canadian cultural industries. The negotiation process revealed and consolidated the pivotal position of the American communication and information industry in the creation of what Reagan hailed as "a new economic constitution for North America."[45] It also revealed and consolidated the limits of Canadian opposition to it.

This first trade agreement, signed by Canada despite widespread popular opposition, has had significant implications for the legislation, production, and dissemination of culture. Through its provisions corporate entities acquired the legal rights of individual citizens on both sides of the border. The acquisition of "personal rights" by corporations was thus extended beyond the provision for "corporate speech" and First Amendment rights in the United States, to be consolidated in international law.[46] Through such trade agreements the U.S. government has successfully extended the right of corporations to organize, process, store, retrieve, and disseminate information that had been established within its own borders to an internationally ratified, legally guaranteed right of corporations to override government policies and public rights in other countries.

By interpreting culture, information, and consumer services as commodities, the Free Trade Agreement established in law the corporation's right to challenge any protectionist policy whether in the public or private sector of the sovereign territory, and set a precedent for future international agreements. The European Economic Community (EEC) was widely cited as precedent to the FTA, but the FTA was the first to supersede the policies of national governments. Where the EEC organizes international trade between sovereign nations, the FTA pursues transnational integration and the suppression of public policies. By writing into bilateral legislation the right of transna-

GABLE, *Regina Leader Post*, 1986, comments on the debates surrounding the proposed Canada–United States Free Trade Agreement signed in 1989. Courtesy of the artist.

tional corporations to override national policies, these agreements extend beyond the redefinition of culture as a marketable commodity to encompass an entire political concept of the relationship between marketplace and state. It represents "a model that the U.S. is offering to the world as its way of forging and managing the global economy," precisely because it guarantees the United States the right to commercial retaliation against any policy it interprets as "unfair competition."[47] Such retaliation can prohibit any measures taken to retain control of any form of manufacturing, services, or information conceived by government in terms of social policy rather than as unregulated commodity exchange. In this way the 1989 FTA exemplifies the process now called globalization, which Boaventura de Sousa Santos defines as "the process by which a given local condition or entity succeeds in extending its reach over the globe and, by doing so, develops the capacity to designate a rival social condition or entity as local."[48]

It is no coincidence that the authors of *The Corporation*, a documentary film tracing the legal history of corporate rights back to the freeing of the slaves, are Canadians who witnessed the terms and outcome of this debate. (Earlier filmography of these authors includes *The Canadian Conspiracy*, discussed in "Writing on the Border" and "Weathering the North," chapters

1 and 7.) Even today, few Canadians support the demise of the public sector. Its institutions have historically provided indispensable resources for indigenous cultural production where economies of scale otherwise prohibit it. However energetically this sentiment is expressed, the privatization of culture proceeds apace. The split between citizenship and consumption in Canada as in other countries around the world drives a wedge into the concept of political sovereignty.[49] By situating Canada as a country with the economic and political dependencies of the Third World (a traditional rallying point for Marxist literature on national sovereignty) and the information and cultural needs and capacities of the First World (a theme generally overlooked in such literature),[50] these trade agreements extend center-margin relations into the heart of cultural administration. Through such agreements, the U.S. and Canadian governments and corporate allies expand the reach of corporate interests and initiatives while disenfranchising growing portions of the population. These changes have furthered the erosion of social service programs, public health insurance, social housing, unionized jobs, native communications, women's services and organizations, cultural and educational subsidies, public broadcasting, public transportation, public hospitals, public control of natural resources, and other services previously defined as unprofitable rights. Recent protests against the World Trade Organization, the World Bank, the Pentagon, and other corporate entities are an important response to the perceived shift of power from government to capital. Creative works that explore such issues are being evicted from the screens.[51] These political tensions have consequences for the social and institutional production of culture, suggesting that what is being displaced is arguably as important as what is being received, and animating continuing debates in the critical commentary on culture.

five

The Musicking Machine

While environments as such have a strange power to elude perception, the preceding ones acquire an almost nostalgic fascination when surrounded by the new.—MARSHALL MCLUHAN, *Essential McLuhan*, 287

What do musicians with traditional training—in my case, eleven years of piano lessons—have to offer the musical culture of the twenty-first century? It is not hard to believe we are completely obsolete. A host of digital and Internet services provide studio time and sound resources (I am not sure whether to call them instruments), online services, and live or digital collaborators to people interested in making music on their computers. To some musicians and music theorists, and to me when I'm gloomy, the digitization of musical production signals the end of music. But nothing can bring the end of music, and obsolescence is a far more complex process than we may imagine. "Post-music" production involves longstanding critical debates surrounding sound reproduction, musical authenticity, authorship, and transformations of listening.[1] My more modest purpose here is to revisit the history of the keyboard in the context of changing dynamics of space and time, automation, and embodiment (or disembodiment) that have so profoundly altered sound reproduction in the last century.

The piano was a central player in the transformation from Victorian culture to the practices and ideals of modern consumerism. The mechanization of the piano placed speed and convenience at the heart of North American consumer culture. Technical and commercial innovations designed to en-hance musical reproducibility have challenged and altered modes of musical performance. Through this process the piano has played a notable role in the modernization of culture. It has been an important agent in the eleva-tion and containment of creative work performed by women, the dissemi-nation and adaptation of bourgeois cultural practices and values across the new world, the symbolic glorification and commodification of entertain-ment, and the efficacy of mechanization in fostering new ideologies of con-venience and efficiency in leisure time as well as in work. These dynamics have characterized a broad range of interactions between humans and ma-chines. But the history of the piano evokes questions about time, embodied memory, and the technologies of creative expression that would be hard to explore in an examination of washing machines or computers. The his-tory of every modern technology raises questions about progress, agency, technological determination, and power, but musical instruments uniquely articulate motion and emotion, feeling and doing, individual subject and social space within the flow of material history and symbolic expression.

In *Musicking: The Meanings of Performing and Listening*, Christopher Small recommends the interpretation of music as cultural practice rather than as text. In the contexts with which we are concerned, this means devel-oping an account of changing relations between musicking and machines. The history of the piano highlights historical interdependency between musical practices, the mechanization of sound production, and new tech-nologies of the self, and illustrates how such interdependency has defined and transformed musicking over the last century. As a musical instrument, the piano articulates the sensual and semantic experience of music through an interface between human hands and a mechanized stringed instrument. A growing tension between convenience and duration has altered the tem-porality and agency of the human body and constitutes an important part of this history.

A related theme taken up here is McLuhan's concept of obsolescence in the media. McLuhan argues that new technologies create changes in the media environment much as the emergence of a new species, according to evolutionary biology, alters the interactions of species within its environ-ment. While dubious about analogies between biology and technohistory (see chapter 9, "Cultural Technologies and the 'Evolution' of Technological Cultures"), I accept McLuhan's challenge to situate media innovation in the context of a material ecology of the media environment. As each new medium establishes its place in the marketplace, it transforms meanings and practices in older, now "residual" (in Raymond Williams's terminology) or "obsolescent" (as McLuhan worded it) technologies. We see this process clearly in the design of sound technologies, which are constantly re-engineered to simulate and displace the instruments, sounds, and practices preceding them. Early pianos were embraced in prosperous homes in part because of their ability to replace more costly chamber ensembles patronized by the aristocracy. The piano could sound multiple notes simultaneously and replicate the effect of many instruments playing together. Later, in an extension and reversal of this process, some mechanical pianos housed multiple instruments that could be sounded within their frame. Today the virtual piano may be selected as one choice among many in the digital archive of sampled sounds. Sampling is a stage in a long process of technological alteration that has blurred conventional distinctions between the consumption and production of music, and transformed instruments, performance practice, and the larger ecology of musical production.[2]

A Brief Geography of the Keyboard

A Newly Invented Musical Instrument.—Two handsome cabinet pianofortes, that play themselves in a most brilliant and correct style all the fashionable country dances, waltzes, reels, etc., one of which will be parted with on reasonable terms. Would particularly suit a foreign market, as a great curiosity.—ARTHUR ORD-HUME, *Pianola: The History of the Self-Playing Piano*

The upright piano appeared in England in 1795 and in Austria in 1835.[3] The first upright piano in Ontario was produced in 1853, but uprights did not replace square pianos, which were susceptible to damage from Canadian climate changes, until around 1875.[4] In this era pianos were primarily an import business, an arrangement between Europe and the colonies clearly evoked in the 1816 advertisement cited above. By the end of the century, following technical adaptations to the Canadian climate (specifically the wood that was used, for Canada's extensive old-growth forests provided exquisite sounding boards), piano manufacturing had become a major contributor to the economies of several Canadian cities. In the early 1900s piano manufacture became one of the most profitable industries in central Canada, and

Canadian pianos were being exported worldwide.[5] The piano was by then well established as part of the civilizing process bringing culture to the New World. For many immigrants, possession of the piano was seen as a crucial, even mandatory part of the colonial settlement process. Many settlers of European descent would not enter the Canadian wilds without one, and popular histories are replete with stories of pianos being hauled over mountains into mining towns, brothels, and remote northern communities.

The first Canadian piano company opened in 1844, offering instruments, sheet music, and sewing supplies.[6] The congregation of musical and sewing supplies was not unusual in the nineteenth-century marketplace; musical and sewing supplies were important tools for women seeking to create a comfortable, respectable life in a frontier society. They both supported the important association between gentility, femininity, and domestic well-being which dominated Victorian culture and formed a bridge with its modern successors. Then as now, amateur pianists were predominantly women. In settler communities, music education was gradually established for the daughters of the well-to-do, and wives-to-be of pioneers in the west often insisted that they be provided with this civilizing instrument before tying the knot.[7]

The domestic piano may have been a reassuring possession for women in this environment, but the prospect of a musical culture possessed by women was not a reassuring sight for the visionaries of the new society. "Music . . . was considered a frivolous pastime and considered important only as part of the education of young ladies," notes the music historian Clifford Ford. "Should a talented young man or woman manage to survive both the prevalent social attitude towards music and the jungle of charlatans and frauds in the music teaching profession, he would still have to seek advanced training in the musical centres of Europe."[8] If piano playing lacked prestige outside the parlor, it was not only because of the distance from those cultural centers in Europe; it was also because the affinity between femininity and piano performance was already inscribed in the social meanings of the instrument. This association permeated popular fiction, social commentary, visual art, and commercial advertising across Canada and the United States in the late nineteenth century and early twentieth. Through her connection to the piano, the lady of the house was expected to provide solace, prestige, and aesthetic sensibility to her family and community, while the husband supported ties to Europe through his occupation and social stand-

"Music was considered a frivolous pastime and considered important only as part of the education of young ladies." Clifford Ford, *Canada's Music: A History*. Courtesy of GLP Press.

ing. In this early stage of household consumerism, the wife's function was to appropriate and preserve the values and commodities which her competitive husband, father, and son had little time to honor or enjoy; she was to provide an antidote and a purpose for their labor.[9] Together the piano and the player accomplished this perfectly, participating in the constitution of a domestic household that was simultaneously private (the domain of sexual regulation, moral strengthening, and parental discipline) and, through display to the outer world, public: a necessarily visible site for the practice of conspicuous consumption. The instrument helped both materially and rhetorically to constitute the modern categories of public and private life. It served to mediate and maintain conventional heterosexual power relations within the domestic sphere and played an important role in the modernization of domestic space in the capitalist societies of the West.

If these responsibilities represented an explicit acculturation of women's work, the social meaning of the piano often prevailed over the creative horizons open to its interpreters. A good life housed elegant deportment, sensitivity, and discipline: in short, a piano and a good woman to play it.[10] Buying one for his wife or daughter provided a man with a conventional representation of public success and private felicity. If women took their music seriously or sought different purposes for their art, then the usual barriers to public space came into play. Professional concert pianists were almost exclusively men, amateurs mainly women.[11] The piano offered itself as a vehicle for women's personal expression, and helped to keep them in their place. As Massey argues, "The attempt to confine women to the domestic sphere was both a specifically spatial control and, through that, a social control on identity."[12] However ambivalent, this aspect of piano performance helped to shape its ensuing history.

The idea that music's association with gentility was in this context stronger than its capacity as a medium of expression is illustrated in an 1884 short story by the then popular writer Isabella Valancy Crawford, "Five O'Clock Tea." "Musical girls," she notes,

> Generally with gold eye-glasses on chill, aesthetic noses, play grim classical preparations, which have as cheerful an effect on the gay crowd as the perfect, irreproachable skeleton of a bygone beauty might have, or articulate, with cultivation and no voices to speak of, arias which would almost sap the life of a true child of song to render as the maestro intended.[13]

This caustic narrator, finely attuned to the cultural dynamics of colonial society, already associates the piano with a "bygone" era, and she counterposes that "grim" sound to the imaginary songs of a child of nature—presumably one uncorrupted by glasses and lessons. For Crawford the piano represents a geography of colonization as well as a normative cultivation of girls, and at least this observer was not captivated. On the other hand, the piano was not just popular in the salon rituals of genteel society; casual frontier communities, such as the gold rush areas of British Columbia and the Yukon, found a valuable use for pianos in the dance halls and bars.[14] A mechanical piano was as satisfying as a conventional one for many settlers in these frontier societies.

Canadian schools of music presented little similarity to European conservatories; they were not professional schools but taught all comers, anyone who would pay a fee.[15] Music was considered a "frivolous pastime," important only as part of the education of young ladies, notes Ford.[16] For many women and some men, however, musical performance helped to constitute a subjectivity that was simultaneously a refuge from and a product of new, more intimate, regimes of everyday life being established through capitalism, colonialism, and the bourgeois family. The feminine gendering of the instrument and performance upon it helped to constitute its history as an instrument of modern culture that was simultaneously sacred and disposable.

The growing public for instrumental music in Canada through the second half of the nineteenth century was drawn by powerful concepts and

THE "*Autopiano*"

is a Pianoforte of excellent tone, graceful appearance, and of absolute durability. The illustration shows the Autopiano as played with music roll, but for use in the ordinary way the two panels can be closed and no one would think it other than an ordinary Piano. The Autopiano is the first complete Piano, as it also enables those who have not studied Piano-playing to perform the most difficult music in a natural and most artistic manner, with the same human expression and perfect technique as the most famous pianists.

As the Autopiano can be played by every member of the family, how much more useful is it than an ordinary piano, especially as it only costs a little more, either for cash or deferred payments. The price is—

75 GUINEAS,

and pianos of any make are taken in part exchange. The Autopiano Lending Library opens the World's Music Repertoire to anyone.

YOU ARE INVITED TO CALL AND SEE THE ENORMOUS ADVANCE OVER ANY PIANO-PLAYING DEVICE HITHERTO KNOWN, OR WRITE FOR CATALOGUE No. 12.

Kastner & Co., Ltd., 302, Regent Street (near Queen's Hall). *Principal Showrooms:* 34, 35 & 36, Margaret Street, LONDON, W. *City Branch:* Salisbury House, London Wall, E.C.

The home was redefined simultaneously as a cultural space and as "free" from the constraints of public space, a sociotopographic premise that carried with it the threat of declining artistic standards.

feelings about music's importance to the cultivation of useful individuals in a flourishing modern society. The piano may have been a reassuring possession for women in this environment, and accomplished women were at least potentially marketable candidates for marriage, but the prospect of a musical culture possessed by women was not reassuring to visionaries of the new society. Crawford's opinions were not unique in this respect. For a colonial society dominated by European settlers, a musical culture made up predominantly of women pianists and itinerant fiddlers, categorically devoid of aesthetic and professional standards, was an insufficient vehicle for the articulation of a solid, respectable middle-class culture. The accomplished playing of wives and daughters could enhance the gentility of the family and select parts of the local community, but it was not an adequate vehicle for the constitution of a cultural elite.

The repertoire of European musical culture was favored for this purpose not only because so many middle-class immigrants came from there, but also because it was already associated with artistic practices and conventions through which superior individualities were thought to evolve. By nurturing players and audiences for such performance, the nascent community could meld together the dynamic search for aesthetic experience and social status. The commercial sphere of instrument manufacture, the satisfactions of accomplished self-expression, and the mutable intensities of sound combined to generate a growing market of middle-class listeners for these performances. The piano was an important mediator in this process, for despite (or, really, because of) its complex mechanical nature, it favors fluctuating chromaticism and intensities and rewards players with the sense of a fully realized musical voice if they maintain the self-discipline necessary to actualize it. These attributes appealed to middle-class women who found ways to express themselves without disrupting their social situation. Other attributes of the piano—its size, its solidity, its interdependency with the self-discipline of practicing—lay the foundation for a new approach to the culture of the home. Through the symbolic and material effects of the piano, the home was redefined not just as a site for family life, with the wife at the center, but also as a site of leisure. If home was still only secondarily a site of leisure (particularly for women), the piano helped to redefine it as a site of cultural activity and musicking as something that helped to constitute and even to enrich this site. Music was becoming something one did privately, in conditions of individual preference and relative ease, rather than something that primarily occurred in the public domain.[17] The home was redefined simultaneously as a cultural site and as "free" from the constraints of public space, a sociotopographic premise that carried with it a number of internal tensions, including the threat of declining artistic standards.

By the early years of the twentieth century, middle-class domesticity was being redesigned and revalorized across Europe and North America through the rise of department stores, commercial decorating, new domestic appliances, and advertising.[18] Aesthetic aspirations for the home were being intensified by the deliberate targeting of women as consumers of beautiful things. The notion of convenience was introduced at the same time through the invention of various timesaving devices for the modern housewife. The piano was promoted as indispensable to and indexical of the social process through which the middle-class home was becoming a site of leisure, of space and time set apart from work and commerce. Piano-playing women and children were central to the affective images and material practices of this changing domestic space.

But "practicing" sounded too much like work, and failing to practice produced dispiriting results. The marketing for newer mechanical players evoked the same semiotics of domesticity and cultivation but linked these to explicit rejection of the discipline of practicing. As the market was inundated with new status-enhancing instruments and appliances for the home, it was not only the piano being displaced but also an accumulated history of feminine culture and cultivation. The increased accessibility of electronic music reproduction went hand in hand with the loss of listeners for their performances. Stan Godlovitch suggests that the expectation of an audience is integral to musical performance. "Lectures and performances alike look for ears to fill," he writes. "Lacking the ears, nothing remains to fill save the room, scarcely a surrogate." A player without an audience is not a performer but a demented person, "almost pathological"; proceeding to play without listeners "smacks of desperation."[19] Godlovitch describes the "defiance" of such a player in the context of an empty hall, not a living room. But amateur pianists—attached through training, disposition, and embodied memory to obsolete skills and archaic instruments, so many of us women—might feel some resonance with his description.

Mechanical Pianos

Changes in musical production are so rapid today that they seem to turn the knowledge gap into microfractions of biological time. Such microfractions will not serve us well in tracing this history, however, for experiments in mechanizing keyboards began well before the piano had been embraced as the preferred instrument for domestic entertainment and musical education. As early as the fourteenth century, when organs were the exclusive property of monasteries, builders were seeking technical improvements to them, not only in terms of sonority and temperament, but also in terms of their interface between human and machine.

"The organ is an instrument strongly bearing the character of a machine," notes Max Weber in his study of industrialization and music. "In the middle ages its manipulation required a number of persons, particularly bellows treaders. Machine-like contrivances increasingly substituted for this physical work."[20] The desire for more sublime registers of sound had already begun to conflict with the limited capacities of the human body. Once the

split between body and spirit was inscribed in these instruments, technological improvement was dedicated to furthering this end, and pianos and
organs were subject to continuous renovation. The lighter harpsichord (or
clavecin), the piano's other precursor, was played by amateurs—"particularly
and quite naturally all folk circles tied to home life"—including women.[21]
The greater accessibility of this instrument helped to accompany and advance new harmonies in popular music, but it was soon left behind in the
evolutionary trajectory of mechanical augmentation.

This search for mechanical progress was not derived purely from a spiritual vocation. Henry VIII is known to have left behind "an instrument that
goethe with a whele without playing upon" at his death in 1547.[22] The mechanical ingenuity of such instruments was a source of pleasure that was
surely enhanced by the exclusivity of possessing them. By the early seventeenth century, such mechanical devices were no longer the exclusive property of monasteries and kings. A builder of musical automata in Germany
made spinets that could be played by a drum or barrel, and mechanical instruments were heard in early performances of Shakespeare;[23] mechanical
singing birds were a favorite toy for those who could afford them. The piano
emerged in mid-eighteenth-century Europe as the favorite instrument of
the northern middle classes, reinforcing their greater focus on indoor life
and the culture of the bourgeois-like home with its increasing preoccupation with effort and discipline.[24] Clockwork instruments and self-playing
pianos were subject to widespread technological innovation. By the mid-
nineteenth century, mechanical pianos were popular in bars and music
halls as well as some homes. By then a substantial market was emerging for
musical commodities—sheet music, instruments, public performances by
artistic celebrities—that were no longer restricted to aristocratic or religious
settings.

While we should be cautious about imposing a retrospective evolutionary narrative on the life of these instruments, there is one general dynamic
that shapes this process of change. With the emergence of mechanical instruments, musical notation, and mass printing of musical scores, music was
increasingly mobile; it belonged less and less to a particular place or time.
Obviously the piano itself was never a mobile instrument. But the compositions, the sheet music, the fashions, and the performances were able to
spread laterally through "better" parts of society. The piano's appearance
in so many homes constituted a solid link between culture as a distinctive

activity and the economic and domestic achievements of the middle class, which proudly assumed the earlier, more limited privileges of monastery and court. In an increasingly secular, market-oriented milieu, the piano expressed the height of middle-class achievement, acquiring a mythological status that resonates nostalgically in film and literature today.

Such achievement was not popular with everyone. To some contemporary minds it was appropriate that mechanical experiments would thrive in this context. With the prospect of musical compositions being purchased by nameless grocers' daughters, as Arthur Loesser put it, "composing for the market seemed unworthy of a skilled, deliberate effort; it seemed almost like something that could be equally well done by a machine."[25] It was not the technical reproduction of sound that irritated such writers, but the human one—the proliferation of automatic-sounding musicking performances arising from fashion-conscious purchases of instruments, lessons, and popular compositions in print. The synchronized training of human hands was perceived as blurring the boundary between bodies and machines. Innovations in sound reproduction would henceforth be understood as further interventions in and diverse delineations of that fluid boundary.

Sheet music was the first music-related mass medium, and along with sewing supplies and other resources for the home, helped to generate the new consumer culture of the mid-nineteenth century. In this situation "art is made mechanical," as one disenchanted music teacher concluded, "by fast and furious amateurs."[26] The spread of amateurism invited the scorn of sensitive critics such as this one, who saw culture as opposed to mechanization or mass production of any kind. But the mass production of musical scores, combined with pressures to cultivate domestic performance, established a central cultural technology of the Victorian middle class. The combined embrace of self-discipline and fashion put thousands of piano students to work practicing away, "one eye on the music . . . the other on the mantelshelf clock."[27] If musicking has been liberated from the exclusive spaces of pre-bourgeois institutions, note how deeply it has become imbricated with a specific embodied measurement of time. The student is required to practice a half hour, an hour, two hours, depending on discipline, accomplishment, and commitment. From these descriptions, it doesn't sound as though these fledgling impresarios were having much fun. We need to be wary of this conclusion, however, for the feminized and domesticated context of such practicing was bound to earn contempt from some quarters.

The changing technology of musical production incorporated and went beyond the simultaneous repetitive discipline of practicing identical pieces; their designers set out to automate those same movements through mechanical reproduction. Entrepreneurs in the music industry learned to profit from the experiential downside of the practices they themselves promoted. Experiments in designing machines for composing and performing were flourishing by the nineteenth century, not only because it was technically possible but also because a hospitable social context was emerging for them. Responding to the increased middle-class focus on interiority and domesticity and the growing willingness of households to invest money in such objectives, inventors explored ways to enhance instruments as playback mechanisms for the home. They worked assiduously on shrinking sound sources to fit within the frame of the mechanized piano and on mechanizing the playing of them.[28] More advanced player pianos offered greater verisimilitude through recordings of professional pianists while providing a regular keyboard as well. By the beginning of the twentieth century, retailers for player pianos and acoustic pianos were competing for the same market.

McLuhan suggests that when a medium is displaced by a newer medium, it becomes a work of art, imbued with the aura associated with art in the modern era. Its former transparency as a medium disappears behind its newly foregrounded materiality, which, remediated by the newer technology, acquires the status previously denied to it as an object. Nowhere is this process more clear than in the history of the keyboard. With pianos competing with their technological successors, advertisers retreated from the conventional claims of superior technological prowess formerly used to promote the acoustic (nonmechanized) piano, and emphasized rather the status of the older instrument as a work of art. Turn-of-the-century promotion for Steinways exemplifies the manner in which high-end pianos were marketed as great works of art in contrast to their mechanical competitors.[29] Some advertisers commissioned new graphic art to accompany their depiction, so that the instruments appeared simultaneously as technological achievements, and artifacts of an age not yet taken over by mechanical reproduction.[30] Shifting their emphasis from the instrument as a marvelously intricate manufacturing achievement, advertisers now associated the acoustic piano with fantasies of exquisite taste and individual expressiveness, promoting what Craig Roell terms the basic *uselessness* that allowed the Steinway to thrive in the consumer's imagination. The piano was offered not as something one did, but as something one had. Meanwhile "doing" was being reattached to a very different set of activities and skills.

The first decades of the twentieth century were crucial in cementing ties between fashion, consumption, and the ideology of the modern. Emphasizing the enhanced role of consumption in domestic management and the growing retail sector of department stores, advertisers and magazines drew upon new design strategies that positioned feminine taste and discrimination as central to the cycle of production and consumption. Celebrating what had previously been described paternalistically as "female accomplishments," this campaign depended on a heightened appreciation of distinctive items of domestic use and display that women could buy rather than make.[31] The newly coined phrase "the democratization of luxury" described the process through which items of traditional feminine craftsmanship were entering department stores and graphic arts, their manufacture continuously updated by the temporal rhythms of contemporary fashion. Feminine craftsmanship was promoted to consumers as a decorative resource just as it was being displaced from the process of production. In this campaign, notes Penny Sparke, Art Deco offered "a distinctively feminine version of the modern" which was richly decorative, openly commercial, and closely tied to domestic consumption. "It appealed to consumers internationally," Sparke notes, "and was central to the transformation of the modern from an elite to a democratized base, a shift which helped to construct a bridge between masculine and feminine cultures."[32] In Europe, traditional feminine crafts were disseminated in new commercial contexts, while in the United States, Sparke suggests, fashion rather than craft emerged as the central link between art and commerce. The emphasis of this new social engineering was not on effort or accomplishment, but on taste and aesthetic judgment; here, as in other contexts, "the liberal subject was reformulated from an individual moral being into a subject of need."[33]

This new taxonomy of doing and having was equally visible in musical culture. Practicing was discursively redefined through negative connotations of kitsch, social ambition, and drudgery. Piano design and marketing sought to displace the need to practice through purchasable substitutes that were doubly valorized as conduits to pleasure and tools of democratization and freedom. Pianos began to register two temporalities at once, representing both the knowing sophistication of the up-to-date twentieth-century consumer, with a good eye for design and innovation but no time to spend on unproductive leisure activity, and the harmonious stability of the nineteenth-century bourgeois home, where individuality was an expressive act and musical achievement the result of socially approved effort. Time and the benefits of saving it, carefully articulated to rhetorics of pleasure and need, formed central themes in early twentieth-century marketing. It only seems ironic that it was the piano that led the way. The mechanized piano embodied America's most fervent ideals. The automated instrument offered the pleasure of creating without work, practice, or the taking of time; the opportunity to participate in something valued by others without needing to understand it; and a fascination with exceptional talent. The idea of enhancing personal power through mechanization was advanced through ads for machines ranging from washing machines to automatic pianos. The latter drew on the support of recording artists, who found they could correct mistakes and perfect the recording before it was released, shifting onto the recording technology the qualities of power and "natural" inspiration that justified the performance and the technical preservation of it in the first place.

Not surprisingly, the popularity of these techniques aroused a nascent anxiety about mechanization in the culture. This concern is evident not only in the advertisements for traditional pianos, where heritage and prestige are now emphasized, but also in ads for the more up-to-date mechanical instruments. It was not necessary to invest time, these texts implied, to reap personal rewards from music; nonetheless music could maintain, even enhance authentic and profound listening experiences. The implicit anxiety about the authenticity of such technologically mediated performance inspired copywriters to produce rhapsodic prose on the expressive possibilities of the new machines. The following instance appeared in 1921:

> The tel-electric piano player. It is the *one* player which you, *yourself*, whether an expert musician or not, can quickly and easily learn to play with all the individuality of a master pianist. It permits you to interpret perfectly world-famous compositions with all the original feeling, all the technique, and with all the various shades and depths of expression as intended by the composer.
>
> In using electricity as the motive force of the tel-electric we not only eliminate the tiresome foot-pumping and noisy bellows of the pneumatic player, but we place the instrument under your absolute control—ready to answer, instantly, your slightest musical whim.[34]

The idea of enhancing personal power through mechanization was advanced through ads for many kinds of machines for the home.

The constellation of pleasure, self-expression, ease, and heightened individual power invoked here clearly encapsulates the attraction of the new mechanical instruments. Like the conventional piano, the mechanical players were celebrated for their ability to enhance self-expression and social status. Both were advertised in terms of their ability to create clearly individuated sounds, their technical superiority to their competitors, and their indispensability for the creation of enviable domestic space.[35] But the mechanical piano offered a greater sense of personal power with a fraction of the effort. Making music no longer depended on the drudgery of practice, with its now negatively connoted emphasis on digital dexterity and its capacity to make capable and obedient machines of the fingers.[36] The joint purpose of instrument and owner was to entertain the guests and keep the offspring busy at home without making them feel like dexterity machines, advancing what Roell describes as the gradual replacement of the Victorian work ethic with the leisure-oriented consumer ethic.[37] By sidestepping the need to practice, the pianola was able to "satisfy growing daughters and sons with a natural craving for some form of entertainment . . . who will seek it outside it if is not provided within the home."[38] Musical skill, formerly enshrined as the favored symbol of Victorian culture, was now subjected to a systematic downgrading through promotional rhetoric. The piano was still a crucial item for small or family parties, but the embodied skill, discipline, and time it took musicians (still mainly women, judging from illustrated advertisements of the time) to perform on it had been made dispensable.[39] Women could continue to perform traditional feminine roles such as playing the piano or managing the household even if they had taken a job; thus anxieties about gender roles were neatly transferred to (and presumably solved by) the domain of consumption.

Player pianos were marketed in terms of their promise to reproduce faithfully the brilliance and nuance of the most accomplished performances, without the user having to acquire such accomplishment herself. By playing on a special piano, professional pianists produced piano rolls that created markings to exactly correspond to the performer's strokes on the keys; these rolls were then played back on a reproducing piano powered by an electric motor.[40] The pianists recorded in these rolls also worked as "part-time merchants," promoting piano manufacturers in concerts and testimonials.[41] In fact the piano was the first major consumer commodity to be attached to brand loyalties. Steinways and Chickerings were endorsed as brands by musical celebrities in live performances and magazine advertisements. Through player pianos the cult of virtuosity extended into the home, where music-loving consumers could also listen to these performers on their mechanical pianos.

By the late nineteenth century, patent offices in Canada and the United States were deluged with applications by inventors seeking to improve the mechanisms of the piano and the sound of pianists playing them. The first self-contained pneumatic piano appeared in 1880.[42] The first commercially successful reproducing pianos for the home appeared in Europe and North America in 1901—just before the phonograph, another technology intensifying the move toward a more separated geography of family and domestic life. By the First World War, with sales of player pianos and piano rolls booming, the silent piano seemed on the verge of obsolescence; it seemed inevitable that, as Roell recalls it, the benefits of music would soon be enjoyed by all.[43] In this democratic sonictopia, musical events displayed not the homely skills of the amateur performer but rather the more entertaining recorded skills of the virtuoso, which could be purchased and brought home to enjoy in the family salon.

In his history of recorded sound, Michael Chanan describes the phonograph as the first sound technology to produce both hardware and software (record players and records) as interlinked commodities.[44] But that initiative actually arose earlier, with player pianos and the marketing of piano rolls by famous performers. As Lisa Gitelman shows, "The terms 'hardware' and 'software' might not have been applied at the time, but something of the relation that later emerged between them was already recognizable, working in the construction of 'self-playing,' as it would in the construction of machine-readability and of digital 'wares.'"[45] The sale of piano rolls depended on inciting a desire, in consumers who already possessed player pianos, to purchase multiple recordings. While sheet music sales continued to depend on the ownership of instruments, "the newer makers of music rolls suffered the hardware obsession of the music trades."[46] If pianos had been marketed on the basis of womanly skills and middle-class domesticity, player pianos and piano rolls were advertised on the basis of new innovations in faithful sound reproduction, enhanced by the claim that through such innovations world-class musical performance could be appreciated on a more democratic basis. Here democracy and consumerism were adamantly joined, together promising that individuals could flourish musically while bypassing the acquisition of musical skills. Rather than practicing, or submitting to someone else practicing in the home, one should simply develop one's musical discrimination and learn to appreciate the fine points of recorded performances.

Today, looking back at the enthusiastic testimonials that pianists offered to the faithful reproduction of their artistry on player pianos, it must be remembered that they were contrasting these mechanical reproductions to the still elementary technique of acoustic recording, which made the sound of the piano thin and tinny, liked the plucked string of a banjo or guitar. Sergei Rachmaninoff claimed that the early recordings of his playing made the piano sound like a Russian balalaika.[47] More successful recordings were made of the singing voice, most famously Enrique Caruso, whose voice, recorded in 1902, was so rich it drowned out the surface noise and made the inadequate apparatus sound rich and vibrant.[48] Attempts to modify the piano to make it record more clearly with these early techniques did not improve the effect. The more sonically effective player pianos conquered the home market and made their way into the movie theaters by the early 1920s. Reproducing the work of professional musicians while enabling pro-jectionists to switch in a timely manner from one genre of musical drama to another, they put thousands of pianists (typified in one account as a jaded female beating a scarred upright whose duty it was to scare away the ghostly silence that otherwise enveloped the screen)[49] out of work. Between 1925 and 1932, with the growth of synchronized sound, the number of musicians employed in motion picture theaters declined from 19,000 to 3,000 in the United States.[50] The transformation of music performance was even more dramatic for amateurs, who by the 1920s were being encouraged to imagine themselves as consumers, rather than producers, of music for the home.[51]

By the end of that decade, pianolas were being stockpiled, having fallen victim to the attractions of radio.[52] With the progress of sound reproduction, the piano, embraced and promoted as the center of middle-class domestic and musical life across North America, both expanded and lost that role. This paradoxical change transformed the economies of domestic musical culture. The larger scale of factory production necessary to produce such complex instruments in large numbers led to greater corporate concentra-tion and the disappearance of multigenerational family businesses, which mainly did not survive the Depression. Like the nineteenth-century music halls later overtaken by cinemas, the piano as a human-machine interface was complicit in its own obsolescence. We cannot see or hear the transformation of music production or domestic space in the body of an individual piano. A well-made piano, constructed as mine is from good Canadian wood, can sound as harmonious now as when it was made eighty years ago. It is through the instrument's changing relationship to other technologies and practices that we must reconstruct this transformative process. The piano's agency as a medium or instrument of interaction between composers and performers, performers and listeners, teachers and students, people and machines, has altered over time in interaction with social and technological changes. While the materiality of the instrument has remained more or less the same (aside from the wood, for old-growth forests are now largely depleted; only the most expensive pianos could use such wood today), it performs different kinds of agency at different moments and in different geopolitical spaces. Today we can best understand the piano as the bearer of different, sometimes even incompatible, registers of temporality and social memory.

The Mechanical Ideal

Musicking is the creation of human performers interacting with one another and with their instruments. The modernization of instruments contributed to an inventive search to create inanimate objects that could duplicate the work of performers. The emergence of virtual performance concerns not just whether audiences witness a performance live or mediated, but how the performance itself is produced.[53] The piano offers a suggestive case study of this transformation. The mechanization of piano performance involved the transfer of compulsion from individual effort to technological innovation, with a new emphasis on the saving of time and the happy avoidance of unnecessary discipline. This transition introduced the capacity for performers to correct details in their performance before they reached their audiences. More generally, the production of "virtual fingers and hands," as Gitelman describes it, produced new senses of "'the self' in 'self-playing.'" Embracing the pleasures of sound separate from the earlier physical requirements of producing such sound, they enacted a new kind of subjectivity that was socially supported by the surround-sound ideals of democratic access. These experiences reinforced the commitment of aspiring musicians to ongoing innovation in musical machines and new cycles of stylistic innovation. It was no longer the pressure of parents or teachers, but the novelty of player pianos and the currency of music "software" commodities available to program them, that were held out to inspire young people to learn. For students competing to memorize their music pieces, reproducing pianos were replacing mothers as memory guides.[54]

It was natural that such innovation would take convenience one step further. With mechanized pianos, one could perform beautiful pieces of music without having to spend time learning to play them. All you had to do was push a pedal or lever. The idea that mechanization of instruments made music accessible to the unskilled efforts of toddlers and children became a central motif in their promotion, and quickly became the chosen strategy for advertising automatic pianos. Most well known was the image of the Gulbransen baby, accompanied by the slogan "easy to play": "all the family will quickly become expert . . . Without long practice! All the joy without hard work!"[55] Of course, as Roell notes, musical performance was thereby challenged as a vehicle for domestic harmony and virtue; if playing does not need to be nurtured and cultivated, if good performance doesn't demonstrate the sensitivity and self-discipline of the player, what is its value? And what is the worth of those who had achieved the skills the old way? From being a key symbol of feminine virtue and artistic self-discipline, playing a keyboard was converted to something that anyone can do, without regard for embodied or gendered constraints of time, learning, sensitivity, or skill. Consequently, "poor sister has hardly touched the keys," as a critic noted in 1919, recording a hearer's ambivalent response to the horseless pianoforte.[56] A similar gendering of the player's dilemma also appears in John Philip Sousa's 1906 contestation for authorial rights over music rolls: "Printed notes, spots, and marks were no more equal to his musical thought or 'living theme,' he was sure, 'than the description of a beautiful woman is the woman herself.'"[57]

A 1903 article published in the *Chicago Indicator* assessed the instrument as follows:

> The increasing vogue of the piano player . . . is now regarded—and rightly regarded—as one of the most significant phases in the life and advancement of this mechanical age. It is heralded by the enthusiastic as a portent of the dawning of a new epoch, when machinery will still be the motive power of civilization, but will be applied to uses hitherto

deemed sacred from its invading banners. . . . If this vision is to be realized, the piano player will certainly be the most prominent factor in its accomplishment. The public in general will be pleased, and the piano trade will certainly not lag behind the rest of the world in similar feelings; for it is plain that, when the day of the player [piano] arrives, the field of piano enterprise will be greatly enlarged.

Note that this ode to mechanization (and its conquest of "hitherto sacred" activities) appeared in the same decade that biomechanical research entered the sphere of factory production. Frederick Taylor conducted detailed research on workers' physical movements in order to calculate ways to maximize their efficiency and the productivity of the assembly line. The idea of reducing to its essentials the motion required to produce a specific mechanical action was not restricted to the factory but was being promoted with similar zeal in the voluntary domains of cultural and leisure activity.

What causes the vogue of the player piano to reach such heights? First, the author of the newspaper article suggests, the popularity of the piano as an instrument of the home; second, the American habits of economizing time:

> Our citizen loves music, but he has no time to spend in studying a complex technique. His daughter, perhaps, who would be the proper person to fill this want in his household, is busy working in a store or factory, or goes to high school and must study her Caesar or geometry when she gets home. And then there are many people who have no daughter, or none of the proper age. These matters seem trivial, but they nevertheless have a potent influence.

The author lists additional reasons:

> The third fact is this: with a piano player in your house you can give a friend musical entertainment and discourse with him at the same time. Or if you have nothing to talk about—and this is a contingency that happens with remarkable frequency at social gatherings, especially small ones—you may set your piano at work.
>
> Still another cause lies in the admiration of the public for anything which acts, talks or plays automatically. They wonder at the thing. A wonder is a good thing to subdue and make your own. It pleases you; it will please others. Perhaps it will make them envy you; and what so sweet

as envy to the envied? Again, the piano player is a novelty. In all ages novelties have been eagerly sought for, but never has there existed such a craving for them as now.[58]

Appearing at the same time Sousa was attacking the adequacy of automatic playback, these comments are strikingly prescient. The author gives expression to now familiar themes in the rhetoric of technological advocacy. We see the fascination with mechanization both for its own sake, and for what it portends in terms of future progress; the promise of greater freedom from the constraints of embodiment; the pragmatic advantages of economizing time, even in leisure, following the ambivalently viewed move of women into the workforce; the advantages of musical reproduction for allowing listeners to enjoy a state of genial distraction, without the need to converse with one another; the importance of up-to-date technologies for conspicuous consumption; the civic duty of contributing to industry through consumption; and, perhaps most poignantly, yet with such calculation, the magical qualities of sound reproduction with their ability to produce a childlike sense of wonder. If mechanization and rationalization were responsible for the growing disenchantment of the world, as Sousa implies, then paradoxically sound reproduction, with its magical siren song, promised to counter that process.

By the end of the 1920s, however, these effects were all being celebrated in and accomplished by radio. The dramatic drop in piano production was absorbed financially (for those protected by corporate mergers) through the dramatic rise in the sales of radios. This theme is another defining motif in discussions of the technological transformation of musical reproduction. The evocation of magical moments evoking wonder and desire occurs within the framework of a social and corporate process wherein technical invention and planned obsolescence accumulate and recur. As soon as a technology has captivated and conquered its market, its interconnected network of machines, performers, performances, and related commodities crumbles in the wake of a newer device. Between 1900 and 1930, 2.5 million player pianos were sold in the United States,[59] and only 650,000 acoustic pianos a year were produced worldwide.[60] As player pianos supplanted the sheet music industry, they were in turn supplanted by the phonograph (1907) and radio (1928). The market for pianos partially regrouped in Canada and the United States in the 1930s and 1940s, but it would never again reach levels from the First World War period, when there were seventeen piano firms in Toronto.[61] The Canadian piano industry reached its peak in 1966, but by the 1970s had given way to foreign subsidiaries. By then, Japan was the major producer of pianos, and worldwide production was only slightly higher than it had been half a century earlier. By the early 1980s, an estimated 40,000 pianos were being discarded—junked—annually in the United States.[62]

The rise of the piano coincided exactly with the rise of modern industry and modern culture. We can understand its moment of dominance and its later replacement by more mechanized means of sound reproduction in the context of industrial modernism and postindustrial postmodernism as sociocultural formations. The history of the piano's technological evolution and displacement offers a cogent instance of McLuhan's idea of obsolescence, and provides an exemplary case study in the paradoxical progress of cultural technologies in the twentieth century. By advancing the Victorian virtues of hardworking domestic morality, and by articulating these values with the more casually compulsory imperatives of currency and innovation encouraged by modern consumerism, the piano contributed to both the creation and obsolescence of modern culture.

Obsolescence

McLuhan approached the media as an environment, and argued that this environment framed the conditions for our general perception and our understanding of individual media. When a new medium emerges, the media ecology shifts, and the role and meaning of each medium are altered. That doesn't mean that the older media disappear or even that they lose their social or material efficacy. In McLuhan's language, it means that the new technology, having as yet no medium-specific content to fill it, embraces the contents of its predecessor. It is this process that translates the earlier medium into art. McLuhan's account of technological change resonates with what Winner calls the process of "reverse adaptation": with a complex technological system in place, investors in a new technology search for applications and thus reverse the conventional relationship of means and ends.[63]

It may have been the invention of radio that first elicited this idea of reversed ends and means. It was not the public that waited for the radio, Brecht argued, "but radio that waited for the public; to define the situation of radio more accurately, raw material was not waiting for methods of production based on social needs but means of production were looking anxiously for raw material. It was suddenly possible to say everything to everybody but, thinking about it, there was nothing to say."[64] Pursuing the idea of uneven development between a medium and its contents, Friedrich Kittler echoes McLuhan's hypothesis; he describes the housing of one form in another in terms of a kind of piggyback from one technology to the next, bypassing the exploration of any salient features present in each new development.[65] Radio was solidified socially and commercially as a means of distribution, to borrow Brecht's phrase, only to be overcome by television. Nonetheless radio is still omnipresent in everyday life, artists continue to explore the medium, and it forms a favorite content for film and the Internet.

McLuhan and Winner both emphasize the interdependency of human and technological actors within such ecologies and the complex reversals (as distinct from ruptures) brought about by technological change. In McLuhan's account, speech becomes the content of writing, drama the content of film, film the content of television. Critics lost their grasp of the specific effects of television, to take one notable instance, because they relied on critical methods derived from drama and film rather than finding what was specific to the television medium. Because live performances were reproduced by mechanical means, the pianoforte was the content of the player piano. This displacement elevated the levels of competence and expressivity expected from piano performance and reduced the amateur to a marginal place in musical culture. Subjectivity and expressiveness were important reference points for marketing mechanical instruments and music rolls, but these were now actualized better by machines for reproducing, not creating, such qualities. Listeners were encouraged to prefer the sonic representation of expressiveness in others.

Mechanical pianos permitted consumers to reattach themselves physically to the music-making process. They could sit at the piano in their accustomed position and inflect the mechanical recordings by means of the manipulation of pedals, buttons, and levers that could alter volume, intensity, and speed. No musical training was necessary. It would take eighty years and the mergence of DJ practices before this idea really succeeded as musical practice. Then, in another technical reversal, digital sampling made the DJ's recycling and manipulation of records, or "scratching," the content of a new software that removed the necessity of working with turntables, reviving interest in issues of musical memory and presence and generating new practices in the musical landscape.

With newer media taking up older forms as their content, McLuhan argues, the profound changes occurring with these technological shifts are sensorially and culturally obscured. We struggle to understand their significance in an environment in which our modes of understanding are shaped and altered by the technological extension and suppression of our various senses. Today the reconstruction of sound occurs at an enhanced level of technological remove, with samplers and drum machines deconstructing and reprocessing musical performance that has been broken down to digital bits and reorganized via the language of the computer. These digital capacities suggest a radically new category in the process of obsolescence. It is not specific media—pianos, turntables, or vinyl—or specific genres, but rather conventional modes of performance that provide the "content" of new digital media. The sounds produced through this process of radical abstraction could challenge our understanding of music, although so far they have not widely done so. Rather than the player completing the instrument through her performance, now it is the instrument with all its digital resources, including previous performances, completing the on-site performer. While both involve symbiotic relations between body and machine, the hinge of dependency has shifted further toward the machine and its accumulated resources. Now, as in the time of the bellows organ, possibilities for innovative collaboration in musicking are being organized by new techniques. Now, as then, it is individual mastery of new technologies that dominates the horizon.

Individuals acting as composers, producers, and engineers stretch the conventional boundaries of music to encompass techniques such as scratching, looping, condensing, or otherwise distorting sampled sounds. These techniques ostentatiously confuse boundaries between music and machine, human and other sounds. It was this confusion of boundaries that first inspired the early modernist art of noise. But the newer forms of composition imagine music, not cannons or streetcars, as the "content" of the newer media. Most commentary has obscured rather than illuminated this potential transformation. It emphasizes downloading recordings that are sonically indistinguishable from what we could buy at the music store, and the copyright issues arising from this practice. By conceptualizing the Internet as a kind of player piano, as provider of prerecorded musical content, and by focusing on the economic and legal controversies that arise from this use, both users and critical commentaries have obscured the potential significance of the media there conjoined.

To make sense of such developments, Marshall and Eric McLuhan developed a *tetrad* of the laws of media. They pose these as questions: (1) What does an emergent medium enhance or intensify? (2) What does it render obsolete or displace? (3) What does it retrieve that was previously obsolesced? (4) What does it produce or become when pressed to an extreme?[66] For instance, television enhances multisensuous experience; displaces radio, film, and point-of-view perspective; retrieves the occult; and reproduces the inner trip.[67] The car enhances privacy, displaces the horse and buggy, retrieves the knight in shining armor, and in extreme form produces traffic jams and corporate piracy.[68] Just as television foregrounds and then displaces sensuality, the car emblemizes and then displaces speed.

Can new digital resources for music making be read in terms of these laws? What is enhanced? The spatial reach of sound technologies, interaction between digital and musical technologies, and the accessibility of musical tools. What is obsolesced? Conventional contexts and experiences of interaction between musicians, audiences, skills, and instruments—everything that once constituted what we call music—and the time it took to bring these together. Musical performance as a representation of previous playing (practicing); live (and therefore finite) performance in real time. Spatially, the physical boundaries of the home, the studio, the concert hall, and the CD. What is retrieved? Collaboration for musicians who might retreat to the isolation of their studios, or who have lost access to individual expression in the highly "Taylorized" worlds of classical or commercial music. Sounds of the natural environment. The historical archive of sounds. And what is produced in extreme forms? Soundtracks for every space? The end of record companies? The dissolution of music from property rights; the disappearance of signature styles? Copyright wars between friends? The replacement of music education with computers in the classroom, and a limiting of access to learning musical skills to the elite? These are all possible. Such speculations shape our dreams, and these modern dreams interact with social and material forces to shape the contours of our technologies and our selves.

"You Push the Button, We Do the Rest"

Changes introduced by digital music-making have transformed not only instruments and the role and scope of playing, but also the wider ecology of performance, reception, and meaning.[69] We need to look at this in the context of everyday life. Today you can turn on lights without hitting a switch; search a library without going to it; shop without entering a store; move up, down, or across a building without moving your legs; turn up the radio, change the channel, or flip to another CD without leaving your chair; cook without chopping or stirring; and then, bereft of physical motion, "sculpt your body shape without strenuous time-consuming exercise!!" as a recent TV commercial enthuses. There are few bodily functions that haven't been enhanced and displaced by technologies of convenience. As a widely promoted value, convenience translates as two interrelated advances: something that reduces the time it takes to perform a task, and something that permits us not to use our bodies, to substitute extensions or amplifications of the body in their place.

This advocacy depends on the premise that there is not enough time in the day and that final solutions to this problem must be found at an individual level. Thus 70 percent of the $30 billion now spent annually on food advertising in the United States promotes "convenience" foods, which rely extensively on product promotion (the advocacy of practical solutions) while obscuring links between farm and table and beyond.[70] In Elizabeth Shove's exemplary account, "Convenience is now associated with the capacity to shift, juggle and reorder episodes and events. . . . It is the ambition of maintaining standards in the context of an increasingly fragmented temporal environment that drives the pursuit of convenience." Over time the terminology of convenience has "legitimized new forms of consumption and located them as self evident and sensible."[71] This discourse normalizes the routine which requires such convenience (we are all implicated; we are all overworked); promises calm solutions to hectic lives; focuses problem solving on individuals, mainly women; and implicitly characterizes the failure to comply as undesirable, unmodern, even unclean, regardless of environmental impact.[72]

Driven by the allure and escalating social necessity of convenience (for time is money), North Americans increasingly find physical endeavor too inconvenient to undertake—unless done *for its own sake*, like art, in pursuit of expression or a better body. Transcending the body through technological improvement redefines it, shifts its meanings from achievement to limit, and offers in its place endlessly renewed marks of privilege and power. Seeking power, we empower our extensions. The paradoxes of this translation return inevitably to haunt its subjects.

The influential campaign to enhance pianos with electronic playback mechanisms was part of the construction of a consumer culture whose import goes well beyond the animation of consumerism as an economic practice. For it is embedded in, and serves to persuade its readers and listeners of these twin ideas: saving time is a universal good, and physical effort is best avoided. Happiness is redefined as access to abstraction from time and the human body. In this "modern obsession with present-mindedness," if something *takes your time* (even to think about), this is simply a problem in search of a solution.[73] In music as in the other domestic arts, the technology offered for this purpose deskills its domestic users, obviates their empirical knowledge, and "has the cumulative effect of redefining what people take for granted."[74] It was the struggle for time that fueled the social embrace of technological innovation. The detritus of this quest inspires the popular preoccupation with "slow food," craft, yoga, and even piano lessons, by means of which people try to get in touch with a residual sense of embodied time.

Conclusion

While instruments have changed over the centuries, the fascination with them remains attached to a similar rhetoric of improvement and delight. Technological innovations in musical performance promise to endow their owners with the marvels of up-to-date knowledge and technical prowess. They deliver the convenience of simulated performance and enhance the user's sense of individual expression. They mediate ingenuously between human and mechanical agency, offer an enduring magic of sound reproduction whose mechanisms are increasingly invisible, and enhance social status through possession of these wonders in their newest form. The time once required to acquire musical skill has not disappeared; it has been transferred to another kind of *dispositif*, to borrow Foucault's terminology. Foucault defines the dispositif as a heterogenous ensemble consisting of discourses, institutions, architectural forms, regulatory decisions, laws, administrative measures, scientific statements, philosophical, moral and philanthropic propositions—in short, the said as much as the unsaid. Such are the elements of the apparatus. The apparatus itself is the system of relations that can be established between these elements. . . . I understand by the term "apparatus" a sort of—shall we say—formation which has as its major function at a given historical moment that of responding to an *urgent need*. The apparatus thus has a dominant strategic function. This may have been, for example, the assimilation of a floating population found to be burdensome for an essentially mercantilist economy: there was a strategic imperative acting here as the matrix for an apparatus which gradually undertook the control or subjection of madness, sexual illness and neurosis.[75]

To subject the earlier piano-centered apparatus to the scrutiny of Foucault's archaeology is to unravel the way it brings together human and machine to combine and animate the potentially incongruous discourses of uplifting aesthetics, personal discipline and musicking as a technology of the self, together with musical professionalism, and gender, together with small-scale industrial craftsmanship (the making of the piano), routine training, the culture of the home, the colonial outreach of Europe, and so forth. The newer dispositif shifted the relations between these disciplines, objects, and skills, placing the young musician in front of a mechanized piano, a digital keyboard, and then a computer screen, where he or she engages just as fiercely with new interfaces and old ambitions, spatially freed from the family salon and momentarily oblivious to time.

The question of the acceleration of time takes us to the boundaries of music and even further, to the boundaries of what we know about the "natural" rhythms of the human organism. As Richard Beardsworth notes, "contemporary technoscience . . . constitutes an unprecedented speeding up of the dynamic relation between the human and the technical that 'risks reducing the difference of time, or the aporia of time' . . . to an experience of time that forgets time."[76] This is an apt description of the interface between music and digital technologies today, which is exacerbating a radical asynchronicity of time among humans and other species. If art really can, as McLuhan suggests, teach us about our environment through which we swim like oblivious fish, then new musical practices will draw our attention

"The music machine," Toronto, 1999.

to these processes in some way. They will illuminate the tension between old and new techniques and the new possibilities that arise from them. They will remind us of music's ability to evoke history and memory, of changing configurations of the human body, and of the social production of time and space. Such technological changes have created not only alienation but also freedom; the freedom, as Steve Talbott eloquently suggests, "to form new hypotheses, to see things from fresh, previously unimagined perspectives, and even to consider how we ourselves might contribute to the future evolution of things."[77]

six

Locating Listening

I don't think we should consider the "modern state" as an entity which was developed above individuals, ignoring what they are and even their very existence, but on the contrary as a very sophisticated structure, in which individuals can be integrated, under one condition: that this individuality would be shaped in a new form, and submitted to a set of very specific patterns.—**MICHEL FOUCAULT,** *Power*

That is why this apparently modest notion (listening does not figure in the encyclopaedias of the past, it belongs to no acknowledged discipline) is finally like a little theatre on whose stage those two modern deities, one bad and one good, confront each other: power and desire.—**ROLAND BARTHES,** "Listening"

It is said that music knows no boundaries; it is more accurate to say that it redefines them. Similarly, broadcasting is said to know no boundaries (the 49th Parallel being notably contentious in that regard), while one of its major effects has been to extend or alter them. Like music, broadcasting is in part about the constitution of space. In establishing territoriality, there was sound long before there were fences. The ongoing reshaping of listening is tied to a changing sense of location: where we are, "where the music takes us,"[1] where we belong.

Radio history presents us with an interesting quandary. On one hand, radio has been a significant tool in the establishment of colonial and anti-colonial regimes and national territories. On the other hand, the spread of sound reproduction technologies makes our relationship to place increasingly complicated. Electronically mediated space is not one with itself, and neither is the listener. Over time, technologies of sound reproduction have formed a fluid striation of listening situations in which global, national, local, industrial, natural, vehicular, pedestrian, and other kinds of scale create hybrid options for the individuated consumer. Radio's articulation to regimes of citizenship has been supplemental to, and is in North America widely overshadowed by, a plethora of individuated listening events that produce the mobile, adaptive, and individuated subject so important to the contemporary cultural economy.

This chapter addresses radio as a cultural technology of sound mediating bodies in space. Radio locates and connects listeners through the sounds they receive and increasingly through the sounds they select. But how radio does this, in relation to what kinds of location, and with what effects vary profoundly in different political and historical circumstances. In North America, radio has been transformed by historical, economic, and technical changes which contribute to deep transformations in the practices of listening. As an assemblage of technologies and social relations, radio mediates political and regional territories, tools of sound reproduction, commercial owners, regulating agencies, the journalists and employees who speak through them, the musicians who record their music, the technologies that reproduce the music and carry it across the topographies of everyday life, corporations that design and produce these technologies and choose these recordings, advertisers that promote their products, and communities that form and disperse around them. The medium actualizes and depends on a conjuncture of isolation and connection shaped by specific relations of space, identity, art, politics, and profit.

As technologies converge, they spawn new "revolutionary" possibilities for listeners. A changing constellation of musical and digital technologies naturalizes what Timothy Luke calls the "industrial ecologies of ephemeracultures," which morph from one technoform to the next, fusing the desiring ear, the shifting space, and the rapid obsolescence of reproductive media.[2] This process can be explored historically in relation to the changing social contexts and spatial subjectivities of the listener-citizen-consumer. "Our epoch," Foucault claims, "is one in which space takes for us the form of relations among sites."[3] The study of cultural technologies helps to reveal how these "relations among sites" are produced. Music has played a special role in this process, for its dominance of the media soundscape enables listeners to find a sense of belonging in the midst of widely dispersed situations. This dominance represents both the promise and the failure of radio in Western capitalist cultures. Wherever it locates you, whatever it comes up against, music shapes the place you're in. It speaks to the heart of where you are, and tells you something about what it means to live there. With the emergence of these industrial ecologies, space and location become explicit; then space is recognized as a social construction, and music as one of its codes.[4]

For almost a century, music has provided the crucial content for radio, and it remains central to both radio programming and the newer technologies that expand or displace it. It is through music that such technologies follow or pursue listeners into listening spaces, which are mobilized, dispersed, and reconnected by these same technologies. Radio can be understood then as a form of musicking, a concept which "prompts one to assume responsibility for delineating how different stroking interpellates different folks—how it works not simply as an expression of different identities, or, for that matter, as a solicitation of particular identities, but rather as an event where the differences 'folks' share (however unequally) are called up and assembled, in effect, constituted."[5] As a constellation of cultural technology, radio is capable of colonizing speech as well as space, but it is also capable of giving voice to anticolonial movements and feelings, as Frantz Fanon demonstrates in his study of Radio-Algers. Before it became a voice for the Algerian Revolution, "Radio-Alger was listened to only because it broadcast typically Algerian music, native music. In the face of this budding Algerian market, European agencies began to look for 'native' representatives."[6] Where, how, and to whom listeners connect is the complex subject of the cultural technologies of sound. Whether the "global village" of digital convergence marks the end or the beginning of difference in this constitutive process depends on a complex interaction of technology, affect, and power, in which music plays a crucial role. Knowing how the struggle progresses means learning how to listen.

One result of this teletopographic reality is that music, indeed any mode of address in sound, seems to articulate time, but not space, whose overcoming nonetheless provides the occasion for the listening event. Nowhere is this perceptual displacement more evident than in radio, which organizes our sense of morning, of daily activity, of the discipline of time. It's like the experience of driving a car along a familiar road at high speed. On the road, it seems to be the driver's body that remains still, and everything around the car that rushes past, into the past. In fact, the landscape stays (relatively) still and it is the driver, locked in a body in the driver's seat, who rushes across the space. This actuality doesn't account for the

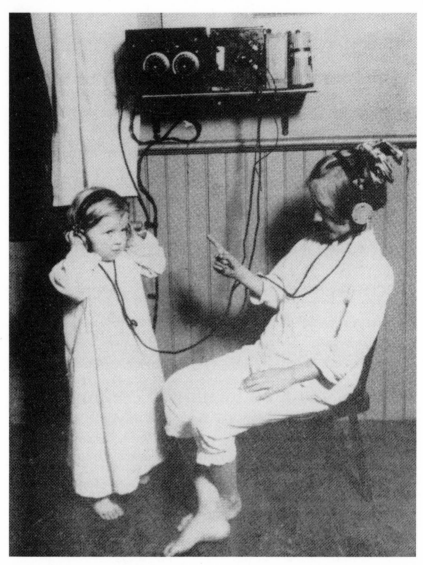

Young sisters experiment with new ways to listen. Where, how, and to whom listeners connect is the complex subject of the cultural technologies of sound. *Public* 4/5 (1990/1991). With permission of the editors.

experience that comes with driving. It doesn't feel like space that interrupts the affinity between driver and her destination, but rather time, punctuated by music and landmarks which together signal the episodic triumph of individual movement over density and distance, of time over space. This focus on time is a convenient apprehension (or misapprehension). For the driver, it is actually space—its stubborn facticity and the intent to traverse it—that dominates the action. The experience of time is defined by practices of producing space. This makes driving a quintessentially modern activity.

This misapprehension of space preserves the location of experience in the singular. The driver's perception does not extend laterally to the local topography of fields, cables, railways, factories, malls, and houses, constellated by a network of roads with steel boxes rushing across it. Instead, it contains the viewing subject and the view within a single steel box. This ultramobile car-radio assemblage does not belong anywhere in particular; rather, it draws its user into an "abstract technoregion" which gradually overcomes the "concrete communal ties" between people and their surroundings.[7] Cultural technologies of listening encourage this same apprehension. It is no accident that technologies of travel such as the railway, automobile, airplane, or urban bus developed interdependently with the technologies of listening. What is a car without its music?

"Separation and division in order to unify . . . atomization in order to encompass; segmentation in order to totalize; individualization in order to obliterate differences and otherness."[8] Technical resources "evolve" in the direction of enhancing the mobility and autonomy of bodies and sounds. Producing or entering musical space requires little physical effort and no longer involves sharing it with others—unless you are a youthful clubber or concertgoer, a soundscape artist, or a driver who to likes to open your car windows and crank the sound way, way up.[9] The separation of performers from one another in the recording studio is mirrored by the dispersal of their listeners. By enhancing their mobility, new media such as CDs, digital audio editing, digital audio broadcasting, satellite-based digital audio radio services, and Internet radio promise a radically decentered listening experience. They appear to exemplify the promise advanced for all technological innovations of the twentieth century: the capacity to enhance technical reproduction, program diversity, and democratic engagement for listeners who would "conceive of themselves as citizens rather than consumers."[10] Like other technologies, they both enhance and curtail the freedom of the listener. The convenience and mobility inscribed by new technologies reinforce yet fatally undermine the expectation that identity and freedom can be defined and completed by them.

As human agents in this "industrial ecology," DJs and VJs, composers and performers, sound mixers and producers, jingle writers, radio programmers, and their political and corporate administrators are all mobilized by the injunction to create and reproduce sound in compliance with this apparatus. Music producers consider the technical capacities of the platforms through which the music will be recorded and heard; radio programmers think about the social spaces in which the sound will be broadcast; electronics manufacturers study the behavior, demographic profile, spending habits, and perceived desires of their intended users.[11] Sound production thus measures and influences the fluid locales and boundaries of our listening formations. As Paul Theberge writes, "Specific activities related to making or consuming music result in differently structured listening habits. . . . Listening [is then] both context and effect."[12]

As radio history suggests, such technological mobilization alters the listener's engagement with her surroundings. It is not coincidental that the introduction of "revolutionary" digital audio technologies over the last decade or two to mobilize listeners coincides with intense deregulation of the broadcasting sphere. "Regardless of format," one analyst observes, "commercial music services will likely continue to program in a way that values the guidance of consultants and other industry insiders over input from local audiences."[13] In this regard radio establishes a pattern for subsequent technologies. "For the most part," Barney suggests, "we citizens just take what we get when it comes to technology. We live in the world of the cell-phone, the automobile, the jet airliner, pharmaceuticals, plastic, video surveillance, the computer, gas pipelines, the supermarket and endlessly proliferating screens, whether we like it or not: *nobody asked us*."[14] Through these processes, technology is ironically confirmed as the all-important means of free choice through which consumer citizenship is produced. We can even turn the radio off.

This is not to say that there is no discussion of the "radiosphere." Indeed the Canadian communication policy archive offers an extensive literature on radio and its connection to citizenship. Texts about radio, music, and identity circulate through cultural and communication policy, market research, music education, musicians' magazines, fanzines, advertising, and so on. Like the discourse of entertainment summarized in "Angels Dancing" (chapter 4), such texts play an important role in defining and legitimating the currents of musical culture. Since music plays so strong a role in "the cultural placing of the individual in the social,"[15] tracing these multiple contexts helps to identify some of the processes through which the listener's sense of location is defined. We can view these processes in terms of the representation of sound, representation through sound, and practices of listening, thus emulating the trilateral approach that Lefebvre employs to analyze the making, conceiving, and perceiving of social space. Through radio, music mediates our interactions with space and our contradictory senses of belonging. Each spatial organization and scale of locality—the city, the nation, the ancestral home, and the space between the ears—is organized by cultural technologies of space, and each offers its imprimatur to the mix.

Locating the Question

In 1919, a Montreal radio station (XWA) owned and operated by the Canadian Marconi Company of Montreal, broadcast some music taken from recordings that had been borrowed from a music store on St. Catherine's Street in exchange for on-the-air acknowledgment. This was the first broadcast of gramophone records on the continent, the first live voice having been transmitted by wireless by Reginald Fessenden, a Canadian living in the United States, in 1906. Marconi had been granted exclusive license to develop broadcasting in Canada after leading the commercial development of wireless in Britain, the United States, and the seas between, with the aid of the British Post Office.[16] It is unlikely that the music aired that day was recorded in Canada; most phonograph companies were owned by Americans, the lonely Canadian Vitaphone Company having gone out of business in 1916.[17] The first Canadian wireless broadcast thus featured music probably recorded in the United States, while the first American radio broadcast featured a live performance by an ex-patriated Canadian.

That same year, the federal government took over several bankrupt railroads and formed the publicly owned Canadian National Railways which later carried the first cross-Canada public radio broadcast. As described in "Spatial Narratives" (chapter 3), the national railway and the public broadcasting system traveled together across Canada in search of nationhood. During the same year, Britain extended preferential tariffs to goods manufactured in Canada, establishing a branch plant export strategy that encouraged foreign corporations to develop manufacturing operations within the country. This policy redefined relations between Canada and its trading partners while maintaining the imperial structures at their base. In 1919, Canada was also elected as an independent member to the League of Nations. These events were part of a turning point in the modernization process wherein the nation-state, the entertainment-industrial complex, and communication technology were joined in an apparatus of unprecedented scope. Mobilized by both colonial and anticolonial agendas, these events contributed to the building of an infrastructure that laid the groundwork for both national space and transnational capital expansion.

By 1922 thirty-nine broadcasting licenses had been issued to commercial stations by Ottawa, but they were mainly short lived. The airwaves were swamped by powerful transmitters in the United States, which were interrupting each other as vigorously as they were obliterating weaker Canadian signals. Few Canadian stations could broadcast farther than ten or twenty miles; in the evenings, in particular, they were overtaken by transmissions from American stations.[18] Disputes about licensing, program imports, royalty payments, and the dominance of American stations in listening polls led to the formation of the Canadian Association of Broadcasters in 1926. In 1928 broadcasters joined a furious debate about the government's right to withdraw a radio license from a Jehovah's Witnesses' station in Saskatchewan following an address by a member of the Ku Klux Klan. This tempest led to the 1928 appointment of the Aird Royal Commission on Broadcasting, which submitted its report in 1931. Ether was a limited natural resource, the commission stated, and it was reasonable to regulate its use. The Aird Commission had found "unanimity on one fundamental question—Canadian radio listeners want Canadian broadcasting."[19] From 1931 until the last years of the twentieth century, connections between radio, public ownership, citizenship, and national space were at least rhetorically entrenched in this same principle.

Commentators emphasize the close connection between nation-building and communication technology in government rhetoric and in the writing of history.[20] The reiteration of this rhetoric obscures a changing political and institutional milieu. If "public interest" and "communication technology" became interchangeable terms for policy advisers and communication scholars, how they connect, what they mean, and what kinds of spaces they co-constitute have changed substantially over time. In the 1930s, the Canadian government instituted federal agencies to intercede as owner-regulators in the name of public interest as a response to the proliferation of American commercial radio transmissions across southern Canada (a protectionist move), and to intense political pressure from citizens north of the border (a strategy of political legitimation). This dual mandate, supported by an intermittently aroused political consensus, has continued to inform negotiations between the two countries for control over both commerce and public legislation. The Canadian Broadcasting Corporation was originally created to connect public and private stations, create national community, offset foreign influence, and advance communication and technology in the public interest. The bond between music, listeners, and space is always already linked to government policy, and the attitudes of listeners can not escape association with such intervention.[21]

At the same time, the state's politics and actions have been contradictory in purpose and effect. From 1936 to the 1950s, the CBC had "the responsibility of creating, single-handedly, the conditions which would support an active music life in Canada."[22] During that period the schedule encompassed a diverse range of music: fiddlers, opera singers, accordianists, local orchestras, and big bands from across the country. Such heterogeneity had begun to fade by the 1950s, when the National Report on the Arts, Letters, and Sciences highlighted culture as a component of national defense. As high commissioner in London during the war, Vincent Massey, one of the report's authors, "had seen at first hand the importance of culture to a nation fighting for its life."[23] Following this report, support for the arts was transferred to the secretary of state, arts funding was separated from communication policy, and the regulation of the broadcasting system was severed from the CBC. Music production within the CBC was largely dissolved, to be reinstitutionalized by universities, granting agencies, and commercial producers. Following the 1957 Fowler Report on Broadcasting, commercial broadcasters won regulative autonomy from the public agency they victoriously defined as their competition.[24] With the institutional separation of professional music, public broadcasting, and commercial radio and television—and of the agencies administering them—such divisions would be reiterated in how musicians learned to play and how listeners learned to listen.

Today, suffocated by competition and lack of funds, the public system forms a small fraction of the listening environment. The agencies formed to regulate broadcasting now defend "Canadian culture" through industry-friendly regulation of the private sector, mimicking the United States regulatory regime while appearing to counteract it. Canadian content quotas for broadcasters introduced in the 1970s have enhanced access to commercial recording facilities for Canadian musicians, but they have not counteracted the capitalization and corporate appropriation of Canadian cultural industries. With increasingly lax regulation of foreign ownership and distribution, the recording industry is regulated like any other sector of the economy.[25] Indeed the social purpose of government regulation has grown more and more elusive. More Canadian musicians produce commercially successful recordings, but their distribution via CD or radio is concentrated in the hands of cross-media oligopolies. More than 90 percent of Canadian radio listening is claimed by commercial broadcast and satellite radio. The commercial market's ascendancy has created a system of radio and satellite stations and music labels that belies the anti-market logic of public interest and nationalist objectives espoused by regulators and listeners alike.

Canadians are amongst the highest consumers in the world in per capita expenditures on recorded music, and the most prolific downloaders of on-line music. Hundreds of millions of dollars—over 80 percent of revenues from the domestic market—"flow south" each year as a consequence of this branch plant economy, with only a small portion of revenue reinvested in Canadian music.[26] Most records manufactured and sold within Canada are made from imported master tapes. Canadian record labels are like high-tech companies in the Ottawa Valley; they function as innovative "farm teams" for multinational conglomerates who buy them out once they have achieved the requisite level of financial success. The interest in Canadian music among these conglomerates is restricted to recordings which can be marketed across the continent (or in the case of French language recordings, abroad).[27] This updated branch-plant substitution policy is a tangible reality for English language songwriters, who are encouraged to record songs about dying in Texas or mornings in Minnesota (rather than Manitoba—where's that?) because of their industry's economic dependency on the American market.[28] Texas, Nashville, and Georgia appear in songs performed by and for people who have never been there. The words become doubly or triply coded signs evoking an intertextual map of genres and styles rather than an experience of place. The semiotic depletion of meaning from place suggests an analogy between the mode of address in popular music, and a comparable mode of address in cinematic enunciation, which does not "normally identify itself as proceeding from anywhere in particular: a film seems simply to be 'there' as it unfolds before our eyes."[29] When a band refers to a local place by name (The Tragically Hip's "Bobcaygeon" is a favorite example), the act seems almost daring—it interrupts and defamiliarizes the abstract signs of musical location through which the "industrial ecologies of ephemeracultures" are materialized in sound. The task of signifying space falls to radio and music television hosts, and now—further disarticulated from any politically viable scale—is shrinking to the size of a computer screen.

Whether marginal or indistinguishable, the relationship between Canadian music and Canadian listeners is established within this context and shaped by it. Of course, local music is marginalized from Liverpool to LA through similar relations of production. But this process is also shaped by a political discourse which positions such questions within the problematic of Canada itself. Despite the rhetoric of public interest that accompanies subsidy for their projects, producers tend to encourage musical qualities that, regardless of their vernaculars, can succeed equally in Vancouver or New Jersey. Listeners assure pollsters that they like to hear Canadian music and that the public sector should ensure that they can do so. Having proclaimed their good citizenship, they turn on the radio or pick up their iPod and slide sideways into a punctuated landscape in which territory goes no farther than the listening body and her chosen pleasures.

These experiences perpetuate the double bind that structures listeners' identity. Their soundscape celebrates the success of local musical celebrities while government policy readjusts to transnational economies of scale that continue to define and circumscribe such success. This structural paradox is reproduced in, and reinforced by, the ways Canadians think or talk about and listen to music. Radio's legacy is strong in history and myth, as well as in the everyday soundscape; so much so that many public and community radio producers evoke its memory and find ways to reconnect radiophonic space with the topos of its listeners. Such echoes confirm that for many media producers and listeners,

the public presentation [of identity] is far from a purely economic issue. The state's legitimacy is often drawn from its capacity to speak for its citizens, to be their vocalizing agent. This is achieved . . . in part through the doctrine of nations, the concept of a particular space defined by the state itself but informed affectively by a sense of cultural belonging."[30]

Through its various trajectories, music plays a crucial role in advancing and undoing this legitimation process.[31]

Locating Listening

The experience of pop music," Simon Frith writes, "is an experience of placing: in responding to a song, we are drawn, haphazardly, into affective and emotional alliances with the performers and with the performers' other fans."[32] We do not have to be next to performers or other fans to have this experience. Musical space is embodied but diffuse; it draws us into a cartography of affective alliances which can defy as easily as it reproduces the experience of proximity. A solitary headphone or a radio station mix can evoke a sense of belonging as powerfully as a single song, and alter the spaces of meaning for the songs they play. Just as listening to a song mediates our feelings with our social surroundings, so reproductive technologies add diverse levels of mediation to the bonds between musical experience and social space. Cultural technologies of sound mediate between the production of music and the production of us as audiences, and between such audiences and the heterotopias we inhabit. These mediations are articulated to diverse spatial scales and social agendas.

The idea that commercial broadcasters are mandated to serve "the public interest, convenience and necessity," for instance, is "crucial to the endeavors of American radio broadcasters [who] . . . have their own economic interpretation of the term 'public interest.'"[33] The idea that consumer sovereignty dictates the circulation of music has historically held less influence among Canadian observers, who have witnessed the expansion of a corporate system that is aggressively indifferent to borders, publics, and localities. No Canadian scholar would so readily celebrate the hit parade as "a floating totem of public pleasure."[34] Of course, the idea of a unifying "hit parade" has been overtaken by multiple venues. The digital "revolution" carries affective investment over to the technologies themselves, and their sound effects contend for space as well as time. For Adorno, these "floating totems" of public pleasure turn to objects of hatred and contempt because we unconsciously resent our submission to intensely promoted songs or devices in the first place. While my experience confirms his insight—there is nothing more irritating than last year's overplayed songs, nothing more disposable than last year's playback device—the machinations of the marketplace are hardly obscure from this vantage point. Perhaps the ambivalent history of participating in this hyperactive process from the vantage point of the margin, a vantage point that may be different ideologically as well as geographically, explains the greater willingness to accommodate the musical past manifested in musical and broadcasting practices north of the border. Canadian radio has a more elastic temporality, a greater readiness to revisit sounds of the past in playlists than its American counterparts. This difference is instantly discernable by listening to radio playlists on either side of the border. It is harder to identify differences in the music itself produced in the two countries; far easier to hear such difference after the fact of knowing its place of origin. Does it matter? In her essay "Lesbians and Popular Music: Does it Matter Who is Singing?," Barbara Bradby looks to feminist literary theory to explore the question of lesbian identification in popular music. "In the area of popular music," she explains, "it seems that everyday listening practices raise similar puzzles around the performer as are raised around the author of a text."[35] It's not just that listeners can't automatically "know" whether a singer is or isn't one of them. In the very act of posing the question, they experience, like thoughtful readers of women's writing, a contradiction between history and desire, between the intellectual recognition that the category "lesbian" is historically constructed and arbitrary, and the emotional need for a "dream of a lesbian nation, even as we recognize its fictionality." Listeners can realize the social nature of such mythmaking, Bradby suggests, and yet still participate imaginatively in the "interplay between personal identity and the identity of a performer, a process which is socially mediated through the everyday practices of the lesbian 'community.'"[36]

Notwithstanding the tenuousness of connection between lesbians and Canadians (although a survey of Canadian films directed by women suggests otherwise), both identities emerge in knowing relation to their construction proximate to more authoritative social formations. Both are peripheral to and yet forced to observe the mainstream; both are linked by shared communication and experience that is better understood by those who belong. Both pose the challenge of difference within as well as beyond their perimeters. Whether Canadian musicians and listeners attribute their desire for difference to the uniqueness of their values, experiences, or landscapes,[37] or seek rather to produce such difference through their interactions with media, record labels, and fan communities, "Such meanings are not simply inherent in musical or song texts, but . . . are embodied in material practices such as the exchange of cassette tapes, deejays' promotion of certain music, dancing at discos."[38] Since Canada is not a "natural" space with a singular identity, but rather a hybrid and produced space involving distinct activities, regions, ethnicities, and styles, there is no point in searching for a single identity, a common sound. This does not prevent performers and listeners from wanting access to the means of communication.

Radio, Radio

The modern practice of song rotation within a limited playlist arose in the United States following a study of jukebox selections which showed that listeners tended to select the same recordings over and over again, and "would tune in if they could be sure of hearing their favourite records." The decision to capitalize on the discovery and to "ensure that the biggest current sellers were played at set intervals" led to a major renovation of American radio, in which "a whole range of audience-catching elements—time checks, weather reports, station call-signs, trailers and typewriter sound effects [were] added to the mix."[39] As a result of such changes the "bandstand" concept, in which stations broadcast fifteen-minute segments of a single artist or band, was abandoned. In the new radiophonic regime, "Nothing was left to chance."[40] Thus, format practices observed in one spatial setting were extended into another. The spread of Top Forty radio mobilized a youth market for advertised commodities such as cosmetics and clothing, transistor radios, fan magazines, and new releases. The combined regime of radio, music, and advertising quickly spread beyond the U.S. borders. British and Canadian radio broadcasters were forced to adapt to be able to deliver audiences to their own local advertisers. Today nearly 100 percent of Canadians listen to radio each week for an average of around eighteen hours. Such listening mainly takes place as a "secondary activity," which means that programmers don't care whether or how much you are actually listening, so long as you don't turn it off. This principle has been embraced by public as well as private broadcasters, shaping everything from the compression of the dynamic range to the choice of programming through which radio programmers become complicit in their own peripheral use value.

"Repetition," charges Jacques Attali, "produces information free of noise." This is not an entirely sustainable objective, for if there is no noise, there is no point in listening. How to compensate for the calculated low noise threshold of "wallpaper" radio?[41] Commercial radio announces itself by emphasizing its localness. Radio's localness has been widely emphasized in textbooks and industry commentaries about on-air practice, and successful DJS account for their popularity by claiming special contact with the local scene. "Radio is very much a local medium," advise Johnson and Jones, authors of an influential American textbook on radio station practices. In the same paragraph, however, they acknowledge that "in fact, no local station really originates all of its programming material. Phonograph records are nationally distributed, as is the news from wire services. Most ideas are borrowed, not originated."[42] Radio has relied heavily on recorded music "for reasons of tradition, convenience, and economics." Recorded music is cheaper than other programming; since the reliance on recorded music subjects radio to "the corporate grip of the record industry on radio," broadcasters replicate the music industry's tendency to downplay local talents and to promote national trends at the local level.[43] Broadcasters become "localizers" of international content, rather than the reverse.

If commercial radio represents itself as the local medium, most of what we hear is not local. The studio or transmission tower may be housed up the street; it might even be subject to extensive government scrutiny each time the station renews its license. But the sum of relations upon which radio depends is as definitively transnational as it was in 1919, before Canada's government intervened on behalf of domestic broadcasters. Radio might be a low-tech medium, but it is rarely an autonomous one. As a commercial enterprise, radio performs the dual function of localizing and delocalizing space. Its programming is designed to attract the highest possible proportion of listening hours for sale to local advertisers. "Local" content is reduced to paid time slots for advertisers and the traffic and weather reports. The emphasis on local relevance is instrumental in radio's competition with television, its dependency on local advertising revenue, its interdependence with transit, and its promotion of music sales and events in the local area.

In this context it falls to the DJ's voice to provide an index of radio's authenticity as a live and local medium, and to offer evidence of the efficacy of its listeners' desires. It is through his or her voice that the community hears itself constituted; through this voice that radio assumes authorship of the community, which is woven into itself through the voice's jokes, advertisements, music, all represented recurrently and powerfully as the mapping of local life. The DJS do not choose the music and rarely discuss it. In this respect it is not surprising that satellite radio has largely eliminated them. Commercial broadcasters calculate song rotation through an administrative orchestration of stylistic and chronological range, moving from new to old and back again depending on the target demographic's affection for older songs relative to its willingness to pay for new ones. As musical programming is emancipated from local control, it is rearticulated to the semiotics of time. The format weaves together a pattern of new and old music and talk addressed to the composite listener's tastes, temporal habits, and perceptions, and, lest we forget, working needs.[44] Each radio station is constantly updated to enter and to fill (without drawing critical attention to) the listener's home, place of work, or mode of transport; each station is programmed to draw listeners willingly into its temporal flow and disperse them into productivity. Competition between broadcasters ironically prevents the play list from being too diverse, too hybrid, or too local. Music broadcasting is designed for people who need to relax and (almost) forget where they are: working, driving, washing dishes, waiting. The music connects them to fantasy, pleasure, and community without separating them from the rhythms of everyday life. Listeners are brought *together in time* and *independent of space*, in a virtual sonic location both occupied and removed from perception.

Public broadcasters are meant to provide alternatives to such practices, but they function in the same "ecology" of listening choices and must provide the option of a more distinctive difference for select audiences. The mandate of public broadcasting is to elevate its listeners from the work discipline of mere hearing by more complex artistic and narrative demands which join listening to the project and territoriality of citizenship. "To say that citizenship is a practice," writes Barney, "is to say that it is something not merely borne but more precisely something done, not just an attribute but an act, not simply a status inherited passively or won through due process or struggle but a habit motivated by circumstance and obligation, cultivated through education and experience, consistently performed."[45] Is this too much to ask of radio? Not for theorists such as Brecht and Fanon. Some radio critics now predict that the democracy of producing and listening will be restored by the digital and satellite dispersion of radio into multiple sites. Someday, we may look back at the advocates of digital democracy with the same poignant hindsight with which we regard the history of broadcasting. But I am getting ahead of myself.

Public broadcasting's mandate is not just filled through music and public affairs. Producers of radio documentaries and dramas conventionally forefront on-location sounds in their soundtracks. We hear the sounds of trains moving, children laughing, bullets flying, and rivers running, and participate vicariously in an affective investment in place. Hosts identify performers by where they come from and where they are. Here place signifies as an index of public representation. The rhetorical synthesis of technology and presence signals that the vehicle is public (Canadian) culture, and therefore inhabitable. Listeners are joined through the sonic connection of space and time, like the national subjects Benedict Anderson describes in *Imagined Communities*. Framing the fragments of voice and musical kinship, a weather report recites the mantras of place, ceremonially mapping the forecast for Penetanguishene, Kapuskasing, Sault Ste. Marie, Timiskaming, or Thunder Bay, and providing spatial word-signs that anchor the music. This sonic tradition can be seen as a temporal extension of early radio's importance to dispersed settler cultures, for whom radio enhanced the sense of security and the right to inhabit the land. Fanon calls this colonial communication a "daily invitation not to 'go native,' not to forget the rightfulness of his culture."[46] The constitution of listeners through sonic representation of space inscribes varied geographies. Commercial stations now use a brief musical signature to identify their corporate identity within a saturated urban field, while the CBC indexes its programs by distinct musical signatures that can be heard across the country. CBC Radio 2—"where the music takes you"— offers a demographically adept blend of classical music, indie rock, and jazz, reminiscent of the "light classical" format that dominated CBC programming in the 1940s.[47] You can listen to it while you work, as do the Korean owners of the convenience store at the corner, and as I do when the time is right. CBC Radio 1 combines the news, weather, and traffic crucial to local stations with talk, phone-in discussions, and music.

Between 1982 and 1997, CBC 1's *Morningside* was the most popular program in Canadian radio. Host Peter Gzowski conducted more than 27,000 interviews with artists, politicians, musicians, activists, farmers, letter writers, personalities, and less well-known people. The unpredictability of these events was part of *Morningside*'s attraction, and together with the success of shows such as *This Hour Has 22 Minutes* suggests that Canadians like programs in which the hosts ask the questions and the populace answers them, rather than the reverse arrangement so popular in American media.[48] In such programs citizenship is not signified by musical taste but by a search for connection that encompasses a range of types of music and a broader sense of "public" space. Such interaction produces a sense of process, of unfinished desire. What other explanation can be found for the success of The Barenaked Ladies' tuneful lark, "If I Had a Million Dollars," in a CBC poll identifying the Top Canadian Songs of All Time? But, then, why was there such a poll? CBC programming has fallen into the hands of demographers poached from the private sector, and while it offers outstanding radio, there are few surprises.

Arising in the spaces abandoned by these institutions, college radio and community radio forefront diverse local musical forms and constellate the creative expression of difference within place through an interweaving of musical genre and talk. Programs are generically diverse and represent, at different times of the day, ethnically and culturally diverse communities. The boundary between programmers and listeners is fluid and dynamic. Because different communities take to the air at different times, listeners must either browse the ethnomusical soundscape or learn the schedules. Either way, community radio refuses to become standardized, homogeneous, or habitual. It demarcates and stands back from radio as an "acoustic wallpaper" as Andrew Crisell calls commercial radio, "a music while you work service riddled with commercialism."[49] This refusal is not simply a matter of what occurs within the acoustic space captured by music. Listening to community radio means engaging with heterogeneity; it offers a strategic reversal of commercial radio's production of musically defined environments that simultaneously incite and disperse its listeners. Through music, talk, and actuality, community radio defines and mobilizes its community. By seeking a more activist, informed, and diverse listening audience, community radio reduces the distance between the public and private meanings of the music. It doesn't always reduce the distances between its listeners.

Canadian radio producers and sound artists have produced a rich aural vocabulary for evoking shared space. At the same time, an uninformed listener can't automatically identify a piece of music coming from (English)

Canada, though if you listen (after the fact), you can hear a different grammar of musical sound, recognizable perhaps in the grain of the voice, a less
driven sense of time, a proclivity for lyric-driven tunes, an adept vocabulary
and blurring of generic borders.[50] If Canadian music is diverse, hybrid, and
regionally based—if the radio archive offers a continuing topos for sonic self-
recognition—commercial radio formats do little to sustain such qualities.
They are designed to calculate and convey genre and currency, not locale
or fusion. Toronto hip-hip artist k-os describes commercial radio as a form
of "genre apartheid."[51] For those thriving on what k-os terms the "continuous multidirectional diasporic multi-cultural influences" of black Canadian
music, hearing the music is like piecing together a puzzle. "Because Toronto
in the actual aboriginal language means 'meeting place,'" explains k-os:

> And I think that's what comes out of our music. Like, there is no par-
> ticular sound. There's just a *bunch* of sounds. . . . Like, if you listen to a
> Saukrates or Kardinal, they're going to sound like they're from an At-
> lanta. They're going to sound like they're from LA on a track. They're
> gonna sound like they're from New York. They're going to do something
> where they switch to soca and West Indian twang, then, they'll do some
> straight Toronto hiphop over a jazz beat, and you'll know that's the stuff
> 'cuz it's fried by Queen or Yonge St.[52]

This music resides somewhere in the movement between places and between pleasure and knowledge, a version of the "bifocality" of immigrant
cultures: a "common experience of being betwixt and between," without
leaving the country.[53] Such betwixt-and-betweenness calls for a different
kind of attention. As Mark Fenster reminds us, "The local is a critical site
for the making and remaking of the social in musical practice."[54] What k-os
describes as "genre apartheid" is one of the conservative pressures through
which localities attempt to purify themselves. Just as radio is not inherently
an inclusive medium, so "the local" is not inherently a progressive force.
K.d. lang sang bluntly critical neocountry songs about meat and sexual
politics until members of the Alberta legislature, prodded by powerful
cattle ranchers, sabotaged her local career. Her next album won an award
for best female "adult contemporary music" at the U.S. Grammy Awards.
A decade later, k.d., no longer a resident of Canada, released "Hymns of
the 49th Parallel," an anthology of smooth, highly orchestrated covers of
Canadian singer-songwriters. It sells well in the national megabookstore,

whose owners forbid their staff to play k-os on the sound system. We all bump up against the limits of the "local."

The search for belonging can separate us from as well as join us to the discourses and entitlements of citizenship. When broadcasting oligopolies govern and rationalize so much of what we hear, the surprises of "multi-directional diasporic multi-cultural influences" must migrate from the airwaves. As the airwaves fall to privatization, program managers hope that more people will listen, but not really. This radio depends on distraction for its existence. Its primary goal is to accompany us through breakfast, travel, and work without stimulating too much attention or any thought of turning it off. In this respect radio is mutually interdependent with the daily life for which it provides the soundtrack. Its programming is designed to harmonize the contradictions of domestic and working life (and the stalled spaces between them) that radio could potentially illuminate and transform.

Sonic Spaces

As with all mediated spaces, we are concerned not only with "What kind of space is it?" but more importantly, "What kind of space does it help produce?"[55] Lefebvre, like McLuhan and Innis, reprimands us for focusing on communication rather than on the spaces it makes.

> Our illusion of transparency goes hand in hand with a view of space as innocent, as free of traps or secret places . . . closely bound up with Western 'culture,' this ideology stresses speech, and overemphasizes the written word, to the detriment of a social practice which it is indeed designed to conceal. . . . Such are the assumptions of an ideology which, in positing the transparency of space, identifies knowledge, information and communication.[56]

This misapprehension of spatial relationships may be commonplace, but it is not silent. It is articulated through a proliferation of sound which tumble into our ears at the flick of a hand. This "ideology" of transparent space produces a sonic discourse that traverses space but ignores its facticity: call it aggressive expressionism; call it "We are the World." Alternatively sound can place you somewhere familiarly exotic, like Jamaica or Nigeria.[57] There are sonic vocabularies that make you feel as though you could be anywhere, a transcendent body, a dancing body, a selfless self, an American; as if you might be sunning in California or find your happiest state floating nowhere in particular. Lefebvre's "ideology" of transparent space is exemplified by the way sound reproduction alters the perception of physical distance. Because recorded sounds can be played at various volumes, they can dissolve the experiential knowledge of the relationship between sound and distance, or what Kittler terms "acoustic self-perception."[58] Musicking can enhance or contest this effect. The categorical familiarity of everyday radio soundscapes provides the kind of pleasure Brecht condemns in his 1930 essay "The Modern Theatre Is the Epic Theatre." Brecht associates the conventional opera's seamless integration of words, music, production, listener, and environment with the "Gesamtkunstwerk," or "integrated work of art," advocated by composer Richard Wagner. In this art the music accompanies and heightens the text, paints a psychological situation, "dishes up" the music to the listener with the effect of sacrificing thought to the "culinary principle."[59] As Hans Eisler shows in his 1951 study *Composing for the Films*, Hollywood soundtracks are suffused with Wagner's influence, in that they are orchestrated to heighten and intensify the feelings evoked by the narrative and visual performance.[60] Like format radio, which "leaves nothing to chance," such entertainment carefully fuses sound with actions which can "continue fulfilling its function with or without them. . . . [Audiences] absorb what they need; and all they need is a given amount of stuff."[61] In place of this heightening of emotion, Brecht calls for a transformed relationship between music, text, and listener or spectator in which each component "adopts attitudes" in relation to the other. To break the spell of spectatorship is to introduce fissures between the elements, to turn the spectator into subject matter *and* observer and so arouse his or her "capacity for action."[62] This is the sound of citizenship, which seems to resonate in spite of, as much as because of, regulatory policies. For citizenship is "not simply a status inherited passively or won through due progress or struggle" but rather, as Barney argues above, "a habit motivated by circumstance and obligation, cultivated through education and experience, consistently performed."[63] Despite the obvious differences between opera and radio, Brecht applies this argument to both genres. The work must not only make sense of reality, it must alter it; it must not only disrupt the sedating fusion of music and feeling, it must do so in a hedonistic manner; it must not only take advantage of the existing apparatus, it must expose its political foundation. It only seems ironic that the seamless, emotionally compelling blending of music and action promoted by Wagnerian opera should later inflect the everyday soundscapes of millions of radio listeners. Brecht's ideas, like Lefebvre's, remind us to address not only the content of radio but also how radio practice absorbs or illuminates social space.

Changes in music reproduction technologies enable consumers to carry their preferred soundtrack from one location (or geopolitical scale) to another. Such soundtracks personalize the sense of place, sometimes in connection with actual spaces, sometimes in place of them, and increasingly through a complicated combination of the two. Playback technologies have further reshaped listening practices, producing precisely delineated musical constituencies cutting across multiple spaces and mediations. Consumers are deluged with messages about the necessity of possessing up-to-date technologies in the name of the values so vital to the North American pulse: status, mobility, currency, convenience, total affect, and (paradoxically) the opportunity to choose. These values are realized in the cumulative miniaturization and bundling of consumer electronics in ever-new tasty packages, whose convenient mobility advances and reverses the "secondary activity" assigned to radio. Music is everywhere the listener is; there is a soundtrack for every occasion. The listener's feelings, purchasing habits, and technological horizons are constantly implicated and referenced in these innovations.

The now traditional representation of radio as a local medium is strategically extended into this environment. In the 1990s stations began to rely on centralized music program networks, and satellite radio was licensed commercially despite opposition from broadcasters. "In essence," a radio columnist wrote in *Broadcaster* of one such station, "it's a local station gone national. This illusion exists because Canadian Radio Network (CRN) jocks steadfastly refuse to identify their location. As well, the service offers toll-free 1–800 request lines, so listeners can call in and talk to a jock, wherever they may be."[64] For this columnist, the only drawback of this innovation is unemployment for hundreds of DJS, who like film accompanists of an earlier generation are being replaced by automation. While community stations find wider audiences through Internet and satellite dissemination, they are dwarfed by the all-music satellite radio services recently licensed by the Canadian Radio-Television Commission (CRTC), which are financed by user fees. Satellite radio abolishes DJS and advertising altogether and is exempt from national content quotas applied to conventional broadcasters.

Over time, shifts in recording and listening technology and marketing push radio programmers toward an ever-increasing rationalization of musical selection. Their techniques reduce program noise and cut labor and programming costs rather than flexing the boundaries of musical taste. If ensuing glitch-free radio practices assure listeners of their right to habitual pleasures, they suppress equally fundamental rights. Lefebvre speaks of the right to the town (how often do you hear DJS—those aural icons of local culture—encouraging debates or actions on urban development, racism, pollution, day care, land rights, public transport?) and the right to be different ("the right not to be classified forcibly into categories which have been determined by the necessarily homogenizing powers") which are endangered by the economic and political management of urban space.[65] As Liette Gilbert and Mustafa Diceks point out, "claiming the right to the city does not simply translate into a relocalization of claims from the national to the urban level. Urban citizenship does not necessarily replace or negate national citizenship. The right to the city, or what Levebvre also referred to as the right to urban life, is a claim upon society, not simply a claim to territorial affiliation."[66] Having been forcibly classified into categories, urban radio does not invite us to make significant claims upon it. In fact radio's management of urban space may be its primary accomplishment. We turn to local radio not just for music but for news and events, and for help in managing traffic, time, weather, and temperament in relation to the rhythms of the working week.

Given its skillful mediation of sound, locale, and imaginary community, radio comprises an ideal instrument for collective self-construction. Fanon argues that the Algerian Revolution emerged conterminously with the people's embrace of Radio-Alger; as radio brought them a sense of themselves, "the Algerian at this time had to bring his life up to the level of the Revolution. He had to enter the vast network of news; he had to find his way in a world in which things happened, in which events existed, in which forces were active."[67] If radio exists "only to make others present, an invisible machine for making the world visible to itself,"[68] the community which is spoken through the medium is also constituted by it, and altered by its structures and selections. For Brecht, radio's potential would be realized only when radio became a means of communication, rather than distribution. Contemporary radio functions as the latter, but represents itself as the former. As radio multiplies and intersects with other technologies, listening communities are similarly fragmented and reconstituted. With just a touch of the radio dial, you can be somewhere and someone else.

The more seamlessly the radio soundtrack joins diverse places, the more it approximates placelessness or what Lefebvre calls abstract space. This makes it difficult to separate love from economies of scale. Love songs in particular seem to overcome every kind of conceivable distance—a connection that would be more apparent were pop music critics less reluctant to talk about the lyrics. Music-while-you-work is all about love. Love provides the affect for routine processes of abstraction and deterritorialization that never fully succeed, and musicking breaks the surfaces of the soundtrack just as affect punctures the surface of the photograph.

"Schizophonics"

Listeners in Canada occupy two dreams simultaneously. One is the dream that we are American; the other is the dream that we are not. The two dreams are lived simultaneously, like a split screen or half-awake hangover, and they are intimately intertwined with material structures of cultural production. Years of negotiation have divided broadcasting and the cultural industries between private and public sectors, national and transnational players, and increasingly segmented groups of listeners, all unequal partners in what legislators call a national system. The compromises responsible for this arrangement speak to us simultaneously as significant political achievements of the nation-state and as the triumph and expansion of populist American culture. As these apparatuses move closer together, the listeners move farther apart; both dream spaces lose their association with territorial entities, and both condone a diminishing space for citizenship and civic engagement. Wizard technologies propel cultural industries into the vortex of the global soundsphere while enhancing listeners' fading sense of personal power. Tuned in, hooked up, wired into—we see ourselves as part of a global culture and claim hybridity as the essence of who we are. The only way to resolve this contradictory state is to engage in transformative practices: making music, devising accessible strategies of electronic reproduction, redefining these practices in relation to viable ecological trajectories, and drawing these struggles into broader discourses about sound and musicking in action.

A theory of the contradictory nature of location is crucially important. Otherwise no account of the role of culture in modernization, no recognition of the diverse roles of nation-states, and no analysis of the complex interaction between popular culture and imperialism is possible. To place location on the auditory horizon is not a call to unify audiences by geography, nationality, ethnicity, or taste. Only commercial broadcasters, commercial demographers, and the CBC do that.[69] To the extent that it represents collective identity as a unified totality, each construction is a work of ideology, continuously disassembled by the famous creative disloyalty of listeners, for whom "freedom of listening is as necessary as freedom of speech."[70] As ethnomusicologists of the Americas have realized, residents in the New World are "people whose ways of being share [only] the common quality of a foreign past . . . and the long heritage of colonial rule."[71] Our musical landscape can tell us about their past, those migrations, this rule, their struggles and achievements. In this context, access for white, native Canadian, or Afro-Canadian music, in any combination of identities and styles, becomes the electronic equivalent of land claims on the ground. Like the current struggle for local foods and biodiversity, such claims remind us to ask whether and how place, location, and access to the means of production are to be valorized or contested as sources and contexts for speech. To the extent that they are not, the issue of territory is erased, made abstract, subsumed by the production of reproducible space. Then entertainment reproduces itself in a condition of reification, insofar as pleasure defines itself as the exclusion of everything but itself, a privileged discursive feature of both patriarchy and imperialism.

seven

Weathering the North

A tourist inquiring how cold the winter was in Banff, we told him it was so cold last winter that the ice froze in the Upper Hot Springs Swimming Pool. One boy's feet went through the ice, and he got his foot scalded.—Oh, we've lots of stories like that.—E. FOWKE, *Canadian Folklore*

Modifications of the physical environment by man may be compared with technological advances. They often proceed on their own momentum, with or without a philosophy—or they might create their own.—CLARENCE GLACKEN, *Traces on the Rhodian Shore*

The weather, like music, mediates between our physical and social bodies. Its rhythms and irregularities, and the rituals we construct around them, shape what it means to be part of the social, both within a particular time and space, and across to other times and places as we imagine or remember them. For many people, certain summer smells are reminders of childhood adventures, and fresh autumnal winds evoke the harvest ritual of going out to buy new books and sweaters. Every year the commercial "mediascape" bombards us with sounds and images of a "white Christmas," only to turn around just after the New Year and assail us with images of the tropics. In November we long for snow; just a few weeks later, we are dying to escape winter weather and make our way south.

Images of place are intimately tied to mythic or remembered notions of its weather. Our sense of what is desirable in the weather, like our response to music, seems perfectly natural, indeed to express our sensitivity to nature itself. But, again like music, this embodied experience of the environment arises from technological, social, and cultural mediations between the individual and collective body. This is especially complicated when you consider today's weather. Current changes in weather promise, according to some experts, to make a warmer and more fecund Canada the center of empire in the next century. Such transformation will present major challenges to the constitution of Canada's political, temperamental, and cultural life. Given the importance of weather as the storied foreground of our natural environment, an ethnometeorological study of our interaction with weather promises important insights about changing constructs of nature, culture, and identity.

Weather contributes to the sedimentation of culture in two respects: as an inescapable part of shared experience in everyday life, and as part of a hierarchically mediated set of observational and scientific discourses woven through and across the every day. Just as weather varies from one bioregion to another (as well as across days and seasons), so the cultural technologies of nature vary across regions and social contexts. Just as weather defines the natural habitus of human cultures in a particular bioregion, so the cultural technologies of weather locate us at a complicated intersection of nature, representation, embodiment, and science, part of a web of mediations involving the seasons, inside and outside, convenience and disruption, civilization and the uncivilizable, colonizer and colonized, tourism and money, agrarian logic and scenic beauty. These mediations shape our understanding of human pleasure and achievement, and of Nature itself as evident measure and meaning of this achievement. The structures that mediate the weather are shaped and shifted by historical experience, and particularly, as I show in this chapter, by successive practices of colonization: the colonization of indigenous peoples by European settlers; the colonization of Canadian by American culture; the global expansion of American technological prowess and, then, arising from and yet indifferent to these geopolitical dynamics, the colonization of air and water. The result of this history is that our weather is now constituted by a set of rituals with deeply conflicting expressive and instrumental functions.

Weather and Empire: The Northern Dilemma

Climate change is constituted by a more intense polarization of seasonal extremes, the summers growing hotter and the winters colder, which could quickly become unbearable. But the greenhouse effect could provide northern regions with significant relief, at an experiential level if not in terms of political cognition. Scientists predict that the average annual temperature could rise from two to nearly five degrees in the coming decades, which is almost as much as our present global average temperature has increased since the last ice age. Winters will grow shorter, and growing seasons longer. It's pleasant to think about warmer weather, but unpleasant to think about droughts: dry earth, dying animals, dwarfish plants, dust, and other agricultural disasters. We long for an early spring, but the ice cap is melting. This development carries important implications for culture north of the 49th.

Weather is the condition that mediates between our bodies and the landscape that (as it is so often claimed) defines Canada as a distinctive culture. In some weird way, we *are* our weather. This idea is evoked frequently in everyday icons and comments about the body politic. Media polls reveal that Muslims and other Canadians have more than the winter weather in common. Thus citizens' reciprocal recognition is naturalized by their shared encounters with the weather. Like any myth this one has some truth to it. Unfamiliar faces acknowledge their kinship through shared encounters with danger, mutual assistance, and endurance. Voices speaking different languages are compelled to connect, to enact the ethical belief that the survival of one depends on the care of the many. The libertarianism found in the American South, where trailer park residents in hurricane zones refuse safety regulations in their building codes, is virtually unimaginable in this climate, whose prospective fatalities are a mundane fact of life. I am aware that there are parts of Canada where it doesn't snow much, and parts of the United States that stretch north of Toronto and see far more of it. But nation and weather are linked through a powerful technocultural assemblage which continuously reconnects and articulates territory to northernness, inhuman wilderness, human stamina, racial tolerance, and snow. The prospect of radical change in the weather north of the 49th challenges the foundation of the collective imaginary. In farming, politics, culture, trade, temperament, and the continental balance of power, it is Canada's geography and weather, its "nature," that have provided the most convenient explanation for its subjects' plights.

Usually the claim that a certain discourse "naturalizes" power has little to do with what we mean by *nature*, which is being evoked metaphorically here (in a reverse "naturalizing" process) to stand for phenomena that are unchangeable and untouched by human agency. Nature functions rhetorically to establish the distribution and boundaries of human agency, and weather offers definite proof of nature's intractability. This binary construct of human-other is a problematic way to think about nature, as many critics and philosophers have argued. The weather conditions mediating between human beings and "nature" are themselves mediated by networks of discourse involving management and meaning that shape how nature embodies and is embodied by us. How we encounter the weather is shaped by ritual, technology, economy, and geopolitics, and by the systems of representation that mediate these social relations. In the north, weather has been made intelligible in relation to colonial transformations of language and landscape by European and American machineries of power. That is to say, weather had a history even before it began to change.

As travel extended the reach of early modern science, European encounters with other cultures provoked troubling questions about the nature of mankind. When explorers and missionaries began to travel to the Americas, the "New World" became the subject of considerable speculation in Europe about relations between character and environment. This was a "New World," said one arrival, "because the ancients had no knowledge of it."[1] Obviously they meant their own ancients, not the ancestors of the people they encountered there. From the sixteenth to the eighteenth century, natural philosophers dedicated themselves to theorizing the connections between geography, migration patterns, distant cultures, and the foundation of human nature. Understanding relations between human dispositions and natural environments was said to be the new prerogative of princes, who could rule best by drawing on the expert advice of scholars versed in geography to understand their subjects.[2]

According to the classification system advanced by such scholars, Europeans are capable and reliable in work, culture, and health because of their moderate climate, while those who live in more extreme climatic conditions are less able to moderate and control their lives and body politics. People from the north were thought to be "bold but lack cunning; . . . physically vigorous, simple and straightforward, but frequently under the influence of Bacchus." People from the south were deemed to be cunning, superstitious, subtle, soft, and lacking in boldness.[3] A temperate climate could be expected to produce temperate characters, who are, like the third chair found by Goldilocks, just right! "What was more logical," muses Clarence Glacken, "than to interpret the spectacle of sleepy natives lying in the shade in the hot warm climates as creatures held in thralldom by their climate? The age-old ideas of environmental influence, far from being discredited, actually increased in effectiveness—not only in the voyages to the New World but in the travels through Eurasia and in the reports about Persia and China."[4] Building on these ideas, Giovanni Botero, whose sixteenth-century publications established a pre-Malthusian approach to the study of populations, judged that people whose conditions were adversely influenced by climate could be altered and improved—through the effects of music.[5] Readers familiar with McLuhan's speculation about the potential political advantages of adjusting hot and cold media on a global scale may recognize this uncanny precursor; both authors associate the rule of distant culture with a geopolitical thermostat subject to central regulation. Later remedies for such adverse influences were found in more pedestrian technologies, which the Americas (despite their avowedly temperate climate) have been particularly anxious to employ. "Given the ideological, political, not to mention racial significance of these ideas," writes one historian, "the prospect of air-conditioning was of immense importance: here was a 'tool that would allow all humanity to progress beyond the accidents of climate.'"[6] In retrospect, we can see that air conditioning has helped to produce its own "accident of climate," placing in doubt the happy modern equation between climate management and human progress.

The natural philosophers of the Enlightenment period were not expected to draw their knowledge of climate and character from a study of foreign local traditions. It was only later that settlers would be called upon to "settle the country rhetorically, rather than etymologically," as Paul Carter suggests in his groundbreaking study of language and power in colonial space. It is one thing to describe a climate as injurious to human progress; it is another thing to occupy such space, to "transform a former boundary into a communicable space."[7] Such boundaries were constituted by geography, nature, or the "nature" of indigenous peoples. Spaces cleared for settlement in the "New World" had to be inhabited, and before they could be properly colonized, they had to be translated and made intelligible to the encroaching culture. This process inevitably involves the cognitive as well as physical violence of colonial intervention. Even today, the people of English Canada remain ignorant of the oral and material traditions through which indigenous cultures established and transmitted their intimate knowledge of their physical environment. The challenge of climate change presents an opportunity to revisit the long-distorted dialogue between different kinds of knowledge, to see what relearning can offer to redress a situation in which all of us, but especially aboriginal communities who now confront the worst effects of global climate change, need all the help we can get.

Informed by the residual ideas of early modern science, postsettler cultures have embraced moderate temperatures and managed interiors as prerequisites for the practice of confident modernity. This process exemplifies a larger trend wherein the rights of citizenship associated with modernity have been distributed proportionately to the perceived capacity to manage nature. We see residues of this discursive logic in practice when immigrants of color are asked how they are coping with the cold, thus reinforcing their distance from established citizenship; when Canadians are satirized by Americans in terms of their envelopment in cold—"Canada needs a *climate*!!" (see "Writing on the Border" [chapter 1]); when southerners from either country express paternalistic condescension toward northern populations on these same grounds; and when citizens of two closely proximate national territories learn to see weather systems as part of an asymmetrical geopolitical terrain.

This chapter explores this historical tendency in terms of an underlying dilemma. It is only by trying to overcome or disguise its climatic challenges that Canada could appear as a confident subject on the world stage. Yet national identity, like any other signifying entity, requires confirmation of its difference. As Harvey reminds us, "The process of state formation was, and still is, dependent upon the creation of certain kinds of geographical understandings (everything from mapping of boundaries to the cultivation of some sense of national identity within those boundaries)."[8] Such differences are formed and regulated through practices of arriving, mapping, naming, perceiving, and managing the land. What an interesting quandary this has been. The colonization and modernization of this landscape have produced tensions in our interactions, our senses, and even our meteorological conditions, and its cumulative history has produced a colonized morality of the body as well as a polluted sky. We don't have to look far for symptoms; everyday choices resound with meaning. Only a contextualized body politics can explain the young men tramping around Montreal in subzero weather wearing T-shirts and open jackets, carrying steaming Styrofoam cups but

American forecaster, Canadian forecaster. Photographs by Vid Ingelevics.

otherwise declaring their indifference to the cold (after all, Montreal is in Quebec, not Canada), or the young girls whose puffy winter jackets are not long enough to sit on (after all, teen fashion is peremptorily global), or the hunky suv drivers declaring their semiotic affinity with nature while sailing through the city in perfectly controlled interior environments (after all, the city is dirty). For some subjects, fashion deviance is more frightening than frostbite, and the air that suv drivers feel on their skin is categorically more important than the air produced outside by artificial climate machinery. Whether defying the weather or hiding from it, the actions of these subjects carry meaning, forming, like the weather itself, a web of relations between bodies and the spaces in which they live.

Perhaps it goes without saying that this enculturation, this shaping of diverse uses and representations of the cold that is our indigenous condition, contains subtle but profound political consequences. Now that weather is the subject of grave international controversy, perhaps it is apparent that the inverted significance of northern weather presents a key to our past and future. Is it not obvious that colonial history has transformed the weather from privileged medium (the wind carrying messages, the rain carrying water) to privileged object (something to be measured and predicted) and then prominent victim (who knows what military-industrial blot has caused the wind to blow so catastrophically, the rain to fall so strangely, the water to seep so poisonously) of global capital? Just as Canada is especially equipped to read the language of technological forms, so it is in a special position to trace the history and implications of this eco-colonization process. Citizens are forced to second-guess the premises of neoliberalism for the simple reason that people who sleep in the streets can freeze to death. Fantasies of control over nature are brought to earth by frostbite, and the neoliberal dream of limitless mobility is frozen in its tracks.

Should we then welcome global warming? When it comes, should we congratulate ourselves for having rescued our fellow citizens from the snow and ice? For some theorists, the environmental movement has been slow to combat public indifference because of its internal oscillation between the dramatization of catastrophe and the banalization of everyday response.[9] Coming to terms with this oscillation could improve our understanding of the fundamental dilemmas of Canada's existence. From this reappraisal, a new anticolonial, postnational collective self-consciousness can surely emerge. But have the evening T V weather reports said anything against the problematic improvement of the nation's climate? Does the local weatherperson say: "Good forecast for you patriots. It will be cold today!"? Would it make sense if she did? Will the newspaper's daily "50 years ago today" column remind its readers of an earlier golden age of arctic cold, and nudge them into stoic protest against the colonizing intrusion of greater warmth, with its accompanying rhetorics of profit and pleasure? Or will Canada's comprador bourgeoisie celebrate this climatic change on behalf of its potential fiscal benefits, renegotiating agricultural subsidy and trade agreements with the increasingly destabilized United States, voicing platitudes about the manageable price of progress in connection with growing problems in more arid zones of the west, and once again ignoring the extraeconomic ethics of the nation's destiny? Will peoples of the north wield more power when their climate is less cold? What happens when there is nothing left to hunt, when the ice cap melts away, when the Arctic becomes a field of oil wells, a speedy route for shipping goods to Asia, a war zone? What does it mean in this context to embrace a body politics?

Shaped by the legacy of empire, it seems a perversity of progress to appreciate the cold, or the social architecture of a culture shaped by cold, in a public domain occupied with the valorization of efficient pleasure. Such pleasure depends on the overt elimination of displeasure as its complement; it relies on the strange idea that displeasure (as this is dominantly defined) can never be pleasurable, and vice versa. We are instructed continuously in an apoliticizing, narcissistic, and xenophobic construct of pleasure itself. Such instruction interferes with our right to the unpredictable pleasures of transgressive nature through which we find our collective place in the world.[10] Living as we do in the shadow of the world's most powerful "technocracy of sensuality"[11] what could affection for this natural habitus (outside of overrepresented, well-regulated episodes of white Christmases and carrot-nosed snowmen, distantly photogenic mountain landscapes, and winter skiing) reveal other than a masochistic toleration for inferior conditions? Wouldn't any normal person prefer Florida? How can the indomitable, unpredictable, and antidisciplinary excesses of winter precipitation be admitted into a public discourse that is ordered and enabled (as satellite views remind us daily) by an immense technological apparatus of progress and mastery, without appearing to be caught in a premodern, preadult condition of perverse glee?

It is not in response to climatic change that adults of my acquaintance complain so much more about the weather. Nor is this sensitivity due simply to the aging process of this same segment of the population, which no longer cheers lustily at the invigorating prospect of after-school hockey or leisure skating-dating at the local rink. At first glance, the explanation is simple. It's television. It's not only that the forecast offers a simple morality play each day as it fills its slot in the local news: sun is good; cloud cover is bad. When was the last time you saw a blizzard on prime time? It never snows in California; people never freeze to death in Florida; there's never nasty slush in those nameless Ohio or New Hampshire towns that provide the archetypal setting for daytime television, and reality show contestants are never held back by a snow day. Admittedly television is full of such apparently harmless deceptions. Is one form of idealistic representation the same as any other? From the present vantage point, no. The issue can't be neatly resolved with a critique of representation. It is not sufficient to object that this mediated landscape is *unrealistic*; no one believes in realism any more, and the concept has nothing to do with television, whatever they call the programs. Television's effects work through and beyond the level of signs; indeed television represents (its coverage of the weather being exemplary in this respect) a major disciplinary apparatus whose main effect is to supervise the movement, location, ethos, and temperamental tolerance of our physical being while "naturalizing" this surveillance and supervision as (in the context of the present subject) an act of nature.

Thus we are forced to concede that our shivering intolerance of the cold reveals more than the visceral effect of spectatorial fantasy, that this unpatri-

"The weather outside is . . ." Photograph of Toronto by Paul Tichonczuk, courtesy of the artist.

otic misery exposes the explanatory limitations of thinking about televisual mediation in terms of representation, at least as representation is ordinarily conceived. It is our bodies that are at issue. The predictive scientific assemblage has done its best to eliminate the serendipity and surprise of the great outdoors. With forecasts available 24/7, you need never be caught or delayed by unexpected weather; with mobile communication devices you never have to hear an unanticipated sound. This is sad, because this is the surprise you long for. In this hyper-mediated environment, to submit to such surprise is pathological; it is like forgetting to pay for lunch or espousing politics in a clinic. To *not* anticipate the weather, to bring the wrong equipment, make the wrong plans, or wear the wrong clothes is like not knowing the time: it is a symptom of personal mismanagement, a failure to employ the technologies of everyday normal living. Comfort and convenience are obligatory resources for the successful management of daily life, and their pursuit justifies increasing rationalization and normalization in modern routines and practices.[12] Central heating, air conditioners, climate-controlled cars, underground malls and pathways, and weather forecasts participate in a process of technical mediation which teaches consumers to structure and manage routines of everyday life with ever greater control over spatial and temporal conditions. This cult of efficiency and its required distancing from the natural environment creates "an arguably new and certainly niggling tension between the production, appropriation and maintenance of standardized and localized interpretations of normal practice."[13] With these warming and cooling technologies in place, it is simply not acceptable to be overcome by any local weather, except in the case of Acts of God, which are categorized as disasters.

So it is not surprising that people really do feel colder, even as the winters are growing milder, and the result of our maladjusted bodies is an enormous, imperceptible, geological shift of our loyalties, our values, our morals, our very beings. That's the point I want to make about the weather.

A Brief History of the Forecast

Before weather forecasting became an everyday ritual in broadcasting, weather prediction was the subject of everyday readings of natural signs: the color of the evening sky, the direction and force of the wind, the behavior of animals and insects, the sound of trees, and the distance covered by ordinary sounds. These were supplemented by the reading of barometers, which were widely available to Europe and Europeans by the eighteenth century. Knowledge of local weather was transmitted across generations in the form of rhymes, proverbs, and mythic figures. The shortcoming of such weather lore was not inaccuracy; weather literature is replete with stories of scientists and explorers being shown up by local oral tradition. Shortly after I undertook this research, the CBC featured a fourteen-year-old prairie girl who outpredicted Environment Canada, the federal government's weather bureau, two weeks running. In the wake of the catastrophic 2004 tsunami in Indonesia, it was revealed that one island community survived without casualties because their longstanding culture of storytelling told them what the winds meant. In both cases, the traditional observation of natural signs produced short-term predictions as reliable as modern meteorological forecasting, as climatologists themselves concede. "You can go with all your magic markers and your electronic equipment and your satellite photos and in the final analysis it's Mother Nature who's going to decide exactly what to do," one weather analyst remarks cheerfully.[14] "A ring around the sun or moon, brings snow or rain real soon," adds Environment Canada's senior climatologist, is "70% right—almost as good as Environment

Canada."[15] This acknowledged limitation produces a natural ambivalence in viewers, whose desire for prediction is structured by the historic disavowal of nonscientific knowledge and yet sutured with the ever-present knowledge that the weather will cheat the forecasters and do what it wants.

Obviously an economy built on (relative) predictability and security cannot rely on traditional knowledge, for such forecasts rarely extend reliably past a couple of days.[16] Indeed an improved capacity to predict the weather was a fundamental precondition for the emergence of modern capitalism. The task of gathering weather observations simultaneously in a number of places originated briefly in the seventeenth century but was undertaken regularly only after 1780. By 1820, systematic weather observations were being organized across Europe and the United States, introducing the process of time-space compression later described by theorists of the modern. To extend the temporal range of weather prediction, and to respond to the needs of travelers and scientists, rapid communication across space was a prerequisite. The observation of weather across a larger region led to the realization that storms generally travel from west to east, so that one could anticipate tomorrow's weather as today's weather "a day's storm-travel to the west."[17] Of course such knowledge is useful only when it can travel more quickly than the storm itself; otherwise, inconvenient weather would come and go before the local inhabitants could be warned of it. Thus the telegraph was a crucial innovation in the history of modern weather, conveying daily weather information by 1849 and storm warnings as early as 1855. The telegraph, which "freed communication from the constraints of geography,"[18] also freed weather knowledge from the constraints of local knowledge networks, drawing ever larger units of time and space into the circumference of scientific forecast and planning.

The most crucial technological changes have transpired since the 1960s, when technical advances in meteorology were articulated with military and aeronautical research on one side, and television on the other. By 1965, images of the earth disseminated from satellites were being used for television weather reports; by 1975, private companies were contracting out satellite photo services for television weather reports.[19] Most of the present-day forecasts on television or the Internet are gleaned from sophisticated satellite-based and computer-based visual observational technologies fed through digital information processing, as I explain in the next chapter. These technologies have developed rapidly since U.S. president Dwight Eisenhower established NASA in 1958 to manage United States nonmilitary aeronautical and space activities.[20]

After the Second World War, meteorology underwent a simultaneous process of institutionalization and privatization in Canada and the United States. In 1955 two Canadian government meteorologists went into business for themselves and made a lucrative living selling weather forecasts and cloud-seeding services to businessmen. Canadian journalists were quick to speculate on the political implications of the new technology: "The day approaches when a government may be thrown out of office because voters disliked its weather," one wrote.[21] (I pray that this forecast comes true as soon as possible, before our current government's obsequious abandonment of the Kyoto Accord invites the kind of disaster that turns the very idea of government into a bitter nostalgic fantasy.) By this time, weather forecasting was becoming a regular feature of television news. Introduced to early television by men with military training, weather forecasting exploded in the 1950s in a riot of jokes and gimmicks. "Weathergirls" were a favorite feature of live television in the 1950s.[22] We might think of them as "vanishing mediators," whose visual appeal accomplished the transition of weather from specialized science-based communication to television entertainment.

In the climate of Cold War technological prowess, the new technologies of meteorological prediction were the subject of considerable journalistic enthusiasm. *Maclean's*, Canada's national news-magazine, opened the door with a gossipy portrait of the daily life of the weatherman.[23] This kind of coverage embraced the forecast as a new source of entertainment in the exciting new medium of television. But there was (as there always is) more to this than entertainment. The emergent science of forecasts was headlined as a "crystal ball for profits" in *Saturday Night* magazine's business column; the writer points out that weather affects agriculture, logging, oil, employment, airplane travel, consumer sales, advertising, storage, pollution reduction, insurance claims, and general litigation, and that foreknowledge of future weather can benefit investment in all arenas. "The point of all this," the writer concludes, "is that the business man, in casting about for help in the more profitable operation of his activities, should glance weatherwards."[24] A *Financial Post* report on McGill University's "stormy weather group" traces the group's scientific adventures in searching for appropriate instrumentation for radar photography and for photographing and transmitting "constant altitude" photographs of a 200-mile radius circle. The author notes the significant broadcast, transport, and military uses of such photographs. "Weather can cause great economic losses to many others who do not know before hand what to expect. It can be a source of great monetary gain to those who can understand and anticipate it."[25] By this time, ex-government meteorologists were making a good living selling short-term weather modification and long-term weather forecasts to enterprising businesses.

The introduction of weather satellites in the early 1970s coincided with the professionalization of television weather, the temporary disappearance of women forecasters, and the proliferation of commercial firms distributing syndicated weather data. By then television could display weather forecasts across the continent, illustrated with color radar, electronic lettering, and live satellite photos. The claim that enhanced image processing improves weather prediction was crucial to the emergence of television, but it remains empirically questionable: in general, the forecast is not more reliable, but more people have faster access to the knowledge that is available. Weather's effects on the circulation of commodities are managed not so much through prediction but through frozen anticipation in built form, as our enclosure in tunnels and malls—Canada has the largest and the most per capita in the world—demonstrates. Despite masterful observational and digital technologies, meteorology—the uncontroversial rationale for such technologies—still encounters definite limits in the truth value of its forecasts. What we can see and where we see it are not necessarily commensurate with what we can predict. Farmers and drivers still suffer incalculable damage from the weather's wrath. Eluding the optical and digital extensions of human vision, weather still outwits the computers. With the predictive claims associated with the new technologies, however, meteorology joined medicine as "one of the first scientific disciplines . . . to develop science-based services for the public."[26]

In this manner—via the "neutral" instrument of North American scientific surveillance—weather entered the representational landscape of Canadian culture. By the 1970s, when satellite observation technologies and weather system prediction systems came together in a compelling televisual rhetoric of observation and mastery, it was finally admissible to show the weather. Only then could it be depicted without bringing trauma or apocryphal folklore in its wake. Acting out the wondrous energies produced by this turn of events, weather reporters were the celebrities of the new medium. They were gregarious and comforting. They had charisma and long, friendly careers. Like DJs, they mediated private and public spaces and cemented viewers' friendly relationship with the televisual environment. By helping viewers to avoid the cognitive and physical complexity of unplanned natural encounters, television colluded in a process of infantilization, seeking to protect its viewers and altering their attitude to what they did, inevitably, confront. When weather prediction entered the home, the children come indoors. Among the Inuit, this was the first change reported as a result of the introduction of television into their community. They had begun to find the outdoors just too cold.

"And Thus You See a Strange Abundance"

I want to resituate this brief history of predictive technologies in the context of Canada's colonial history, and to show that the strategic intertwining of social and semiotic practices with natural forces has much older roots than the story so far suggests. The history of weather is inseparable from colonial technologies of space in the most encompassing sense of the term. With weather, as with other forms of natural mediation, discourse makes our human practices meaningful; shapes the forms of literacy and skill that arise in relation to them; and defines fissures and spaces within which alternatives or oppositions can be imagined. Nowhere is this claim more relevant than in relation to colonial travels and encounters in the so-called New World.

Journals written by the early explorers and missionaries who traversed the north on behalf of European church and state reveal the difficulties of their encounters with different spaces and peoples. A Jesuit missionary named Paul Le Jeune wrote of "the great trials that must be endured" by those who "cross over the seas, in order to seek and to instruct the Savages."[27] In a 1634 passage entitled "What one must suffer in wintering with the Savages," Le Jeune describes the ordeal of navigating between the suffocating smoke and the pitiless cold, between famished dogs and disagreeable foods, compelled all the while to sleep, and drink, and walk plunged to the knees in the snow. This would not have been novel information for the intended readers of his journal, as French official circles (thoroughly committed to the establishment of a New France) had already learned of the severity of Canadian winters and the superiority of Amerindian housing in surviving them.[28] In fact the French, committed as they were to the conceit that climate determined character, maintained a strong belief in cold's beneficial effects upon the health and strength of its subjects. Of course, they were not freezing in the midst of it. Missionaries such as Le Jeune shaped their journals for their sponsors so as to "re-create the circumstances in New France in a manner conducive to the adoption of desired courses of action."[29] Just as the frontier requires a back tier, to echo "Space at the Margins" (chapter 2), so the missionary's epistolary relation to his French readers was one of complex codependency on the decisions of readers, "a dependency exacerbated by the mission's material and environmental vulnerability."[30] Strategically, Le Jeune needed the Native; he needed to depict "the indigene, whose soul remained the mission's professed object, as at once 'Savage' and capable of redemption."[31] By describing the "Savages" as both incomprehensible and redeemable, the missionary hoped to convince his superiors of the value of his endeavors and of his ability to struggle for their souls in competition with their own barbaric spiritual leaders. Only then could he gain further material support for his endeavors.

Perhaps thoughtful of such considerations, Le Jeune averts any suspicion of petulance by writing about how he had given away the mantle off his shoulders, along with some other available comforts, under the evil and covetous gaze of "the Sorcerer." This powerful member of the community insisted on playing Prophet, he writes, "amusing these people by a thousand absurdities, which he invented, in my opinion, every day. I did not lose any opportunity of convincing him of their nonsense and childishness, exposing the senselessness of his superstitions." (We do not learn what those superstitions were, nor how Le Jeune, who is strategically demonstrating the salvageability of the Savages through the projection of evil onto the single body of the Sorcerer, can detect the suddenness of their invention.) "Now this was like tearing his soul out of his body; for, as he could no longer hunt, he acted the Prophet and Magician more than ever before, in order to preserve his credit, and to get the dainty pieces."[32] In this passage the battle between Savage and mission concerns the just allotment of food, warmth, and comfort. But it was conducted most vigorously, if we are to believe Le Jeune's longer account, on the terrain of language, leaving both protagonists very much exasperated.

Le Jeune's artful account of these encounters was informed by strategic knowledge of the climates, languages, and customs of the indigenous populations.[33] His journal informs church authorities that the language of the Savages was "full of scarcity" on matters of piety, devotion, and virtue, and on theology, philosophy, mathematics, "all words which refer to the regulation and government of a city, Province or Empire"; along with justice, flowers, punishment, kings, science, and wealth. By noting the lack of words for these spiritual and governmental obligations, the missionary communicates the belief that he alone is guided by them. The poverty of language indicated here is reversed in areas where richness prevailed in "the tongue of our Savages." Note the plural possessive of the modifying term: "*our* Savages." Their vocabulary seems excessively alterable in accord with different kinds of substantives, thus yielding entirely different terms for cold: *tabiscau assini*, "the stone is cold"; *tacabisisiou nouspouagan*, "my tobacco pipe is cold"; *takhisiou khichteman*, "this tobacco is cold"; and, moving to larger objects, *siicatchiou attimou*, "this dog is cold"; and so on. "And thus you see a strange abundance," observes the author, which both impresses and depresses the visitors in their attempts to influence the Savages.[34]

The saying that "Eskimos [*sic*] have many words for snow" is a commonplace among schoolchildren, for whom images of the Inuit people wrapped in fur parkas provide an index of quaint or childlike adaptability to their inhospitable terrain. Such children are mistranslating from a vantage point not so far from Le Jeune and his contemporaries, and not just through the name they give the Inuit people. They are trying to understand the prolific descriptive resources of the Inuit in terms of a functional nominalism parallel to their own, as though there could not exist any fundamentally different spirit of naming. English language terms for snow have a quantitative and instrumental purpose, which is to encourage us to continue our business with as little delay as possible. They convey how difficult it is to get to work, how far its excesses might go in immobilizing us or relieving us from our duties, what the sports conditions are, in extreme situations threatening to turn us into irresponsible citizens (not showing up for work, deserting our cars, stopping to care for one another in the streets) in its own willful image. Our language does not grant agency to the elements. Other ways of "naming" snow represent a childish inability or refusal to subjugate weather in the appropriate manner. Thus we learn that a technology of everyday life without a plan for mastery of the elements is no technology at all.

This instrumental and regulative approach to the northern environment was further consolidated and spatially disseminated with the introduction of broadcast weather reports, when meteorology was introduced as both entertainment and an indispensable resource for the management of daily life. The forecast's importance for regulating everyday regimes is evident in the normalizing language we share today, which, following the same disciplinary logic, subjugates the weather by measuring its nuisance value. Words such as *flurry* (don't worry), or *storm* (cause for alarm) communicate strong underlying premises about the need to maintain routines when possible future conditions are transported into the present. This snow is a functional condition requiring appropriate redress; it must have no independent life or logic. Another missionary, François Le Mercier, touches on this theme in a "relation" from 1666–67 entitled "Of the false gods and some superstitious customs of the savages of that country." Here we find further evidence of that incomprehension with which colonizers approached the "Savages." A Father Allouez cited by Le Mercier asserts that "These people are of gross nature, they recognize no purely spiritual divinity, believing that the Sun is a man, and the Moon his wife; that snow and ice are also a man, who goes away in the spring and comes back in the winter."[35] This anthropocentric snow lacks divine authority, and represents no explicated cause. It cannot be attributed to a technologically displayed mass of cold fronts, nor to the vengeance of a willful god, as our forecasts are wont to conclude (often simultaneously), especially when it snows after Easter. This "Savage" snow is part of a cosmos in which origin, life, suffering, justice, and time can be made sense of in stories of the seasons.

Journals of first contacts such as those of Le Jeune and Le Mercier offer vivid descriptions of the difficulties of this spatial and discursive project. In a similar vein, Father Louis Hennepin offers European readers the first description of Niagara Falls, having arrived there in December 1678 with the assistance of Iroquois guides. Unable to accept what he saw—a waterfall sourced from a lake, rather than a mountain, as is typical of Europe—Hennepin made the falls three times their actual height, added an upstream mountain range, and magnified the ferocity of snakes to support his representation of the falls as a Christian hell on earth.[36] Evidently such reports were not published too widely, or the population would not have grown so quickly. European settlers of the eighteenth century and nineteenth were inspired to migrate to the New World by the European romance of natural beauty and the American ideal of conquerable frontier, and were ill prepared for what they found. This experience led to a condition of representational confusion, precipitated by the compelling urge to evoke the natural milieu without being able to confront or accept it in familiar hermeneutic terms. The struggle to accommodate experience of the landscape was voiced in a language that was awkwardly imposed upon it. As they participated in "unhoming indigenous protocols and ontologies [through] perpetual colonialism,"[37] as Robinder Sehdev puts it, they could neither articulate the land's actuality nor celebrate the physical resourcefulness, collective interdependency, and environmental knowledge that shaped itself around it. In response to this crisis, colonial culture did its best to eliminate further "naturalistic" reference to nature, and only permitted its return when representational conventions had been properly tamed by the successful entrenchment of the conventions of American and European landscape painting, frontier literature, and the weather forecast.[38]

Through their early encounters with indigenous cultures, these colonial explorers struggled to adapt to the conditions they encountered in these first contacts, learning indigenous languages, as Le Jeune illustrates, and even writing dictionaries for some of them, while fur traders learned to be fluent in local languages. Later, as settlers sought to take possession of the land and establish their precedence in the "New World," the common good was discursively redefined as a relationship with nature based on mastery and control. Because the indigenous person did not produce or reciprocate an adequately instrumental language, he could not possess the world and no longer deserved to be master of it. Le Mercier's dismissal of the cognitive abilities of the "Savages" in his "relation" confirms Fanon's description of the contradictory importance of language to the colonial relationship. In Sekyi-Otu's discussion of Fanon, power in the colonial relationship is founded in an asymmetrical relationship to instrumentality in language. He writes: "The idea that the colonized subject's 'human status in the world' is disclosed by the experience of language has foundationalist resonances to the extent that it is framed by a normative view of the interactive and cognitive functions of linguistic competence." This linguistic competence has everything to do with its understanding of the environment. The normativity of the white man's assessment rests on "the claim, unwarranted in the colonial context yet implicit in its language game, to the possibility of an objective truth and a common good in the face of a manifest antinomy, in the face of the absolute social dichotomy that divides and separates the colonizer and the colonized as knowing, speaking, judging, and acting subjects."[39]

This normativity served to prevent harsh winter conditions from enter-ing into wider representation until its harsher realities could be properly mediated and distanced by available representational techniques. This dis-cursive absence can be understood symptomatically, as evidence of trauma. Early colonial settlers were brutally challenged by the environment they "discovered." As the art historian Anne Marie Willis shows, the history they relate describes "a basically European society spreading itself across a very un-European landscape. It is rooted in that first settlement process in which the pioneer faced two main obstacles: the new land and the old culture."[40] In this narrative, the new nation (in her study, Australia) is settled by "people, artists most particularly, coming to terms with the uniqueness of the land, learning to love it, leaving behind their European aesthetic frameworks and seeing that Australian landscape 'with new eyes.'"[41]

Like Paul Carter, whose work has been so influential in the rewriting of the history of colonial landscape, Willis takes issue with this characteriza-tion.

In these narratives, the land is endowed with an unquestionable truth, it becomes a final resting place of meaning—its character is declared as evi-dent, the problem being that of observers needing to remove the scales from their eyes in order to see the land fully revealed. Nature is posited as culture, when in fact nature itself is a cultural construction and the his-tory of Australian landscape painting is not one of progressive discovery, the building up of an ever more accurate picture, but a series of changing conceptualizations, in which one cultural construction plays off another, in ever more complex webs of invention and in which the picturing of the local intersects with other, including imported, aesthetic and cultural agendas.[42]

The landscape, like the border, actualizes cultural and political as well as natural processes. Strategies for "picturing of the local," largely "natural" landscape in countries such as Australia and Canada were strongly shaped by the ambitions and expectations of early modern explorers. Travelers en-acting the "age of discovery" came looking for a natural paradise suffused with abundant riches and savage wilderness, an enterprise I have already described in "Space at the Margins" (chapter 2). By the eighteenth cen-tury, travelers had begun to assume the powerful, magical qualities they had already projected onto the land.[43] They themselves were powerful and magical because they were able to survive and conquer in such remarkable conditions. In this crucial act of displacement, what they survived (the cold, for instance) came to stand in for whom they conquered. In this way the weather served to mediate changing political relations between communities and their cultures.

In the early twentieth century a new self-consciously national art extended this displacement, creating a landscape full of trees and animals but largely empty of humans. The painters known as the Group of Seven set out to create a new landscape vocabulary expressive of the face-to-face confrontation between the explorer-painter and the stark, beautiful (so it appears to us now, as beneficiaries of this art) landscape of north-central Ontario. Canada's most visually and touristically elaborated symbol came to be its landscape—an uncontroversial means for its citizens to imagine and aestheticize a "natural" white (I don't simply mean snow-covered) collectivity otherwise deprived of identity. The depiction of an uninhabited state of nature implacably returning the artist's gaze was a dominant trope through which colonial settlers came to possess and define the country as their own. It is not unusual for a nation to come to consciousness of itself through its archive of landscape imagery; as Willis observes, landscape painting is a "necessary rite of passage" for the settlement of colonial cultures in new worlds.[44] It is part of the process through which settlers adapt to a culture marked by radical difference, through which the topos is gradually altered by colonizers' efforts to possess the landscape.

But these topia betrayed their contradictions. When we say there was no language for Canada's weather, we are uttering a complex idea. It is not reducible to the number of words for snow. Through a combined mobilization of wilderness imagery, artistic solidarity, and institutional canonization, the artists and dealers who invented the Group of Seven called Canada into being as a modern nation through representations of a place where no one appeared. Having been evicted from their lands by colonization, First Nations peoples were evicted a second time by the European settler's magically renewed love of nature. Setting forth to touch the wilderness with the same masculine prowess with which explorers crossed the country, these painters discovered a nature without adversaries or equals. The deadlier ravages of winter rarely appear in these landscapes. Equally conspicuous by their absence is evidence of pastoral or agricultural settlement, industry, smoke, machinery, or other signs of human presence that might attend the implied lonely observer. These images testify to the difficulty of establishing a sense of ownership over an unwelcoming nature. This difficulty is celebrated as a source of beauty.

Precisely so, this visual topography involves a subtle deceit. In fact, early colonists often rapidly adapted to the unexpected cold, transforming the long winter months into a season of indoor conviviality, highlighted by traditional religious and secular feasts. Friesen notes how adeptly settlers in Labrador learned to live and work in their new environment, and emphasizes the generosity of aboriginal guides who helped them to survive periods of great difficulty.[45] As Miller reminds us, it is important to differentiate diverse relations between colonists and aboriginals, depending on whether the newcomers were explorers and hunters who depended on indigenous knowledge for their success and their survival, or settlers who were determined to acquire possession of land and free it from all previous inhabitants.[46] These fragments of cross-cultural experience and settler adaptation are largely absent from the painted landscapes that came to represent Canada's nature. This dichotomy between experience and representation shaped the entry of the land into the representational field.

This history poses old and new questions to the meanings of the natural environment. Different approaches to knowledge, possession, and the land left an enduring rift between races and classes of early Canada, and to a diminishing of possibilities on all sides. The wind still carries messages, for those who are willing to listen to them, but they are not the same messages. Meanings of the land are changing through intensities of exploitation that could not have been imagined a century ago. Diverse knowledges of nature are coming together to make sense of the shared violence of their denaturalization. Signs are separated from their seasons, animals from their habitats, forms of life from their ways of life. It is not the task of indigenous knowledge to reassure others about an unchanging nature or unchanging culture. Quite the opposite: because of how and where they live, indigenous peoples are forced to know best how the changing weather is changing everything.

Snow Removal

By the early twentieth century, Canada's settler society had become complicit in the manufacture of romantic images of the landscape of the New World that would help attract new settlers to cross the ocean. The first film crew traveled across Canada on the Canadian Pacific Railway in 1902. Their purpose was to make films to send abroad to encourage emigration. The crew was instructed to show "the premium that western Canada offers for home-making and independence to the man of energy, ambition and small capital; to picture the range cattle, fat and happy, roaming the foothills of the mighty Rockies; to tell the piscatorial enthusiast of cool retreats beside rushing streams where the salmon and trout lurk beneath the rock's over-hanging shade."[47] The crew worked under a strict directive from the CPR "not to take any winter scenes under any conditions."[48] Canada was already too much thought of as a land of ice and snow. The films were premiered in London in 1903 without any evidence of it. This was the first, but not the last, injunction to Canadian filmmakers encouraging the production of winterless films.

This doesn't mean that no one made films about Canada with snow in them during the early years of movie history. Quite the opposite was the case! After 1920 Hollywood produced "Northwoods" movies by the hundreds, and they all had snow in them. "In the eyes of the moviegoing public," Pierre Berton writes, "Canada seemed to be covered by a kind of perpetual blanket of white—an unbelievably vast drift that began almost at the border and through which the Big Snow People plodded about like the denizens of Lower Slobbovia."[49] Through its articulation to costume, body language, primitive behavior, and primitive sexual politics, snow was made indexical of a childlike civilization: a landscape in need of conquest, industry, and law. The image of the Mounties fulfilled a crucial mediating function in the entry of this wilderness into the narrative conventions of civilized popular culture. The battle for law and order can hardly be fought in the wilderness without appropriate iconographic representatives of disorder. Hollywood's Mounties were as strongly subjected to the symbolic as was the snow that was their inevitable backdrop, which no doubt contributed to the humorous affection with which we retain them, in our more ironic modern iconography, in that frozen sphere. In 1995, as if to complete this crude infantilization, the Mountie image was acquired by Disney. Marketing and distribution of the Mountie icon was later returned to the Royal Canadian Mounted Police Foundation.

The pre-Disney films were rarely *made* in Canada, as Berton notes, but they entertainingly *signified* Canada with juxtapositions of pine trees, dishevelled French-Canadian villains, Mounties, snow, and uninhabited virgin forests. Once again colonial subjects are defined by their failure to manage their natural environments, a perceived failure tied indelibly to their less-than-civilized social competencies. Notwithstanding the thrilling and commercially successful adventures of Hollywood's top actors in this woodsy, mythical north, it takes little imagination to understand why Canadian officials were determined to counteract the uncivilized aura thereby attaching itself to their winter.

Though Hollywood's love affair with the "Northlands" faded away, anxiety about snow in Canadian film production did not. With the rise of its own commercial film industry, indigenous film production was no longer dedicated to attracting emigrants, but rather to producing exportable films. An exception to this new pattern can be found in the films made under the infamous 1947 Canadian Cooperation Project, which resulted in the practice of inserting small, more or less arbitrary (and presumably snowless) references to Canadian locations in American films as a means of attracting tourists to visit their northern neighbor. This agreement was a humiliating trade-off for permission granted to Hollywood to continue its suffocating economic control of film production and distribution within Canada. The attempt to enhance exports of films made in Canada helps to explain the production processes signaled in headlines such as "Shebib's Ordeal: Faking California in the Snow." As the film director describes it, he put ice into his actors' mouths to eliminate the steam issuing from their breath when they opened their mouths to speak their lines.[50] No one would guess they were in Canada! Here the difficulty posed by winter is not so much how to survive the cold as how to disguise it. The pressure to export cultural commodities is now as depressingly familiar as a spring freeze, but few of its effects have been as graphic as this one.

The landscapes of Canadian films and television series have grown picturesque in accord with the scenic conventions of North American pastoral spectatorship and abstractly regional pastoral nostalgia. Anglo-Canadian feature films tend to forefront the local topography but forfeit its fearfulness. The camera pans across the local landscape with a rough affection (perhaps the wheels bounce, or the sound drifts, but the leaves are gloriously green) that is just this side of post-Wordsworthian convention, and the seasons are never later than the autumnal burst of golds and reds. What remains of the natural milieu is a technicolor panorama fit for tourists and foreigners, which we all become in the momentary drift of sentimental

Hollywood's Canada: *The Heart of the North*, 1921.

pleasure. Whether appearing in feminist features or middle-brow social-issue "Movie of the Week," the landscape comforts the viewers and distances them from a significant part of what they know. Behind this pastoral picture, history, weather, and language intertwine and disappear.

Quebec film is a different matter. As Barrowclough notes with regard to the films of Lefebvre, landscape, seasons, and snow are "characters in themselves and determining factors in either the depiction of character or event."[51] In *Kamouraska* (1973), *Mon oncle Antoine* (1971), both directed by Claude Jutra, and other classics of Quebec cinema, snow provides a cinematic frame in a multiple sense: it appears as the content of opening and closing shots; as the central feature of a peculiarly stark, black-and-white pictorial aesthetic; and as the unyielding framework within which space and time, character and action, are measured and obscured. Animating this narrative motif is the presence of snow, not just as synecdoche, as referent for some external and sensually intangible physics, deity, or power, but as an autonomous entity with its own movements and laws, its own effects in the sphere of character and collective history, its own singularly powerful poetics.

Clinical Report

"Everyone talks about the weather, and no one does anything about it," Mark Twain observed a century ago.[52] This infantilizing caricature of pre-industrial folk humor in the face of implacable nature allows for a poignant paradox in our case. Weather is our most intimate subject and yet forms an indifferent frame and metaphysical limit of the social realm. Just as the border represents the limits of Manifest Destiny, so the north's seasonal harshness imposes limits on the fantasies of power and control through which science claims possession of the New World. Weather has agency you can't deny. At the same time it is a site of continuous colonization of representational and technological practice. Even the most "natural" of the elements is shaped by culture and inevitably enters into its logics.

The idea of climatically determined cultures was instrumental in helping to spread artificial climate control through the Western world, turning heat and cold into intolerable inconveniences.[53] The most brazenly unruled of all of "Nature" succumbs to differently empowered imaginaries, which haunt our material and symbolic expressions through inversion, distortion, condensation, and absence. Winter weather provides the subject matter of constant, highly ritualized, usually humorous conversational exchanges ("cold enough for 'ya?") in the face of looming discomfort and possible catastrophe, signaling a mature stance of complicit unrequited hedonism (any sane person prefers summer) and heroic resignation. However difficult it is to be gracefully hedonistic when tying up one's boots or digging out one's car, one can expressively indicate with a minimum of effort that we all deserve better. A great equalizer, the subject serves as uncontroversial glue for all everyday social encounters.

"Talking about the weather" is a double-edged détente; it means, let's bond by making small talk, *and* let's stay distant by saying nothing. It's hard to find a better encapsulation of the civilly unrevealing English Canadian temperament. (So much for northern boldness and lack of cunning.) And yet, however nonchalantly we approach the subject, however well we shield ourselves from it, however little we want to say about it, nothing is less trivial. Because of the weather, people live or die; communities are sustained or lost; futures beckon or collapse. This actuality creates a dilemma for the audiences of the daily forecast as they experience their daily injection of postcolonial meteorological instruction. How can a complaint against winter and the heavens' injustices be reconciled with the stoic collectivist morality that is said to differentiate us from our hedonistic neighbors? Why hate cold, when it explains what is best about us? As a student climate activist queried through his megaphone in 2008, why deprive the north of its "right to be cold," just so we can drive our cars? Why long for warmth, when the ice caps are melting?

In this situation, a "realistic" depiction of wintry weather works metonymically to represent the political will for regional self-determination and social justice. This motif, already described in the Quebec films of the 1970s, can be traced across the archive of English Canadian film and television. In the CBC drama *Street Legal* (1987–94), progressive urban lawyers were shown walking down Toronto's Queen Street in falling snow. The opening sequence for *Due South* (1994–96) featured light-handed associations between snow, justice, and ghosts of the dead. In *Canada: A People's History* (October 22, 2000 to November 18, 2001), patriots perform or recollect historic acts while warmly wrapped against the cold. And so they were. It is a mistake to imagine that settlers lacked the resources to negotiate their environment, or that they occupied a separate universe from the aboriginal inhabitants, who shared their skills and resources.[54] European settlers learned from the indigenous peoples how to eat, how to sleep, and how to travel in winter. As a residual memory of this debt, parkas returned in post-Iraq favor in the fashion news. The balancing act between different skills and forms of social capital is a central, often invisible, part of the political environment. Acclimatized by the ordinary practices of the *habitus* (in Bourdieu's sense) of television and the office, sheltered by an increasingly privatized and globalized audiovisual culture, nervous about the outdoors and open to the universe, it's impossible to survive a winter free from betrayal. Can we detect a symptomology of sublimated guilt?

The pathology of Canada's relationship with weather is revealed at a glance. Canadians are obsessed with the weather. We talk about it endlessly.

Yet there is a strange ghostlike space between the ritual grumblings and the public space of the official forecast. There are few cherished myths, other than symbolic condensations such as hockey players and the Mounties, whose endlessly recycled iconography both references and counteracts the lawless powers of northern winters hinted at so decorously in the inevitable snowy backdrop. To reclaim this space is to enter into an insurrection in language. Patterson Ewen, one of Canada's great painters (1925–2002), produced a large and beautiful corpus of work exploring the confrontation of cosmologies in visual representations of the weather. But the prestigious catalogues and critical essays addressing his work do not mention the subject of weather once. The authors do not want the weather to speak for them; they are sidetracked by the sublime. In truth they do not want the weather to speak at all. The weather occupies a zone of bad conscience, and in the approved spheres of symbolic and public cultures we would much prefer to keep quiet about it.

In popular culture, as in art, there are important exceptions to this claim. In television commercials for gasoline companies, an intemperate hysteria lurks behind the reassuring face talking at "you the driver" through the snow-screened window. Careful timing offers the viewer a comic reading: just when the driver (you) starts to panic about being trapped and freezing to death, the gas company pops in with a brotherly word. They were joking! They were there all along! We understand this country; the voice-over assures us as the gas station disappears into the whiteout. This reassurance is meant to inoculate viewers against their anxiety about driving in winter weather. Do not worry about mobility, the commercial insinuates; we can get you to work; you can transcend this condition and reap the rewards of your labor. One wonders whether this homey hysteria sidetracks viewers from recollecting that this same gas company has been transferred to private hands and no longer belongs to them.

Only within a comic trope—almost as a "return of the repressed," you might say—do we recognize ourselves under the whiteout of a blizzard. Trudging, half-human figures bundled in wraps, obscured backdrops, a demolished and demonic landscape, the sound of spinning tires, the "snow" on the screen—this is not grandeur, but uncontrollable absurdity. In the SCTV production *The Canadian Conspiracy* (1985), for instance, Canada is evoked in sudden blips within a series of rapid edits. A half-invisible Ottawa, submerged under still falling snow, appears suddenly and violently between serene palm-tree-lined poolside vistas of California and Florida. "Meanwhile," says the voice-over, "in Canada . . ." An enraptured laugh erupts upon hearing it shown like this. This is not entirely a friendly image; this grotesque canopy filled with plodding blobs bears little relation to the white magic that falls from the sky each November and turns everyone into children, amenable and transgressive in equal measure, hoping for that benign powerlessness that appears when snow forces everything to stop and you can stay home without rebuke. You know that your laughter at this depiction is also not entirely friendly; it's not clear whether it's the snow, the plodding, or the hyperbole that invites your chortling hostility. Assuming an amphibious position, you prefer not to know. And you don't have to, for so much discourages you from bringing that subject into thought.

Understanding the silence that otherwise surrounds the terrain of weather requires a complete toolbox of historical, psychoanalytic, semiotic, mythical, and political critique. To unbury this cultural presence and absence, we must deploy these tools within a reflexive analytic mode. We need to acknowledge complex strategies of repression, inversion, and displacement. Who could otherwise believe that in a mythic landscape long dominated by "Nature," such capable forces of repression could have taken our weather from us? Under such circumstances it is only natural that the indigenous examination of weather threatens to be snowed under by the heuristic arsenal.

Weathering the North

As modern nationalism loosens its hold on the cultural apparatus, wilderness landscapes have been supplemented by a different iconographic repertoire that heralds a more habitable future. Images of explorers, the railway, transmission towers, satellites, and remote robotics celebrate the lineage of technical wonders enabling the citizenry to master topographic and vertical space. Aerial photography can be traced to the period just before the Group of Seven, and, as I show in the next chapter, it excited special patriotic affection. In the course of pursuing partnerships with United States military and corporate enterprise, Canada has sought to enhance its national prestige through technological achievement, and photographs of satellites and satellite images proliferate in political advertising, postage stamps, government publications and websites, television and computer graphics, outdoor guidance maps, academic public relations, and weather reports. These communication technologies are the subject of preferred science projects for school children (as distinct from their American counterparts, who prefer to study frogs), and provide the jewel in the crown of Canada's self-representation abroad.

The exemplary combination of television and weather prediction is part of an ontological as well as a topological shift. Like weather reports arming us against unexpected storms, the rhetoric of technological advance shields us from that cognitive insistence on confronting necessity which constitutes the physiological fuel and aesthetic potential of northern cultures. In this sheltering domain of the technological sublime, the only currency is pleasure and the only pleasant land is green. This is not vision, not exactly language, something beyond temperament, beyond signs or science, something which approaches an ethos of the body. This ethos is betrayed by the condition of classic repression (of which one cannot speak) that erupts in an uncanny vision of the powerful yet ambiguous powers of snow and ice. The components of this ethos and repression are also decipherable in the management of contemporary information about the weather. The forecaster's cheeriness about sunshine obscures the power of global warming to make and destroy governments, fortunes, crops, and even countries.

It's lovely to think of a sunny summer day and the promise of sensual awakening, warm skin, effortless motion. This unification of pleasure and mobility assumes ever greater power as the matrix against which experience is assessed. An unruly climate expresses collective disorder, constraint, delay, anxiety, and inefficiency. A moderate climate validates individual convenience, efficiency, comfort, and pleasure. In a moderate climate, humans can savor without noticing their natural environment. In an immoderate climate, humans confront the limits of their own capacities. Weather is a condition through which we unequally negotiate our powers. Each region has its jokes and prohibitions, its seasonal festivities, its fears and forecasts become proverbs over time. Each region embraces and excludes the rights of bodies to claim citizenship on the basis of these kinds of knowledge. These form the ambivalent harvests of memory and place and create the foundation for "topophilia": the pleasure of the located body.

Such experiences diminish in value in the city, where bodies are protected by television and other forecasts, subways and snowplows, grocery stores and restaurants, and the visceral pleasures of beaches and sand at the end

Monitoring the Storm (24 seconds) (detail). Twenty-four black-and-white photographic prints on fiber-based paper, edition of February 2007, Christina Battle. Christina Battle is a Toronto artist with a BSC in Environmental Biology from the University of Alberta and an MFA from the San Francisco Art Institute. Working with film, video, photography, and installation, her works often investigate the intersection of natural and industrialized environments and violent weather phenomena.

of a plane ride. We are still waiting for that miracle which—following other miracles of science that brought us floating sound, electricity, three-dimensional images, and fluoride—will do something about the weather. Like the hopes attached to radio, this dream is inspiring in its paradoxical inventiveness and its vulnerability to disappointment. Such desire fails to confront its own regressive character, stepping sideways into a sardonic humor that imagines citywide domes, global warming, and other devices too close to reality, too far from heaven for true salvation. Beyond all this, beyond the winter wraps, the clumsy boots at the door, the mess of melting snow, the beauty, the predictable aggravation and pointless suffering, and then springtime and the unreasonable summer heat, there is something that cannot be mastered or controlled by the individual or liberal subject, something hinted at when we think of the winter deaths of the homeless, the haunted dreams of survivors, stranded trains, cancelled flights, certain knowledge that it rains on Sundays and will freeze in April forever—or until the ice caps melt.

The winter reminds us about best-laid plans, managerial hubris, and the limits of progress. In information theory, noise is anything which interferes with the intended communication; it is a rude interruption, a foreign word, uninvited sound, crackle over the wires, dirt on the lens. White noise is noise without meaning, a physical fact which justifies the arbitrary categories through which sound enters culture. In the modern canon, good weather is silent. Like light, it forms the inaudible conduit for other information: the sound of birds through an open window, the sparkle of waves, the sun warming the skin, smooth morning traffic. Bad weather is weather that makes itself audible, that introduces noise to the body's interface with the world, that threatens to demolish the discipline of everyday routine with no reason or need to explain. Bad weather is a transgression of silence and a threat to order. There is nothing in the world like the sound of rain. When you hear a cold wind, even on the radio, your spine tingles.

eight

Mapping Space

IMAGING TECHNOLOGIES AND
THE PLANETARY BODY

For communication purposes, a satellite is any heavenly object off which radio signals can be bounced.—BRIAN WINSTON, *Misunderstanding Media*

If the modern Constitution invents a separation between the scientific power charged with representing things and the political power charged with representing subjects, let us not draw the conclusion that from now on subjects are far removed from things. On the contrary.—BRUNO LATOUR, *We Have Never Been Modern*

When we check the weather reports to find out what's coming, we now take the viewpoint of the angels: looking down at the earth, rather than up at the sky. Our ancestors looked upward, and saw in the stars what they already knew: the twinkling outlines of goddesses and gods, mythic animals, and other astrological figures caught in the timeless spin of cosmic destiny. Looking downward through the satellite lens, we too see what we already know: a map of boundaries and arrows drawn over an abstract landscape, showing a battle between cold and warm fronts and the flow of meteorological systems rendered visible by the jerky movements of digital clouds. These instruments provide us with a reassuring vision of earth from a distant but attentive eye, which can translate atmosphere, turbulent air, land, movement, and sensation into the legible surface of a screen.

What does it mean that we now examine the skies looking down, rather than up? What do we read in these images, and why do they seem so eloquent? The question invites diverse genealogical, meteorological, sociospatial, utopian, visual, ecological, and military readings, presented in no particular order and with no initial compunction to separate science from myth or infrared radiometers from other practices of divination. This is not a general principle, as a consequence of which, for instance, intelligent creation would constitute as valid an account of history as the theory of evolution. These readings build from the premise that the accuracy of prediction, the instrumental objective of atmospheric observation from space, is not significantly improved by recent technological innovations, as most people know in a common-sense sort of way but forget, with classic Orwellian doublethink, while watching the television screen.

The weather report is brought to us by a technically sophisticated image production apparatus which displays its achievements on a daily basis. To make the weather forecast more accurate would require a software program able to simulate weather and climate at a level far beyond what meteorology can now accomplish. Its calculations would have to be able to produce climate models at an adequate level of complexity to meet the exigencies of nature itself, a capability which the images imply but can not actually produce. There are powerful residues of premodern cosmology in our response to these images, notwithstanding their instrumental rhetoric. The forecast is like science fiction. We watch, we see, we skeptically believe. This describes the "attenuated fiction effect" of television, which produces "a semifiction effect akin to but not identical with split belief—knowing a representation is not real, but nevertheless momentarily closing off the here and now and sinking into another world." As Margaret Morse asserts, this effect is built on television's distancing effect, which finds "complicity with the viewer against an 'outside world' represented as 'hostile or bizarre,' and the viewer's delegation of 'his or her look to the TV itself.'"[1] This idea has double relevance when it comes to the weather report, which displays advanced surveillance and measurement technologies yet often gets it wrong.

Poised between heaven, rain, and the digital sublime, the weather forecast offers its viewers a seductive reconciliation of science and art. By articulating the mysteries of nature to the technologies of intelligent imaging, forecast imagery forestalls the indifference to questions of reality and simulation that are so vexing in other arenas of media culture. Nature is "real" because (and to the extent that) its representation is scientific, object reliant, and brought to us from a great height. Our indoor environments mirror this deferral of sensation by being (for middle-class Westerners at least) carefully insulated against the vicissitudes of nature. We can look at storms without feeling their wrath, for we have satellite views for the big picture and storm chasers for the close-ups. The urban weather forecast speaks to urban culture's desire to experience nature at a distance and to keep it there.

There is nothing like the weather, on the other hand, to remind us of the limits of our powers. "What goes on inside the machine are imitations only, schematics of storms, line drawings of the weather," writes climatologist Thomas Levinson. "Outside, overhead, the real thing dominates. The occasional failures of the computers become a kind of reminder, a relatively gentle warning: for all the power of the latest computers the weather itself remains in some way intractable, out of control."[2] Recent disasters such as the tsunami in Indonesia and Hurricane Katrina in the southern United States offer harsh reminders of that intractability. Everyday weather delivers this same message in a more banal language. By checking the forecast, we hope to protect ourselves from and even to enjoy the unpredictability of the temperature. Viewers can celebrate both technique and nature's resistance to technique in one powerful viewing experience. Nature, like war, is reenchanted by the technological sublime.

In *The Machine and the Garden*, Leo Marx documents the nineteenth-century transfer of collective experiences of awe and reverie from natural sources such as mountains and waterfalls to technological wonders such as the railway. This shift transcends the romantic or pastoral distinction between country and city, and generates a new form of transfixed attention linked indelibly to ideas about progress. By combining the natural power of climatic events like blizzards or heat waves with the visual power of digital graphics and telematics, the weather forecast simultaneously combines and inoculates us from two distinct planes of discursive power and wonder. The weather forecast "works" even when it does not fulfill its promise. Its imagery is predicated on a long chain of digital and communicative processes which break down previously invisible natural elements into information that can be translated into visual data. An analysis of this data produces a statistical likelihood about how weather will unfold over the near future. This predictive calculation offers the reassuring sense that science can grasp the future and draw it cognitively into the present so that we can benefit from its authoritative knowledge. Joining together these disparate digital processes, the forecast's claim to authority is a consequence of vision (nice color images), efficiency (checking it involves little time), conscience (it monitors air quality and uv indexes), and omnipresence (through instant accessibility via radio, television, and the Internet). The act of checking the weather marks the routinized insertion of future time into the providence of today, and provides a ritual element to the navigation of temporality and self-preservation to which I am personally quite dedicated. If weather forecasts contribute less than we might hope to the needs of those who depend most on the weather, they are nonetheless part of the everyday discipline of the media age.

Landscapes in Space

If you look at satellite views in American newspapers and television forecasts, such as those shown in chapter 7, you will notice that Canada appears without internal markings. Lacking visible geopolitical identification, the country is represented metonymically by air currents entering the United States, mainly the cold "Canada" sends south. Arguably this is part of the same trajectory that produced "Hollywood's Canada":[3] that snow-covered, meteorologically overdetermined, uninhabited if not uninhabitable landscape which American cinema represented as Canada for some sixty years (see "Weathering the North" [chapter 7]). The fact that Hollywood's Canada is traditionally covered in snow may explain how it came to disappear on the maps. Just as the word America semantically excludes Canada, its movies and maps construct a marginal politicoeconomic identity for Canada based on its topographically determined, that is, "natural" geopolitical destiny. Canada's peripheral but resource-rich status in the continental economy is thereby reproduced as a natural consequence of its "posterior destiny,"[4] rather than as a consequence of politics and power. Canada remains visually off-center, graphically empty if not absent altogether, marginal to America's triumphant conquest of nature and the world. In these images Canada signifies those lagging parts of the world in which nature still holds sway.

In the satellite pictures and maps broadcast by Canada's weather channel, on the other hand, Canada displays most of the continent and its weather systems in one inclusive view. Viewers thus learn that weather moves in more than one direction. There is a material and technical context for this difference in the production of knowledge: our weather forecasts are transmitted across the country by Canadian broadcast satellites, but the information is collected from American satellites which map the terrain from a more southern vantage point. These satellite-based weather images are thus maps of technoterritory—they indicate who is watching whom, with whose instruments—as much as they are maps of geophysical terrain. Canada's

Weather map, *The Weather Channel*, Canada, 2007.
Photograph by Vid Ingelevics.

satellite status is reproduced by the geopolitics of satellite communication. The weather forecast materializes the technical convergence and economic interdependency of a specific technological assemblage of satellite communication transmission, GPS monitoring, television, digital information processing, digital graphics, security systems, and the management of urban space.[5] The images produced by this apparatus present us with an interesting anomaly, for their presence in our media landscape looms larger than their modest functionality as meteorological science would suggest. The mediation of technological and geographical landscapes extends the colonial history of scientific-technological mapping and administration of the land to the digital grid of three-dimensional space. Like maps, canoes, and politics mediating the border, satellite weather images mediate land and language, surface and depth, distance and myth, politics and money, and sovereignty and globalization, woven with all their fascinating contradictions into surface and outer layers of the earth.

Satellite image production extends a history of landscape depiction which prefers its nature at a distance. This tradition together with the history of scientific and technical achievement provides a context for the development within Canada of an aerial-visual technological apparatus unequaled (we are told) in the world. The images shown in the weather forecast are both derivative and distant from that pictorial history. To understand this trajectory, we need to define more clearly the object of which we speak. Satellite images originate from the trajectory of mapmaking, and in a sense are maps themselves; graphic and indexical images of digital clouds and cold fronts are made flat and topographically legible by means of superimposed political boundaries which reiterate the maps that came before. Maps celebrate simultaneously the love of surfaces and the inspiration of movement in which surfaces morph and disappear. Like these images, maps unite the dream or record of transport with the passion for appropriate measurement. Like travel, war is impossible without maps; both are transformed by the digital elaboration of actual and virtual space. Whether composed for civilian or military purposes, maps constitute a visual index of traversable space which is pragmatically linked to the anticipated exigencies of unaccustomed, uncharted, or unfriendly movement.

To historians, anthropologists, and some cartographers, maps also offer a visual encyclopedia of the myths, values, and political assumptions of a particular culture at a particular time. All maps state an argument about the world, Brian Harley reminds us,

> and they are propositional in nature. All maps employ the common devices of rhetoric such as invocation of authority. This is especially so in topographical ... or in thematic maps. ... Maps constantly appeal to their potential readership through the use of colour, decoration, typography, dedications or written justifications of their method. Rhetoric may be concealed but it is always present, for there is no description without performance.[6]

Preindustrial maps provided iconic justifications for travel with decorative images of wind gods, cupids, sea monsters, heraldic icons, and other deities appropriate to potential conquest. Colonial maps portray the topographies of lakes and mountains imprinted with new place names, the previous inhabitants having been relegated to a rhetorically differentiated margin of the terrain.[7] Extending this trajectory, satellite images search out and depict useful spaces from the vantage point of excellent technologies while pleasingly referencing their own capabilities in this regard. In the weather forecast, they confirm their indebtedness to maps through rhetorical flourishes in the direction of digital artifice (spasmodic shifts in cloud cover or continental currents, for instance), which celebrate the inventiveness of their execution without interrupting the screen's unearthly silence. This accommodation provides a regular public celebration of the technological mastery of space which is progressing rapidly within the purview of the Pentagon. Their graphic capacities arbitrarily and instrumentally redraw spatial relations and boundaries, up and down in geometric space as well as side to side, conveying the possibility of traversing and managing as well as representing this vastly extended space.

In their promotion of digital image production, satellite weather images celebrate their own ability to pierce beyond the surfaces of physical and human topography and to show what was previously unseeable by humans, literally to "unconceal" what lies behind them,[8] as though landscape, or nature in general, was heretofore "veiled," as the language of Western science so persistently implies.[9] The concept of a precognitive natural world hiding behind its surfaces is a disingenuous response to the productivity of digital imagery. Nature is always interpreted by contemporary frameworks of meaning and use. These images do not function simply as maps; they are also documentary photographs, technically inscribed visual simulations made to record the earth's "real" surface as it appears in a specific moment of time. "The photographer," claims Lewis Mumford, "must take the world as he finds it."[10] That is, the photograph emphasizes temporality by separating the image from it, lifting its imprint from the living flow of passing minutes just as these images do. Of course the world changes not only from one moment to another, one view to another, but also from one lens to another. The world the photographer finds, as Mumford puts it, is the world made legible by the photographer's purpose and equipment. Like photochemical photography, these digital pictures capture a moment of visual data lifted from time. While their photographic transparency enhances their legitimacy, they are not actually photographs, either, for they do not duplicate what the photographer sees. Rather, they are digital simulations of photographs, or to be precise, virtual images digitally processed to look like photographs, inscribed onto the residues of maps.

The observational technologies that produce these virtual images have grown considerably more advanced than those used in early LANDSAT pictures, when measurement of visible and near-infrared radiation allowed scientists to measure atmospheric temperatures, vegetation cover of land surfaces, and biological activity in the oceans. In the years following the first LANDSAT launch, the development of radar, Doppler, infrared, and microwave radiometers further enabled satellites to measure water vapor and condensation, atmospheric temperature and radiation patterns into the upper atmosphere, surface and cloud temperature, levels of ocean waves and sea salinity, and the ozone. In each instance, information is produced by scanning an atmosphere which is highly complicated in texture, movement, and dimensionality. Selected information about this atmosphere—including heat, light, and the presence of other measurable materials—is produced by converting data into numbers and radioing these numbers to an earth-based computer where data "becomes imagery on photographic film," which, in turn, explains an editorial in *National Geographic* July 1976, "can be put to a variety of uses." With the digitization of "imagery on photographic film," it's not only the photograph that is virtual but also the imagery itself. Without these instruments, this image would not exist. As atmospheric surveillance technology progresses, additional conditions—such as temperature, clouds, and the presence or absence of light—become measurable entities translatable to visual data. This translation into image has a dual advantage: weather conditions can be predicted and displayed for the "postpanoptic" observer, while these same conditions cease to be obstacles to the accuracy of ground surveillance that can be monitored from above. Darkness and cloud cover are visible to us halfway across a continent, if we check the weather forecast, but they no longer serve to hide beneath. The satellite has indeed "unconcealed" the earth's surface, and we are complicit with it.

Like other information about the earth surface and atmosphere, the natural conditions of the changing climate—day or night, heat or cold, windiness, cloudiness—are computer processed into a composite image of brilliant colors that are gorgeous to behold and only arbitrarily related to earthly manifestations. Infrared satellite images produce virtual photographs showing us that white is cold, black is hot, the winds range from blue to yellow, and the oceans move from red to purple, while the hole in the ozone is gray or violet. We are looking at a new type of landscape literacy, in which the "modern" perspective of the terrestrial human eye is rendered obsolete—arguably turning Galileo's telescope, the first direct optical challenge to the combined rule of divine authority and common sense, backward to view the earth, and creating a radically new type of sacred knowledge.

Ushered into visibility, the elements seem to have undergone a process of reenchantment. "It is curious," McLuhan muses in his essay on radio, "how much more arresting are the weather reports than the news, on both radio and TV. Is this not because 'weather' is now entirely an electronic form of information, whereas news retains much of the pattern of the printed word?"[11] Gesturing toward a larger vision of technological transcendence, McLuhan finds electronic information more magical than print, and considers knowledge mediated electronically to bear the marks of this sublimity. How prescient this idea was. "Weather," like "space" and or "the body," has become a charismatic abstraction, embroiled in political, epistemological, and critical reflection and yet constantly eluding its grasp. Our knowledge of the weather, like that of the body, is increasingly shaped by information gathering and digital image processing, which "makes it possible to rationalize activities more comprehensively than if they had been undertaken by a human being."[12] In "The Musicking Machine" (chapter 5) I describe this process at work in the automation and digitalization of piano performance. In the context of satellite image production, the digital integration of information and communication networks is contributing to what Christopher Coker calls the reenchantment of war, whereby "the survival of the fittest" is replaced by the "belief in the survival of the best informed."[13] The productivity of this idea in the transformation of military practice led Haraway to describe war as a "cyborg orgy, coded by C31, command-control-communication-intelligence, an $84 billion item in 1984's U.S. defense budget."[14] By integrating war and computers in one cyber-military network, the Pentagon has confirmed that "Knowledge is paramount. . . . The unprecedented level of battle space awareness that is expected to be available will significantly reduce both fog and friction." Such awareness depends on the transformation of elements into pictures together with the transformation of hypothetical futures into statistical prognostications. The uncertain future, like the unseen cold front, becomes an administered object of data processing. "To be better informed," Coker explains, "is to know of every change in circumstances in the external environment. Wisdom has largely become a matter of information processing."[15] There is 30 percent chance of precipitation tomorrow, 60 percent the following day; measuring the odds, the graphic shows rain. The quality of digital knowledge, the efficiency of the agencies acquiring and processing this knowledge, and the usefulness of this knowledge to capable self-administration are profitably translated into spectacle and promoted in the daily forecast.

The Planetary Body

Satellite-based observational technologies render the earth's surface together with its surrounding atmosphere into usable visible information. Like medical X-rays, which extend and replace the human eye with optical technologies, they render surface or body boundaries obsolete. They reveal to us what is hiding in the oceans, and the deserts, and the jungles, and the wind. As each space is rendered transparent, the planet and its resident bodies are urged to greater productivity, a more efficient yielding of secrets, contents, products, knowledge. This rendering-into-image is closely linked to processes of medicalization performed by modern science, particularly on the woman's body, which paradoxically disappears behind its contents. Symptoms are translated into discrete visible information that can be acted upon by the physician, with or without the participation of the patient. Perhaps this connection, and the equivalent hierarchization of knowledge that results, explains the sympathetic bedside manner of many weather forecasters.

But the analogy is limited in at least one respect: we already think of organs and the unborn as tangible objects, as visualizable, if not actually visible, like vehicles moving or buried in enemy territory under a cloud-filled sky. In contrast, satellite optics create images, that is to say, surfaces, out of materials which were not previously conceived as tangible entities. Before telescopic imaging technologies, we did not conceive of air, wind, or temperature as visible matter. Satellite photos create a virtual photo from a virtual surface that is actually a three-dimensional environment in flux. Without digital technologies these images would not exist. The hyperreal technical design makes the image look as veritable as a photograph, whatever the origins and veracity of its digital parts. Such veracity is a function of rhetoric, not reference, for digital techniques create images with qualities brazenly independent of their referents. Given this artifice, how do we know whether the images are real? If satellite surveillance and digital processing are part of the militarization of information, how do we know where one ends and the other begins? At the conjuncture of science and war, the boundary between image and artifice is particularly vulnerable. The 1991 "Desert Storm" invasion in the Persian Gulf was known as the first environmental war, a concept that has more recently been applied to Darfur. A wary observer might pay particular attention to the daily circulation of images of the weather in the region and the occasional disparity between weather depictions and military reports. If weather can be altered either inadvertently (in the case of global warming) or deliberately (as we know with respect to military interventions), fiddling with its representation has its own enticing possibilities.

One effect of satellite images of the earth is that they encourage viewers to view the elements as part of the planet's body, and to imagine unexpected changes as symptomatic of the planet's health. Thunder and lightning are no longer read as the expression of deistic rage (although multicultural Toronto constantly reminds me how relative this assertion is), or as proof of a natural sublime force moving through the universe. Rather, we (by which I mean Western-educated agnostics) view it as a battle between warring physical elements threatening a fragile body, the body of the earth, into which we, as viewers, are doubly implicated in the act of looking. We experience a weather that performs like nature, yet we know it is not "natural," that industrial development has been an active agent in weather composition, and that we are thus both subject and object of its misdemeanors. Like the woman on the table, we become both viewer and viewed through the image of the postpanoptic planet. Like her, we see almost to the center of things, extended through a postphotographic surveillance that penetrates surfaces and finds new optimizable realities. Like her, our double identity as clinical subject and observer is mediated by a scientific instrument which brings hidden truths into view. Just as her body disappears, like a ghostly container, behind the fetus, so we discover our own invisible culpability in the act of display. Those extensions of ourselves with which we share the planet—the hamburgers, air conditioners, chemicals, "e-waste," and factory farms destroying the atmosphere inside and out—are nowhere to be seen in these images. We see empty landscapes pregnant with weather, and defer gratefully to the lens's pragmatic achievement.

As we know from the look of TV weather reports, meteorology has been quick to employ new space-based digital and observational technologies as they develop. In fact, meteorology was the first practical (by which they mean "nonmilitary") application of NASA's satellites and satellite-based technologies when they were first deployed in the 1960s, and it remains their most prominent client. Observations from satellites "transcended the atmosphere, which opened up a whole new field of scientific endeavour. . . . Before space-based satellites, weather tracking and predictions had been sketchy at best, relying solely on ground observation and sightings from ships and planes, with great geographic areas of the planet left unreported. Now satellites could record developments all over the earth."[16] This improved capacity meant that "any person on earth could be located immediately by satellite [and] parts of the earth that had never been photographed could now be mapped."[17] These satellites quickly became a central resource for the Weather Bureau, part of what was optimistically described as a "range of revolutionary commercial services reliant on the use of outer space [involving] the sharing of technology and operating systems with all the countries of the earth, the establishment of multinational corporations, and joint satellite ventures by over fifty cooperating countries."[18] The improvement in weather forecasting was less dramatic than expected, as previously noted, "not because of the quality or quantity of image data provided by weather satellites, but because of the lack of a model of the atmosphere exact enough to make reliable weather predictions even from plentiful data."[19]

The weather service was NASA's first commercial application; television and then the Internet became the weather service's most important customer after the military. Meteorology is thus ideal ground and favored progeny of growing tactical alliances between satellite-based optical technologies and communications, data processing, computer graphics, and commercial television, each of which has become technically and economically essential to the survival and growth of the other. Television culture would not be the same without satellites, because the distance it traverses makes satellite transmission indispensable. In turn, satellite communications are impossible without advanced computer programs; space exploration would not have obtained adequate political backing without various "useful applications" which are also useful to military missions; and weather makes lousy TV without computer graphics. This is finally how we have to understand these images. They are social constructions arising from the complex imperatives and alliances of three interdependent industries: paramilitary space exploration, computer software, and television. Following the so-called Revolution in Military Affairs guiding the Pentagon since the mid-1990s,[20] these functions are increasingly integrated with military needs. Because these institutions need each other more than we need them, we have the weather forecast. Thus (echoing George Orwell once again) we learn to celebrate science while forgiving its errors on a daily basis.

Yet what the images evoke is more compelling and eloquent than all this would suggest. For satellite views of the earth's surface show us not only the weather (if you are trained to read them) but also the following: This is one planet, one life, one world, one dream. This is the view of the globe from the eye of God. This is the promise of earth without its wars and bestiaries. This is our planet, its orbs humming with light and shadow in praise of the benevolent eyes of the celestial panopticon. This is the magic of a revitalized myth of origins, addressing us personally in our domestic spaces and rituals of the every day, but still in possession of its mysterious, inaccessible, distant power. This is the gorgeous metaphysical triumph of the technological sublime, displaying itself in perfect harmony with the arcane laws of nature. Satellite images of the planet are thus a contemporary version of what Walter Benjamin termed the aestheticization of politics, a concept he first used to critique his contemporaries' "avid romanticization of the technology of death."[21]

In a review of a 1925 collection of essays entitled *War and Warrior*, edited by the conservative Ernst Junger, Benjamin anticipates with horror the technical innovations that would permit "the tongue twisting chemical vocabularies" of the new killing tools being manufactured in Germany. Like the Futurists, Junger "relished the dramatic colours of gas and fire, exploding fireworks and the metallized nature of the battlefield" and responded to their display as a "new techno-sublimity."[22] Writes Martin Jay: "Noting its contributors' avid romanticization of the technology of death and the total mobilization of the masses, [Benjamin] warned that it was 'nothing other than an uninhibited translation of the principles of l'art pour l'art to war itself.'"[23] Like gas and fire, satellite images of the planet were not created to serve purely spectacular ends, any more than the immersive environments of contemporary digital simulation were created purely for artists' projects or video games. But their rich polysemic beauty travels well from their conditions of origin, fueling the iconographic arsenals of divergent social formations. The United States' National Aeronautics and Space Administration, global telecommunications groups, nongovernmental organizations, scientists, and environmentalists translate the visual-virtual accomplishments of the military-entertainment complex into an instantly recognizable icon of world peace, ecological interdependency, and love for a fragile planet, Gaia. James Lovelock, the founder of the Gaia theory, claims that the concept came to him when he was inspired by the first photographic views of earth from space. "Ancient belief and modern knowledge have fused emotionally in the awe with which astronauts with their own eyes and we by indirect vision have seen the Earth revealed in all its shining beauty against the deep darkness of space."[24] This earth as Gaia is a biospheric "self-regulating entity with the capacity to keep our planet healthy by controlling the chemical and physical environnment."[25] The simple and self-sufficient enormity of this system (Lovelock hopes, comparing earth simultaneously to cybernetic systems and the human body) demonstrates that it can survive whatever we might do to it.[26] But we will need better information-processing capacities and better feedback loops between space travelers and earth-based model builders to understand how the earth-as-system works and how it would be possible to manage its future. As industrial society increases its consumption of energy, Lovelock suggests, we have increased our "responsibility for maintaining planetary homeostasis," but such an obligation depends on the successful application of cybernetics to the analysis of the system as a whole.

Once again the science of weather exemplifies and advances a model for successful information management. "Present-day weather forecasting makes use of the most comprehensive and reliable data-gathering network yet available," Lovelock asserts, "the most powerful computers in the world, and some of the most talented and able members of our society. Yet with how much certainty can the weather be predicted even a month ahead, let alone into the next century?"[27] What is important here is not a particular forecasting function, but the ecology of managerial functions implied by the imaging of space. The photograph of planet Earth inspires us by communicating "our optimal role in relation to other forms of life around us."[28] This "optimal role" involves increased vigilance on the part of us humans. But which humans, what kind of vigilance? To take this discussion beyond cybernetic management, it is necessary to locate the source of the aestheticization of power involved in the production of these images. As the image of the planet emerges from what was previously invisible, the instruments producing the image grow lighter, more mobile, more elusive. As Virilio argues, "visibility and invisibility now began to evolve together, eventually producing invisible weapons that make things visible—radar, sonar, and the high-definition camera of spy satellites."[29] James Der Derian describes the "technostrategic origins" of surveillance technologies in terms of "the perpetual dream of power to have its way without the visible exercise of will that would produce resistance."[30] Coker describes the Pentagon's embrace of "postconflict" fighting of wars as the intent to mold information, weapons, and peoples into an all-encompassing network "greater than the sum of its parts."[31] This new regime contributes to "a cybernetic system that displayed the classic symptoms of advanced paranoia. . . . We see and hear the other, but imperfectly and partially—*below* our rising expectations."[32]

The first photograph of the whole planet Earth, taken on November 10, 1967, is said to have inspired the impulse to save the planet. Photograph by NASA.

In fusing together monumental technological, commercial, and military resources, the panoptic lens arouses ecological awakening *and* cybernetic management, and the militarized technological sublime is reharmonized as a planetary icon.

"We look at earth differently," claims SPAR Aerospace in a national magazine advertisement, "to guide our challenges in the 21st century." The image is a distant planet emerging from darkness. "Pictures from space of our planet Earth have been instrumental during the past 15 years in increasing the awareness of the earth as a finite resource," boasts the photo album advertisement in *National Science and Technology Week*, a special 1992 newspaper supplement on Canada in space.[33] The publication was part of a combined government and industry campaign to increase Canada's investment in space technologies, whose technical and economic imperatives are reorganizing countries and industries into dependent entities propelled ceaselessly forward by the global pressures of the joint corporate-military enterprise.

Satellites and the Theory
of Reverse Adaptation

Information produced by satellite-based optics has scientific, commercial, and military importance. As the history of mapmaking and of more contemporary observational technologies shows, the needs of scientific, commercial, and military interests are increasingly difficult to distinguish. As distance and connection are produced by one technology (the railroad, the radio, satellites), another emerges to master a more distant space. Space exploration continues a trajectory that begins with the mapping of the unfamiliar territories of the New World. Such exploration has combined with modern science to produce useful knowledge through which ever more distant spaces are brought into administrative reach.

The development of technical capacities for producing images of land from a distance laid the foundation for Canada's technical niche in American space research. Climate and territory are widely cited as motivation for and subject of Canada's most important contribution to space science: remote sensing technologies, which ride piggyback on NASA satellites to produce brilliantly improved images of the earth's surfaces. These technologies make possible beautiful landscapes of the earth's surface in which changes in the atmosphere, topography, and vegetation, or human and mechanical activity, can be detected from many miles above our heads. This colorful digital landscape is also put to work as a metonym for our uniquely cosmopolitan, multicultural, and globally sensitive nationhood, realizing symbolically and materially the fusion of a continental technoapparatus with the land of a nation defined as here and nowhere else. Threatening to override this sentimental link to national history is the satellite view's privileged status as metonym for global technocratic power and thus (paradoxically once again) out of our hands.

The first American satellite was sent up in 1958, the year Eisenhower formed NASA to administer the space race of the United States with Russia. The space administration was fraught with contradictory pressures: for national prestige (four months after becoming president, Kennedy committed NASA to placing a man on the moon and bringing him back by the end

The Atlas of Canada 1906-2006 L'Atlas du Canada

"Atlas 1906–2006." This Canadian stamp, launched in 2006 to celebrate the history of Canadian mapmaking, echoes the visual geometry of satellite measurement.

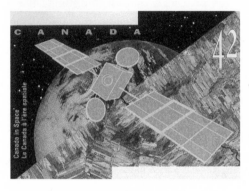

"Canada in Space," 1992. This stamp celebrates Canada's widely celebrated, publicly subsidized contribution to space exploration, the CANADARM, which is currently for sale to a United States military contractor.

of the decade); for scientific research and development in space, portions of which had been taken over from the Pentagon; and last, for what was called "applications," including weather satellites containing meteorological instruments, the first of NASA's applications programs to be put into operation.[34] Its genealogy exemplifies what Winner calls the process of "reverse adaptation": with a complex technological system in place you search for applications, and thus reverse the conventional relationship of means and end.[35] In earlier chapters I have explored the relevance of this trope to the development of sound reproduction technologies. The interdependency of satellite surveillance and weather forecasting provides another example: a visible end for an emergent technological means.

Early in the development of space research, Canada committed itself to developing and interpreting satellite communications, initially to help communicate across the vast regions of the country's north. Canada was the third country in the world to launch a satellite, Alouette 1, in 1962. In 1972, the launch of Anik A1 made Canada the first nation to place a do-

U.S. stamp, 1981. "The duty of intelligence is to be the eyes of the state."

mestic satellite in geostationary orbit. At the same time, Canadian earth-observation technologies were being tested on United States satellites. The process of reverse adaptation acquired a spatial dimension through military and civilian exploitation in the northern part of the hemisphere. Aerial photography had been an important part of military and commercial activity from as early as the 1920s; by the 1930s the National Research Council was developing equipment for plotting maps from highly oblique aerial photographs and a stereoscopic plotter. Canada's Air Force activity was concentrated on photographic surveying during the First World War.[36] The ability to display the country from above made Canada visualizable as an integrated, differentiated whole. RADARSAT was designed to continue Canada's expertise in aerial optics, introducing a new generation of remote sensing from space and raising earth surveillance capabilities to a new level.

Canadian scientists pioneered the use of satellites to observe, map, and communicate with remote areas that were previously out of bounds for geological science or electronic media. Communications and aerial photography were by the 1960s well established as Canadian fields of expertise. Space research activities quickly focused on these as an appropriate means to develop a science and technology sector useful to continental investors. Through the North American Air/Aerospace Defense Agreement (NORAD, initially signed in 1958) and other agreements, Canada's partnership in continental defense research has greatly enriched companies and universities specializing in aerial surveillance, optics, and measurement.

Canada's vast topography and small population are said to provide a geo-physical destiny that "naturally" compels scientists to map, survey, represent, and communicate across the mountains, the tundra, or the ice fields. Today this expertise is harnessed by larger projects funded by NASA, the U.S. and Canadian departments of defense, and the European Space Agency.

The implosion of land, landscape, and LANDSAT witnessed by these im-ages can be understood metonymically as evidence of the same dynamic paradox that shaped Canadian broadcasting. Canada built one of the most technically sophisticated communication infrastructures in the world, de-signed to reach remote regions of the north with the purpose of extending citizenship to those it could not be profitable for private broadcasters to reach. It became, in what communication historians term a "tragic paradox," a superb vehicle for the dissemination of American television. Similarly, the satellites that provide weather data to Canadian meteorological services are no longer owned by Canada. In this context, the "natural" logic of east-west continental space is re-adapted to a "natural" continental system through a relationship that is at once geographical, technological, administrative, and cultural. Canada is constituted by a specific topography, which it brings to earth through a continental aerial gaze. The United States continues to take its borders—topographic, technical, even meteorological—for granted.

North of Empire

In 1961, President Eisenhower made a "Farewell Address to the Nation" warning his listeners of the increasing power of the "military-industrial complex" and "its ability to shape U.S. foreign policy."[37] In 1967, Prime Minister Pearson spoke strongly against the militarization of space by the superpowers, arguing that "the deployment of such a system would be an enormously costly undertaking, which, in the end, would probably lead, as the ballistic-missile race did, to ever-mounting defense budgets without any permanent increase in national security or international stability."[38] Five months later, Robert McNamara announced that the United States would proceed with the "Sentinel" Anti-Ballistic Missile (ABM) system. Pearson "regretted very much" the American decision, but would not rule out the possibility that Canada might eventually participate in such a system. Government positions taken in 1968 and in following years followed this pattern, expressing political disapproval of ballistic missile defense systems while being reluctant to take a firm position against them, particularly once specific plans had been undertaken in Washington.

Like Pearson, Prime Minister Trudeau enacted an ambivalent approach, asking the UN to ban space weaponry altogether, while on the other hand, "refusing to rule out Canadian participation in the SDI program. Indeed, [his government] has gone somewhat further in positively endorsing SDI 'research' while continuing to express reservations about actual 'development and deployment.'"[39] In a 1985 report on "Canada's Territorial Air Defense," the Senate Committee on National Defense again warned against major commitments to ballistic missile defense, arguing that the project was exceedingly costly and antithetical to the ABM Treaty. It would "run counter to the spirit of current arms control accords concerning outer space and might well destroy any hope of establishing new accords banning space weaponry." Canada should avoid becoming a "junior partner" in the United States military space program, the committee maintained, and limit its activities to "passive detection and surveillance."[40]

One could assemble an inspiring anthology of such globally attuned, politically moderate statements by Canada's leaders. They advance a philosophy of foreign policy centered on internationalism, multilateralism, and diplomacy. Yet, actual foreign policy has moved toward a "more assertive free-trade-oriented economic foreign policy; a diminished concern for sovereignty except where tested by national-unity crises involving Quebec; and a broadening view of security to include environmental threats and sustainable development."[41] The willingness to engage in paramilitary research and innovation is part of the rise of "trade-led internationalization," which was attended by a number of political changes, including the move of trade to the foreign ministry (1982), the collapse of foreign policy into the larger context of security and defense, the decrease in federal budget assigned to foreign policy, and the increased influence of business interest group lobbies in the development of foreign policy.[42] These developments helped to create the political context in which negotiations for the initial Canada–United States Free Trade Agreement were conducted. The pattern evident in 1985 remains the same today: Canada expresses "concern and commentary" about military space projects; it demonstrates "a current ambiguity in policy reflecting the tension between Canadian preferences and those of the U.S. Government"; and it expresses far stronger and "more forthright" criticism before policy has been confirmed in Washington. As Purver says politely, "it is easier for Canada to make known its reservations on this subject before actual decisions have been made to go beyond the research phase."[43]

Popular opinion opposes the militarization of space, even in the aftermath of 9/11, as well as Canada's involvement with it. While the Conservative prime minister Steven Harper has carefully avoided this topic in talks with the White House, the research consortium attached to the Canadian department of defense continues to follow principles of bilateral defense and research cooperation established by NORAD. Why has public opinion not resulted in an autonomous national defense policy? This anomaly needs to be understood in its economic and geopolitical context. Between 1959 and 1983, the U.S. Department of Defense spent $160 billion on military space programs, and a separate $308 billion dollars on NASA. Between 1984 and 2002, the United States spent over $311 billion on military space programs through the Department of Defense. If you combine this expenditure with the NASA budget for the same period, 1984–2002, together with "other" space funding, American expenditures on space research amount to $570 billion dollars during this period.[44] O'Hanlan calculates the total United States expenditure on space defense between 1959 and 2002 at approximately 1 trillion, 106 million, 200,000 dollars.[45]

The "pathological prosperity" suggested by these sums has been part of a massive state subsidy to high-technology industrial research in the United States. It has "generated breakthroughs in medicine, computer software design, and laser technology, which U.S. private capital then sought to exploit commercially. At the same time, it acted as a slush fund for projects which failed to win support elsewhere."[46] This astronomical level of state investment provides space technology needs with unequaled power to determine scientific, technological, and economic activity within the United States and (with various degrees of coercion) in countries engaged with trade and security relationships with them. It is no accident then that, according to a 1995 government statement on foreign policy, "states have been increasingly willing to enter into agreements that voluntarily cede aspects of economic sovereignty." As Bruce Doern and John Kirton note in their summary of this text, "Together with the information highway and cross-border individual and group ties, technological innovations, and the outward-looking political and economic policies, [international capital markets] diminish the 'ability of states to act independently since they can no longer isolate themselves from the world without unacceptable domestic consequences.'"[47] Of course, joining "the world" on these terms also has domestic consequences.

As Ann Denholm Crosby's research on NORAD demonstrates, the Cold War exerted "significant determining effects on Canada's defense policy decision-making" and continues to shape its conception, administration, and command.[48] Cooperation between the United States and Canada during the Cold War laid the groundwork for ongoing defense-related production in five respects. First, the Canadian defense production industry depends on the United States for sales, research and development contracts, and special privileges in connection with American defense production. Second, ongoing cooperation between the two countries has encouraged firms from the United States to establish subsidiary firms in Canada, which adds further American voices friendly to American interests to the Canadian industrial lobby. Third, military production cooperation has encouraged a growing coincidence of economic interests between the Canadian government and the defense production industry. "An industry that is on the leading edge of high-tech production contributes substantially . . . to employment, to the country's GNP, and to industrial competitiveness, which reflects positively in Canada's international balance of trade figures."[49] Fourth, these industry representatives play an important role in the formulation of defense policy. And fifth, Canadian and United States military personnel "assume positions in the corporate structures of the defense production industry upon retirement from the military, . . . [bringing] a history of cooperative relationships forged in joint military projects and programs." These developments have cultivated a Canadian defense production industry that depends on the United States for sales, research, and development contracts. United States subsidiaries north of the border increase American influence in the Canadian military-industrial lobby and strengthen the "coincidence of economic interests between the Canadian government and the Canadian defense production industry," which further enhances military industry influence on government policy.[50]

In light of these facts, it is pointless to separate international capital markets from U.S. government policy in terms of space research and what used to be called its technological spinoffs. Canada must secure its place in this high-technology marketplace, or it will be left far behind, frozen, as former progressive Conservative prime minister Mulroney said of Canada should its citizens reject the Free Trade Agreement with the United States, in the headlights of progress. Citizens might be slow to come to terms with this reality, but the government is up to speed. Repeated renewals of NORAD sustain the context and terms of reference for extensive cooperation between Canada and the United States in space-based defense. For military, technological, and increasingly economic reasons, Canada participates actively in American military planning and production in space. The Defense Research and Development Canada (DRDC) consortium, formed in 1994, is dedicated to "ensur[ing] that the Canadian Forces (CF) remain technologically prepared and relevant." Together with "Canadian industry, universities, other national partners and our allies," the DRDC promises to "contribute to defense modernization by demonstrating the use of technology for defense solutions."[51]

The Reagan administration announced the launching of the "Star Wars" outer-space "defense" project in 1983, on the same day *Star Wars: Return of the Jedi* was released in theaters across the United States. Since that day the American discourse of national security has been strongly tied to the military superiority of vision technologies and the power to rule outer space. Such projects entice viewers to believe that they (or by extension, their government) can safely assume the viewpoint of the angels, perfectly informed and unseen above the earth and that by virtue of this power, their safety and authority is assured. Derek Ellington, a Canadian policy advisor, formerly with the Weapons Division of Canadair before becoming director of scientific and technological strategic planning for Canada's Department of National Defence (DND), offered a far more pragmatic rationale to convince a 1983 conference of government and corporate leaders of the importance of space.

> Canada, as a member of the Western Alliance, will become increasingly dependent on a strong technological infrastructure to support her commitments to collective defense. Yet, paradoxically, that very infrastructure is the essential element needed to build a reliable lifeline to a sound economic future. Clearly in the years ahead, industrial strategies will need to be devised which accommodate the parallel, and indivisible, objectives of national security and national socio-economic development. Space is one area that holds considerable promise.[52]

NASA's Apollo program was more than recompensed, the author notes, by savings that accrued through the use of space in such areas as weather information, agricultural development, resource exploitation, and communications. Future uses will include mining the asteroids situated between Mars and Jupiter; mining and processing resources on the moon; space colonies; and the use of laser beams transmitted from satellites to propel aircraft and spacecraft. "As always," Ellington concludes, "military applications will likely continue to pace technological progress."[53]

The report from which these predictions are drawn highlights the theme of paradox and contradiction that defines Canada's approach to this prospect. "High technology is recognized as a key determinant of social progress and economic well-being," Ellington writes, "and it seems *paradoxical* that the attainment of these socio-economic objectives should be paced by an impetus arising from military needs."[54] The paradox arises from the conflict between the nation's rhetorical commitment to diplomacy, peace, and social and economic well-being, and its transnational military commitments. Space technology magically resolves this conflict by contributing simultaneously to both objectives. This solution has created a consensus on policy and research in the "high-tech" arena that justifies itself by reference to a "trickle-down" effect connecting military research to employment, research, manufacture, and GNP. According to this logic, military cooperation with United States space research and defense is crucial for the viability of a peaceful, nonmilitary sovereign nation and its civilian well-being. The ethical paradox of this arrangement (to which each successive government pays necessary lip service) is outweighed by the political-economic imperative of attracting investment in technological innovations with possible military applications. The foundational Cold War logic of the NORAD agreement thus continues to inform relations between government, industry, and university research today, notwithstanding the technological changes transforming the landscapes of war.

This is how the paradox works. Space technologies are so complex that they require huge technical and political investments, which have major implications for the economy. This investment is justified by the idea that we in the West are a democracy unlike our enemies who (being undemocratic) spend more than they can afford on space. To defend ourselves from aggressive hostile forces, we have to develop competitive capabilities and R&D in high tech industries, which will have dramatic implications for public policy and industrial strategy. Satellite surveillance, aerospace robotics, fiber optics, digital image processing, robotics, and virtual reality technologies are hypothetically useful to any government, corporation, or individual who can pay the price for them (and the more of these, the better). Fortunately the development of these expensive and potentially destructive capabilities, for which government spends more than it can afford, has economic benefits which will trickle down to the rest of society, since we are a democracy.

Canada's military advisors are not necessarily thinking of this irony when they call space a "paradox of opportunity." If we continue to develop peaceable space technologies, they argue, we can simultaneously advance our technological resources, increase our usable knowledge of nature, develop peaceful and profitable spinoffs, and keep our place in the continental military-economic system. They would approve of my dentist, who can fill my teeth with nontoxic white matter and X-ray them from outside my head because of research in space. Their position is an indirect acknowledgment that Canada is itself a kind of satellite, a poor relative with higher altitude and moral consciousness whose economic survival depends on remaining useful to the surveillance requirements of continental military defense. Once again Canada disseminates its humanist impulse through its technocratic trajectory. Governance travels from the imperatives of continental technical systems to the policies of the state, rather than, as any sensible person might wish, in the reverse direction.

In the 1990s, space policy advisors more neutrally emphasized the Canadian government's growing needs for "surveillance over a variety of activities through her vast and largely uninhabited area and the approaches thereto."[55] Like other middle powers, Canada called for "internationally controlled satellites that would verify arms control agreements and monitor troop movements."[56] Military and corporate research policies were linked by the need to equip armed forces of the future with the most advanced equipment, whose selection "must be based primarily on the requirements for security," but which should be able to "perform tasks that make valuable contributions to the country in times of peace." Nonmilitary threats cited in this scenario include environmental degradation and international drug traffic, whose monitoring calls for the same technologies as those needed to verify arms control agreements and other surveillance and monitoring tasks "for national civil as well as defense needs."[57] Our security from unexpected weather, drug traffickers, and Iranian or North Korean military conspiracies was thus assured. The convergence between military and communication technologies has accelerated since the mid-1990s, when the "Revolution in Military Affairs" placed unprecedented emphasis on information supremacy in terrestrial, virtual, and outer space.

Science and technology research, financial growth prodded by the accumulation of information and space technologies, and the commercial exploitation of "defense" contracts increasingly take priority in domains that were once defined as dedicated to the public interest. The trickling down is not economic; it creates technical, cultural, and institutional effects in diverse contexts, including academic institutions. Canada's Expert Panel on the Commercialization of University Research encourages increased traffic between business, government, and university administration, to the extent that distinctions between academic and commercial research grow ever more nebulous.[58] Researchers in the humanities and social sciences have been able until recently to avoid the implications of this shift, for the trend toward commercialization within the academy appears to be driven by economic rather than political concerns, as though the shift to "innovation" was uninformed by state policies. Academics remain cannily agnostic about research alliances between university and corporate partners, accepting them as a pragmatic response to current exigencies rather than recognizing a political process with destructive effects on science, public policy, and academic freedom.[59]

In the 1960s and 1970s, academics who accepted funding from military agencies for research in science, medicine, information, or culture were subject to heated public criticism and exposure.[60] In response to institutional mediators such as the Canadian Research and Development in National Defense and other bodies, it appears to be commercial pressures that circumscribe our research environment. As the former CAUT executive William Bruneau puts it, "Performance indicators encourage universities and governments to strive for instance relevance and industrial utility. . . . At a time of constant pressure to replace public funds with private money, to participate wholeheartedly in private-sector markets of all types, and to use Performance Indicators (PIS) to judge how quickly universities are making these moves—the naïve social mechanics of another era are gone, replaced by knowing neo-liberals."[61] Academics who explore networked spaces, biotechnologies, and the digital frontier appear to be simply helping the university (and themselves) in an era of reduced circumstances. As the expansion and integration of telecommunications and informatics, or telematics, come to dominate technological R&D, the questions of whether or how such research is connected to national defense loses its saliency, and activist critiques of university-military complicity lose their bite. After all, the commercialization of knowledge makes research "accessible."[62]

My university supports and promotes a number of laboratories dedicated to space research, focusing (as Canadian tradition warrants) on vision, optics, and virtual reality. Weekly press releases promote consortiums made up of university and corporation joint initiatives in various areas of outer-space technology and science. Lacking access to university records, we don't always know who funds these projects and to what ends.[63] We see that scholars who conduct research on or with "new technology" are rewarded with lucrative grants, research chairs, laboratories, and teaching exemptions while the classrooms of their colleagues swell and rumble. The income generated by such research is described as an important source of support for higher education. Needless to say, this is an ideological as much as it is a fiscal truth.[64]

Rods from God

For American religious fundamentalists, America is singularly and uniquely blessed, but the sky above them is perceived as empty of benign spirits and friendly visitations. Space is the last frontier, the zone in which the final battles will be won. "The United States," declared the White House as it inaugurated Star Wars,

> will pursue activities in space in support of its right of self-defense. . . .
>
> The United States considers the space systems of any nation to be national property with rights of passage through and operation in space without interference. Purposeful interference with space systems shall be viewed as an infringement upon sovereign rights.[65]

In this statement, new sectors of outer space are being constructed as territorial extensions of empire for the purposes of battle. The UN General Assembly had already passed the 1963 "Declaration of Legal Principles Governing the Activities of States in the Exploration and Use of Outer Space," which insists that "No sovereignty or ownership can be claimed in space."[66]

In 1967, such principles were materialized as law with the passage of the UN "Treaty on Principles Governing the Activities of States in the Exploration and Use of Outer Space, including the Moon and other Celestial Bodies," or the Outer Space Treaty. This treaty's second article specifies that "Outer space, including the Moon and other celestial bodies, is not subject to national appropriation by claim of sovereignty, by means of use or occupation, or by any other means." As Helen Caldicott and Craig Eisendrath hopefully add, "The modern counterparts of King Ferdinand and Queen Isabella will not own outer space."[67]

The UN passed another agreement in 1979, the "Agreement Governing the Activities of States on the Moon and Other Celestial Bodies," prohibiting any country from claiming, occupying, or using celestial bodies for military activity. However, many countries have not ratified it. Despite these international treaties and laws requiring peaceful uses of outer space, "the United States, in particular, the most technologically sophisticated country in the world, continued to explore expanding military uses of outer space.... Decades of military research finally surfaced in the 1990s, when outer-space satellites became involved not only in target identification but in a whole new area: guiding weapons to their targets." As Caldicott and Eisendrath note, the "smart bombs" employed in the 1991 Gulf War could overcome bad weather and fire from extreme distances without pilots, and cost relatively little—"a bonanza of long-distance killing, courtesy of space-based satellites."[68]

Today the satellite gaze is being superseded by integrated webs of telematic interconnectivity through which all entities connect under the powerful supervision of a central host. The newest weapons designed for the war in space are the so-called Rods from God, comprised of a pair of satellites orbiting several hundred miles above the earth. One side functions as a targeting and communications platform while the other carries tungsten rods that can be dropped on targets with less than fifteen minutes' notice. When instructed from the ground computer, the targeting satellite commands its partner to drop its darts. The guided rods enter the atmosphere at 36,000 feet per second, comparable to the speed of a meteor. Like a cell phone in a horror film, it locates and destroys its target even if it's buried deep underground.[69] By developing weapons specifically designed to be deployed in outer space, the United States is defying international efforts to ban such weapons and encouraging other countries to develop defensive arsenals.

"Rods from God," a proposal for satellite-based tungsten
weaponry orbiting hundreds of miles above the earth.
Photograph courtesy of John MacNeill.

Thus the paradox of space research extends beyond this or any nation's borders. As Caldicott and Eisendrath argue, "If the United States does indeed
weaponize the heavens, it will put at risk the entire new world of global
communications, weather prediction, mapping and location, and scientific
exploration. And weapons once employed will eventually be used; that is
the history of the human race."[70]

Members of the previous Canadian Parliament voted against participation in the Star Wars initiative, and an overwhelming majority of Canadians
oppose such collaboration. The government of Canada says there are no
weapons deployed there as yet, so why not help lay the technical foundations? Are telematics-cybernetic optics, communicating robots, and satellite communications not part of our own communication infrastructure?
Meanwhile the White House wonders, why does this neighboring country
refuse to defend itself in space? When these weapons are mobilized, as they
must be once so much capital is expended upon them, whom will they attack, and whom will they defend? These instruments of flight register and
invite threat. Their inventors are afraid of the sky which they have liberated

for their own purposes. They are afraid that what they have raised up will fall back down. This is where war and ecocatastrophe collide.

The Weather Forecast

We have traveled some distance in this discussion of the weather forecast. Today's forecast can be seen to be continuous with the modern scientific approach to weather and climate, which sought to map and measure the natural elements in order to develop greater control over their effects. European science began to measure climate and temperature in the seventeenth century at least in part because of new questions and needs created by travel. Canadian exploration and research set the technical framework and goals for Canadian science and technology to explore and connect Canada's unique climate and topography. The popularity of weather forecasts has helped to legitimate huge expenditures on space and telematic technologies which will extend a mainly military genesis and purpose.

Continuous satellite-based weather forecasts add twenty-four hours to a four-day forecast, but predictions are still wrong over 20 percent of the time. They also create a lucrative market for satellite surveillance services that otherwise would have to be funded entirely by government and military agencies. Our everyday need and aesthetic appreciation for these services (much aided by the entertaining sophistication and gorgeousness of constantly improving visuals and computer graphics, for which we pay with our television and cable bills as well as our taxes) are both facilitators and by-products of space and defense policy and are threatened by this same policy. Weather forecasts rely on a set of technological tools originating in what, in this context, it still makes sense to call the military-industrial complex—everything from satellites, radar, and other optical equipment to software and television itself—whose socially beneficial applications are thereby demonstrated on a daily basis. The forecast we have come to know and love depends on near-instantaneous telematic transformation of extremely distant atmospheric data into two-dimensional images on a monitor. Military and civilian research on space technology continue to emphasize the need to expand and accelerate this capability and to point to commercial applications in the development of new frontiers. While journalists ponder Stephen Hawking's recommendation that earth should colonize space before it implodes, space researchers ponder whether corporations or nations should be allowed to lay claim to the planets waiting to be colonized. Since the Outer Space Treaty prohibits territorial sovereignty, they argue, private investors, not NASA or other public agencies, should rule the development of space territories.[71]

Yet there are signs of rupture in the political and institutional contexts in which such science is produced. Growing concern about global warming and the complicity of many industrial products in producing this threat; opportunistic attempts to develop and profit from satellite-monitoring devices that can track such changes; lack of human security in the face of high-risk environments; the proliferation of e-waste; and lunatic fantasies for settling or commercializing space are all potential storms in the placid atmosphere of the planetary orbit. Such problems have not troubled the aura of the planetary image because part of its magic is its distance from these travails. As Hannah Arendt observes, "Modern humanity's submission to the call of the distant has succeeded in shrinking the earth into a ball. The earth converges to a ball in space, to a mathematical point within a scheme of universal motion, to the degree that we withdraw ourselves from it."[72] Satellite images of the earth remain compelling because they signify a longed-for reunification of science and art at the disposal of the viewing subject. They offer the pleasure of panoramic distance and the spectacularization of landscape by means of which imaging technologies culminate 200 years of colonial geography.[73] They resanctify yet qualify longstanding gender-based metaphors of earth and observer by elevating the act of perception into the higher reaches of cosmic science, and they remind us of the utopian possibility of a grounded universal totality. Most of all, their power to draw our gaze derives from their very ambiguity, the way these images oscillate with perfect majestic equivocation between sublime beauty and unseen powers of scrutiny and domination, the way they stand for, and between, an inhabitable world in lasting harmony, a connected world united by digital intelligence, and a distant world of smart and desultory death.

Cultural Technologies and the "Evolution" of Technological Cultures

If evolution cannot rationally be viewed as a way to get from ape-like creatures to man, then cannot the use of evolutionism as an ideological belief system get us from man to an ape-like creature? Such a capability would be of enormous value in politics.—PETER MEDAWAR, *The Future of Man*

The arrival of the new millennium was accompanied by a fanfare of pronouncements and speculations about our technologically enhanced future. The association between new technology and progress unified otherwise quite disparate voices: business and feature writers in the daily press; government and the broader arena of public policy; postmodernist and "cyberfeminist" manifestos; television and science documentaries; university and arts administrators; granting agencies for academic research and the fine arts; and the more overtly spectacular entertainments offered up by science fiction, children's television, and the military. It seemed impossible to avoid or reject the invitation to participate in revolutionizing the world through technological innovation. Following the 9/11 attack on New York, which revealed the failure of high-tech security measures, together with increasing concern about the environment and anxiety about children and youth so wired they forget who or where they are, the unanimity of public discourse has faded. Nevertheless, I stand by the argument this chapter makes. The scene may have shifted, but in the context of educational, scientific, telematic, and cultural technologies, the tune remains the same.

The consensus of these discourses is that digital and networking technologies have the capacity to reorder every domain of social and personal life, transforming gender and the body politic, work and knowledge, health and science, domestic life and entertainment, national economies and international relations, democracy and the distribution of power. If teleology has vacated the discourses of history, religion, and even science; if utopia has expired in the cultural imaginary, as many critics now believe, this is only so that it can gather and condense in the narrative of "technoevolution," which draw us irresistibly toward the holographic world of technological futures.[1] I cannot read these texts without appraising their claims against the world we live in. As the institutions that govern our everyday lives invest millions in network technologies, global military expenditures surpass $1 trillion a year, with the United States and its "Revolution in Military Affairs" spending more than all other countries combined. The transnational corporations involved in this project hold unprecedented power over the political process. These corporations effectively set the boundaries for the possible in every sector once considered (on this side of the border, at least) public interest. Their foraging habits are destroying the habitat of the planet, while their technological achievements have done less than promised to enhance its population's abilities to scrutinize, reflect upon, and collectively change their environments.

The belief in the technological revolutionization of society is not new, but there have been some alterations in its terms of reference. For Serge Moscovici, writing in the 1960s, new technology "signals a new moment in mankind's consciousness of its role in instituting natural processes and regulating its own structure in relation to them." Here ecology and human self-regulation are seen to be moving toward unity: "Ecology will be truly political when it admits that what is characteristic of our history is to choose among the states of nature that exist at a given moment."[2] Similarly, drawing on the idea of a posthuman ecology, Edgar Morin asserts that technologically mediated systems ecology has the capacity to "civilize civilization," a claim echoed in the work of Alain Lipietz, Guattari, and other ecological humanists.[3] Such cybernetic systems have enabled us to know states of nature in new ways, as we have seen with the weather, but they don't seem to be "civilizing" society in the more general scheme of things. Of course evolution never works as intelligibly as neo-Darwinists have implied, and the history of human-machine relations is no exception. As the "Information Age" matures, computers and cell phones fill the classrooms and homes across the continent. By the time a user graduates into the next grade, these tools will have been tossed into toxic landfill in favor of newer models. While children are increasingly screen literate, educators claim that their verbal, mathematical, and social skills are declining. Their cognitive and social skills are so altered by these wired worlds that a moral panic is arising around them. Many don't know how to read and have no idea how to find themselves on a map. While these children are ready to toss out their digital toys after half a year, millions of children live below the poverty index and suffer from poor health, malnutrition, and poisoned environments. While some children leap into the future, others die in its debris.

New research on biotechnologies gives a jump-start to the evolutionary process in the name of advancing health and freedom. While such research has expanded reproductive choices for women, few women are economically or legally empowered to make such choices meaningful. A 2005 UN Population Fund review revealed that "millions of women are still dying from preventable complications of pregnancy, as well as abuse and neglect. . . . In 2003, donor governments spent $69 billion (U.S.) on development aid. That same year, global military spending totaled approximately $1 trillion."[4] Millions of women and children see little change in their life prospects despite these biotechnological advances, many of them deprived of prosperity, health, and physical safety, some of them in my own country, the most wired nation in the world.

Narratives of technological progress continue to reassure anxious subjects that the world's problems can be solved by new technology. The interdependent mantras of innovation and convenience have played a central role in the adoption of new technologies, as earlier chapters of this work have illustrated. "Convenience" seems to involve personal choice—how you travel, how you listen to music, how you practice birth control, how you navigate the city—but it is not a personal preference. "Convenience" is an organizing discourse that plays a pivotal role in mobilizing social practices in domestic, cultural, industrial, and "natural" space, making them accessible to corporate growth through the normalization of technological change.[5] Addressing the strategic link between capitalism, technology, and convenience in postwar North America, the philosopher George Grant warned that corporate leaders would "seek a justice which is congruent with those conveniences, and gradually sacrifice the principles of liberty and equality when they conflict with the greater conveniences." In his commentary on Grant in *Technology and the Canadian Mind*, Arthur Kroker adds that "'Injustice for the very weak' is the political price to be paid for the unfolding of the technical age as the broader destiny of the liberal account of justice."[6] If Grant's prognosis seems too bleak for forward-looking thinkers, we need new evidence to prove him wrong.

In this chapter, I explore the narrative of technological evolution as a cultural technology that extends the production of space into the digital frontier. Digital technology is constantly changing, but the hopes and fears played upon in its promotion are not. Such promotion represents the strategic articulation of two discursive fields, biology and religion, within the dominant framework of technological progress.[7] If biology and religion are still opposed in the pedagogies of the Christian Right, the digital "revolution" has benefited from its ability to replay central themes of early Christianity. Early enthusiasts emphasized cyberspace's capacity to enable individuals to transcend their physical bodies in a realm "beyond" the physical, and to remake themselves in a free, disembodied virtual space.[8] The idea that special knowledge ensures some kind of transcendent salvation connects the Christian with the technological sublime. As Margaret Wertheim shows, cyberspace was "a repackaging of the old idea of Heaven but in a secular, technologically sanctioned format."[9] Digital utopians are not in search of a godlike entity so much as a new self, reborn in a community in which bodies no longer matter, accessible to anyone regardless of earthly conduct or constraints. In the secular version, the seeker bears no responsibility toward the earthly realm he seeks to leave behind. This is a convenient kind of transcendence; the self is made flexible and free, not just from physical location but also from the mundane requirements associated with place or virtue. This ethos extends the fantasy advanced through the promotion of player pianos, when the piano roll promised to release the music lover from the responsibility to practice, practice, practice (see "The Musicking Machine," chapter 5 in this volume).

Technoevolutionism proposes a digital space emerging from a self-evolving system that expands and changes according to immanent developmental laws. Insofar as technology follows its own evolutionary laws, it subverts or rewrites all others, including evolution itself, which comes to be understood as "the steady advance towards the 'increased complexity of an organization' in which survival *is* information processing."[10] Because it represents a more efficient mode of collecting and analyzing data, the electronic frontier challenges and transcends smaller-scale levels of organization, such as the region, the academy, or the nation-state. Its logic combines total voluntarism (in cyberspace you can be, find, make, or play at anything) and hyperdeterminism (if you don't adapt to this innovation, you are lost). It is this latter threat, the social Darwinist undertow of cybernetic evolutionism, rather than the ecological humanism described by Mendovici and Guattari or the transcendent idealism described by Michael Benedikt and Wertheim, that drives this orientation toward the imaginary future.

Like many publications, the *Toronto Star* entitles its weekly technology section "Fast Forward." There is no time to wait, the title says—jump ahead of where you are, or you will be flattened beneath the headlights of progress. Canada's Department of National Defense publishes an Annual R&D report on science and technology entitled "Looking Forward, Staying Ahead," while the "fast forward" mantra is chanted routinely by university administrations and research-funding bodies. The "forward" promises not just a spatial logic (as we saw in "Writing on the Border" [chapter 1]), but also an intensified temporality in which we must jump ahead of ourselves. With the emergence of the artistic avant-garde, as Antoine Compagnon notes in *The Five Paradoxes of Modernity*, the term *avant-garde* shifts from a spatial to a temporal meaning. "Art desperately clings to the future, no longer seeking to adhere to the present but to get a jump on it in order to inscribe itself in the future . . . art is irrevocably linked to an evolutionary model." With this shift, "the avant-garde, substituting the pathos of the future for acceptance of the present, doubtless activates one of the latent paradoxes of modernity: its claim to self-sufficiency and self-affirmation inexorably leads it to self-destruction and self-negation."[11]

Keeping in mind that self-destruction presents spatial implications at a scale that could not have been anticipated 50 or 100 years ago, this same paradox characterizes the logic of technoevolutionism. According to the rules of this discourse, being ahead resides in technological rather than aesthetic, judicial, ethical, or ecological domains. Digital technologies propel us into postnational, posthuman communities as a consequence of tactics and innovations generated by the evolutionary laws of these same technologies. This evolutionary process contradicts the logic of its biological underpinnings (metaphorical or otherwise) by proceeding independent of its environmental contexts—which in the case of human society involves power, money, risk, and social order as well as ponds, bugs, and predators, as evident in the ways these entities are being poisoned by the toxic waste produced by "made-to-break" patterns of innovation and obsolescence. The Internet progresses faster and faster, its proponents maintain, because it is "a collective cyborg system of individuals and machines, ruled by strict evolutionary laws."[12] In cyberspace, as opposed to pond space, technological reflexivity inevitably advances the rate of progress. This claim situates technoevolutionists as modernists who, like the artistic avant-garde in the early twentieth century, project themselves into a future in which the achievement of their objectives might bring about their own obsolescence.

The technology-biology-evolution connection is so pervasive that its metaphorical nature has become invisible, and evolutionary biology is offered as an objective, scientific model of history, of technological change, and of the necessary trajectory of human nature. Even critical perspectives on technological change are shaped by this trope, so that participants in the discourse begin to perceive evolution solipsistically as both cause and effect of technological change. Within this tautology, the question of whether "evolution" is metaphor, model, or empirical description cannot and need not be answered. The interdisciplinary ascendancy of metaphorical thought has its own role as agent in the new digital media, given their celebrated capacity for what Marshall McLuhan prophetically called "a new tribal encyclopaedia of auditory incantation."[13] Put two or three concepts from different knowledge paradigms next to each other, and it's magic! They become one. Functioning simultaneously as scientific trope and ontological metaphor, the technoevolutionary motif evokes a confidence in science that in part counteracts the disquiet about science and technology haunting North American culture.

Technoevolutionism relies on an analogy between biological and technological evolution whose underlying premises we need to examine. The claim that technological progress creates greater reflexivity in the technical environment invites comparison with the concept of cultural technologies introduced by Foucauldian theorists to describe the orchestrated production of self-conscious social subjects under capitalist modernity. Both paradigms emphasize the productivity of new technologies in creating systemic reflexivity; both point to the ways that such technical systems contribute to the formation of new human subjects. At the same time, these two modes of analysis advance different approaches to history, politics, and nature. My purpose is to orchestrate an encounter between the discourses of technological evolutionism and cultural technologies, and to explore them critically in relation to one another. In the following pages I explore technoevolutionism as a still-hegemonic discourse guiding our understanding of and relationship to technological change. I survey several influential texts connecting biological and technological evolution, and question the assumptions on which their theories are based. I suggest that differences in evolutionary models when applied to culture produce differences in how the future is conceived. My object is finally to consider how the technoevolutionary discourse is itself a "cultural technology" that works in conjunction with the digital information technologies it describes to produce tangible effects in how we think about, socially produce, technologically mediate, and viscerally experience our social and embodied selves.

Future Conditional

Hyperbolic promises for the technological future have played an important role in bringing technologies into use throughout the modern era. Early commentaries imagined dry cleaning by sound waves, colonies on the moon, the transformation of low-income countries into wealthy nations, and the twenty-hour work week. Not so long ago it was thought that

> the smashing of the atom would release cheap energy in abundance; the Pill would limit population growth; computers and automation would do all dirty, dangerous and heavy work in factories and on the land; television would bring education into every home; and telecommunications would link all people on the globe. And once people were freed from dull, stultifying, and dangerous work they would become enlightened and considerate of one another. A new and better age would dawn, hallmarked by humanism, solidarity, and well-being for everyone.[14]

In a similar vein, experts predicted that the so-called Information Revolution would give rise to a leisure society; yet between 1973 and 1994, leisure time declined by 37 percent.[15] By 1995, two-thirds of Canadian workers reported that they were working longer hours compared with a few years earlier; only a quarter of these said they were being paid for the extra effort.[16] Experts predicted that the emergence of the home-based electronic cottage would alleviate urban transportation problems, but subsequent evidence (and daily experience) points to the opposite effect.[17] Today, urban gridlock is held responsible for devastating economic, social, and environmental effects. Commentators claimed that virtual communication would revolutionize gender roles, but the personas roaming the Web replicate the most "stereotypically spectacular" gender stereotypes of the predigital age.[18] Social policy advisers claim that a knowledge-based economy requires an educated workforce, and, while a growing proportion of young people attend university, that institution is being rapidly transformed into a managerial nexus of technocratic encounters and ideas. Advocates predict that computer-mediated communications (CMC) will enable citizens to cast off the hierarchical distortions of the mass media and develop a more genuine alternative democracy. How far this alternative can revive democratic politics, and whether this alternative can affect more than a small part of the world's population, are still in dispute.[19] Others speculated that mass computing would reduce the need for paper and thus encourage a more sustainable environment. Not only did this not occur, but electronic manufacture and waste are more toxic than paper ever was. Cyberspace designers claim that new technologies are going to "make the body obsolete, destroy subjectivity, create new worlds and universes, change the economic and political future of humanity, and even lead to a posthuman order."[20] Whether we find this a plausible prospect, an ambitious utopia, a naïve virtual translation of Adorno's negative dialectic in which humans whirl themselves into hyperrational oblivion, or merely a reminder of the growing redundance of human labor under advanced capitalism, we cannot escape the grandiose speculations in social engineering that inform such claims.

Today such hopes are being revised to address the increased mobility of digital devices that carry connectivity and entertainment into every inhabitable space. As *Time* Magazine puts it: "One of the big trends of 2007 was the idea that computing doesn't belong just in cyberspace, it needs to happen here, in the real world, where actual stuff happens. This is just the beginning."[21] Cyberspace evidently lost its claim to being part of "the real world." If yesterday's technology was guilty of distracting users from "actual stuff," the convergence of mobile digital technologies promises to restore them to a universe in which they once again occupy the center. Just as the focus on "reality" as a measure of representational value led to the toppling of the concept of the real, so the newer focus on "communication" is troubling the larger meanings of the term.[22]

These pundits seem oblivious to the irony of the situation. Anxiety about the indifferent powers of technology and the impersonal environments of large institutions is stimulating a poignant desire for human connectedness. This desire is carefully aroused by the design and promotion of telematic services and commodities that promise a sense of place and community in these new wired "spaces." "Webness," assures Derrick de Kerckhove, is "connectedness."[23] Thus most home-based leisure Internet use is dedicated to electronic mail. In industry-sponsored studies, however, researchers found that Internet use made family members isolated and depressed, and actually decreased the size of their social networks: "We were surprised to find that what is a social technology has such anti-social consequences," say one group of researchers.[24] People are communicating more, yet feeling less "in touch" than ever.

Such findings may assist with the design of new consumer technologies, but they have had little impact on the representation of digital media. Neither past nor present appears to blemish new predictions. Loneliness, ecological destruction, urban chaos, spreading unemployment, the monstrous military, unimaginable growth in corporate and biotechnological power whose effects are increasingly visible in the impoverished university—these problems magically disappear in the utopias of technoevolutionism. The discarded bodies of last year's computers and phones vanish as fast as containers can be built to carry them away. In order to maintain its evolutionary logic, technoevolutionism must continuously separate itself from such history. Drawing on the evolutionary paradigm permits commentators to privilege mythic metanarrative over empirical analysis, technological and psychological obsolescence over sustainability, and the contagion of corporate discovery over public research and debate. This promotional magic creates what Kroker terms a "Techno Topia," a promised cornucopia that makes no space for ethics, critique, or the actuality of experience.[25] In this climate, questioning technological innovation is ridiculed as a naïve dismissal of science, democracy, and hope.

The conflation of human and technological evolution works not only to envision electrifying futures, but also to displace alternate strategies for imagining our futures. Technoevolutionism displaces alternate imaginings by positing the technological imperative as coming from outside ourselves, outside of culture, through a self-generating evolutionary progression rather than through the culpable logics of our own social system. The logic of autonomous technological change, so carefully disassembled by Winner,[26] possesses a largely unchallenged authority in political discourse, commerce, big science, and the far-flung spectacles of culture and popular myth. As a result, technology—like previous known religions—enables people to live toward an imaginary future while disciplining the hopes and expectations of the present. "A mechanised world," McLuhan observed, "is always in the process of getting ready to live."[27] George Grant echoes this thought in his observation that in modern science and philosophy, "the possible is exalted above what is."[28] Virilio adds that the "technologies of real time . . . kill 'present' time by isolating it from its presence here and now for the sake of another commutative space that is no longer composed of our 'concrete presence' in the world, but of a 'discrete telepresence' whose enigma remains forever intact."[29]

He could have been writing about the planet. One could not ask for a better description of the experience of the Internet, with its oft-noted ability to produce a cumulative oblivion to time, one's body, and one's physical surroundings. The technotopian discourse displays a deep ambivalence toward presence and embodiment that permits the most striking anomalies of perception. While technology is the agent that will inevitably bring about the transformations we long for in the future, it has, by contrast, nothing to do with the present, whose dissatisfactions are severed from last year's promises of utopic transformation. Enthralled by the sense of "aheadedness," Samuel Mallin claims, the pursuit of the future as the "pure image of the cognitive" unveils a present that "thrusts forward inhesitantly and with full faith and confidence, [but] has all about it the most astonishing wreckage and waste."[30] The technological narrative blooms in the fertile ground of amnesia, in our reluctance to remember the actualities of the present or the past.

Commentators on the digital future fit this portrait very well. They "forget" that the current collapse of economic and social security was precipitated, at least in part, by the wide-scale deployment of smart technologies which directly preceded the newer technologies they propose will rescue us from our current difficulties, by means of their greater realism, mobility, access, or convergence. This is a convenient oversight, particularly for dealing with a populace that is becoming skeptical about progress. For this recollection might provoke the idea that more than technological change is necessary for a truly transformed future; that different kinds of change might produce different kinds of evolution. It might provoke the realization that just as human evolution is not primarily genetic, so social evolution may not be primarily technological, that some evolution involves aspects of human behavior and commitment that have nothing to do with technology. Acknowledging this idea would help to move beyond the impasse described by Sioui:

> The belief in the superiority of European culture and morality, which has served as a foundation for the acquisition of other people's territories and resources. Its scientific name is the theory of social evolution, which puts forward, as a truth, the principle that those people who possess the most "advanced" technology and the "capacity of writing" are in the vanguard of the process of "evolution," and thus have the right, inherent to their culture, and the responsibility, to bring about the "development" of the "less advanced."[31]

The dream of human unfolding has been projected onto technology, which stands in for the future. It is not actually we who unfold; or rather, if we do unfold, it is forward into a specifically technological space that, ever evolving, draws us in to meet our more hopeful, more convivial, more evolved selves. These future selves beckon from the other side of the screen. What is evolving here is really technique.[32] No one outside of Hollywood asks whether the technoevolutionary trajectory might play a role in the *de*volution of human capacities. Cheered on by the apparent consensus of mainstream and marginal voices, technoevolutionism relies on the assumption that human culture, democracy, freedom, and intelligence must and will progress along with our technology. And surely this is the secret of the technological utopic: technology both signifies and guarantees that change can only go forward, never backward, and so human intentionality is magically confirmed as both causality and effect of a technologically evolved future that is in any case inevitable.

So mythic thinking has not relinquished its hold on the marketplace of contemporary thought. This presents both ontological and political challenges to critical cultural studies. Supposedly we are on the brink of unprecedented and fundamental transformation. But who is changing what? Hasn't technology changed the nature of evolution itself? If so, does this change give us greater or less control over our futures?

Technology and Evolution

Whether concerned with finance, culture and entertainment, information processing, or science and medicine, many journalists and academics view *technology* and *progress* as interchangeable terms. If this conviction seems questionable in the wake of post-Enlightenment thought, which has offered searing critiques of human presumption, its exponents justify their claim in the language of science. They rely on evolution to explain the progressive nature of technological change, and technological change to demonstrate the progressive nature of historical change. The evolutionary trope is not seen as metaphorical or even transdisciplinary. Because technological change has become so rapid, it does not seem inappropriate to collapse thousands of years of geological and genetic change into a generation. Evolutionary rhetoric may depend on a conceptual mashup of metaphor, model, analogue, and replication, but its users have an apparently neutral and incontestable alibi for an otherwise questionable claim to progressive change.

"It seems hardly open to dispute," writes Joel Mokyr in his book on technology and economic progress, "that what has happened to people's ability to manipulate the laws of nature in the service of economic ends is unidirectional and deserves the word progress."[33] Mokyr explains the dynamic of this unidirectional progress in relation to evolution as "a specific dynamic model governed by mutation and selection." The concept of natural selection is helpful for understanding technological progress because

> techniques—in the narrow sense of the word, namely, the knowledge of how to produce a good or service in a specific way—are analogues to species and changes in them have an evolutionary character. . . . Some cultural, scientific, or technological ideas catch on because in some way they suit the needs of society [note that "society" has, or is, a single interest] in much the same way as some mutations are retained by natural selection for perpetuation. In its simplest form, the selection process works because the best adapted phenotypes are also the ones that multiply the fastest.[34]

Here technological innovation is perfectly analogous with competitive adaptation and the survival of the fittest, whose universal truth is thereby corroborated. Because natural law accounts for the process whereby some technological prototypes succeed on the marketplace while others do not, there is no need to seek other kinds of explanation.[35]

Another influential historian of technological change, James Beniger, situates this technoevolutionary drive within the larger drive for control manifested across the expanding domains of biology and genetics, information and communication, intelligence and cybernetics. Technology takes on the function of order and control in societies that are too complex to be guided by primitive sociality or the reciprocal altruism of more evolved societies. Here, evolution is redefined in relation to cybernetics. Because cybernetic systems are adaptable, or capable of "learning," the development of computer programs approximates our definition of evolution, and the two processes become interchangeable. Thus "evolutionary" changes in the virtual creatures inhabiting simulated environments are metaphorically interchangeable with organic evolution. Progress or mutation in information processing becomes a metonym for progress in intelligence, which in turn stands in for the totality of progress in human evolution. "All that is required for evolution to occur," Beniger explains, "are the static and dynamic aspects of its essential control function: replication of programming and its differential selection relative to other programs. It is the emergence of precisely this capability, in the earliest ancestors of DNA that marked the origin of life on earth, that is the beginning of evolution through natural selection."[36] Having established prehistoric identity between laws of nature and laws of history, Beniger can now account for the history of industrialization, the intensification of processing speed, and the crisis of control in post-industrial society. It's evolutionary.

Not surprisingly, the merger of natural, cybernetic, and economic histories finds wider application in the resurgence of social Darwinism in social thought and economic policy. If specific technologies are human made, the underlying logic of technological change replicates the laws of nature. This means not only that human evolution is coextensive with technological evolution, but also that technological evolution follows the bioevolutionary principles of adaptation and the survival of the fittest.[37] According to Herbert Spencer, founder of the theory of social Darwinism and source of the term "survival of the fittest," "There was a principle of social selection operative in history, and because this was so it was extremely important that men didn't interfere with it, and in particular that governments didn't interfere with it."[38] Since social selection is a natural process, successful adaptation will bring "human happiness of a general kind": "If you really believe that there is a system of progressive social selection going on," Raymond Williams observes, "it can seem wild infamy to interfere with it."[39] This is, of course, the organizing principle of neoliberal economics and the leading rationale for global capitalism.

The depiction of technology as a self-evolving link between natural law and progressive change serves to communicate the idea that individual struggle, hypermobility, and rapid technical obsolescence are at one and the same time laws of the environment, and components of adaptation required to survive environmental change. The imperative of technological progress assumes the place of the natural environment to which humans adapt with greater or lesser success. Social Darwinism simultaneously narrows the definition of evolution, and broadens its applicability: all aspects of human endeavor are advanced by competitive struggle and adaptation to laws of change. Mary Midgley attributes this belief to the "irresistible escalator" of Lamarckian evolutionary thought, which assumes that evolutionary change inevitably draws us upward and onward.[40] As diverse commentators have observed, this assumption lends nature "a highly moral colouring that Darwin himself was eager to avoid"; for Charles Darwin, "nature had no teleology, apart from the better adaptation of species to their environment."[41] Indeed Darwin resisted the term *evolution* precisely for that reason; he saw natural selection not as progress, but merely as a description of local adaptation to changing environments. Darwin's own theory of natural selection proposes "no perfecting principles, no guarantee of general improvement; in short, no reason for general approbation in a political climate favouring innate progress in nature." Thus, Stephen Jay Gould concludes, adaptive changes that enable animals to survive in local environments "do not mark intrinsic trends to higher states."[42]

In his primer *The Evolution of Technology*, George Basalla concludes that

> neither the historical record nor our understanding of the current role of technology in society justifies a return to the idea that a causal connection exists between advances in technology and the overall betterment

of the human race. Therefore, the popular but illusory concept of technological progress should be discarded. In its place we should cultivate an appreciation for the diversity of the made world, for the fertility of the technological imagination, and for the grandeur and antiquity of the network of related artefacts.[43]

Despite these cogent interventions, the Victorian belief in progress still dominates the public understanding of evolution and forms a bridge between its scientific and nonscientific meanings. Nature is represented as a constellation of fixed laws from which principles of cooperation, community, altruism, and stability are necessarily evicted.[44] Given the dominance of this paradigm in media and corporate and political narratives, part of the critical task of redefining technological evolution, as feminist critics like Evelyn Fox Keller have shown, is to restore principles of cooperation and solidarity to the interlocked domains of society and nature as these are understood and enacted in the public sphere.

For some commentators, this is precisely the mission of the Internet. Drawing on an alternative evolutionary narrative, they see the Internet as a means to transcend the hierarchy, isolation, and disempowerment produced by earlier technologies, drawing us into a more evolved "posthuman" collectivity in which human alienation, social injustice, and the quandaries of embodiment are transcended and made obsolete. If social Darwinist thought dominates mainstream discourse on technology, society, and justice, evolutionism is equally popular among more specialized critics and theorists writing about cybernetics, digital subcultures, classroom pedagogies, and the technologically oriented fine arts. Like the "wired" communities of cybernetic subcultures, these groups celebrate a technologically advanced future dominated by smart machines.[45]

However technocritics define technology—as a specific set of tools, a historical process, or the discursive work of a political or cultural formation—they share the tendency to situate technological development within the narrative of evolutionary law. Positing a link between technological and human evolution bridges the knowledge domains of genetic biology, the history of technology, and social and cultural history. Bioengineering plays a special role here: remapping of the human body as digital information transforms and cements the relationship between human and technological developments, which can now replicate one another in more explicit ways. The distinctions among social, biological, and genetic evolution appear to diminish, and technological change appears as "an inevitable evolutionary process mapped on the anatomy and physiology of the [human] body."[46] The evocation of the human body as subject and object of technological change both locates and naturalizes the evolutionary process. This rhetoric produces a powerful animation of the machine world, accompanied by "an extraordinary proliferation of images of, and narratives about, the obsolescent body."[47]

Evolutionary Bodies

If the body is obsolescent, it must be left behind by something better, an emergent species more adaptive within the more "evolved" environment. Some economists find a parallel between this replacement process and the period of the industrial revolution, when the focus of human labor and culture shifted from the farm to the city. Neoconservatives, such as the president of Canada's Business Council on National Issues, reason that just as horses were replaced by tractors so the role of humans must diminish and then be eliminated by the computer.[48] Newer, more evolved species will be able to move effortlessly through simulated three-dimensional space; new forms of posthuman intelligence will inhabit an alternative spatial universe whose utopian qualities are tautologically derived from this same scenario. As Shoshana Zuboff wrote in the early years of the "digital revolution," "Information technology not only produces action but also produces a voice that symbolically renders events, objects, and processes so that they become visible, knowable, and shareable in a new way.... In its capacity as an automating technology, information technology has a vast potential to displace the human presence."[49] Researchers and science fiction writers have explored the idea that protein-based life forms are moving toward obsolescence, to be replaced by silicon-based life forms that can be downloaded and reproduced via computer.[50] Marvin Minsky, MIT's cybernetic pioneer, envisioned artificial intelligence as a release from what he called "the bloody mess of organic matter"; what is important about life is the mind, whose structures are replaceable by a thinking machine.[51] Writers such as William Gibson, Kevin Kelley, and Hans Moravec all celebrate a future "freed from bondage to a material body."[52] This narrative rejection of the flesh dismisses the social and biological complexity of neuron life in favor of a reified form of human intelligence that is reducible to digitally replicable information. Not surprisingly, these authors focus on the evolution of technical forms (3-D information processing, digital environments, genes and nanotechnologies, AI, robotics), rather than on the interaction between technical and human agents. The human role is limited to the organization and extension of the "technical ensemble," in order to pass it on to the next generation. In this scenario, as Winner observes,

> The mortality of human beings matters little, for technology is itself the immortal and, therefore, the more significant part of the process. Specific varieties of technics can be compared to biological species that live on even though individual members of the species perish. Mankind serves a function similar to that of natural selection in Darwinian theory. Existing structures in nature and the technical ensemble are the equivalent of the gene pool of a biological species. Human beings act not so much as participants as a selective environment which combines and recombines these structures to produce new mutations, which are then adapted to a particular niche in that environment.[53]

In other words, individual humans do not create or shape the techno-evolutionary process; they merely enable and respond to it. It is technologies, not people, that propel the evolution of new species or taxonomies. By developing its technologies and tools, the human body learns to multiply its strength (they mean, of course, the strength of human instruments and prostheses). These prosthetic technologies serve to extend human capacities in space and time, an advance which, as the influential archaeologist and historian V. Gordon Childe argues, is quantifiable and constitutes "tangible proof of human progress."[54] What characterizes technology as progressive in his account is its ability to accomplish new tasks, to aid in the growth of human populations, and to extend human capabilities in time and space.

We are concerned here with the last of these accomplishments, the virtual extension of the human body across time and space until it dissolves in the "electronic frontier." The more that technology comes to function as a prosthesis of the human body, as critics have observed, the more the body itself becomes *immaterial*. One presumes they use this term metaphorically, to mean extraneous, afunctional, devalued; note that the idea of the immaterial is itself dematerialized. "In this electric age," McLuhan hypothesizes, "we see ourselves being translated more and more into the form of information, moving toward the technological extension of consciousness.

That is what is meant when we say that we daily know more and more about man. We mean that we can translate more and more of ourselves into other forms of expression that exceed ourselves."[55] This prediction anticipates descriptions of the Internet as a new form of disembodied collectivity, and virtual space as a new posthuman environment. McLuhan's comment also anticipates the conception (if this is the right word) of artificial life, whose researchers and advocates rely on "the feasible separation of the 'informational' from its material substrate."[56] As Jean Baudrillard notes, "It is as if the extension of the pleasures of the body to its representations, the extension of biology into ideology, is itself 'a process of craving and pleasure,' a sort of addiction to the pleasure of overcoming the body that, in turn, 'it is necessary to overcome.'"[57]

This comment offers a cogent reflection on another implicit problem in the evolutionary narrative. For the collaboration between technical development and human evolution, which is accompanied in these utopian narratives by the promise of a revived sense of collectivity, coexists with a progressive vanishing of the human body, which gradually disappears into the "hypervisualizations" of cyberspace. "Over hundreds of thousands of years," Kathleen Woodward writes,

> the body, with the aid of various tools and technologies, has multiplied its strength and increased its capacities to extend itself in space and over time. According to this logic, the process culminates in the very immateriality of the body itself. In this view technology serves fundamentally as a prosthesis of the human body, one that ultimately displaces the material body, transmitting instead its image around the globe and preserving that image over time.[58]

Of course bodies are not literally displaced, however much their nervous systems are modified or extended; it is the "information" transmitted through the act of communication that is dematerialized, not the body. But the disconnection between the body and the messages it sends is apprehended in terms of a hypermobile functionalism that reverses them: through new technologies of communication, information is animated with life and movement, and the human body is left behind, inanimate and abject, conceptually displaced by the more significant movement of information. In this account, the collectivization of consciousness and intelligence (de Kerckhove's "Webness") occurs in direct proportion to—and can only be realized by—the disembodiment of subjectivity.

This particular equation of communication and disembodiment stems from a century-old description of the impact of electronic media's ability to commune instantaneously with others without physical proximity to them. The physical body remaining behind in the telecommunicative event, sitting there in front of the telephone or computer, is erased not so much by the technology as by the written account of it, which continuously affirms the idea that the human body has been supplanted by the act of communication and will find its power restored only with a newer tool. The common rhetoric of bodily displacement now associated with the Internet thus makes a double move that displaces its own rhetorical effects. Of course, this reification is not just a function of rhetoric. Cyberspace is designed precisely to create the sensation of leaving one environment and entering another, three-dimensional, virtual space. Let us take up this premise on its own terms. If communication displaces the person, if simulation nullifies the original, what actually happens to the communicating body? Is its experience merely a function of postmodern simulation? When we nullify the body in these narratives, do we not make ourselves obsolete or at least unaccountable as a species? What are the origins of this metaphysical assassination, this revenge against the "meat" (in William Gibson's oft-quoted phrase; see discussion in the next section), the "bloody organic mess" as Minsky put it, that characterizes organic life? Why does this theme so dominate our fantasies? Are we imagining a more evolved human nature, or are we willing our species, like the chatty homicidal virologist in Terry Gilliam's *12 Monkeys* (1995), into obsolescence? His will to obsolescence declares its altruistic motivations; the human species must disappear not because we are godlike in our creative capacities but because we have believed ourselves to be so. As Robert Romanyshyn writes in *Technology as Symptom and Dream*: "One can still imagine technology as *vocation*, as the earth's call to become its agent and instrument of awakening. But in the shadows, the imagination falters and technology seems less the earth's way of coming to know itself and more the earth's way of coming to cleanse itself of us."[59]

This dystopian narrative shows evolution leading to the supplanting of human cultures by other, more "advanced" moral and technological systems. In this way our only-human irrationality is simultaneously justified and defeated by the accomplishments of our science. In one popular motif in contemporary science fiction (*Terminator 2* [1991], *Millennium* [1989], Gene Roddenberry's *Earth: The Final Conflict* [1997], *12 Monkeys*, *Star Trek*, and so on), technologically enhanced future societies create "cyborgian" angels who can travel backward in time to rescue us from catastrophe, thereby simultaneously exposing and redeeming our collective Frankensteinian pathologies. Echoing Darwin's own understanding of evolution, this trajectory displaces humanity from the center of the cosmos. In the Hollywood version, however, the cosmos—or rather, the further-evolved future—arrives just in time to rescue hubristic humankind as it teeters on the brink of apocalyptic natural and other catastrophes.

Evolutionary Technologies

The literature of evolutionary biology records a series of challenges to those versions of evolution that define adaptation purely in terms of self-interest, and self-interest purely in terms of competition and struggle. As Keller observes in her study of this literature, however, biologists who seek to elaborate general theories proceed as if these challenges were without foundation or had never occurred. If the scientific community has tended to foreclose this discussion, how much more easily these tensions disappear by the time evolutionary theory has spread to the nonscientific world, where it maintains enough scientific credibility to uphold the mythic imperative of technological progress. This myth relies on a mimetic equivalence between biological and technological evolution that has helped to situate and explain technological innovation within a regressive economic and political climate. The evolutionist ideology thus produces definite effects in the production of technologies themselves, which in turn work to shape our perceptions of social, cultural, and physiological possibility. These technologies may not change us at a genetic level, unless they are genetic technologies; but they do shape and direct the fabric of the social, and the values and conditions of possibility for our lives as embodied social beings. Social and economic relations, ethics and justice, aesthetics and symbolic culture, and evolutionary narratives themselves are all part of the human evolutionary process. The West's idealism about the transcendence of nature cohabits with its dark side: a deeply rooted antipathy to the vulnerability of physical bodies which can be seen across contemporary cultures of the human body. Women are said to have greater control over their bodies than in any time in human history. We can (we are told) choose whether, when, and how to have children, when and with whom to have sex, and even (so we are told) what to wear, how to look, how much to weigh, and how (or ideally, whether) to wear our age. All these represent sites of unprecedented individual freedom. How ironic, then, that women feel themselves to be the subject of such regulation of and intimate antagonism toward their own embodied selves. Unless they are enthusiastic co-agents in the control strategies of new reproductive and cosmetic technologies, they may not feel that the evolutionary narrative is unfolding to their benefit. Rather, one might feel that her body becomes a "body of evidence" of her failure to transcend worldly temporality and physical aging, to the degree that every moment "after" this one is a step closer to seeking the "before."[60]

Since Donna Haraway's "Cyborg Manifesto," many feminists accept the limitations of thinking about bodies in contrast to technologies as though they were independent and opposed entities. The cyborg is not subject to Foucault's biopolitics,[61] Haraway writes optimistically, arguably contradicting her own findings and paving the way for a longstanding feminist ambivalence toward the subject of embodiment. This important scruple sometimes disguises an underlying reluctance to talk about the body at all in other than representational terms. The technologically mediated body is constituted in this discourse as an instance and function of representation. Whether in reference to science fiction or biotechnology in practice, this representational body resides outside of space and time, potentially freed not just from gender and other polarities but more profoundly from all the dangers, banal and otherwise, that actual bodies encounter in the early twenty-first century. Yet the disembodied subject has unparalleled power to control her history and environment. For Avital Ronell, the blurring of simulated and real worlds represents "a tendency to retrofit the technological prosthesis to a metaphysical subject—the sovereign subject of history, destiny's copilot."[62] This Cartesian approach to thought has far older roots in the Enlightenment with its emphasis on observation and rational cognition and its rationalist rejection of embodied experience. At the same time, a number of factors have come into play to disseminate this mode of thought into the wider culture.

The idea of a frontier waiting to be overcome by a metaphysical subject has long defined the American imaginary. "In so far as real places elsewhere have been exhausted," Kevin Robins observes, "it has become necessary to find new kinds of place and frontier to sustain the needs of the modern imaginary. Now the new frontier opens up onto cyberspace, the place of virtual life, and it is there that the proclaimed pioneers of the new techno-culture . . . believe they will find another beginning."[63] For McLuhan, the new subject is born in changes in the media of communication, which affect our perceptions of space and our actions upon it. "Every new technology," he claims, "gradually creates a totally new human environment. Environments are not passive wrappings but active processes."[64] In both of these descriptions cyberspace represents a palimpsest of historical and technological space reconstituted by technological mediations which build on earlier ideas to make them meaningful. Like Foucault, McLuhan emphasizes the constructivist and disciplinary characteristics of modern culture, and the extent to which perception is organized by the self-conscious formation of the individual subject. Drawing on the work of Walter Ong, McLuhan traces this emphasis on self-consciousness to the birth of print, which facilitated a new separation of inner and outer space and of speech from text. For McLuhan (who arguably manifests his technological determinism most strongly on this very point), print thereby produces the hyperrationalized, alienated, and aggressive ego of modern civilization. Virilio develops this insight by noting that "individuality or individualism was thus not so much the fact of a liberation of social practice as the product of the evolution of techniques of the development of public or private space."[65] In other words the hyper-individualism which protoscientific culture ascribes to the genetic code of human nature is a historical and sociospatial product, a lived consequence of the cultural technologies of modern power.

The same understanding can be brought to bear on the rhetoric of disembodiment surrounding cyberspace and the Web. Many critics trace this theme to the cyberpunk fiction of William Gibson, whose 1984 *Neuromancer* popularized the image of the body as meat to be shed as quickly as consciousness can be uploaded onto a computer. Clearly the opposition between body and intellect has much earlier roots. But the idea of a machine as a three-dimensional environment to be explored and lost in can be traced to the mid-1960s, when Douglas Engelbart's invention of the mouse transformed the computer screen into a new three-dimensional "informationscape." That innovation, argues Steven Johnson, changed not only how we use machines but how we imagine them. "The bitmapped data-sphere he unleashed on the world in 1968 was the first major break from the machine-as-prosthesis worldview. For the first time, a machine was imagined not as an attachment to our bodies, but as an environment, a space to be explored."[66]

Note that this is precisely the argument McLuhan was then making about the media environment. Engelbart's move to "endow that data with spatial attributes"[67] occurred within the context of a popular and scientific culture in which a spatialized, technologically enhanced intelligence was both comprehensible and desirable. The term *interface* appeared at the same time, when an inventor working on flight simulation merged the real-time imaging capabilities of the digital computer with mechanical flight simulators to help train military pilots. By the 1970s, techniques for rendering objects and spaces with apparent three-dimensionality were being perfected, "laying the foundations for lifelike computer animation, and for the illusion of immersion in the image field."[68] The virtual space created by flight simulation offered the sense of "an open world where your mind is the only limitation."[69] As Arendt has shown, this widespread disavowal of limits effectively eliminated ethics from the virtual field.[70] It also fueled the inventiveness of the United States military in its drive to force the Soviet Union into a technical and military contest it could not win. Like the notion of evolution with which this illusory "space" has been so closely linked, the idea of an alternative, three-dimensional, purely informational environment open to exploration by an appropriately disembodied intelligence has subsequently been thoroughly naturalized.

As a discourse working across the semiautonomous domains of science, technology, commerce, journalism, and culture, technoevolutionism functions as a cultural technology which privileges individuation, mobility, disembodiment, and the continuous conquering or abolition of space. The Internet is an ideal manifestation of these principles. As an extension of what Williams termed "mobile privatisation," it promises its users the ability to inhabit an increasingly everywhere-yet-nowhere space of hypertechnological mediation. As the interface between self and virtual "space" recedes, users learn to overlook the socially mediated nature of such technology.[71] But technoevolutionism also offers a countering narrative, in which the Internet, supported by innovations such as Google and Open Source software development, enables users to transcend the hierarchy, isolation, and disempowerment produced by earlier technologies, and to evolve toward a postcapitalist, postnationalist collectivity. The history and practice of this idea have also contributed to the evolution of the Internet, first through the influence of communitarian values among designers in the 1960s and subsequently through the influential ideals and practices of first-wave Web practitioners.

According to Murray Turoff, an influential designer writing in 1976:

> I think the ultimate possibility of computerized conferencing is to provide a way for human groups to exercise a "collective intelligence" capability. The computer as a device to allow a human group to exhibit collective intelligence is a rather new concept. In principle, a group, if successful, would exhibit an intelligence higher than any member. Over the next decades, attempts to design computerized conferencing structures that allow a group to treat a particular complex problem with a single collective brain may well promise more benefit for mankind than all the artificial intelligence work to date.[72]

But what "complex problems" were addressed? Early users were primarily affluent, employed, unmarried men, who subjected themselves to punishing programming schedules and commonly "deaestheticized" the body by ignoring its needs and appearance.[73] The predominance of teenage boys and young men is not surprising, argues Allucquere Rosanne Stone, since young males are particularly driven to escape the proximate world of physical awkwardness and embarrassment, and to find a space where they can regain a sense of power and control.[74] If CMC or telematic technologies indeed produce greater "collective intelligence," its designers have tended to dissociate intelligence from the organic and social situatedness of human life, preferring its "higher," disembodied form with its machinelike adaptability. As Katherine Hayles writes, "The body's dematerialization depends in complex and highly specific ways on the embodied circumstances that an ideology of dematerialization would obscure."[75]

The emphasis on the Web as a constellation of "virtual communities" has also obscured its importance as a site of control technologies. As Dale Bradley emphasizes,

> Cyberspace is more usefully understood as an active strategy through which various forms of control are enacted . . . than a static space 'in' which individuals and information are somehow digitally (re)produced. . . . The importance of the presumed "split" between the physical and the

virtual (whether in terms of space or the body) cannot be overstated because it is only by positing a profound separation between the physical world of society and the virtual world of cyberspace that the utopian claims made with regard to cyberspace can be deployed. If there is no separation, then cyberspace's utopian possibilities dissolve as one is forced to consider its historical production within and by, rather than beside or beyond, social power relations.[76]

Evolutionary Trajectories

The discourse of evolutionism functions as a socially neutral alibi for corporate expansion and innovation unimpeded by collective democratic participation. The rendering of technological change as a law of nature works to defend economic and technological relations from social debate and critique, and to direct implementation toward the development of competitive rather than collaborative spaces. The widespread representation of technological innovation as following systemic, autonomous, progressive laws provides a context and alibi for the anxious desire to "make something of oneself" so central to modern Western culture. At the same time it tempers the seductive anxiety of self-formation with the cool neutralities of technological imperative and scientific law. Thus it reiterates the managerial imperative of constant technological updating.

The technoevolutionist discourse has a utopian side, which continues to play an important role in technological innovation and diffusion. As Michelle Kendrick observed in the mid-1990s,

> It is . . . no surprise to read so many manifestos of "cyber-liberation" by those involved in promoting the sale and dissemination of computer technologies. Cyberspace fictions regularly channel anxieties regarding technology into romanticized notions of a reconfigured subjectivity that represents the triumph of the algorithmic mind over a physical body that refuses to be fully computed. Shifting the focus from the constructed nature of subjectivity to the "need" for technological enhancement, such fictions create a desire to be connected, a desire not to be left behind on the information superhighway. To escape the anxieties of being violated by an "inhuman" technology, therefore, becomes (paradoxically) a process of producing the desire to desire more technological intervention in order to become more fully human.[77]

This process has created a growing market demand for technologies that satisfy the desire for emotional connection in the ordinary consumer. Howard Rheingold, grand uncle of Web utopianism, notes that "when people who have become fascinated by BBSS or networks start spreading the idea that such networks are inherently democratic . . . they run the danger of becoming unwitting agents of commodification. . . . The hopes of technophiles have often been used to sell technology for commercial gain."[77] These hopes are not only part of market strategy; in complex, even paradoxical ways, they are incorporated in the design of the technologies. Now that cyberspace is no longer really "real," Facebook sites and Blackberries connect users who want to feel more directly connected. Discourse and technology are inseparable agents in the reconfiguration of space, encouraging us to believe that a well-connected postembodied life dispenses with gender troubles, loneliness, disability, even death. A deeply rooted cultural symptomology thus gives form, through complex technological mediation, to the horizon and limit of conceivable futures.

The posited future actualization of authentic connection reinforces the perception that our bodies are the only thing standing between us and the phantasmagoric future. This ambivalence about the value of the human body contains an important if unacknowledged truth. The human body is not reducible to pure information. Thus it is threatened by irreversible damage from petrochemical industries, plutonium, pesticides, chemical additives, nuclear testing, global warming, the hole in the ozone, and the escalating toxicities of speed. Our imperfect abilities to withstand these stresses threaten to impede the highway to progress. We are not ready to transport ourselves to Jupiter or Mars, Hollywood (and Stephen Hawking) notwithstanding, and cyberspace seems the next best place to hide. Our immune and reproductive systems are the roadkill of the information highway. Without bodies, there are no obstacles to the evolution of Technotopia. With bodies, we confront divergent evolutionary paths: digital rapture and metal body parts for the privileged few, or extinction, or a more habitable planet.

If we want other kinds of futures (some say, any future at all), we need better ways to imagine and connect with the physical world. If we are truly committed to the emergence of collective intelligence, we need to begin by querying how "intelligence" and "communication" (and "we") are being shaped and pursued by corporate strategies, by alliances between the military and telecommunication industries, and by the security state. We should demand more intellectually rigorous and modest understandings of these terms if we are to reclaim them from parties and practitioners in thrall to the technological sublime. We need to reconcile the dream of renewed community associated with digital communication with the sustainable future of human and other bodies. Only by doing so can we intervene usefully in the process of technological change, or hope to reconcile its so-called imperatives with the dreams of renewed connection and solidarity that have for so long kept them alive and well in the cultural imaginary.

When I began working on this project, people were wondering whether Canada could last, given the combined pressures of an uneconomical geography and an acquisitive neighbor. Now, I hear people wondering if President Obama can save the United States. This book was written in the context of volatile change between these two sets of circumstances. This change has involved significant shifts in the political landscape and in the kinds of disposition, commitment, and analysis informing both critical scholarship and popular culture. I would be betraying my understanding of both arenas, however, if I overestimated the degree of historical transformation such changes suggest. Is this a new epoch, or just a new chapter?

A postscript such as this one might reasonably argue that the social and intellectual contexts in which I wrote this work, like their subject matter, have passed into historical record. Free trade may be disputed in its particulars, but the principle is now taken for granted. Bush is out of office, the economy is in crisis, and the American empire is broke. Global warming is widely accepted as the result of human action (except among a portion of the American population), more classical musicians are being trained in China than anywhere else, music reproduction has gone digital, and half the people I see in the streets of Toronto were not born in this country. They (we) are the truth of this country's future. Given such changes, the context for this work, like the moment that gave rise to the cartoon reproduced on page 153, has surely passed. "What's really scary is that we Canadians could lose control of our culture. . . ." Which Canadians? Which culture? What kind of control does that husband want anyway?

But time does not work like this. For one thing the husband's comment was already a complicated joke in 1986, and for another, we are still rehearsing its meanings. Just because something is past, as the political cartoon reminds us, does not mean it is not present, whether as tragedy or farce (or more likely—on this subject, at least—as an ironic blend of the two). Otherwise, we would not need a theory of articulation, we would not be debating the implications of postcolonialism, and cultural meanings would never matter politically in contexts that varied from those through which they emerged. Constantly resituated in what Butler has termed the politics of "the exasperated 'etc.,'" Canadians are repeatedly implicated in an incomplete politics of nationhood, culture, and justice.[1]

During the 1980s, my graduate student days, negotiations for the first Free Trade Agreement between Canada and the United States provided a raw preview of the strategies of neoliberalization that have subsequently transformed fiscal and social policies in many countries. The debate involved a discursive confrontation between understanding culture as a public good dedicated to sovereignty and culture as a private good dedicated to profit. While hypothetically this conflict applied equally to policies and rights on both sides of the border, its implications were perceived in Canada in more geopolitically specific terms. The conflict between culture as social right and culture as commodity had particular weight and took particular forms in Canada because of the extent to which it was articulated to the body politic. Corporations had been granted the constitutional rights of individuals in the United States, as the Canadian film *The Corporation* reminds us, since the abolition of slavery. But extending such rights for corporations into Canada, notwithstanding the economic rationality for such a move, involved a substantial change in the political fabric of the country. Debate about this agreement renewed an alliance of academics, artists and cultural activists, trade unions, nurses and educators, church groups, farmers, women's groups, and others who had previously emerged between the wars. Both drawing from and distancing themselves from the ever greater prominence of culture as the site of a systematized governmentality, this alliance was concerned not so much with defending an identity as with fighting to preserve social and cultural policies and interests that had been won in the name of the identity known as Canada. This performative aspect of sovereignty is a complicated legacy of the colonial settlement of the country. In Canada, as in other Second World or settler cultures, colonialists have energetically dispossessed the indigenous populations of their territory while struggling against the shifting colonization of their own resources and powers. Identity was always already subject to question.

I was recovering from the political defeat of the anti–free trade alliance when I attended the 1990 conference in Urbana, Illinois, organized to celebrate the Anglo-American ascendancy of cultural studies. In "Angels Dancing" (chapter 4) the early progeny of these two formative but contentious processes, I sought to demonstrate that American cultural studies scholars were failing to grasp the workings of culture and commodification and their imbrication with empire because they were situated in the heart of it. Those of us outside this center were part of the "exasperated 'etc.'" peripheral to the founding assumptions of Anglo-American cultural studies. I had traveled to Australia and learned what this meant. My understanding of this formation was influenced by Henri Lefebvre's *Production of Space*, which offered complexity and depth to my growing belief that there was nothing to be gained by approaching electronic media as two-dimensional text; by the centenary of Harold Innis, whose ideas on communication and empire inform "Angels Dancing" and other chapters; and by the achievements of feminist scholars like Judith Butler, Teresa de Lauretis, Donna Haraway, Meaghan Morris, Margaret Morse, Lynn Spigel, and Judy Wacjman (among many) in theorizing culture's importance in the materialization of private and public space, gender and narrative form, nature, technology, and discourses of embodiment.[2]

These chapters elaborate these ideas while foregrounding the contexts in and about which they are written. They trace some key historical, symbolic, and technological processes through which culture has been mobilized by colonialists and politicians, artists and writers, intellectuals and housewives, teenagers and professionals, and media conglomerates and political entities on both sides of the border as they organize their practices in and thinking about space, belonging, and history. I wanted to analyze culture not just in terms of representations and identities, and the ways they may act as conduits for power, but through the ways meanings and identities are materialized, embodied, disseminated, and transformed through specific cultural technologies in specific geopolitical circumstances. This is both the context and the theme of the work. As I argue in "Space at the Margins" (chapter 2), the rationale for focusing on cultural technologies as spatializing mediators of power has not disappeared. It's not only that this rationale survives our changing understandings of space and the geopolitics of the nation-state; this focus has also proven to be important for addressing the environmental consequences of cultural technologies. It prepares the ground for a study of media not just in terms of representations of nature but also in terms of the degree to which, as my analysis of weather forecasts in chapter 7 suggests, media are increasingly constitutive of our relations with what we think nature is.

It quickly became evident that just as there is no such thing as a discretely determined identity, so there is no such thing as an autonomous cultural technology. They are constituted together and work within changing assemblages of space, technology, identity, and meaning. I was drawn to attend to particular technologies, beginning with radio and later moving precipitously to satellites and screens. But they always came back to me assembled. *North of Empire* pursues multidimensional analyses of the convergences that spoke most eloquently to me during this time: the time-space-habitus of radio, as it connected with recording technologies, railway trains, musicians, and politicians; or television, as it converged with weather forecasters, satellite optical technologies, and digital graphics; pianos, which brought together colonial settlements, wood manufacturing, the enculturation of women's work, and European musical pedagogies; or home computers, part of the global networking of cybernetic technologies, virtual communities, and social Darwinism. Each case conjoins specific technologies, social spaces, government or corporate policies, and the (re)schooling of the body. These conjunctures are not just technological; each is also mediated by gender, colonization, narrative, and corporate interests. Furthermore, people inhabit and act within these assemblages, providing complicated shapes and meanings to them and altering how we live and understand culture. Feminists know that these incomplete processes, these *etcetera*, involve embodied experiences like affect, desire, performativity, conviviality, and contradiction. Postcolonial theory calls upon us to revisit these processes in relation to historical themes of conquest, space, knowledge, and power. These intellectual resources have proved essential to theorizing Canada, and how we pursue such connections may be useful beyond its borders.

Only by translating across the assumptions and vocabularies of the disciplines can we comprehend the moment when cultural symbols or practices collide with historical change or the politics of belonging or the trajectories of the physical world. This reminds us that cultural studies works best when it works across the boundary lines inscribed by history, theory, or subject matter. Cultural studies can never be singly about culture because that is a misinterpretation of what culture is. Culture makes meaning in relation to power, geography, technology, race, language, sex, memory, time or space, weather or animals or food, *et cetera*, as well as what we ideationally share with others or what we hope for.

I have described the foundation of this work in relation to the rise of left cultural nationalism alongside Anglo-American cultural studies in the 1980s. I situate my understanding of cultural technologies in this history without offering any sense of closure on questions about how far this history has passed into the past or how much it belongs in the discursive present. There are theoretical and ethical reasons for leaving this question open to the contingencies of politics and time. I have already mentioned the theory of articulation, which emphasizes the temporary unity of discursive and political elements within particular social contexts.[3] I have also implicated the history of colonialism, and in particular how European colonists subjugated indigenous peoples and knowledge in the New World by situating them as other in self-justifying narratives of social progress and the domination of nature. Such juxtapositions unravel and reconnect over time according to logics that are far more complicated than the conventional representation of history suggests. For the French theorist Michel Serres, time is "dynamic and 'topological' rather than linear and repetitive."[4] Serres calls upon us to understand history multidimensionally and in spatial terms. "As we experience time—as much in our inner senses as externally in nature, as much as *les temps* of history as *les temps* of weather—it resembles this crumpled [handkerchief] much more than the flat, overly simplified one."[5] However minutely we trace the folds of the wrinkle, however singular the events of which we speak, the very conditions of tracing and speaking are transforming beneath our feet. Power pursues its ends by variously disrupting or preserving the exigencies of the present. Our ability to recognize the uncertainty of outcomes in politics and history surely owes something to the way that nature now manifests itself to us in the name of chaos rather than natural order. Guattari writes: "There is a principle specific to environmental ecology: it states that anything is possible—the worst disasters or the most flexible evolutions. Natural equilibriums will be increasingly reliant on human intervention. . . . There is at least a risk that there will be no more human history unless humanity undertakes a radical reconsideration of itself."[6] In both politics and nature, and the relations between them, there is an ethical dimension to negotiating disruption and preservation.

It is difficult to assess the timeliness of the time in which this book was written just as it is difficult to navigate this balance. We are living with a more vividly disjointed temporality than earlier ideas could account for, with punishing reversals that speak of progress and self-consciously progressive theory that speaks of eternal returns. How can we appraise and evaluate our theories and interventions without time-traveling into the future? In what circumstances is the emphasis on culture as experience that opens into collective emancipation a salutary idea, and at what point does it become a form of wishful thinking or even collusion? What kinds of assumptions are embedded in working definitions of culture as formation, flight, mobility, growth, or stasis? What kinds of futures have been presupposed by these frameworks and commitments as cultural studies moves from the margins to the centers (and now, perhaps, back to the margins) of our academic institutions?

Imagine we are writing our own history of the present. Tell the story of cultural studies from two hundred years in the future, my brother suggested when I mentioned writing a postscript. "Once upon a time," I thought, "culture was established as the gravitational center of power in building a self-consciously modern regime." "Once upon a time," I interrupted, "race and gender interrupted the orchestration of the Enlightenment's claims." "Once upon a time," the story goes, "peoples were vanquished because their cultures failed to change." "We must consider the fertile contradictions of building a polity through the government of culture." "The emergence of cultural studies coincided with the time people watched the same television shows. And then they didn't." "World government? No one cared." "Originally, researchers identified production and consumption as different stages in the formation of the cultural subject." "Back then, before the Internet . . ."

"In the twentieth century cultural studies stubbornly restricted its attention to people."

Of course there are many stories of cultural studies and many imaginary futures. It is not as easy to imagine yourself into the future as you might think. You have to choose your site of speculation. Imagine that the borders that now separate us are gone. Imagine armed borders between here and the other side of the street. Imagine our races mixed into a pointillist dance with pigment. Imagine listening to music and voices through implants in our brain which we will struggle to command. Imagine life without air travel, car radios, or cars. The animals will be gone. The world will be powered through windmills and solar power. Environmental catastrophe will have precipitated the ruinous collapse of governments, and neofascist troops will roam the cities and the reservations with GPS devices and second-hand armaments. We won't have bodies as we now understand them. White people will leave Earth and colonize cleaner planets. We will grow crops on our roofs. Addiction to Facebook will be genetically enhanced at birth. Nanotech-enhanced intelligences will save us from ourselves. The territories of political management will shrink to the size of neighborhoods, grow to the size of planets. We will rise and pass through walls. Everything will be fundamentally the same.

We seem to need these imaginary futures to gain insight into our wrinkled histories. John Keane's "Whatever Happened to Democracy?" was one visitation I heard recently from the future; Terry Eagleton's "From Celts and Catastrophe" was equally dystopic.[7] Neither was optimistic, and how could they be, conjured as they were—like Margaret Atwood's *Oryx and Crake*, published in 2004—in the midst of the Bush regime? In these narratives science and technology have destroyed the hopes invested in them, having served as Frankensteinian tools in the demise of both democracy and sustainability. No doubt this fracture helps to explain why animals have become so visible in popular and scholastic imaginings, including my own.[8] They are part of an energetic project to re-enchant the technological landscape. This re-enchantment comes with a price that begins (as the animal iconography suggests) with children and ends—again, probably with children—with the dilemma of unsustainable risk at the heart of magic. As *The Spiderwick Chronicles* (Mark Waters, 2008) shows, you could find yourself in an enchanted world in which special optical lenses reveal the many creatures around you. How wonderful to have such powers! But the failure to attend rightly to others could unleash monsters that trespass time-space borders from their virtual world to yours, heralding alternative outcomes in which freely morphing ("flexible") animal shapes ruthlessly crush human and other bodies (leading perhaps to the devastated landscapes of *Wall-E*, the brilliant 2008 animated film playing out of the trajectories of risk society) or burst forth from flowers and take flight in a swirl of hope. "Their world is closer than you think," advises *Spiderwick*'s motto. And so we end where we began, in a cinematic exploration of other spaces and how they should be known.

We elaborate critical resources appropriate to the contexts in which we find ourselves. Sometimes we just need to remember what we know already so we can work through the interruptions, affirming our rights and the rights of others to dream their different dreams about life on earth. As the growing crisis of the university, the increasing fragility of humanistic research, and the untimeliness of natural emergency suggest, such affirmation may be harder than it sounds. We need to learn new ways of thinking and talking just to defend the thinking and spaces for talking we already have. Once again, for cultural studies as for other critical interventions, the work begins.

introduction

First epigraph: Raymond Williams, *The Politics of Modernism*, 151. Paul Hjartarson explores the relevance of this text to Canadian cultural studies on his TransCanada Institute website (visited May 2007; printed-out pages on file with author).

1 Moore is obviously a special case. In *Bowling for Columbine*, he exposes the myths underpinning gun violence in the United States by a trip to Toronto, where he goes around opening unlocked doors. It's a solo performance of the mock invasions of his earlier film, *Canadian Bacon*. He made another reference to invading Canada in an appearance on *The Daily Show* in 2007. I think it's meant to be funny.

2 Smith, *The Geopolitics of Information*.

3 Dubois, *The Souls of Black Folk*; Fanon, *Black Skin, White Masks*; Gilroy, *Against Race*.

4 McLuhan, "Canada."

5 O'Neill, *Plato's Cave*, 16.

6 In a renowned 1972 cross-country radio competition to complete the sentence "As Canadian as . . ." the enduring winning entry, by eighteen-year-old Heather Scott, was "possible under the circumstances." The story is told by her father, R. W. Scott, May 18, 2004, on http://www.oratory.com//hscott.html (visited June 2006; print-out is in the author's files). The phrase is taken up in countless contexts, including an essay on irony in Canadian literature by Linda Hutcheon, *As Canadian as Possible—Under the Circumstances*.

7   See, e.g., Innis, *Staples, Markets, and Cultural Change*; Kroker, *Technology and the Canadian Mind*; McLuhan, *Essential McLuhan*; Melody, Salter, and Heyer, *Culture, Communication, and Dependency*; Patterson, *History and Communications*; Donald Theall, *The Medium Is the Rear View Window*; Stamps, *Unthinking Modernity*; Acland and Buxton, *Harold Innis in the New Century*; Angus and Shoesmith, *Dependency/Space/Policy*; Angus, *A Border Within*; Babe, *Ten Canadian Thinkers*; Barney, *Prometheus Wired*; Carey, *Communication as Culture*; Cavell, *McLuhan in Space*; Berland and Hornstein, *Capital Culture*; Franklin, *The Real World of Technology*; Friesen, *Citizens and Nation*; Genosko, *Marshall McLuhan*.

8   McLuhan, *Understanding Media*, 23, reprint. in McLuhan, *Essential McLuhan*, 151.

9   According to Williams, "paradoxically, if the book works it to some extent annihilates itself"; see also *Television*.

10   Innis, "The Bias of Communication," in *Staples, Markets, and Cultural Change*, 326. In *Unthinking Modernity*, Stamps compares Innis with Adorno in connection with this passage, 92.

11   Carey, *Communication as Culture*, 160.

12   O'Neill, *Plato's Cave*, 132, 135.

13   Osborne, "Whoever Speaks of Culture," 42.

14   Adorno and Horkheimer, *The Dialectic of Enlightenment*, 121–22. In his commentary on this essay Mark Poster notes that broadcasting "offends the intellectual's sense of authorship and that this is so regardless of the qualities that pertain to the cultural objects in question." *The Information Subject*, 50.

15   "Culture is ordinary; that is where we must start. To grow up in that country was to see the shape of a culture, and its modes of change. I could stand on the mountains and look north to the farms and the cathedral, or south to the smoke and the flare of the blast furnace making a second sunset. . . . The making of a society is the finding of common meanings and directions, and its growth is an active debate and amendment under the pressures of experience, contact, and discovery, writing themselves into the land."

16   Stamps, *Unthinking Modernity*, xiii.

17   Ibid., 57.

18   Ibid., 62.

19   McLuhan, *Understanding Media*, 153, 159.

20   Innis, "Industrialism and Cultural Values," in *Staples, Markets, and Cultural Change*, 316.

21   "As a result of the social dynamic, culture becomes cultural criticism, which preserves the notion of culture while demolishing its present manifestations as mere commodities and means of brutalization. Such cultural consciousness remains subservient to culture insofar as its concern with culture distracts from the true horrors. . . . What distinguishes dialectical from cultural criticism is that it heightens cultural criticism until the notion of culture is itself negated, fulfilled and surmounted in one." Adorno, "Cultural Criticism," in *Prisms*, 28–29.

22 "The alternatives—either calling culture as a whole into question from outside under the general notion of ideology, or confronting it with the norms which it itself has crystallized—cannot be accepted by critical theory." Adorno, *Prisms*, 31.

23 For Tom O'Regan, Bennett's position offers "a 'pragmatic' politics as the horizon of the thinkable." Cited in McGuigan, *Culture and the Public Sphere*, 18.

24 Stamps, *Unthinking Modernity*, 19.

25 McLuhan, "The Gutenberg Galaxy," in *Essential McLuhan*, 118.

26 See Hanke, "McLuhan, Virilio and Electric Speed in the Age of Digital Reproduction."

27 McGuigan, *Culture and the Public Sphere*, 17.

28 Bennet, *Culture*.

29 De Lauretis, *Technologies of Gender*, 13, 9.

30 Mark Johnson, *The Body in the Mind*, 172. Cited in Cruikshank, *The Social Life of Stories*, xii.

31 Heidegger, *The Question Concerning Technology*, 4.

32 Tomlinson, *Globalization and Culture*, 21.

33 Debray, *Transmitting Culture*, 12; emphasis in original.

34 Eagleton, *The Idea of Culture*, 22. Giddens introduces the concept of "structuration" in *The Constitution of Society* (1984) in an attempt to overcome such dichotomous theoretical categories as structure/agency or subjective/objective. I have extrapolated here to encompass space/time and concept/matter. Cf. Harvey, *Justice, Nature, and the Geography of Difference*, 50–51.

35 Williams, *Television*, 10–14.

36 Barthes, *Mythologies*.

37 Eagleton, *The Idea of Culture*, 5.

38 Lefebvre, *The Production of Space*, 85.

39 Said, *Culture and Imperialism*, 9.

40 Massey, "Power-Geometry and a Progressive Sense of Place," 62.

41 Massey, "A Place Called Home?," 4–5.

42 Banting, "Social Policy," in Doern, Pal, and Tomlin, *Border Crossings*, 34.

43 J. Berland, "Sound, Image and Social Space."

44 Belton, *Orinoco Flow*, 17, 2. See also "Spatial Narratives in the Canadian Imaginary," chapter 3 in this volume.

45 Turner, *Imagining Culture*, 20. As Turner adds in connection with the influential novel *The Double Hook* (1959), "The world can be spoken into existence by will and whim, or can unravel into absence and silence; the ways in which human life has been made possible in the new world are never stable or secure, and cannot be taken for granted." Ibid. Turner's idea of "infinite rehearsal" adds dimension to Derrida's understanding of the archive, which is not "a concept dealing with the past that might already be at our disposal or not at our disposal, an archivable concept of the archive. It is a question of the future, the question of the future itself, the question of a response, of a promise and of a responsibility for tomorrow. The

archive: if we want to know that that will have meant, we will only know in times to come. Perhaps. Not tomorrow but in times to come, later on or perhaps never." Like Belton's topos, Derrida's description of the archive contests the conventional (and environmentally unsustainable) distinction between the conservative embrace of place and belonging commonly associated with Heidegger, and a more cosmopolitan sense of expansion and diversity.

46   See, for instance, Kroetsch, *The Lovely Treachery of Words*; Hutcheon, *Splitting Images*; Schecter, *Zen and the Art of Postmodern Canada*; Turner, *Imagining Culture*; and Angus, *A Border Within*, 209–26.

47   Da Silva and Gomes, "Determining Heights and Altitudes for RF Sites."

48   Charland, "Technological Nationalism."

49   Foucault, "Of Other Spaces," 230.

50   Said, *Culture and Imperialism*, xxvii.

51   Barney, *Prometheus Wired*.

52   Cited in Kroker, *Technology and the Canadian Mind*, 49.

53   See Fredrick Jackson Turner, "The Frontier Hypothesis in American History."

54   Hardt and Negri, *Empire*, 174, 406.

55   Brown and Szeman, interview with Hardt and Negri, "The Global Coliseum" xx.

56   Angus, "Empire and Communications," 4.

57   Ibid.

58   Although I am drawn to Grossberg's discussion of "authentic inauthenticity" as a way of conceptualizing the politics of reclamation in postglobalized place. *We Gotta Get Out of This Place*, xx.

59   Beck, *What is Globalization?*, 20.

60   Massey, *Space, Place, and Gender*, 10.

61   Massey, "Power-Geometry and a Progressive Sense of Place," 63.

62   Chow, *The Protestant Ethic and the Spirit of Capitalism*, ix.

63   Sassen, *Territory, Authority, Rights*, 2.

64   Ibid., 145.

65   Tomlinson, *Culture and Globalization*, 9.

66   See Razack, *Space, Race, and the Law*.

67   Massey, "Power-Geometry and a Progressive Sense of Place," 61.

68   In March 2005 the leaders of Canada (Paul Martin), the United States (George W. Bush), and Mexico (Vicente Fox) signed an agreement called the Security and Prosperity Partnership of North America (SPP). That May, the Independent Task Force on the Future of North America released a document titled, "Building a North American Community." Canadian members of this task force included the Canadian Council of Chief Executives and members of the federal parliament. The report's recommendations included initiatives to establish "a common security perimeter by 2010, develop a North American Border Pass [North American ID card] with biometric identifiers, expand NORAD into a multi-service defense command," share intelligence, develop Mexico's energy resources, "harmonize" areas of energy,

education, military, foreign policy, immigration, and health, expand "temporary" migrant worker programs, and adopt a common external tariff. Marshall, "Security and Prosperity Partnership of North America (SPP)." In September 2006 a North American Forum entitled Continental Prosperity in the New Security Environment was hosted by the Canadian Council of Chief Executives with help from the Canada West Foundation at Banff Springs, Alberta. Political and business elite from Canada, Mexico, and the United States continued the discussion on deepening military and economic ties. Discussions also touched on integrating energy supply, reducing carbon emissions, and closing the income gap between Mexico, the United States, and Canada. Topics included "A Vision for North America," "A North American Energy Strategy," "Demographic and Social Dimensions of North American Integration," and "Opportunities for Security Co-operation." According to reports, "John Larsen, spokesman for the North American Forum, said that the public was not notified of the closed and private meeting and would not confirm or deny that [Donald] Rumsfeld or anyone else was in attendance. He said he did not know who paid for the forum." *Banff Crag and Canyon Online*, September 19, 2006 (visited January 15, 2009; printed-out pages on file with author).

69 Harvey, *Justice, Nature, and the Geography of Difference*, 174.

70 Guattari, *Three Ecologies*.

71 Lee, *Savage Fields*, 7, 9.

72 See Whiteside, *Divided Natures*.

73 Hutcheon borrows the term *amphibology* from Roland Barthes to describe "the opposite of the situation where context forces us to choose one of two meanings and forget the other." Citing Foucault's idea of "the primacy of a contradiction that has its model in the simultaneous affirmation and negation of a single proposition," Hutcheon argues that a Canadian is "a born sucker for anything that will tie her up in knots." *Splitting Images*, 12.

74 "Our language, our story, only uses the poet in order to speak itself. On the other hand, we expect to hear from the poet whatever it is we mean by originality." The solution is to be "the master of listening." Kroetsch, *The Lovely Treachery of Words*, 18.

75 Dan Yashinsky, "Eyes on the Street," 14–15.

76 Williams, *The Year 2000*, 219.

one Writing on the Border

Second epigraph: Seymour Martin Lipset, "Pacific Divide: American Exceptionalism—Japanese Uniqueness," *International Journal of Public Opinion Research* Vol. 5, no. 2 (1990): 121–66. "A person who knows only one country basically knows no country well. Comparing the United States or Japan with other nations is the best way to learn about each. In a previous work, I dealt with Canada, and argued that 'it is precisely because the two North American democracies have so much in common that they permit students of each to gain insights into the factors that cause variations.' " The author of *American Exceptionalism: A Double-Edged Sword* (New York: Norton, 1996) and other works, Lipset spent some time at the University of Toronto and arrived at this conclusion through researching political and cultural differences between Saskatchewan and North Dakota.

 1 Sauve, *Borderlines*, 119.

 2 A selection of interviews from *Talking to Americans* can be seen on YouTube, http://www.youtube.com/watch?v=BhTZ_tgMUdo (visited October 25, 2007).

 3 Mercer and his 22 *Minutes* collaborators won Canada's top television comedy award five times. Mercer hosted the 2000 and 2001 Geminis (Canada's film industry awards ceremony) and Junos (Canada's music awards ceremony). In 2002 Mercer was awarded a Gemini Award for *Talking to Americans* but renounced it in honor of the victims of the September 11 attack. He went on to host a self-titled weekly comedy program on the CBC which is not as funny.

 4 Knelman, Martin. "Talking to Americans Not as Fun as It Used to Be," *Toronto Star*, January 9, 2005, A2.

 5 See John Robert Colombo's poem "A Canadian Is Somebody Who"
> Thinks he knows how to make love in a canoe
> Bets on the Toronto Maple Leafs . . .
> Possesses "a sound sense of the possible"
> Is sesquilingual (speaks one and a half languages)
> Has become North American without becoming
> Either American or Mexican.
> Knows what the references in this poem are all about."
> Cited in Hutcheon, *Splitting Images*, 13.

 6 New, *Borderlands*, 6.

 7 Eagleton, *The Idea of Culture*, 46.

 8 Georg Lukács, *Essays on Thomas Mann*, 47.

 9 McNaught, cited in McLuhan, "Canada, The Borderline Case," 241.

10 Donna Lypchuk on *Eye Weekly Online* (printout in the author's files).

11 Sauve, *Borderlines*, 27.

12 "The foundations for the Canadian conquest of the American entertainment industry were laid in 1909 when 'America's sweetheart' and Toronto, Ontario, native Mary Pickford arrived in Hollywood on orders from Canadian Prime Minister Sir Wilfred Laurier. Her plan was to endear herself to the American populace through cinema and then use her clout to take over the industry" (http://www.magicalmouse.com/conspiracy/). Thus begins the chronicle of the 1985 TV mockumentary *The Canadian Conspiracy*. According to the Internet Movie Database (IMDb) entry, key conspirators include Lorne Greene, Lorne Michaels ("two Lornes!"), Anne Murray, Wayne and Shuster, Michael J. Fox, Pamela Anderson, Jim Carrey, David Cronenberg, William Shatner, and, of course, SCTV comedians John Candy, Catherine O'Hara, Rick Moranis, Dave Thomas, Martin Short,

and Eugene Levy (see Internet Movie Database http://www.imdb.com/title/tt0285470/). An update names Jim Carrey the Lead Agent, Humor Control Initiative, and Alanis Morissette Lead Agent, Musical Control Initiative.

13 An earlier draft of this essay stated that Molson was purchased by Coors. My error was corrected by a media representative from Molson's who wanted to see a draft before granting permission to reproduce the image. She wrote: "That tends to be the misinterpretation of the Canadian public, that their beloved Canadian beer company is now American-owned. (Interestingly, Americans also often misinterpret the transaction and think that their beloved beer company [Coors] was taken over by Canadians!!) In fact, the two companies merged. The Canadian Molson family and the American Coors family share joint and equal control over Molson Coors Brewing Company." (Lori Ball, personal correspondence, May 2008.)

14   Hey, I'm not a lumberjack, or a fur trader. . . .
            I don't live in an igloo or eat blubber, or own a dogsled. . . .
            and I don't know Jimmy, Sally or Suzy from Canada,
            although I'm certain they're really really nice.

            I have a Prime Minister, not a president.
            I speak English and French, not American.
            And I pronounce it 'about', not 'a boot'.

            I can proudly sew my country's flag on my backpack.
            I believe in peace keeping, not policing,
            diversity, not assimilation,
            and that the beaver is a truly proud and noble animal.
            A toque is a hat, a chesterfield is a couch,
            and it is pronounced 'zed' not 'zee', 'zed' !!!!

            Canada is the second largest landmass!
            The first nation of hockey!
            and the best part of North America

            My name is Joe!!
            And I am Canadian!!!
    See Coolcanuckaward website (http://www.coolcanuckaward.ca/joe_canadian
    .htm) and YouTube (http://www.youtube.com/watch?v=DznoUiiOYLs), visited
    March 2006.

15 Duffet, "Going Down Like a Song," 1–11.

16 Miller, *The Well Tempered Self*, 178.

17 See Taylor, *Multiculturalism*, 36.

18 See Resnick, *Thinking English Canada*, 112.

19 Kroetsch, *The Lovely Treachery of Words*, 57.

20 Angus, *A Border Within*, 26.

21 Levin, *Jean Baudrillard*, 209.

22   Thorner and Frohn-Nielson, *A Country Nourished on Self-Doubt.*

23   Angus, *A Border Within.*

24   Razack, introduction to *Space, Race, and the Law.*

25   Day, "Constructing the Official Canadian," 42–66.

26   Baldwin, cited in Gray, *Canada,* 95–96.

27   Ibid., emphasis added.

28   Frye, cited in Staines, *The Canadian Imagination,* 122–23.

29   Kroetsch, *The Lovely Treachery of Words,* 57.

30   Fowkes, *Giving up the Ghost,* 88–89.

31   Loiselle, "The Radically Moderate Canadian," 258–59.

32   Ibid., 264–65.

33   Ibid., 266.

34   Frye, cited in Staines, *The Canadian Imagination,* 23.

35   Schecter, *Zen and the Art of Postmodern Canada,* 106–8.

36   This theme was taken up by the Pittsburgh journalist Samantha Bennett, in a widely circulated 2003 column that typifies American envy: "It's not just the weather that's cooler in Canada": "The Canadians are so quiet that you may have forgotten they're up there, but they've been busy doing some surprising things. It's like discovering that the mice you are dimly aware of in your attic have been building an espresso machine. . . . Like teenagers, we fiercely idolize individual freedom but really demand that everyone be the same. But the Canadians seem more adult—more secure. They aren't afraid of foreigners. They aren't afraid of homosexuality. Most of all, they're not afraid of each other. I wonder if America will ever be that cool." *Post-Gazette* (Pittsburgh), July 30, 2003.

37   Saul, *Reflections of a Siamese Twin,* 8.

38   Slemon, "Unsettling the Empire." For commentary on this essay and its influence see Pennie, "Looking Elsewhere for Answers to the Postcolonial Question," in Hable, *New Contexts of Canadian Criticism,* 82.

39   Clarke, "What Was Canada? Is Canada?"

40   McGreevy, "The Wall of Mirrors," 8.

41   Cook, "Cultural Nationalism in Canada," 20.

42   Thorner, "*A Country Nourished on Self-Doubt,*" 17.

43   McGreevy, *Imagining Niagara.*

44   Francis, *National Dreams,* 130.

45   Karen E. Smith, ice *Case Studies No. 39: The Canada—United States Border Dispute,* http://www.american.edu/ted/ice/alaska.htm.

46   See Cook, *Cultural Nationalism;* Gray, *Canada: A Portrait in Letters;* and Thorner, *A Country Nourished on Self-Doubt.*

47   Cook, *Canadian Cultural Nationalism,* 32.

48   Canada's more pacifistic approach to Korea and Vietnam "exuded a slightly stuffy moralism that did not sit well with many Americans. In that telling phrase of Dean Acheson's, 'the stern daughter of the Voice of God' was still present all too often." Hillmer and Granatstein, *Empire to Umpire,* 176. Research by Beverley Diamond

shows that political cartoonists have been depicting Canada as the female coun-terpart of the United States since the early colonial period.

49 Sehdev, "Unsettling the Settler State at Niagara Falls," 220; Jill Adams, "Activist Roots Still Thrive in Canadian Border Crossing," *Indian Country Today* online, July 23, 2004, quoted ibid.

50 According to Julia Keller, writing for the *Chicago Tribune*, "Canadians are [as a culture] the last group in the world it's still okay to make fun of." "Can They Hear Us?" *Toronto Star*, July 1, 2000, M1.

51 Sassen, *Losing Control?*

52 Andrew Duffy, "Fortress North America: Canada Seeks Continental System to Stop Terrorists, Illegal Migrants," *Montreal Gazette*, January 29, 2000, A1.

53 This is the premise introducing "The Borderland Project," a series of publications to advance understanding of "transborder attributes" from a multidisciplinary per-spective. See McGreevy, "The Wall of Mirrors"; Merrit, "Crossing the Border"; Blaise, "The Border as Fiction"; and Brown, "Borderlines and Borderlands in En-glish Canada."

54 For a controversial account of the instrumental creation of an uninhabited mythic North, see Mowatt, *Canada North Now*.

55 Saul, *Reflections of a Siamese Twin*, 157.

56 See, for example, Hutcheon, *Splitting Images*; Angus, *A Border Within*; Kroetsch, *The Lovely Treachery of Words*; and Schecter, *Zen and the Art of Postmodern Canada*.

57 Kroetsch, *The Lovely Treachery of Words*, 22.

58 Hayles, *How We Became Posthuman*, 8, 9.

59 Kroetsch, *The Lovely Treachery of Words*, 30.

60 Frye, *The Bush Garden*, 27.

61 McLuhan, "Canada: The Borderline Case," 244.

62 Hable, *New Contexts of Canadian Criticism*.

63 Frye, *The Bush Garden*, 45.

64 Belton, *Orinoco Flow*, 10.

65 Ibid., 10–11.

66 Gagne, *Nationalism, Technology, and the Future of Canada*, 1, 3.

67 Schecter, *Zen and the Art of Postmodern Canada*, 47.

68 Ibid.

69 Turner, *Imagining Culture*, 20.

70 See, e.g., Smythe, *Dependency Road*; Audley, *Canada's Culture Industries*; and Lorimer and Duxbury, "Of Culture, the Economy, Cultural Production, and Cul-tural Producers."

71 See Kroetsch, *The Lovely Treachery of Words*, 158.

72 Hutcheon, *Splitting Images*, 12.

73 This is not to say that all cross-dressing is comical—John Greyson's film *Lilies* shows otherwise.

74 Cited in Brown, "Borderlines and Borderlands in English Canada," 33.

75 Morrison, *Canadians Are Not Americans*, 105.

76   McBride and Shields, *Dismantling a Nation*, 36; cf. Marchak, *Ideological Perspectives on Canada*.

77   Longfellow, "The Crisis of Naming in Canadian Film," 207. *I Love a Man in Uniform* is an award-winning film about an actor who begins to walk the streets of Toronto in his policeman costume and loses himself in his fantasy role, with catastrophic results.

78   See Radhakrishnan, "Nationalism, Gender and the Narrative of Identity."

79   Resnick, *Thinking English Canada*, 81–82.

80   McBride and Shields, *Dismantling a Nation*, 8.

81   Ibid.

82   Black, "Time for American Takeover," *Globe and Mail*, December 1, 2000, sec. A.

83   William, "PM Vows to Fight for Poor, Medicare," *Toronto Star*, March 20, 2000, sec. A.

84   Reid, *Shakedown*, 37.

85   Cited ibid., 15.

86   McBride and Shields, *Dismantling a Nation*, 15.

87   Ibid., 40.

88   "What Border," *Time Magazine*, July 20, 2000.

89   *Time* was the subject of considerable hostility between the two countries through the 1970s, as Canada sought protection for Canadian advertisers in the Canadian edition. See Swanson, "Canadian Cultural Nationalism and the U.S. Public Interest," 33. Swanson notes "the temptation for U.S. officials to misread the overall phenomenon of Canadian cultural retrofitting by interpreting it as a simple case of economic protectionism." Ibid., 61. In 1976 a group of Republican congressmen noted, "The Canadian government has charted a course in communications policy which is discriminatory to trading interests in the United States. How far Canada follows that course will ultimately determine the need for and the character of our response." Cited ibid., 72.

90   Ball, cited in Cook, "Cultural Nationalism in Canada," 33.

91   Liz Armstrong and Angela Rickman, "Winning War on Cancer," *Toronto Star*, May, 22, 2007, A19.

92   Tomlinson, *Globalization and Culture*, 110.

93   Lash and Lury, *Global Cultural Industry*, 6–7.

94   Ibid., 14.

95   Government Accountability Office, testimony before U.S Committee on Intergovernmental Affairs, "Bioterrorism: A Threat to Agriculture and the Food Supply," November 19, 2003. This report was widely covered in Canadian media. Available at Government Accountability Office website (accessed July 20, 2007; printout of Web pages on file with the author).

96   The relations between neoliberalism and the culture of danger can be seen in Foucault's last lectures on the relation between biopower and neoliberal "governmentality"; see Loon, *Risk and Technological Culture*.

two Space at the Margins

Second chapter epigraph: Harold Innis, "Great Britain, the United States, and Canada" in *Staples, Markets, and Cultural Change*.

1   Acland and Buxton, *Harold Innis in the New Century*; Berland and Hornstein, *Capital Culture*; Friesen, *Citizens and Nation*; Innis, *Staples, Markets, and Cultural Change*.

2   Jameson, "Postmodernism, or the Cultural Logic of Late Capitalism."

3   See de Certeau, *The Practice of Everyday Life*, vii.

4   Shields, *Places at the Margins*, 276–77.

5   Bennett, *Culture*, 41.

6   Carey, *Communication as Culture*, 151.

7   Semple, cited in Kern, *The Culture of Time and Space*, 226.

8   Innis, *Staples, Markets, and Cultural Change*, 4. The same trading patterns emerged in Australia as it began to export wool to Britain in the early nineteenth century. As Jan Todd argues, "Australia now had a clear function in the world. Into its colonies flowed capital, labor and technology, accompanied by the transfer of institutions, knowledge and resources. Most of these came from Britain. Out of the colonies flowed exports of foodstuffs and raw materials. Most of them went to Britain. Many of the other colonies within the British Empire developed a similar pattern." *Colonial Technology*, 4.

9   Innis, *Staples, Markets, and Cultural Change*, 5.

10 See Miller, *Skyscrapers Hide the Heavens*, 223.

11 Ibid.

12 Jhally, "Communications and the Materialist Conception of History," 64.

13 Innis, *The Bias of Communication* and *Empire and Communications*.

14 Massey, "The Politics of Space/Time," 261.

15 See Kern, *The Culture of Time and Space*, 206.

16 Ibid., 235–36.

17 For commentaries on the effects of this historical context on Innis's work, see Melody, Salter, and Heyer, *Culture, Communication, and Dependency*, 23; Angus, "Orality in the Twilight of Humanism," 22; Stamps, *Unthinking Modernity*, 44; and Watson, *Marginal Man*, chap. 2 Watson summarizes this effect as "a view of the war as a rite of initiation taking place on the extreme margins of humanity: the trenches." Ibid.,76; thus Innis's bitter awakening to imperial power serving under British military officers during the First World War.

18 Innis, *Staples, Markets, and Cultural Change*, 13.

19 Innis, "A Plea for Time" and "Industrialism and Cultural Values," in *Staples, Markets, and Cultural Change*, 316, 378.

20 Spengler, cited in Kern, *The Culture of Time and Space*, 259.

21 Ibid., 105.

22 Innis, "A Plea for Time," in *Staples, Markets, and Cultural Change*, 378–79.

23   Innis, *Empire and Communications*, 76.

24   Acland, "Histories of Place and Power," 251.

25   Stamps, *Unthinking Modernity*, 21.

26   Lefebvre, *The Production of Space*, 26.

27   Ibid., 85.

28   Gregory, *Geographical Imaginations*, 169.

29   See de Certeau, *The Practice of Everyday Life*, 38.

30   Gregory, *Geographical Imaginations*, 168.

31   Innis, "A Plea for Time," in *Staples, Markets, and Cultural Change*, 80–82.

32   Brooker-Gross, "The Changing Concept of Place in the News."

33   Drache, "Introduction," in Innis, *Staples, Markets, and Cultural Change*.

34   Marx, cited in Smith, *Uneven Development*, 93.

35   Said, *Culture and Imperialism*, 5.

36   Hall, "The Local and the Global," 27.

37   Santos, "Toward a Multicultural Conception of Human Rights," 216.

38   See Kern, *The Culture of Time and Space*.

39   Carey, *Communication as Culture*.

40   Said, *Culture and Imperialism*, 5.

41   Smith, *Uneven Development*, 97–130.

42   "In constant opposition to the tendency toward differentiation, this tendency to-
      ward equalization, and the resulting contradiction, are the more concrete deter-
      minants of uneven development. This contradiction is resolved historically in the
      concrete patter of uneven development." Smith, *Uneven Development*, 114. Smith
      notes that this dichotomous process is evident in the leveling of the quality of
      working life, in the leveling of the urban-rural dichotomy, and in "the transforma-
      tions of nature into a universal means of production." Ibid.

43   Appadurai, "Disjuncture and Difference in the Global Cultural Economy," 295.

44   Chatterjee, *The Nation and Its Fragments*, 26.

45   Ibid., 28.

46   I explore this idea further in "Locating Listening," chapter 6 in this volume.

47   For the authoritative history of this conflict and collusion, see Babe, *Telecommu-
      nications in Canada*, 252–56, which addresses the reversal of national sovereignty
      objectives.

48   See Massey, "The Politics of Space/Time," 265.

49   Carey, "Harold Adams Innis and Marshall McLuhan," 273.

50   See Helms, *Ulysses' Sail*, 224–26. Steven Greenblatt reminds us of the powerful
      association of wonder and greed with which Columbus met—and wrote of—the
      New World. Greenblatt, *Marvelous Possessions*.

51   Helms, *Ulysses' Sail*, 260.

52   Shields, *Places at the Margins*, 175.

53   Sioui, *For an Amerindian Autohistory*, xx.

54   King, *Inventing the Indian*. See Siemerling, *The New North American Studies*, 68.

55   Latour, *We Have Never Been Modern*, 38–39.

56 Innis, "The Importance of Staple Products in Canadian Development," in *Staples, Markets, and Cultural Change,* 4.

57 Ibid., 5.

58 Acland, "Histories of Place and Power," 256. This passage summarizes Robin Neill, "Imperialism and the Staple Theory of Canadian Economic Development: The Historical Perspective," in Melody et al., *Culture, Communication, and Dependency.*

59 Innis, *Staples, Markets, and Cultural Change,* 2.

60 Shields, *Places at the Margins,* 29.

61 Shields, ibid., 182–83, cites the influential historian W. L. Morton (1970): "The ultimate and the comprehensive meaning of Canadian history is to be found where there has been no Canadian history: in the north."

62 Industry, Science and Technology Canada, *Science and Technology Economic Analysis Review,* 1.

63 Significantly this is not the case with electronics, aerospace, or computer industries, all areas of expertise Canada has developed without damage to its branch-plant relationship to industry in the United States. Jan Todd offers an illuminating description of a comparable gap in the research bridging scientific knowledge and technological innovation in nineteenth-century Australia. Agents of local science were active in "the process of assimilation of new technologies into local production systems," she writes. "What they were not generally doing was carrying out research aimed at direct solution of technological problems by means of domestic research activity. . . . Whether through lack of interest or lack of confidence, the ready availability of overseas technology seems indeed to have pre-empted, or displaced, local research programs aimed at development of new home-grown technologies to solve an acknowledged industry problem." Todd, *Colonial Technology,* 224–25. She concludes that Australia's willingness to appropriate and choose technological options from diverse sources contributed to growing technological sovereignty, if not independence; that full achievement of this goal has been blocked by the failure to achieve critical mass in the dynamic interaction between receivers and producers, or "firms, industries, sectors and colonies"; and that dependency theory explains much, but not all, of the structural imbalances of Australian science and technology.

64 See Babe, *Telecommunications in Canada;* and Berland, "Mapping Space" (chapter 8 in this volume) for further discussion of satellites and the Canadian space industry.

65 McLuhan, *Understanding Media,* 47.

66 Ibid.

67 Ibid., 167.

68 Carey, "Harold Adams Innis and Marshall McLuhan," 298.

69 See Franklin, *The Real World of Technology,* 13. Franklin contrasts memory, community, and resistance, on the one hand, to globalization, amnesia, and passivity, on the other, in terms that are reminiscent of Innis's work.

70 See Carey, *Communication as Culture*, 212.

71 Virilio, "The Third Interval," 3.

72 Virilio, *Speed and Politics*, 7.

73 Lefebvre, *The Production of Space*, 333–34.

74 Sassen, *Globalization and Its Discontents*, 12.

75 Harvey, *The Condition of Postmodernity*, 213.

three Spatial Narratives

Second chapter epigraph: Atwood, cited in Godard, "Notes from the Cultural Field," 212.

1 Frye, *The Bush Garden*, 27.

2 Van Wyck, "Telling Stories," 3.

3 Angus, *Primal Scene of Communication*, 4, cited in Van Wyck, "Telling Stories," 4.

4 Angus, *Primal Scene of Communication*, 21–22.

5 Angus, *A Border Within*, 21, 19.

6 Eagleton, "Nationalism."

7 See New, *Landsliding*; Shields, *Places on the Margins*; and Razack, *Space, Race, and the Law*.

8 Friesen, *Citizens and Nation*, 224–25.

9 Bhabha, *The Location of Culture*, 219.

10 Belton, *Orinoco Flow*, 2, 10; cf. Gregory, *Geographical Imaginations*.

11 Belton, *Orinoco Flow*, 10–11.

12 Gagne, "Technology and Canadian Politics," 1, 3.

13 Jameson, "Third-World Literature in the Era of Multinational Capitalism."

14 Devereux, "'Canadian Classic' and 'Commodity Export,'" 180.

15 Ibid., 185.

16 One of the poems set to music by the Perth County Conspiracy:

> I spun you out
> Of my eyes' fire;
> It wasn't you
> But my desire
> For the pure vein
> Of silver
> Running there
> Even if not mine;
> But I have it now,
> Out of my wish
> I created it
> And can slough
> Off the idiocies
> I constructed of you,

> Can look through
> My hopeful lies
> To your sorry
> Hopes of yourself,
> And your mysterious
> Flawed glory.
>
> Milton Acorn, *I've Tasted My Blood*.

17 Moss, *Is Canada Postcolonial?*, 9.

18 R. G. MacBeth, *The Canadian Pacific—Romance of a Grand Railway*, 1924, cited in Francis, *National Dreams*, 19.

19 The promise to transgress or exceed boundaries is highly valorized in contemporary criticism. Visual theorists claim that the Internet's circulation of images across borders will destroy governments and explode global politics. Cultural theorists claim that cyberspace and biotechnologies have transformed and liberated the body. Political theorists claim that immigration has done this for geopolitical identity. For instance, "It is clear that each successive migrant group represented a rupture in the myth of the nation," Rinaldo Walcott suggests; "It is the migration of non-whites that has continuously disrupted the fictions of the nation-state." But the Canadian "fiction of the nation-state" is all about migrant groups. Walcott, "Keep on Movin," 29. While Walcott expresses racial solidarity with "pre-postmodern postmodern voyagers," his narrative structure is solidly aligned with modernist thought. In each case, the perceived break is privileged over the space it exceeds. Through such valorization, postmodernism displays its modernist legacy.

20 Stewart, *From Coast to Coast*, 9.

21 "Another nice thing about radio is you really feel hooked up to the country, can understand what it must have meant in the thirties if you lived in some rural outpost and had only the wireless to keep you in touch. In the long historical perspective, radio really brought about the transformation." Schecter, *Zen and the Art of Postmodern Canada*, 103.

22 Innis, *Empire and Communications*; Innis, *Staples, Markets, and Cultural Change*; Acland and Buxton, *Harold Innis in the New Century*. I address Innis's work in detail in "Space at the Margins," chapter 2 in this volume.

23 Frye, *The Bush Garden*, 220; cf. Morantz, *Where Is Here?*

24 Godard, "Notes from the Cultural Field," 212.

25 Cavell, "Theorizing Canadian Space," 81.

26 Frye, *The Bush Garden*, 221.

27 Rotstein, cited in Angus, *A Border Within*, 14.

28 For a discussion of real and imaginary diversity in Toronto, see Isin and Siemiatycki, "Making Space for the Mosques," in Razack, *Space, Race, and the Law*.

29 E.g., Banning, "Playing in the Light."

30 Daniel Francis, *National Dreams*, 10.

31 O'Neill, "Empire vs. Empire."

32   Said, *Culture and Imperialism*, 9.
33   Slemon, "Unsettling the Empire."
34   Slemon, cited in Pennie, "Looking Elsewhere for Answers to the Postcolonial Question," 82.
35   Clarke, "What Was Canada?," 33.
36   Slemon, "Unsettling the Empire," 38–39.
37   Siemerling, *The New North American Studies*, 25.
38   Ibid., 27.
39   Ibid., 37.
40   Bird, *Documents of Canadian Broadcasting*, 43.
41   Cf. Hable, *New Contexts of Canadian Criticism*, 88.
42   Transcript of William Ging Wee Dere, "United Nations and Human Rights," presentation to the Nova Scotia Human Rights Conference, Halifax, December 9, 1995, at http://www.asian.ca/redress/sp_19951205.htm. Printout of Web pages in the author's files.
43   Thanks to Sarah Sharma for her help in locating these histories.
44   Dere, "United Nations and Human Rights."
45   Hable, "New Contexts of Canadian Criticism," 88.
46   Ibid., 86.
47   Francis, *National Dreams*, 54.
48   Ibid., 63.
49   Mulvey, "Magnificent Obsession," 10.
50   Doern and Kirton, "Foreign Policy."
51   Berland, "Nationalism and the Modernist Legacy."
52   On conservatism and populism in the United States and the United Kingdom, cf. Grossberg, *We Gotta Get out of This Place*.
53   Miller, *The Well-Tempered Self*, 10.
54   Mahon, "Canadian Public Policy."
55   Gordon, "Governmentality," 10.
56   Whitlock, "Exiles from Tradition," 12–13.
57   Ibid., 15.
58   Dean, "Concealing Her Blue Stockings," 33.
59   Ibid., 2, 18.
60   On the subject of irony in Canadian culture, see Hutcheon, *Splitting Images*; and New, *Grandchild of Empire*.
61   Gould, *Anne of Green Gables vs. G.I. Joe*.
62   Loiselle, "The Radically Moderate Canadian," 262.
63   New, *Grandchild of Empire*, 18.
64   Brodie, *Politics at the Margins*, 60.
65   Hillmer and Granatstein, *Empire to Umpire*, 217.
66   Ibid.
67   Ibid., 219.

68 Gould, *Anne of Green Gables vs. G.I. Joe*, 176.

69 Morrison, *Canadians Are Not Americans*, 184.

70 Ibid.

71 Wilson, "The Death of Princess Diana."

72 Debray, *Transmitting Culture*.

73 New, *Land Sliding*, 8.

74 Angus, *A Border Within*, 153.

75 Chow, *The Protestant Ethic and the Spirit of Capitalism*.

76 Berland, "Radio Space and Industrial Time."

77 Mahtani and Salmon, "Site Reading?"

78 PetitionOnline, http://www.petitiononline.com/mod_perl/signed.cgi?romanow (visited July 2006, printout of Web pages on file with the author).

79 Adams, *Fire and Ice*.

80 Lazarus, *Nationalism and Cultural Practice in the Postcolonial World*, 44.

81 Angus, *A Border Within*, 17.

four Angels Dancing

1 Colilli, *The Angel's Corpse*, 57.

2 Serres, *Angels*.

3 Hennion and Meadel, "Programming Music," 186.

4 Ibid., 186–87.

5 Helmut, "Listening Behavior and Musical Preferences in the Age of Transmitted Music," 119–49.

6 De Lauretis, *Technologies of Gender*, 5.

7 Adorno, *Introduction to the Sociology of Music*, 208.

8 On the demographic productivity of special events marketing, see Elmer, "Polarpalooza Beach Party."

9 Du Gay and Hall, *Doing Cultural Studies*.

10 Fischer, "Entertainment," 13.

11 Berland, "Radio Space and Industrial Time."

12 Innis, *The Strategy of Culture*.

13 Carey, "Canadian Communication Theory," 33.

14 Bailey and Crump, "Provincial Musical Hall," in *Music Hall*, vii.

15 Ibid., xvii.

16 Briggs, *Serious Pursuits*, 39.

17 Bailey and Crump, "Provincial Musical Hall," in *Music Hall*.

18 Lefebvre, *Critique of Everyday Life*, 6.

19 Czitrom, *Media and the American Mind*.

20 Lefebvre, *The Production of Space*.

21 Anderson, *Imagined Communities*.

22 Czitrom, *Media and the American Mind*, 77.

23   McLuhan, *Understanding Media*.

24   Brecht, *Brecht on Theatre*.

25   Winner, *Autonomous Technology*.

26   As I argue in "The Musicking Machine" (chapter 5 in this volume), the dominance of the operatic voice was also a response to the technical limits of sound recording at the time.

27   See Mattelart and Mattelart, *International Image Markets*, among others. Crawley makes a similar argument about Canadian television and film. The possibility of different values with regard to production systems and aesthetics is continuously undermined by enforced adaptation to changing technological and economic conditions in the American industry. This adaptation leads to the production of television series that are intended to compete with American series without the advantage of the American production infrastructure. Crawley, "The Canadian Difference in Media."

28   Friesen, *Citizens and Nation*.

29   Poulantzas, *State, Power, Socialism*, 107; cf. Soja, *Postmodern Geographies*, 215.

30   De Lauretis, *Technologies of Gender*.

31   Harvey, "The Urban Process under Capitalism," 127.

32   Lefebvre, "Space, Social Product, and Use Value."

33   Featherstone and Lash, "Spaces of Culture," 6.

34   Helmut, "Listening Behaviour and Musical Preferences in the Age of Transmitted Music," 125.

35   Brecht, *Brecht on Theatre*, 34, 36.

36   Dyer, *Light Entertainment*. Cited in Barnard, *On the Radio*, 154.

37   Foucault, "The Subject and Power."

38   In *The Perfect Machine*, Nelson uses the term *containment* to describe the way in which television assumes the ritual dimensions of collective life.

39   But don't forget the lascivious pleasures of reading Emile Zola, whose moral denunciation of the depraved bourgeoisie takes particularly graphic form.

40   For instance, Brunsdon suggests that the soap opera produces and relies upon three different levels of viewer literacy: generic knowledge (familiarity with the conventions of soap opera: multiple narratives, discontinuity, and weekly cliffhangers are part of the grammar of the genre); program literacy (which requires that viewers understand what happened previously, where characters come from, who belongs to whom); and cultural knowledge (familiarity with "socially acceptable codes and conventions for the conduct of personal life"). The possession of such knowledge serves to reinforce the viewer's sense of her own competence, which is strategically deployed by both producers and viewers in the viewing experience. Brunsdon, *The Feminist, the Housewife, and the Soap Opera*, 30.

41   Braman, "Trade and Information Policy," 288.

42   O'Neill, "Empire vs. Empire," 198.

43   Cited in Theberge, *Any Sound You Can Imagine*.

44   O'Neill, "Empire vs. Empire," 195, 200.

45 Reagan, cited in Mosco, "Towards a Transnational World Information Order,"
    46–53.
46 Patrick, "Global Economy, Global Communication." Braman notes that "The
    focus on information as a commodity by the U.S. is part of an overall rejection
    of cultural, social or political valuation of international information flows that is
    embedded in background studies for policy-makers, congressional hearings and
    policy statements in a quite self-conscious way." Braman, "Trade and Information
    Policy," 288–89.
47 Mosco, "Toward a Transnational World Information Order," 47.
48 Santos, "Towards a Multicultural Conception of Human Rights," 216.
49 Resnick describes the shift from an understanding of sovereignty as the defense of
    the nation-state to a critique of the "claim of the state to represent some absolute
    or ultimate power against its own citizenry." Resnick, *The Masks of Proteus*, 117.
50 Ibid.
51 In 2006 CBC Television controversially dropped its two most popular prime time
    dramas, *Da Vinci's City Hall* and *This Is Wonderland*, which dramatized the effects
    of social restructuring in Vancouver City Hall and the Toronto criminal court sys-
    tem, respectively. CBC Television, now funded as much by advertising as by public
    subsidy, stated that it would no longer produce dramas with less than a million
    viewers and that there was no space for "social issues" programs in its updated
    schedule.

five The Musicking Machine

  I Berland, "Postmusics."
  2 See Theberge, *Any Sound You Can Imagine*.
  3 Kelly, *Downright Upright*, 22–23.
  4 Ibid., 21.
  5 Ibid., 24–25, 27.
  6 Ford, *Canada's Music*, 41.
  7 Ibid., 55.
  8 Ibid., 35.
  9 McDowell, *Gender, Identity, and Place*, 61.
 10 Loesser, *Men, Women, and Pianos*.
 11 Ford, *Canada's Music*, 55.
 12 Massey, *Space, Place, and Gender*, 179.
 13 Crawford, *Selected Stories of Isabella Valancy Crawford*, 22.
 14 Ford, *Canada's Music*, 59.
 15 Ibid., 10.
 16 Ibid., 14.
 17 Negus, "Producing Pop," 114.
 18 Sparke, *As Long as It's Pink*.
 19 Godlovitch, *Musical Performance*, 43.

20   Weber, cited ibid., 120.

21   Ibid., 119.

22   Ord-Hume, *Pianola*, 9.

23   Ibid., 10.

24   Weber, *The Rational and Social Foundations of Music*, 120.

25   Loesser, *Men, Women, and Pianos*, 425.

26   Roell, *The Piano in America*, 57.

27   Ibid.

28   Weber notes that "Orchestra works were made accessible for home use only in the form of piano transcriptions . . . The unshakable modern position of the piano rests upon the universality of its usefulness for domestic appropriation of almost all treasures of music literature, upon the immeasurable fullness of its own literature and finally on its quality as a universal accompanying and schooling instrument." Weber, *The Rational and Social Foundations of Music*, 122–23.

29   Roell, *The Piano in America*, 177.

30   Ibid., 178–80.

31   Sparke, *As Long as It's Pink* , 122–23.

32   Ibid., 123, 125.

33   Rose, "Governing 'Advanced' Liberal Democracies," 40.

34   Ord-Hume, *Pianola*, 102.

35   It is the peculiar nature of the piano to be a middle-class home instrument, Weber states. Weber, *The Rational and Social Foundations of Music*, 124.

36   From the 1901 advertisement "The Pianola: Its Mission," reprinted in Roell, *The Piano in America*, 111.

37   Roell, *The Piano in America*, 155.

38   From the 1904 advertisement "The Present of a Pianola is a Present to *Every* Member of the Family," reprinted in Roell, *The Piano in America*, 110.

39   "A Dr Busby, writing of the new Cylindrichord as early as 1825, explained that in small or family parties, where dancing to the music of the pianoforte is practised, a person totally unacquainted with music, a child or a servant, may perform, in the very best and most correct style, quadrilles, waltzes, minuets . . . or indeed any piece of music, however difficult." Ord-Hume, *Pianola*, 18.

40   Ibid., 12–13.

41   Theberge, *Any Sound You Can Imagine*, 22.

42   Roell, *The Piano in America*, 41.

43   Ibid., 52.

44   Chanan, *Repeated Takes*, 32.

45   Gitelman, "Media, Materiality, and the Measure of the Digital," 204.

46   Ibid.

47   Day, *A Century of Recorded Music*, 10.

48   Chanan, *Repeated Takes*, 30.

49   Loesser, *Men, Women, and Pianos*, 548.

50   Ord-Hume, *Pianola*, 46.

51 Theberge, *Any Sound You Can Imagine*.

52 Roell, *The Piano in America*, 18.

53 Auslander, *Liveness*, addresses whether the performances we see are live or repro-
    duced in media, and critiques the ontological preference for live performance. Aus-
    lander addresses the simulation of liveness from the vantage point of the audience,
    arguing rightly that rock music is mainly recorded music and should not be judged
    through the optics of live performance. But he does not address the changing
    situation of the performer or producer in the recording context. As Gitelman ob-
    serves, "The specifics of materiality continue to *matter* much more to authors, to
    publishers, to 'labels'—that is, to potential owners—than they ever can, could, or
    will to listeners." And to musicians, too. Gitelman, "Media, Materiality, and the
    Measure of the Digital," 214.

54 Gitelman, "Media, Materiality, and the Measure of the Digital," 194–95.

55 Ord-Hume, *Pianola*, 157. For the Gulbransen Player-Piano ads with the famous
    Gulbransen Baby trademark (dated 1921), see 116–17, 156–57.

56 Ibid., 58. An eager public was bombarded with advertisements that emphasized
    how little effort it took to play automatic pianos. Gulbransen advertising poi-
    gnantly illustrates the contradictory ideology of promoting ease of play while
    espousing the individual creativity traditionally associated with the producer
    ethic.

57 Sousa, "The Menace of Mechanical Music" (1906), cited in Gitelman, "Media, Ma-
    teriality, and the Measure of the Digital," 202.

58 Ord-Hume, *Pianola*, 28–29.

59 Ibid.

60 Kelly, *Downright Upright*, 129, 126.

61 Ford, *Canada's Music*, 107, 183.

62 Kelly, *Downright Upright*, 129, 126.

63 Winner, *Autonomous Technology*. See "Mapping Space," chapter 8 in this volume,
    for discussion of reverse adaptation in a different context.

64 Brecht, "Radio as a Means of Communication," 24. Cf. Lander, "Radiocastings."

65 Lander, "Radiocastings," 18; Kittler, "The History of Communication Media,"
    76–77.

66 McLuhan and McLuhan, *Laws of Media*, 7.

67 Ibid., 158–59.

68 Ibid., 148.

69 This section's title is from the famous Kodak advertisement that first appeared in
    1888. See Chernan, *Repeated Takes*, 27.

70 Miller, *Cultural Citizenship*, 117.

71 Shove, *Comfort, Cleanliness, and Convenience*, 170–71.

72 Ibid., passim.

73 Innis, *Staples, Markets, and Cultural Change*, 366, 368.

74 Shove, *Comfort, Cleanliness, and Convenience*, 170.

75 Foucault, *Power/Knowledge: Selected Interviews*, 194.

76   Beardsworth, cited in Wolfe, *Animal Rites*, 75.

77   Talbott, "Technology, Alienation, and Freedom."

six Locating Listening

1   This is the new slogan of CBC Radio 2.

2   Luke, *Capitalism, Democracy, and Ecology*, 64–65; cf. Baudrillard, *For a Critique of the Political Economy of the Sign*, 72.

3   Foucault, "Of Other Spaces," 230.

4   My use of the terms *space* and *place* follows David Harvey, who argues that power derives from the ability to turn space into place. For Harvey, "space . . . is a metaphor for a site or container of power which usually constrains but sometimes liberates processes of Becoming." Harvey, *The Condition of Postmodernity*, 213. Lefebvre adds that "in addition to being a means of production [space] is also a means of control, and hence of domination, of power; yet that, as such, it escapes in part from those who would make use of it." Lefebvre, *The Production of Space*, 26.

5   Mowitt, *Percussion*, 70.

6   Fanon, *A Dying Colonialism*, 74.

7   Luke, *Capitalism, Democracy, and Ecology*, 62–63.

8   Poulantzas, *State, Power, Socialism*, 107; this quote also appears in "Angels Dancing," chapter 4 in this volume.

9   McCartney explains a "soundwalk" as "an improvisation with the sounds of place." "Soundscape Works, Listening, and the Touch of Sound," 183.

10   McCauley, "Radio's Digital Future," 507.

11   See Du Gay and Hall, *Doing Cultural Studies*.

12   See Theberge, *Any Sound You Can Imagine*, 276.

13   McCauley, "Radio's Digital Future," 520.

14   Barney, "One Nation under Google," 24–25; emphasis added.

15   Simon Frith, "Towards an Aesthetic of Popular Music," 139.

16   Stewart, *From Coast to Coast*, 29.

17   Ford, *Canada's Music*, 108.

18   Stewart, *From Coast to Coast*, 21. Details of this history can also be found in Frank Peers, *The Politics of Canadian Broadcasting*, 1969; David Ellis, *Evolution of the Canadian Broadcasting System*, 1979; Dallas Smythe, *Dependency Road*, 1981; Foster, *Broadcasting Policy Development*, 1982.

19   Aird Commission, cited in Peers, *The Politics of Canadian Broadcasting*, 265–67. See Berland, "Cultural Re/Percussions" for a more detailed discussion of this history.

20   Charland, "Technological Nationalism."

21   Straw comments that "Just as until recently government regulators have used the broadcasting system as the exclusive channel through which support for Canadian recordings might be directed, recorded music in Canada has been studied primarily in terms of its role as programming for this system." Straw, "The English Canadian Recording Industry since 1970," 55–56.

22 Crean, "The CBC and the Arts," 6.

23 Ostry, *The Cultural Connection*, 54. For a fuller assessment of this period, see Berland, "Nationalism and the Modernist Legacy."

24 The history of CBC music programming and its relation to changing concepts of public interest and cultural production is addressed at length in my unpublished dissertation, "Cultural Re/Percussions."

25 See Berland and Straw, "Getting Down to Business," for a survey of policies in film, publishing and recorded music.

26 See Audley, *Canada's Culture Industries*; and Berland and Straw, "Getting Down to Business."

27 Straw offers a useful portrait of Canada's recording industry: "While record distribution has emerged, over the last twenty years, as the activity through which oligopolistic control is most effectively ensured, particularities of the Canadian situation have magnified its importance. The geographical expanse of Canada and the existence of two distinct linguistic communities has encouraged the development of distribution operations which are either regional in scope (such as those operating within Quebec), or directed towards dispersed, international markets (such as those for dance music recordings). Most Canadian-owned distributors have confined themselves to such markets, leaving pan-national distribution as the province of multinational firms operating in Canada." Straw, "The English Canadian Recording Industry since 1970," 58.

28 Lehr, "As Canadian as Possible," 16–19.

29 Kuhn, *Women's Pictures*, 50.

30 Miller, *The Well-Tempered Self*.

31 On the legitimation crisis in public broadcasting precipitated by classical music programming, see Berland, "Cultural Re/percussions."

32 Simon Frith, *Music for Pleasure*, 139.

33 McCauley, "Radio's Digital Future," 507.

34 Crane, "Mainstream Music and the Masses," 68.

35 Bradby, "Lesbians and Popular Music," 33.

36 Ibid., 34.

37 In a survey of (Anglophone) musicians conducted in Windsor, Ontario, a number of patterns emerged which may be characteristic of Canadian musicians. Asked about musical preferences and influences, only 12 percent make reference to Canadian nationality, while 18 percent name Canadian bands as models without mentioning their nationality. When mentioning consciousness of their nationality, musicians are more likely to have been affected by experience, rather than by music; by travels in Canada's north: by "wild, untouched nature," or "northern people and culture."

38 Bradby, "Lesbians and Popular Music," 35.

39 Barnard, *On the Radio*, 41.

40 Ibid.

41 Attali, *Noise*, 106.

42   Johnson and Jones, *Modern Radio Station Practices*, 118.

43   Barnard, *On the Radio*, 93.

44   See Berland, "Radio Space and Industrial Time."

45   Barney, "One Nation under Google," 11.

46   Fanon, *A Dying Colonialism*, 71.

47   The Canadian Broadcasting Corporation (CBC) has two national radio networks. CBC Radio 2 features classical music; Radio 1 features alternating music programs, talk shows, dramas, and documentaries. I focus here on the latter. See note 24 above.

48   Gzowski told *Maclean's* soon after he left the show, "The best interviews were the ones that surprised me. They're not (necessarily) the ones with the prime minister or the great author, but, rather, people like Elly Danica, a victim of sexual abuse, or a scientist whose work gives him pride. Donna Williams, the autistic woman, was very moving. She talked about the street lights sparkling pink and the colour of each blade of grass. It was quite wonderful." Canadian Broadcasting Corporation (http://www.cbc.ca/news/obit/gzowski_peter/). Viewed December 2007; printout on file with the author.

49   Crisell, *Understanding Radio*, 17.

50   Canadian music includes (according to my informal interview of local musicians) the traditional musical forms of Quebec and Newfoundland (a mix of Celtic, French, and Cajun); hard rock bands of the 1970s and 1980s; singer-songwriters such as Leonard Cohen, Joni Mitchell, Neil Young, Sarah McLachlan, Sarah Harmer, Alanis Morissette, k.d. lang, Feist, Martha Wainwright, and others (a fusion of pop, jazz, and folk); "roots" or "new country" bands such as Blue Rodeo, Cowboy Junkies, and the early k.d. lang; high-profile alternative rock bands such as The Tragically Hip, Barenaked Ladies, Broken Social Scene, and Arcade Fire; and urban fusions of jazz, West Indian music, and hip-hop represented by the Dream Warriors, k-os, and Sol Guy.

51   Warner, "Hiphop with a Northern Touch!?," 51.

52   Ibid., 59–60.

53   Cohen, "Localizing Sound," 53.

54   Fenster, "Two Stories" 86.

55   See Bradley, *Unfolding a Strategic Space*.

56   Lefebvre, *The Production of Space*, 28–29.

57   "As music is colonized by the commodity form—its use becomes the exchange-ability of its uses—listeners regress to the point where they will not listen to that which is not recognizable without first protecting themselves with an inoculation for the exotic." Mowitt, "The Sound of Music in the Era of Its Electronic Reproducibility," 187.

58   Kittler, "The History of Communication Media," 37.

59   Brecht, *Brecht on Theatre*, 37–38.

60   Eisler in Eisler and Adorno, *Composing for the Films*.

61   Brecht, *Brecht on Theatre*, 35.

62 Ibid. 37.

63 Barney, *One Nation under Google*, 11.

64 Careless, "Canadian Radio Networks," 6–7.

65 Lefebvre, *The Survival of Capitalism*, 35.

66 Ibid.; Gilbert and Diceks, "Right to the City," 254.

67 Fanon, *A Dying Colonialism*, 76.

68 Hennion and Meadel, "Programming Music," 286.

69 Eamen, *Channels of Influence*.

70 Barthes, "Listening," 260.

71 Robbins, "What Can We Learn When They Sing, eh . . ." 193.

seven Weathering the North

1   Glacken, *Traces on the Rhodian Shore*, 362.

2   Ibid., 368.

3   Ibid., 369.

4   Ibid., 358.

5   Ibid., 370.

6   M. Ackerman, *Cool Comfort*, cited in Shove, *Comfort, Cleanliness, and Convenience*, 27.

7   Carter, *Road to Botany Bay*, 137.

8   Harvey, *Spaces of Capital*, 213.

9   Whitehead, "Between the Marvelous and the Mundane."

10 Žižek, *For They Know Not What They Do*.

11 Haug, *Critique of Commodity Aesthetics*, 45.

12 Shove, *Comfort, Cleanliness, and Convenience*.

13 Ibid., 3.

14 Levinson, *Ice Time*, 37.

15 CBC, *Journal*, May 17, 1991.

16 Lee, *Weather Wisdom*.

17 Humphreys, *Ways of the Weather*, 340.

18 Carey, *Communication as Culture*, 204.

19 Henson, *Television Weathercasting*.

20 Mack, *Viewing the Earth*, 12.

21 Peter K. Newman, "They're Selling Packaged Weather," *Maclean's*, January 7, 1956, 35.

22 Henson, *Television Weathercasting*, 80–86.

23 *Maclean's*, August 15, 1950.

24 *Saturday Night*, October 23, 1954.

25 *Financial Post*, November 30, 1957.

26 Hare and Thomas, *Climate Canada*, 159.

27 Le Jeune, cited in Thwaites, *The Jesuit Relations and Allied Documents*, Vol. 7, 35.

28 Dickason, *The Myth of the Savage*, 241.

29 McKegney, "Second-Hand Shaman," 30.

30 Ibid., 29.

31 Ibid., 30–31.

32 Le Jeune, cited in Thwaites, *The Jesuit Relations and Allied Documents*, Vol. 7, 57.

33 McKegney, "Second-Hand Shaman," 30.

34 Le Jeune, cited in Thwaites, *The Jesuit Relations and Allied Documents*, Vol. 7, 21.

35 Allouez, cited by le Mercier, ibid., Vol. 50, 289.

36 Sehdev, "Vanishing at the Border," 6.

37 Ibid.

38 McGregor, *The Wacousta Syndrome*.

39 Sekyi-Otu, *Fanon and the Dialectic of Experience*, 192.

40 Willis, *Illusions of Identity*, 41.

41 Ibid., 62.

42 Ibid., 63.

43 See Helms, *Ulysses' Sail*, 224–26. "A form of paradise already held Western connotations prior to the discoveries, but the attribution of wilderness and its qualities to the West was new and clearly part of the effort to create and identify a new cosmological locale." Tracing this history in a more worldly context, Steven Greenblatt also writes of the association of wonder and greed projected onto the New World. See Greenblatt, *Marvelous Possessions*.

44 Willis, *Illusions of Identity*, 63.

45 Friesen, *Citizens and Nation*.

46 Miller, *The Well-Tempered Self*.

47 Berton, *Hollywood's Canada*, 21.

48 Morris, *Embattled Shadows*, 34.

49 Berton, *Hollywood's Canada*, 25–26.

50 "Shebib's Ordeal: Faking California in the Snow," *Globe and Mail*, November 18, 1972.

51 See Lefebvre and Barrowclough, *The Quebec Connection*, 17.

52 Quoted in Ross, *Strange Weather*.

53 See Shove, *Comfort, Cleanliness, and Convenience*, 27.

54 Friesen, *Citizens and Nation*.

eight Mapping Space

1   Morse, *Virtualities*, 99, 106. Morse is citing John Ellis, *Visible Fictions*, 169.

2   Levinson, *Ice Time*, 118.

3   Berton, *Hollywood's Canada*.

4   Agnew, "Representing Space," 259.

5   There are important economic aspects of weather forecasting that I don't address here, such as insurance and the trade in commodity futures.

6   See Harley, "Deconstructing the Map," 242.

7   See, e.g., *Novae Franciae accurate delineation*, 1657, depicting the Huron (on the left) and the Great Lakes. National Archives of Canada (NMC-6339), reprinted in Morantz, *Where Is Here?*, 36.

8   See Heidegger, *The Question concerning Technology*, 23.

9   Keller, *Secrets of Life, Secrets of Death*.

10 See Mumford, *Technic and Civilization*, 338.

11 See McLuhan, *Understanding Media*, 268.

12 Zuboff, *In the Age of the Smart Machine*, 129, 130.

13 Coker, *The Future of War*, 33.

14 Haraway, *Simians, Cyborgs, and Women*, 150.

15 Coker, *The Future of War*, 33, 35.

16 Caldicott and Eisendrath, *War in Heaven*, xiii–xiv.

17 Ibid., xiv.

18 Ibid., 7.

19 Mack, *Viewing the Earth*, 215.

20 Caldicott and Eisendrath, *War in Heaven*, 7; Coker, *The Future of War*.

21 Jay, "'The Aesthetic Ideology' as Ideology," 41.

22 Junger cited in Leslie, *Synthetic Worlds*, 126.

23 Jay, "'The Aesthetic Ideology' as Ideology," 41.

24 Lovelock, *Gaia*, vii.

25 Ibid., ix.

26 Ibid., ix, 125.

27 Lovelock, *Gaia*, 131, 137.

28 Ibid., 142.

29 See Virilio, *War and Cinema*, 71.

30 Der Derian, *Antidiplomacy*, 29.

31 Coker, *The Future of War*, 43.

32 Der Derian, *Antidiplomacy*, 29.

33 *National Science and Technology Week*, October 1992.

34 Mack, *Viewing the Earth*, 16–17.

35 See Winner, *Autonomous Technology*.

36 Jelly, *Canada*.

37 Eisenhower, cited in Crosby, *Dilemmas in Defence Decision-Making*, 106. Purver notes that they procrastinated on the subject, concluding that "there were 'no major questions of policy in this area which are ready for resolution at this time.'" Purver, *Ballistic Missile Defence and Canada*, 11.

38 Pearson in House of Common Debates on April 11, 1967, cited in Purver, *Ballistic Missile Defence and Canada*, 11.

39 Purver, *Ballistic Missile Defence and Canada*, 13.

40 Ibid., 13.

41 Doern and Kirton, "Foreign Policy," 241.

42 Ibid., 248, 256.

43   Ibid., 14.

44   O'Hanlan, *Neither Star Wars nor Sanctuary*, 6–7.

45   Ibid., 7.

46   Spence, "Lost in Space," 60.

47   Doern and Kirton, "Foreign Policy," 243.

48   Crosby, *Dilemmas in Defence Decision-Making*, 107.

49   Ibid.

50   Ibid., 107–8.

51   Defense R&D Canada, *Looking Forward Staying Ahead 2002*, 6, 13.

52   Ellington, cited in MacDonald, *Canada's Strategies for Space*, 7.

53   Ibid., 18–19.

54   Ibid., 7.

55   Lindsey and Sharpe, "Surveillance over Canada," 31.

56   Der Derian, *Antidiplomacy*, 32.

57   Lindsay and Sharpe, "Surveillance over Canada," 55–56.

58   See Turk, *The Corporate Campus*.

59   See Washburn, *University, Inc.*

60   See, for instance Klare, *The University-Military-Police Complex*. This publication traces the links between military and university research in the United States between 1947 and 1970, and shows that then, as now, research on culture was seen to be relevant to the scientific aims of the nation.

61   Bruneau, "Shall We Perform or Shall We Be Free?," 172–73.

62   On the privatization of space research, see Hudgins, *Space*, which argues that government has failed to keep up with the innovation requirements of space research, and that only the private sector can handle the manufacturing and scientific opportunities associated with it.

63   New legislation in Ontario provides that the Freedom of Information Act should apply to previously classified university records. Faculty will not be required to report research income as part of university records.

64   In *University, Inc*, Washburn argues that of the thousands of university-industry research partnerships pursued in the United States in the last decade, 80 percent of them brought no new income to the university. Indeed the process is better understood in the reverse: such partnerships have become a convenient strategy for transferring public funds to the private sector. University administrators are strangely eager to comply.

65   White House statement, cited in Stares, *The Militarization of Space*, 218.

66   "Declaration of Legal Principles . . . ," cited in Caldicott and Eisendrath, *War in Heaven*, 14.

67   Caldicott and Eisendrath, *War in Heaven*, 15.

68   Ibid., 19–20.

69   Eric Adams, "Rods from God: Space-Launched Darts That Strike like Meteors," PopSci.Com website (visited August 15, 2007, printed-out web pages on file with author); Michael Goldfarb "The Rods from God: Are Kinetic-Energy Weapons

the Future of Space Warfare?," Weekly Standard Web site (visited August 15, 2007, printed-out Web pages on file with author).

70 Caldicott and Eisendrath, *War in Heaven*, 22.

71 See chaps. 6 and 16 in Hudgins, *Space*.

72 Arendt, *The Human Condition*, 250, cited in Romanyshyn, *Technology as Symptom and Dream*, 84.

73 Gregory, *Geographical Imaginations*.

nine "Evolution" of Technological Cultures

1   On utopias or lack thereof in contemporary culture, see Levitas, "The Future of Thinking about the Future"; and Jameson, *The Seeds of Time*.

2   Moscovici, cited in Whiteside, *Divided Natures*, 55.

3   Morin, cited in Whiteside, *Divided Natures*, 74.

4   Olivia Ward, "Countries Failing Women: Report: U. N. Finds Nations Fall Short of 5-Year Goals, Millions of Women Still Dying Needlessly," *Toronto Star*, October 12, 2005, A18.

5   Shove, *Comfort, Cleanliness, and Convenience*.

6   Grant, *English-Speaking Justice*, 78; Kroker, *Technology and the Canadian Mind*, 43.

7   The intellectual history of cyberspace is comprehensively surveyed in Tofts, Jonson, and Cavellaro, *Prefiguring Cyberculture*; cf. Barney, *Prometheus Wired*.

8   See Hillis, *Digital Sensations*. In "A Disappearance of Community," 288, Ronell remarks that this "'intentional reality' . . . takes hold in the control rooms of his majesty the ego," yet simultaneously disavows and disembodies the self. "Intentional [by which she means virtual] reality eliminates the body as organic, finite, damageable, eviscerable, castratable, crushable entity, thereby closing the orifices and stemming leakage and excrement."

9   Wertheim, *The Pearly Gates of Cyberspace*, 23.

10 Coker, *The Future of War*, 33, emphasis in original.

11 Compagnon, *The Five Paradoxes of Modernity*, 37, 32.

12 Terranova, "Digital Darwin," 71.

13 See McLuhan, *Essential McLuhan*, 92. The problem of metaphor in interdisciplinary thought is addressed in Berland and Kember, "Editorial," v. Exchanges among cybernetics, literature, biology, information theory, communications, and evolutionary history are creating a "discursive melee," we argue, in which "biology is now programmed, evolution is cybernetic, communication is evolutionary, and the economy, unlike the human body, partakes of the laws of nature. Knowledge in general seems to be growing simultaneously more technocratic and more metaphorical. Its ability to slip sideways across once impervious epistemological boundaries exceeds all the expectations of a generation of critical intellectuals who once critiqued disciplinary knowledge as a privileged mode of social control."

14 Lazlo, *The Choice*, 8.

15 Castells, *The Rise of the Network Society*, 367.

16 Reid, *Shakedown*, 190.
17 Castells, *The Rise of the Network Society*, 395–96.
18 Millar, "Cracking the Gender Code."
19 E.g., Barney, "One Nation under Google."
20 Escobar, "Welcome to Cyberia," 118.
21 Grossman, "Invention of the Year: Apple's iPhone," 60.
22 Cf. Myerson, *Heidegger, Habermas, and the Mobile Phone*; Barney, "One Nation under Google."
23 See de Kerckhove, *Connected Intelligence*.
24 Kraut et al., "Internet Paradox."29. In 2004 more than 300 million working PCS were discarded (compared to 63 million dumped in 2003); in 2005, more than 100 million cell phones were thrown away, and the number has probably doubled. Slade, *Made to Break*, 1.
25 Kroker, "Virtual Capitalism."
26 Winner, *Autonomous Technology*, 32.
27 McLuhan, *Understanding Media*, 254.
28 Grant, *Technology and Justice*; Grant, *Lament for a Nation*.
29 Virilio, "The Third Interval," 4.
30 Mallin, *Art Line Thought*, 328.
31 Sioui, *For an Amerindian Autohistory*, xx.
32 "This is the flip side of the technical realization of human intent," notes David Rothenberg. "Intentions are themselves renovated through the success of techniques. The entire array of desires is transformed as we are seduced into analogy by the things we have built and constructed." *Wisdom in the Open Air*, 110. I use *technique* as Ellul defines it: "Technique . . . constructs the kind of world the machine needs and introduces order where the incoherent banging of machinery heaped up ruins. It clarifies, arranges and rationalizes; it does in the domain of the abstract what the machine did in the domain of labor." Ellul, *The Technological Society*, 5. For Marx, "The appropriation of these powers is itself nothing more than the development of the individual capacities corresponding to the material instruments of production. The appropriation of a totality of instruments of production, is for this very reason, the development of a totality of capacities in the individuals themselves." Cited in Winner, *Autonomous Technology*, 37.
33 Mokyr, *The Lever of Riches*, 15. "Of course," Mokyr adds, "if technological change eventually leads to the physical destruction of our planet, survivors may no longer wish to use the word progress in their descriptions of technological history. Until then, however, I feel justified in using the term, not in the teleological sense of leading to a clearly defined goal, but in the more limited sense of direction."
34 Ibid., 275–76.
35 An alternative historical approach to the relationship between scientific research, technological invention, and the marketplace can be found in Winston, *Misunderstanding Media*.
36 Beniger, *The Control Revolution*, 118.

37 Mazlish, *The Fourth Discontinuity*, 80.

38 Spencer, cited in Williams, *Problems in Materialism and Culture*, 87.

39 Williams, *Problems in Materialism and Culture*, 88.

40 Midgley, *Evolution as Religion*, 30–35.

41 Ross, *The Chicago Gangster's Theory of Life*, 260–61.

42 Gould, *Ever since Darwin*, 45.

43 Basalla, *The Evolution of Technology*.

44 Keller, *Secrets of Life, Secrets of Death*.

45 Terranova, "Digital Darwin."

46 Woodward, "From Virtual Cyborgs to Biological Time Bombs," 50.

47 Terranova, "Digital Darwin," 73.

48 Reid, *Shakedown*, 128.

49 Zuboff, *In the Age of the Smart Machine*, 10.

50 For critical explorations of this theme, see Romanyshyn, *Technology as Symptom and Dream*; Hayles, *How We Became Posthuman*; Terranova, "Digital Darwin"; and Noble, *Technology as Religion*. Intelligence "downloaded" from humans, creating a posthuman being with unique abilities to save the planet, is explored in many science fiction novels, e.g., David Brin's *Earth*; and John Barnes's *Mother of Storms*.

51 Minsky, *Thoughts about Artificial Intelligence*, 214.

52 Wertheim, *The Pearly Gates of Cyberspace*, 19–25.

53 Winner, *Autonomous Technology*, 58.

54 Childe, *Man Makes Himself*, cited in Basalla, *The Evolution of Technology*. Childe uses evolution to compare human cultural changes to mutations in animal species, and argues that research on prehistoric archaeology demonstrates beyond doubt "the continuous improvement made by humanity since its initial appearance on earth, [and] suggest[s] that what the historian called progress was known to the zoologist as *evolution*." Cited in Bassala, *The Evolution of Technology*, 213–14.

55 McLuhan, *Understanding Media*, 64.

56 Penny, "The Darwin Machine," 61.

57 Baudrillard, cited in Selzer, *Bodies and Machines*, 121.

58 Woodward, "From Virtual Cyborgs to Biological Time Bombs," 50.

59 See Romanyshyn, *Technology as Symptom and Dream*, 3. This reiterates the concept of Gaia; for Lovelock, Gaia is "stern and tough, always keeping the world warm and comfortable for those who obey the rules, but ruthless in the destruction of those who transgress. Her unconscious goal is a planet fit for life. If humans stand in the way of this, we shall be eliminated with as little pity as would be shown by the microbrain of an intercontinental nuclear missile to its target." Lovelock, "Gaia," 212.

60 See Keller, *Secrets of Life, Secrets of Death*; Blum, *Flesh Wounds*, 214–19.

61 Haraway, *Simians, Cyborgs, and Women*, 150.

62 Berland, "Bodies of Theories, Bodies of Pain"; Ronell, "A Disappearance of Community," 288.

63 Robins, *Into the Image*, 15–16.

64 McLuhan, *Understanding Media*, viii.

65   Virilio, "The Third Interval," 5.
66   Johnson, *Interface Culture*, 23–24.
67   Ibid., 20.
68   Ibid.
69   Arendt, *The Human Condition*.
70   Adam, *Artificial Knowing*, 171.
71   Wise, "Intelligent Agency."
72   Turoff, cited in Rheingold, *The Virtual Community*, 113.
73   Castells, *The Rise of the Network Society*, 359–60.
74   Stone, cited in Wertheim, *The Pearly Gates of Cyberspace*, 26.
75   Hayles, *How We Became Posthuman*, 193.
76   Bradley, *Unfolding a Strategic Space*, 33, 101.
77   See Michelle Kendrick, "Cyberspace and the Technological Real," 145–46.
78   Rheingold, *The Virtual Community*, 286.

postscript

1   As Butler shows in *Gender Trouble*, 143:
      The theories of feminist identity that elaborate predicates of color, sexuality,
      ethnicity, class, and able-bodiedness invariably close with an embarrassed 'etc.'
      at the end of the list. Through this horizontal trajectory of adjectives, these po-
      sitions strive to encompass a situated subject, but invariably fail to be complete.
      This failure, however, is instructive: what political impetus is to be derived from
      the exasperated 'etc.' that so often occurs at the end of such lines? . . . It is the
      supplement, the excess that necessarily accompanies any effort to posit identity
      once and for all. This illimitable *et cetera*, however, offers itself as a new depar-
      ture for feminist political theorizing.
2   See Jansen, *Critical Communication Theory*, for an elaborated discussion of theoreti-
      cal intersections of feminism, cultural studies, poststructuralism, and science and
      technology studies.
3   Grossberg and Hall, "On Postmodernism and Articulation."
4   Wolfe, "Introduction to the New Edition," Michel Serres, *The Parasite*, xvii.
5   Serres with Bruno Latour, *Conversations on Science, Culture, and Time*, cited in
      Wolfe, ibid.
6   Guattari, *Three Ecologies*, 66, 68.
7   John Keane, "Whatever Happened to Democracy?," Ioan Davies Memorial Lec-
      ture, York University, 2003; Terry Eagleton, "From Celts and Catastrophe," Ioan
      Davies Memorial Lecture, York University, 2006. See the Ioan Davies Memorial
      Lecture home page, York University.
8   Berland, "Cat and Mouse"; "Animal and/as Medium."

Acland, Charles. "Histories of Place and Power: Innis in Canadian Cultural Studies."
In Charles Acland and William Buxton, eds. *Harold Innis in the New Century:
Reflections and Refractions.* Montreal: McGill–Queen's University Press, 1999.

Acland, Charles, and William Buxton, eds. *Harold Innis in the New Century: Reflections and Refractions.* Montreal: McGill–Queen's University Press, 1999.

Acorn, Milton. *I've Tasted My Blood: Poems 1956 to 1968.* Edited by Al Purdy. Toronto:
Steel Rail Educational Publishers, 1978.

Adam, Alison. *Artificial Knowing: Gender and the Thinking Machine.* London: Routledge, 1998.

Adams, Eric. "Rods from God: Space-Launched Darts that Strike Like Meteors."
Popular Science website, January 4, 2006 (visited July 20, 2007; printed-out pages
on file with author).

Adams, Michael. *Fire and Ice: The United States, Canada, and the Myth of Converging
Values.* Toronto: Penguin, 2003.

Adorno, Theodor W. *Introduction to the Sociology of Music.* Translated by E. B. Ash-
ton. New York: Continuum, 1976.

———. *Prisms.* Translated by Samuel and Shierry Weber. Cambridge, Mass: MIT
Press, 1983.

Adorno, Theodor, and Max Horkheimer. *Dialectic of Enlightenment.* Translated by
John Cumming. New York: Continuum, 1972.

Agnew, John. "Representing Space: Space, Scale, and Culture in Social Science." In *Place/Culture/Representation*, edited by James Duncan and David Ley. New York: Routledge, 1993.

Anderson, Benedict. *Imagined Communities*. New York: Verso, 1991.

Angus, Ian. *The Border Within: National Identity, Cultural Plurality, and Wilderness.* Montreal: McGill–Queen's University Press, 1995.

———. "Empire and Communication." Paper presented to Canadian Association of Cultural Studies, 2003.

———. "Orality in the Twilight of Humanism: A Critique of the Communication Theory of Harold Innis." *Continuum: The Australian Journal of Media & Culture* 7 (1993): 16–42.

———. "The Paradox of Identity in English Canada." *TOPIA: Canadian Journal of Cultural Studies* 10 (Fall 2003): 23–38.

———. *Primal Scene of Communication: Communication, Consumerism, and Social Movements.* Albany: State University of New York Press, 2000.

Angus, Ian, and Brian Shoesmith. "Dependency/Space/Policy: Dialogues with Harold Innis." *Continuum* 7 (1993), 5–15.

Appadurai, Arjun. "Disjuncture and Difference in the Global Cultural Economy." In *Global Culture: Nationalism, Globalization, and Modernity*, edited by Mike Featherstone. London: Sage, 1990.

Arac, Jonathan, ed. *After Foucault: Humanistic Knowledge, Postmodern Challenges.* New Brunswick, N.J.: Rutgers University Press, 1998.

Arendt, Hannah. *The Human Condition*. 2nd. ed. Chicago: University of Chicago Press, 1998.

Armitage, Kay, Kass Banning, Brenda Longfellow, and Janine Marchessault, eds. *Gendering the Nation: Canadian Women's Cinema.* Toronto: University of Toronto Press, 1999.

Aronowitz, Stanley, Barbara Martinsons, and Michael Menser, eds. *Technoscience and Cyberculture*. New York: Routledge, 1996.

Attali, Jacques. *Noise: The Political Economy of Music.* Translated by Brian Massumi, with Fredric Jameson and Susan McLary. Minneapolis: University of Minnesota Press, 1975.

Atwood, Margaret. *The Animals in That Country.* Toronto: Oxford University Press, 1972.

———. *The Handmaid's Tale.* Toronto: McClelland and Stewart, 1985.

———. *Oryx and Crake.* Toronto: Seal Books, 2004.

———. *Surfacing.* Toronto: General Publication, 1983.

———. *Wilderness Tips.* Toronto: McClelland and Stewart, 1991.

Audley, Paul. *Canada's Culture Industries.* Toronto: James Lorimer, 1983.

Auslander, Philip. *Liveness: Performance in a Mediatized Culture.* London and New York: Routledge, 1999.

Babe, Robert. E. *Canadian Communication Thought: Ten Foundational Writers.* Toronto: University of Toronto Press, 2000.

———. *Telecommunications in Canada*. Toronto: University of Toronto Press, 1990.

Bailey, Peter, ed. *Music Hall: The Business of Pleasure*. Milton Keynes: Open University Press, 1986.

Ball, George. *The Discipline of Power*. Boston: Little Brown, 1968.

Banning, Kass. "A Playing in the Light: Canadianizing Race and Nation." In *Gendering the Nation: Canadian Women's Cinema*, edited by Kay Armitage, Kass Banning, Brenda Longfellow, and Janine Marchessault. Toronto: University of Toronto Press, 1999.

Barglow, Raymond. *The Crisis of the Self in the Age of Information: Computers, Dolphins, and Dreams*. London: Routledge, 1994.

Barnard, Stephen. *On the Radio: Music Radio in Britain*. Milton Keynes: Open University Press, 1989.

Barnes, John. *Mother of Storms*. New York: TOR Books/MacMillan, 1995.

Barney, Darin. "One Nation under Google: Citizenship in the Technological Republic." Hart House Lectures, University of Toronto, 2007.

———. *Prometheus Wired: The Hope for Democracy in the Age of Network Technology*. Chicago: University of Chicago Press, 2000.

Barthes, Roland. *Mythologies*. Translated by Annette Lavers. London: Jonathan Cape, 1972.

———. "On Listening." In *The Responsibility of Forms: Critical Essays on Music, Art, and Representation*. Translated by Richard Howard. New York: Hill and Wang, 1985.

Basalla, George. *The Evolution of Technology*. Cambridge: Cambridge University Press, 1988.

Baudrillard, Jean. *For a Critique of the Political Economy of the Sign*. St Louis, Mo.: Telos Press, 1981.

Bates, Charles, and Fuller, John. *America's Weather Warriors*. College Station: Texas A&M University Press, 1988.

Bauman, Zygmunt. *Globalization: The Human Consequences*. New York: Columbia University Press, 1998.

Beale, Alison. "Harold Innis and Canadian Cultural Policy in the 1940s." *Continuum* 7 (1993): 75–90.

Beck, Ulrich. *What is Globalization?*. Cambridge: Polity, 2000.

Belton, Benjamin Keith. *Orinoco Flow: Culture, Narrative and the Political Economy of Information*. Lanham, Md.: Scarecrow Press, 2003.

Bender, Gretchen, and Timothy Druckrey, eds. *Culture on the Brink: Ideologies of Technology*. Seattle: Bay Press, 1994.

Benedikt, Michael. *Cyberspace: First Steps*. Cambridge, Mass.: MIT Press, 1991.

Beniger, James R. *The Control Revolution: Technological and Economic Origins of the Information Society*. Cambridge, Mass.: Harvard University Press, 1986.

Benjamin, Walter. *Illuminations*. Translated by Harry Zohn. New York: Schocken Books, 1968.

Bennett, Tony. *Culture: A Reformer's Science*. London: Sage, 1998.

———. *Marxism and Form*. London: Methuen, 1980.

Bennett, Tony, Lawrence Grossberg, and Simon Frith, eds. *Rock and Popular Music: Politics, Policies, Institutions*. London: Routledge, 1993.

Berland, Jody. "Bodies of Theories, Bodies of Pain: Some Silences." In *Feminism— Art—Theory: An Anthology 1968–2000*, edited by Hilary Robinson. Oxford: Blackwell, 2001.

———. "Culture Re/Percussions: The Social Production of Music Broadcasting in Canada." Ph.D. diss., York University, 1986.

———. "Free Trade and Canadian Music: Level Playing Field or Scorched Earth?" *Cultural Studies* 5 (1991): 317–25.

———. "Nationalism and the Modernist Legacy: Dialogues with Innis." In *Capital Culture: A Reader on Modernist Legacies, State Institutions, and the Value(s) of Art*, edited by Jody Berland and Shelley Hornstein. Montreal: McGill–Queen's University Press, 2000.

———. "On 'Reading' the Weather." *Cultural Studies* 8 (1994): 99–114.

———. "Politics after Nationalism, Culture after Culture." *Canadian Journal of American Studies* 23 (1997): 35–50.

———. "Radio Space and Industrial Time: The Case of Music Formats." In *Critical Cultural Policy Studies: A Reader*, edited by Justin Lewis and Toby Miller. Oxford: Blackwell, 2003.

———. "Sound, Image, and Social Space: Music Video and Media Reconstruction." In *Sound and Vision: The Music Video Reader*, edited by Simon Frith, Andrew Goodwin, and Lawrence Grossberg. London: Routledge, 1993.

———. "Towards a Creative Anachronism: Radio and Sound Government." *Public* 8 (1992): 9–21.

Berland, Jody, and Shelley Hornstein, eds. *Capital Culture: Modernist Legacies, State Institutions, and the Value(s) of Art*. Montreal: McGill–Queen's University Press, 2000.

Berland, Jody, and Sarah Kember. "Editorial: Technoscience." *New Formations* 29 (1996): v–vii.

Berland, Jody, and Will Straw. "Getting Down to Business: Cultural Politics and Policies in Canada." In *Communications in Canadian Society*, edited by Benjamin D. Singer. Scarborough: Nelson Canada, 1991. Rev. ed. 1994.

Berland, Jody, Will Straw, and David Tomas, eds. *Theory Rules: Art as Theory, Theory as Art*. Toronto: YYZ Books and University of Toronto Press, 1996.

Berlant, Lauren G. *The Queen of America Goes to Washington: Essays on Sex and Citizenship*. Durham, N.C.: Duke University Press, 1997.

Berton, Pierre. *Hollywood's Canada: The Americanization of Our National Image*. Toronto: McLelland and Stewart, 1975.

Bhabha, Homi, ed. *Nation and Narration*. London: Routledge, 1990.

Bird, Jon, Barry Curtis, Tim Putnam, George Robertson, and Lisa Tickner, eds. *Mapping the Futures: Local Cultures, Global Change*. London: Routledge, 1993.

Bird, Roger, ed. *Documents of Canadian Broadcasting*. Ottawa: Carleton University Press, 1988.

Blaise, Clark. "The Border as Fiction." *Borderlands Monograph Series*, no. 4. Orono, Maine: Borderlands, 1990.

Bloustien, Gerry, Margaret Peters, and Susan Luckman, eds. *Sonic Synergies: Music, Technology, Community, Identity*. Aldershot: Ashgate, 2008.

Blum, Virginia. *Flesh Wounds: The Culture of Cosmetic Surgery*. Berkeley: University of California Press, 2003.

Bourdieu, Pierre. "The Aristocracy of Culture." Reprinted in *Media, Culture, and Society: A Critical Reader*, edited by Richard Collins, James Curran, Nicholas Garnham, Paddy Scannel, Phillip Schlesinger, and Colin Sparks. London: Sage, 1986.

――――. *Distinction: A Social Critique of the Judgement of Taste*. Translated by Richard Nice. London: Routledge, 1989.

Bradby, Barbara. "Lesbians and Popular Music: Does It Matter Who Is Singing?" In *Popular Music: Style and Identity*, edited by Will Straw, Stacey Johnson, Rebecca Sullivan, and Paul Friedlander. Montreal: IASPM, 1995.

Bradley, Dale. "Unfolding a Strategic Space: A Discursive Analysis of Cyberspace's Power Relations." Ph.D. thesis, York University, 1998.

Braman, Sandra. "Trade and Information Policy." In *Critical Cultural Policy Studies: A Reader*, edited by Justin Lewis and Toby Miller. Oxford: Blackwell, 2003.

Brecht, Bertolt. *Brecht on Theatre: The Development of an Aesthetic*. Edited and Translated by John Willett. London: Eyre Methuen, 1964.

――――. "Radio as a Means of Communication: A Talk on the Function of Radio." Translated by Stuart Hood. *Screen* 20 (Winter 1979–80): 24–28.

Briggs, Asa. *Serious Pursuits: Communications and Education*. Vol. 3, *Collected Essays of Asa Briggs*. Champaign: University of Illinois Press, 1991.

Brin, David. *Earth*. New York: Bantam Spectra, 1990.

Brodie, Janine. *Politics on the Margin: Restructuring and the Canadian Women's Movement*. Halifax: Fernwood Publishing, 1995.

Brooker-Gross, Susan. "The Changing Concept of Place in the News." In *Geography, the Media, and Popular Culture*, edited by Jacquelin Burgess and John Gold. London: Croom Helm, 1985.

Brown, Nicholas, Michael Hardt, Antonio Negri, and Imre Szeman. "The Global Coliseum: On Empire." *Cultural Studies* 16 (2002): 177–92.

Brown, Russell. "Borderlines and Borderlands in English Canada: The Written Line." *Borderlands Monograph Series*, no. 4. Orono, Maine: Borderlands, 1990.

Bruneau, William. "Shall We Perform or Shall We Be Free?" In *The Corporate Campus: Commercialization and the Dangers to Canada's Colleges and Universities*, edited by James L. Turk. Toronto: Lorimer, 2000.

Brunsdon, Charlotte. *The Feminist, the Housewife, and the Soap Opera*. Oxford: Oxford University Press, 1983.

Burchell, Graham, Colin Gordon, and Peter Miller, eds. *The Foucault Effect: Studies in Governmentality*. Chicago: University of Chicago Press, 1991.

Burgess, Jacquelin, and John R. Gold, eds. *Geography, the Media, and Popular Culture*. London: Croom Helm, 1985.

Burnett, Robert. *The Global Jukebox: The International Music Industry*. London: Routledge, 1996.

Butler, Judith. *Gender Trouble: Feminism and the Subversion of Identity*. New York: Rutledge, 1990.

Caldicott, Helen, and Craig Eisendrath. *War in Heaven: The Arms Race in Outer Space*. New York: New Press, 2007.

Calinescu, Matei. *Five Faces of Modernity*. Durham, N.C.: Duke University Press, 1987.

Canada. Royal Commission on National Development in the Arts, Letters, and Sciences. *Massey Commission or Massey-Levesque Commission Report*. Ottawa: King's Printer, 1951.

———. *Vital Links: Canadian Cultural Industries*. Ottawa: Government of Canada, Department of Communications, 1987.

Canadian Heritage. "Canada Music Fund: Tomorrow Starts Today." *Canadian Heritage* website (visited July 6, 2004; printed-out pages on file with author).

Careless, James. "Canadian Radio Networks: A Service for Budget-Conscious Broadcasters." *Broadcaster* (November 1990): 6–7.

———. *Careless at Work: Selected Canadian Historical Studies*. Toronto: Dundurn Press, 1990.

Carey, James W. "Canadian Communication Theory." In *Studies in Canadian Communication*, edited by Gertrude Robinson and Donald Theall. Montreal: McGill University Studies in Communication, 1975.

———. *Communication as Culture: Essays on Media and Society*. Boston: Unwin and Hyman, 1989.

———. "Harold Adams Innis and Marshall McLuhan." In *McLuhan Pro and Con*, edited by Raymond Rosenthal. Baltimore: Penguin, 1968.

Carter, Paul. *The Road to Botany Bay: An Essay in Spatial History*. London: Faber and Faber, 1987.

Castells, Manuel. *The Rise of the Network Society*. Oxford: Basil Blackwell, 1996.

Cavell, Richard. *McLuhan in Space: A Cultural Geography*. Toronto: University of Toronto Press, 2003.

———. "Theorizing Canadian Space: Postcolonial Articulations." In *Canada: Theoretical Discourse / Discours theoriques*, edited by Terry Goldie, Carmen Lambert, and Rowland Lorimer. Montreal: Association for Canadian Studies, 1994.

Chanan, Michael. *Repeated Takes: A Short History of Recording and Its Effects on Music*. London: Verso, 1995.

Charland, Maurice. "Technological Nationalism." *Canadian Journal of Political and Social Theory* 10 (1985): 196–220.

Chatterjee, Partha. *The Nation and Its Fragments: Colonial and Postcolonial Histories.* Princeton: Princeton University Press, 1993.

Cherney, Brian. *Harry Somers.* Toronto: University of Toronto Press, 1975.

Childe, Vere Gordon. *Man Makes Himself.* 1979. New York: New American Library, 1983.

Chow, Rey. *The Protestant Ethnic and the Spirit of Capitalism.* New York: Columbia University Press, 2002.

Clarke, George Eliot. *"What Was Canada." Is Canada Postcolonial?: Unsettling Canadian Literature,* edited by Laura Moss. Waterloo, Ontario: Wilfrid Laurier University Press, 2003.

Clement, Wallace, and Leah F. Vosko. *Changing Canada: Political Economy as Transformation.* Montreal: McGill–Queen's University Press, 2003.

Clifford, James. "On Collecting Art and Culture." In *The Cultural Studies Reader,* edited by Simon During. New York: Routledge, 1999.

Cohen, Sara. "Localizing Sound." In *Popular Music: Style and Identity,* edited by Will Straw, Stacey Johnson, Rebecca Sullivan, and Paul Friedlander. Montreal: IASPM, 1995.

Coker, Christopher. *The Future of War: The Re-Enchantment of War in the Twenty-First Century.* Oxford: Blackwell Publishing, 2004.

Colilli, Paul. *The Angel's Corpse.* New York: St Martin's Press, 1999.

Collins, Richard. *Culture, Communication, and National Identity: The Case of Canadian Television.* Toronto: University of Toronto Press, 1990.

Colombo, John R. "A Canadian Is Somebody Who." In *Splitting Images: Contemporary Canadian Ironies,* edited by Linda Hutcheon. Don Mills, Ontario: Oxford University Press, 1991.

Compagnon, Antoine. *The Five Paradoxes of Modernity.* Translated by Franklin Philip. New York: Columbia University Press, 1994.

Conley, Verena Andermatt, ed. *Rethinking Technologies.* Minneapolis: University of Minnesota Press, 1993.

Conway, John F. "Canadians Who Trust Our Secret Police Should Think Again." *The CCPA Monitor: Economic, Social, and Environmental Perspectives* 31 (2006): 1, 5.

Cook, Ramsay. "Cultural Naturalism in Canada: A Historical Perspective" in *Canadian Cultural Nationalism: The Fourth Lester B. Pearson Conference on the Canada–United States Relationship,* edited by Janice L. Murray. New York: New York University Press for the Canadian Institute of International Affairs and the Council on Foreign Relations, 1977.

Crane, Jon. "Mainstream Music and the Masses." *Journal of Communication Inquiry* 10 (1986): 66–70.

Crawford, Isabella Valancy. *Selected Stories of Isabella Valancy Crawford.* Edited and introduced by Penny Petrone. Ottawa: University of Ottawa Press, 1975.

Crawley, Patrick. "The Canadian Difference in Media: or, Why Harold Innis' Strategy for Culture is More Relevant Today than Ever Before." *Cinema Canada,* June 1986: 19–23.

Crean, Susan. *The CBC and the Arts. A Report on the Involvement of the CBC English Service Division and the Arts Community.* Toronto: CBC, 1974.

Crisell, Andrew. *Understanding Radio.* London: Routledge, 1994.

Crocker, Stephen. "Hauled Kicking and Screaming into Modernity: Temporality and Non-Synchronicity in Post-War Newfoundland." *TOPIA: Canadian Journal of Cultural Studies* 3 (2000): 81–94.

Crosby, Ann Denholm. *Dilemmas in Defence Decision-Making: Constructing Canada's Role in NORAD, 1958–96.* London: MacMillan Press; New York: St. Martin's Press, 1998.

Cruickshank, Julie. *The Social Life of Stories: Narrative and Knowledge in the Yukon Territory.* Vancouver: University of British Columbia Press, 1998.

Czitrom, Daniel. *Media and the American Mind: from Morse to McLuhan.* Chapel Hill: University of North Carolina Press, 1982.

Da Silva, Marcello, and Praco Gomes. "Determining Heights and Altitudes for RF Sites." *Broadcast Engineering* website, March 1, 2000 (visited May 2006; printed-out pages on file with author).

David, Charles-Philippe. "All-out Defence in the Nuclear Age." Canadian Centre for Arms Control and Disarmament / Centre canadien pour le côntrole des armements et le désarmement. *Canadian Perspectives on the Strategic Defense Initiative,* Issue Brief no. 3 (1985).

Day, Richard. "Constructing the Official Canadian: A Genealogy of the Mosaic Metaphor in State Policy Discourse." *TOPIA: Canadian Journal of Cultural Studies* 2 (1998): 42–66.

Day, Timothy. *A Century of Recorded Music: Listening to Musical History.* New Haven, Conn.: Yale University Press, 2000.

Dean, Misao. "Canadian Vulgar Nationalism in the Postmodern Age." In *CANADA: Theoretical Discourse / Discours théoretique,* edited by Terry Goldie, Carmen Lambert, and Rowland Lorimer. Montreal: Association for Canadian Studies, 1994.

Debray, Regis. *Transmitting Culture.* Translated by Erich Rauth. New York: Columbia University Press, 2000.

De Certeau, Michel. *The Practice of Everyday Life.* Translated by Stephen Rendall. Berkeley: University of California Press, 1984.

Defense R&D Canada. *Looking Forward Staying Ahead 2002: Building on R&D Successes for Our Forces.* Ottawa: Defence R&D Canada, 2002.

De Kerckhove, Derrick. *Connected Intelligence: The Arrival of the Web Society.* Toronto: Somerville House, 1997.

De Lauretis, Teresa. *Technologies of Gender: Essays on Theory, Film, and Fiction.* Bloomington: Indiana University Press, 1987.

Der Derian, James. *Antidiplomacy: Spies, Terror, Speed, and War.* Cambridge: Blackwell, 1992.

Dere, William Ging Wee. "Presentation to the Nova Scotia Human Rights Conference: Proceedings of the United Nations and Human Rights Conference (Halifax), 9 December 1995." *Asian Canadian* website (visited July 20, 2007; printed-out pages on file with author).

Devereux, Cecily. " 'Canadian Classic' and 'Commodity Export': The Nationalism of 'Our' *Anne of Green Gables*." In *Cultural Subjects*, edited by Alan J. Gedalof. Toronto: Nelson, 2004.

Dexter, Gail. "Yes, Cultural Imperialism, Too." In *Close the 49th Parallel*, edited by Ian Lumsden. Toronto: University of Toronto Press, 1970.

Diamond, Beverley. "Gender, Music, Nation." Unpublished manuscript, 2000.

Diamond, Beverley, and Robert Witmer, eds. *Canadian Music: Issues in Hegemony and Identity*. Toronto: Canadian Scholars' Press, 1995.

Dickason, Olive P. *The Myth of the Savage, and the Beginnings of French Colonialism in the Americas*. Edmonton: University of Alberta Press, 1984.

Doern, G. Bruce, and John Kirton. "Foreign Policy." In *Border Crossings: The Internationalization of Canadian Public Policy*, edited by G. Bruce Doern, Leslie A. Pal, and Brian W. Tomlin. Toronto: Oxford University Press, 1996.

Doern, G. Bruce, Leslie A. Pal, and Brian W. Tomlin, eds. *Border Crossings: The Internationalization of Canadian Public Policy*. Toronto: Oxford University Press, 1996.

Dorland, Michael. "The Expected Tradition: Innis, State Rationality, and the Governmentalization of Communication." *TOPIA: Canadian Journal of Cultural Studies* 1 (1997): 7–21.

———. "Policing Culture: Canada, State Rationality and the Governmentalization of Communication." In *Capital Culture: Modernist Legacies, State Institutions and the Value(s) of Art*, edited by Jody Berland and Shelley Hornstein. Montreal: McGill–Queen's University Press, 1998.

Dowler, Kevin. "The Cultural Industry Policy Apparatus." In *The Cultural Industries in Canada*, edited by Michael Dorland. Toronto: James Lorimer, 1996.

DuBois, W. E. B. *The Souls of Black Folk: Essays and Sketches*. Chicago: A. C. McLurg, 1908.

Duos, Rene. *Mirage of Health*. New York: Bell Tower, 1993.

Duffet, Mark. "Going Down Like a Song: National Identity, Global Commerce, and the Great Canadian Party." *Popular Music* 19 (2000): 1–11.

Du Gay, Paul, ed. *Production of Culture / Cultures of Production*. Thousand Oaks, Calif.: Sage in association with Open University, 1987.

Du Gay, Paul, and Stuart Hall. *Doing Cultural Studies: The Case of the Sony Walkman*. Thousand Oaks, Calif.: Sage, 1997.

During, Simon, ed. *The Cultural Studies Reader*. New York: Routledge, 1999.

Eagleton, Terry. "From Celts to Catastrophe." Ioan Davies Memorial Lecture, York University, 2003. Ioan Davies Memorial website, York University.

———. *The Idea of Culture*. Malden, Mass.: Blackwell, 2000.

———. "Nationalism: Irony and Commitment." In *Nationalism, Colonialism, and Literature*, edited by Terry Eagleton, Fredric Jameson, and Edward Said. Minneapolis: University of Minnesota Press, 1990.

Eamen, Ross. *Channels of Influence: CBC Audience Research and the Canadian Public.* Toronto: University of Toronto Press, 1994.

Eisler, Hans, and Theodor Adorno. *Composing for the Films.* London: Continuum, 2007.

Ellis, David. *Evolution of the Canadian Broadcasting System: Objectives and Realities, 1928–1968.* Ottawa: Ministry of Supply and Services Canada, 1979.

Ellis, John. *Visible Fictions: Cinema, Television, Video.* London: Routledge, 1982.

Ellul, Jacques. *The Technological Society.* Translated by John Wilkinson. New York: Vintage, 1964.

Elmer, Greg. "Promotional Events in Peculiar Places: Persistent Disasters and Polar Beach Parties." *TOPIA: Canadian Journal of Cultural Studies* 5(2001): 20–32.

Emberly, Peter. "Introduction." In *Lament for a Nation,* by George Grant. Ottawa: Carleton University Press, 1995.

Escobar, Arturo. "Welcome to Cyberia: Notes on the Anthropology of Cyberculture." In *Cyberfutures: Culture and Politics on the Information Superhighway,* edited by Ziauddin Sardar and Jerome R. Ravetz. New York: New York University Press, 1996.

Fanon, Frantz. *Black Skin, White Masks.* New York: Grove Press, 1967.

———. *A Dying Colonialism.* New York: Grove Press, 1965.

Fawcett, Brian. *Cambodia: A Book for People Who Find Television Too Slow.* Vancouver: Pulp Press, 1986.

Featherstone, Mike, ed. *Global Culture: Nationalism, Globalization, and Modernity.* A special issue of *Theory, Culture, and Society.* London: Sage, 1990.

Featherstone, Mike, and Scott Lash, eds. *Spaces of Culture: City—Nation—World.* London: Sage, 1999.

Federated Women's Institute of Canada. Home page. *FWIA Welcome* (visited July 28, 2003; printout on file with author).

Fenster, Mark. "Two Stories: Where Exactly is the Local?" In *Popular Music: Style and Identity,* edited by Will Straw, Stacey Johnson, Rebecca Sullivan, and Paul Friedlander. Montreal: IASPM, 1995.

Fischer, Hans-Dietrich. "Entertainment: An Underestimated Central Function of Communication." In *Entertainment: A Cross-Cultural Examination,* edited by Heinz-Dietrich Fischer and Stefan Reinhard Melnik. New York: Hastings House, 1979.

Flaherty, David H., and Frank E. Manning, eds. *The Beaver Bites Back? American Popular Culture in Canada.* Montreal: McGill–Queen's University Press, 1993.

Ford, Clifford. *Canada's Music: A Historical Survey.* Agincourt, Ontario: GLP Press, 1982.

Foster, Frank. *Broadcasting Policy Development.* Ottawa: Franfost Communications, 1982.

Foucault, Michel. *Discipline and Punish: The Birth of the Prison.* Translated by Alan Sheridan. New York: Vintage Books, 1977.

———. *The History of Sexuality*, Volume 1. Translated by Robert Hurley. New York: Vintage Books, 1990.

———. *Language, Counter-Memory, Practice*. Ithaca: Cornell University Press, 1977.

———. "Of Other Spaces." In *The Visual Culture Reader*, edited by Nicholas Mirzoeff. 2nd ed. London: Routledge, 2002.

———. *Power: Essential Works of Foucault, 1954–1984*, Volume 3. Edited by James D. Faubion, with Robert Hurley, Paul Rabinow, Colin Gordon. New York: New Press, 2000.

———. *Power/Knowledge: Selected Interviews and Other Writings, 1972–1977*. New York: Harvester Press, 1980.

Fowke, Edith Fulton. *Canadian Folklore*. Toronto: University of Toronto Press, 1988.

Fowkes, Katherine. *Giving up the Ghost: Spirits, Ghosts, and Angels in Mainstream Comedy Films*. Detroit: Wayne State University Press, 1998.

Francis, Daniel. *National Dreams: Myth, Memory, and Canadian History*. Vancouver: Anansi Pulp Press, 1997.

Franklin, Ursula. *The Real World of Technology*. Toronto: CBC / Anansi Press, 1990.

Frederickson, Jon. "Technology and Music Performance in the Age of Mechanical Reproduction." *International Review of the Aesthetics and Sociology of Music* 20 (December 1989): 193–220.

Friesen, Gerald. *Citizens and Nation: An Essay on History, Communication, and Canada*. Toronto: University of Toronto Press, 2000.

Frith, Simon. "Towards an Aesthetic of Popular Music." In *Music and Society*, edited by Richard Leppert and Susan Mclary. Cambridge: Cambridge University Press, 1987.

———. *Music for Pleasure: Essays on the Sociology of Pop*. New York: Routledge, 1988.

Frith, Simon, Andrew Goodwin, and Lawrence Grossberg, eds. *Sound and Vision: The Music Video Reader*. London: Routledge, 1993.

Frye, Northrop. *The Bush Garden*. Toronto: University of Toronto Press, 1977.

———. "Haunted by Lack of Ghosts. Some Patterns in the Imagery of Canadian Poetry." In *The Canadian Imagination: Dimensions of a Literary Culture*, edited by David Staines. Cambridge, Mass.: Harvard University Press, 1976.

———. "The Modern Century," in *The Canadian Imagination: Dimensions of a Literary Culture*, edited by David Staines. Cambridge, Mass.: Harvard University Press, 1976.

Gaddis, William. "Stop Player. Joke No. 4. (1951)." *Nettime Listserv* (posted and visited March 4, 2003; printed-out pages on file with author).

Gagne, Wallace. "Technology and Canadian Politics." In *Nationalism, Technology, and the Future of Canada*, edited by Wallace Gagne. Toronto: MacMillan, 1976.

Gasher, Mike. *Hollywood North: The Feature Film Industry in British Columbia*. Vancouver: University of British Columbia Press, 2002.

Genosko, Gary, ed. *Marshall McLuhan: Critical Evaluations in Cultural Theory*. London; New York: Routledge, 2005.

Gentz, Natascha, and Stefan Kramer. "Introduction." In *Globalization, Cultural Identities, and Media Representations*. Albany: State University of New York Press, 2006.

Gibson, William. *Neuromancer*. New York: Ace Books, 1984.

Giddens, Anthony. *The Constitution of Society: Outline of the Theory of Structuration*. Berkeley: University of California Press, 1984.

Gilbert, Liette, and Mustafa Diceks, "Right to the City: Politics of Citizenship." In *Space, Difference, Everyday Life: Reading Henri Lefebvre*, edited by Kanishka Goonewardena, Stefan Kipfer, Richard Milgrom, and Christian Schmid. London: Routledge, 2008.

Gilroy, Paul. *Against Race: Imagining Political Culture beyond the Color Line*. Cambridge, Mass.: Harvard University Press, 2000.

Gitelman, Lisa. "Media, Materiality, and the Measure of the Digital: Or, The Case of Sheet Music and the Problem of Piano Rolls." In *Memory Bytes: History, Technology, and Digital Culture*, edited by Lauren Rabinovitz and Abraham Geil. Durham, N.C.: Duke University Press, 2004.

Glacken, Clarence J. *Traces on the Rhodian Shore: Nature and Culture in Western Thought from Ancient Times to the End of the Eighteenth Century*. Berkeley: University of California Press, 1973.

Gleick, James. *Faster: The Acceleration of Just About Everything*. New York: Pantheon Books, 1999.

Godard, Barbara. "Notes from the Cultural Field: Canadian Literature from Identity to Hybridity." *Essays on Canadian Writing* 72 (2000): 209–47.

Godlovitch, Stan. *Musical Performance: A Philosophical Study*. London: Routledge, 1998.

Goldie, Terry, Carmen Lambert, and Rowland Lorimer, eds. *Canada: Theoretical Discourse / Discourse Theoriques*. Montreal: Association of Canadian Studies, 1994.

Goldfarb, Michael. "The Rods from God: Are Kinetic-energy Weapons the Future of Space Warfare?" *Weekly Standard* website, June 8, 2005 (visited July 20, 2007; printed-out pages on file with author).

Gordon, Colin. "Governmentality: An Introduction." In *The Foucault Effect: Studies in Governmentality*, edited by Graham Burchell, Colin Gordon, and Peter Miller. London: Harvester Wheatsheaf, 1991.

Gould, Allan. *Anne of Green Gables vs. G.I. Joe: Friendly Fire between Canada and the U.S.* Toronto: ECW Press, 2003.

Gould, Stephen Jay. *Ever Since Darwin: Reflections in Natural History*. New York: Penguin Books, 1977.

Grant, George. *Technology and Justice*. Toronto: Anansi Press, 1986.

———. *Lament for a Nation*. Ottawa: Carleton University Press, 1995.

Gray, Charlotte. *Canada: A Portrait in Letters, 1800–2000*. Toronto: Doubleday Canada, 2003.

Greenblatt, Steven. *Marvelous Possessions: The Wonder of the New World*. Chicago: University of Chicago Press, 1991.

Gregory, Derek. *Geographical Imaginations.* Oxford: Blackwell, 1994.

Grossberg, Lawrence. *We Gotta Get Out of This Place: Popular Conservatism and Postmodern Culture.* New York: Routledge, 1992.

Grossman, Lev. "Invention of the Year: The iPhone." *Time Magazine Online,* November 7, 2007 (visited July 20, 2007; printed-out pages on file with author).

Guattari, Felix. *The Three Ecologies.* Translated by Ian Pindar and Paul Sutton. London: Athlone Press, 2000.

Hable, Ajay, Donna Palmateer Pennee, and J. R. (Tim) Struthers, eds. *New Contexts of Canadian Criticism.* Peterborough, Ontario: Broadview Press, 1997.

Haig, Thomas. "Not Just Some Sexless Queen: Note on 'Kids in the Hall' and the Queerness of Canada." In *Semiotexte's Canadas,* edited by Jordan Zinovitch. New York: Semiotext(e), 1995.

Hall, Stuart. "The Local and the Global: Globalization and Ethnicity." In *Culture, Globalization, and the World System,* edited by Anthony King. Binghamton: State University of New York and MacMillan, 1991.

Hanke, Bob. "Media, Temporality, and Environmentality." Paper delivered at Media Change and Social Theory conference, St. Hugh's College, Oxford University, Oxford, 2006.

———. "McLuhan, Virilio, and Electric Speed in the Age of Digital Reproduction." In *Marshall McLuhan: Critical Evaluations in Cultural Theory.* Volume 3: *Renaissance for a Wired World,* edited by Gary Genosko. New York: Routledge, 2005.

Haraway, Donna. *Simians, Cyborgs, and Women: The Reinvention of Nature.* New York: Routledge, 1991.

Hare, F. K., and M. K. Thomas. *Climate Canada.* Toronto: Wiley Publishers, 1974.

Hardt, Michael, and Antonio Negri. *Empire.* Cambridge, Mass.: Harvard University Press, 2000.

Harley, Brian. "Deconstructing the Map." In *Writing Worlds: Discourse, Text, and Metaphor in the Representation of Landscape,* edited by Trevor Barnes and James Duncan. London: Routledge, 1992.

Harvey, David. *The Condition of Postmodernity: An Enquiry into the Origins of Cultural Change.* Cambridge, Mass.: Blackwell, 1989.

———. "The Geopolitics of Capitalism." In *Social Relations and Spatial Structures,* edited by Derek Gregory and John Urry. London: Metheun, 1985.

———. *Justice, Nature, and the Geography of Difference.* Cambridge, Mass.: Blackwell, 1996.

———. *Spaces of Capital: Towards a Critical Geography.* New York: Routledge, 2001.

———. "The Urban Process under Capitalism." *International Journal of Urban and Regional Research* 2 (1978): 101–31.

Haug, Wolfgang Fritz. *Critique of Commodity Aesthetics: Appearance, Sexuality, and Advertising in Capitalist Society.* Translated by Robert Bock. Minneapolis: University of Minnesota Press, 1986.

Hayles, Katherine. *How We Became Posthuman: Virtual Bodies in Cybernetic, Literature, and Informatics.* Chicago: University of Chicago Press, 1999.

Heidegger, Martin. *The Question Concerning Technology.* New York: Harper and Row, 1977.

Helms, Mary W. *Ulysses' Sail: An Ethnographic Odyssey of Power, Knowledge, and Geographical Distance.* Princeton: Princeton University Press, 1998.

Helmut, Rosing. "Listening Behaviour and Musical Preferences in the Age of Transmitted Music." *Popular Music* 5 (1984): 119–49.

Hennion, Antoine. "The Production of Success: An Anti-Musicology of the Pop Song." In *On Record: Rock, Pop, and the Written Word,* edited by Simon Frith and Andrew Goodwin. New York: Pantheon, 1990.

Hennion, Antoine, and Cecile Meadel. "Programming Music: Radio as Mediator." *Media, Culture & Society* 8 (1986): 281–303.

Henson, Robert. *Television Weathercasting: A History.* London: McFarland, 1990.

Hillis, Ken. *Digital Sensations: Space, Identity, and Embodiment in Virtual Reality.* Minneapolis: University of Minnesota Press, 1999.

Hillmer, Norman, and J. L. Granatstein. *Empire to Umpire: Canada and the World to the 1990s.* Toronto: Copp Clark Longman, 1994.

Hobsbawm, E. J. *Nations and Nationalism since 1780: Programme, Myth, Reality.* Cambridge: Cambridge University Press, 1992.

Hudgins, Edward. *Space: The Free Market Frontier.* Washington: Cato Institute, 2002.

Humphreys, W. J. *Ways of the Weather: A Cultural Survey of Meteorology.* Lancaster, Pa.: Jacques Cattell Press, 1942.

Hutcheon, Linda. *As Canadian as Possible—Under the Circumstances.* Toronto: Robarts Centre for Canadian Studies, 1990.

———. *Splitting Images: Contemporary Canadian Ironies.* Don Mills, Ontario: Oxford University Press, 1991.

Industry, Science, and Technology Canada. *Science and Technology Economic Analysis Review.* Ottawa: Supply and Services Canada 1, 1990.

Innis, Harold A. *The Bias of Communication.* Toronto: University of Toronto Press, 1950.

———. *Empire and Communications.* Toronto: University of Toronto Press, 1951.

———. *Staples, Markets, and Cultural Change: The Collected Essays of Harold Innis.* Edited by Daniel Drache. Montreal: McGill–Queens University Press, 1995.

———. *The Strategy of Culture.* Toronto: University of Toronto Press, 1952.

Internet Movie Database. "The Canadian Conspiracy (1995) (TV)." IMDB website (visited July 20, 2007; printed-out pages on file with author).

Isin, Engin F., and Myer Siemiatycki. "Making Space for Mosques: Struggles for Urban Citizenship in Diasporic Toronto." In *Space, Race, and the Law,* edited by Sharlene Ryzack. Toronto: Between the Lines, 2002.

Isin, Engin F., and Patricia K. Wood. *Citizenship and Identity.* London: Sage, 1999.

Jameson, Frederic. "On Cultural Studies." *Social Text* 34 (1993): 17–52.

———. "Postmodernism, or the Cultural Logic of Late Capitalism." *New Left Review* 146 (1984): 53–92.

———. *The Seeds of Time*. New York: Columbia University Press, 1994.

———. *A Singular Modernity: Essay on the Ontology of the Present*. London: Verso, 2002.

———. "Third-World Literature in the Era of Multinational Capitalism." *Social Text* 15 (1986), 65–88.

Jansen, Sue Curry. *Critical Communication Theory: Power, Media, Gender, and Technology*. Lanham, Md.: Rowman and Littlefield, 2002.

Jay, Martin. " 'The Aesthetic Ideology' as Ideology; or, What Does It Mean to Aestheticize Politics?" *Cultural Critique* (1992): 41–61.

Jelly, Doris H. *Canada: Twenty-Fivee Years in Space*. Montreal: Polyscience Publication, 1988.

Jhally, Sut. "Communications and the Materialist Conception of History," *Continuum* 7 (1993): 161–82.

Johnson, Fred. "Cyberpunks in the White House." In *Fractal Dreams: New Media in Social Context*, edited by Jon Dovy. London: Lawrence & Wishart, 1996.

Johnson, J. S., and K. Jones. *Modern Radio Station Practices*. Belmont, Calif.: Wadsworth, 1978.

Johnson, Steven. *Interface Culture: How New Technology Transforms the Way We Create and Communicate*. New York: Harper Collins, 1997.

Kealy, Edward. "From Craft to Art: The Case of Soundmixers and Popular Music." In *On Record: Rock, Pop, and the Written Word*, edited by Simon Frith and Andrew Goodwin. New York: Pantheon, 1990.

Keane, John. "Whatever Happened to Democracy?" Ioan Davies Memorial Lecture, York University, 2003. Ioan Davies Memorial website, York University.

Keith, Michael, and Steve Pile, eds. *Place and the Politics of Identity*. New York: Routledge, 1993.

Keller, Evelyn Fox. *Secrets of Life, Secrets of Death: Essays on Language, Gender, and Science*. New York: Routledge, 1992.

Kelly, Wayne. *Downright Upright: A History of the Canadian Piano Industry*. Toronto: Natural Heritage / Natural History Inc., 1991.

Kendrick, Michelle. "Cyberspace and the Technological Real." In *Virtual Realities and Their Discontents*, edited by Robert Markely. Baltimore: Johns Hopkins University Press, 1996.

Kern, Steven. *The Culture of Time and Space, 1880–1918*. Cambridge, Mass.: Harvard University Press, 1983.

King, Anthony, ed. *Culture, Globalization, and the World System: Contemporary Conditions for the Representation of Identity*. Binghamton: Department of Art History, State University of New York at Binghamton, 1991.

King, Thomas Hunt. *Inventing the Indian: White Images, Native Oral Tradition, and Contemporary Native Writers*. Ph.D. thesis, English Department, University of Utah.

Kittler, Friedrich. "The History of Communication Media." *On Line: Kunst im Netz / Art in the Network*. Graz: Steirische Kulturinitiative, 1992.

Klare, Michael, ed. *The University-Military-Police Complex: A Directory and Related Documents 1970*. New York: NACLA, 1970.

Koselleck, Reinhart. *Geschichte: Ereignis und Ereignis*. Munich: W. Fink, 1973.

Kraut, Robert, M. Patterson, V. Lundmark, S. Kiesler, T. Mukopadhyay, and W. Scherlis. "Internet Paradox: A Social Technology that Reduces Social Involvement and Psychological Well-Being?" *American Psychologist* 9 (1998): 1017–30.

Kroetsch, Robert. *The Lovely Treachery of Words: Essays Selected and New*. Toronto: Oxford University Press, 1989.

———. *The Struggle for a Canadian Prairie Fiction*. Edmonton: University of Alberta, 1977.

Kroker, Arthur. *Technology and the Canadian Mind: Innis/McLuhan/Grant*. Montreal: New World Books, 1984.

———. "Virtual Capitalism." In *TechnoScience and Cybercultures*, edited by Stanley Aronowitz. New York: Routledge, 1996.

Kuhn, Annette. *Women's Pictures: Feminism and Cinema*. 2nd ed. New York: Verso, 1995.

Lander, Dan. "Radiocastings: Musings on Radio and Art." In *Radio Rethink: Art, Sound, and Transmission*, edited by Daina Augaitus and Dan Lander. Banff Centre: Walter Phillips Gallery, Banff Centre for the Arts, 1994.

Lash, Scott, and Celia Lury. *Global Cultural Industry*. Cambridge: Polity, 2007.

Lash, Scott, Bronislaw Szerszynski, and Brian Wynne, eds. *Risk, Environment, and Modernity: Towards a New Ecology*. London: Sage, 1996.

Lash, Scott, and John Urry. *Economies of Signs and Space*. London: Sage, 1994.

Latour, Bruno. *We Have Never Been Modern*. Translated by Catherine Porter. Cambridge, Mass.: Harvard University Press, 1993.

Lazarus, Neil. *Nationalism and Cultural Practice in the Postcolonial World*. Cambridge: Cambridge University Press, 1999.

Lazlo, Ervin. *The Choice: Evolution or Extinction? A Thinking Person's Guide to Global Issues*. New York: Putnam Books, 1994.

Lee, Albert. *Weather Wisdom: Facts and Folklore of Weather Forecasting*. Chicago: Congdon and Weed, 1976.

Lee, Dennis. *Savage Fields: An Essay in Literature and Cosmology*. Toronto: Anansi, 1977.

Lefebvre, Henri. *Everyday Life in the Modern World*. Translated by Sacha Rabinovitch. New Brunswick, N.J.: Transaction Books, 1984.

———. *The Production of Space*. Translated by Donald Nicholson-Smith. Oxford: Blackwell, 1991.

———. "Space, Social Product, and Use Value." In *Critical Sociology*, edited by J. W. Freiberg. New York: Irvington Publishers, 1979.

———. *The Survival of Capitalism: Reproduction of the Relations of Production*. Translated by Frank Bryant. London: Allison and Busby, 1976.

Lefebvre, Jean Pierre, and Susan Barrowclough. *The Quebec Connection*. London: British Film Institute, 1981.

Lehr, John. "As Canadian as Possible . . . under the Circumstances: Regional Myths of Place and National Identity in Canadian Country Music." *Border/lines* (Spring 1985): 16–19.

Leppert, Richard, and Susan McClary. *Music and Society: The Politics of Composition, Performance, and Reception*. New York: Cambridge University Press, 1987.

Leslie, Esther. *Synthetic Worlds: Nature, Art, and the Chemical Industry*. London: Reaktion Books, 2005.

Levin, Charles. *Jean Baudrillard: A Study in Cultural Metaphysics*. New York: Prentice Hall / Harvester Wheatsheaf, 1996.

Levinson, Thomas. *Ice Time: Climate, Science, and Life on Earth*. New York: Harper and Row, 1989.

Levitas, Ruth. "The Future of Thinking about the Future." In *Mapping the Futures: Local Cultures, Global Change*, edited by Jon Bird et al. London: Routledge, 1993.

Lindsey, George, and Gordon Sharpe. "Surveillance over Canada." Working Paper, Department of National Defence, 1996.

Lipschutz, Ronnie. "Reconstructing World Politics: The Emergence of a Global Civil Society." In *Spaces of Identity: Global Media, Electronic Landscapes, and Cultural Boundaries*, edited by David Morley and Kevin Robins. London: Routledge, 1995.

Lipset, Seymour Martin. "Pacific Divide: American Exceptionalism—Japanese Uniqueness." *International Journal of Public Opinion Research* 5 (1990): 121–66.

Local Radio Workshop. *Nothing Local about It*. London: Comedia Press, 1983.

Loesser, Arthur. *Men, Women, and Pianos: A Social History*. New York: Simon and Schuster, 1954.

Loiselle, Andre. "The Radically Moderate Canadian: Don McKellar's Cinematic Persona." In *North of Everything: English-Canadian Cinema Since 1980*, edited by William Beard and Jerry White. Edmonton: University of Alberta Press, 2002.

Longfellow, Brenda. "The Crisis of Naming in Canadian Film." In *Capital Culture*, edited by Jody Berland and Shelley Hornstein. Montreal: McGill–Queen's University Press, 2000.

Loon, Joost Van. *Risk and Technological Culture: Towards a Sociology of Virulence*. London, New York: Routledge, 2002.

Lorimer, Rowland, and Nancy Duxbury. "Of Culture, the Economy, Cultural Production, and Cultural Producers: An Orientation." *Canadian Journal of Communication* 19 (1994).

Lovelock, James. "Gaia: A Model for Planetary and Cellular Dynamics." In *Gaia: A Way of Knowing Political Implications of the New Biology*, edited by William Irwin. Great Barrington, Mass.: Lindisfarne Press, 1987.

———. *Gaia: A New Look at Life on Earth*. Oxford: Oxford University Press, 2000.

Lukács, Georg. *Essays on Thomas Mann*. New York: Merlin Press, 1964.

Luke, Timothy W. *Capitalism, Democracy, and Ecology*. Urbana: University of Illinois Press, 1999.

Lumsden, Ian, ed. *Close the 49th Parallel: The Americanization of Canada*. Toronto: University of Toronto Press, 1970.

MacDonald, Brian, ed. *Canada's Strategies for Space: A Paradox of Opportunity*. Toronto: CISS, 1983.

MacDonald, Rae MacCarthy. "A Madman Loose in the World: The Vision of Alice Munroe." In *Borderlines and Borderlands in English Canada: The Written Line*, edited by Russell Brown. Orono, Maine: Borderlands Project, 1976.

Mack, Pamela E. *Viewing the Earth: The Social Construction of the Landsat Satellite System*. Cambridge, Mass.: MIT Press, 1990.

Mahon, Rianne. "Canadian Public Policy: The Unequal Structure of Representation." In *The Canadian State: Political Economy and Political Power*, edited by Leo Panitch. Toronto: University of Toronto Press, 1977.

Mahtani, Minelle, and Scott Salmon. "Site Reading? Globalization, Identity, and the Consumption of Place in Popular Music." In *Cultural Subjects: A Popular Culture Reader*, edited by Allan Gedalof, J. Boulter, J. Faflak, and C. McFarlane. Toronto: Thompson, 2005.

Mallin, Samuel. *Art Line Thought*. Dordrecht: Kluwer Academic Publishers, 1996.

Marchak, Patricia. *Ideological Perspectives on Canada*. Toronto: McGraw-Hill Ryerson, 1981.

Marchessault, Janine, ed. *The Mirror Machine*. Toronto: YYZ Press, 1996.

Marshall, Andrew. "Security and Prosperity Partnership of North America (SPP): Security and Prosperity for Whom?" Centre for Research on Globalization website, March 2008 (visited February 1, 2009; printed-out pages on file with author).

Marx, Leo. *The Machine in the Garden: Technology and the Pastoral Ideal in America*. New York: Oxford University Press, 1964.

Massey, Doreen. "A Place Called Home?" *New Formations* 17 (Summer 1992): 3–15.

———. "Power-Geometry and a Progressive Sense of Place." In *Mapping the Futures: Local Cultures, Global Change*, edited by Jon Bird et al. London: Routledge, 1992.

———. *Space, Place, and Gender*. Minneapolis: University of Minnesota Press, 1994.

———. *Spatial Divisions of Labor: Social Structures and the Geography of Production*. London: MacMillan, 1984.

Mattelart, Armand, Xavier Delcourt, and Michelle Mattelart. *International Image Markets: In Search of an Alternative Perspective*. London: Comedia, 1984.

Maxwell, Richard, ed. *Culture Works: The Political Economy of Culture*. Minneapolis: University of Minnesota Press, 2001.

Mazlish, Bruce. *The Fourth Discontinuity: The Co-Evolution of Humans and Machines*. New Haven, Conn.: Yale University Press, 1993.

McBand, Michael, and the Canadian Health Coalition. "Implement Romanow Report Petition." *Petition Online* website (visited July 20, 2007; printed-out pages on file with author).

McBride, Steven, and John Shields. *Dismantling a Nation*. Halifax: Fernwood, 1997.

McCartney, Andra. "Soundscape Works, Listening, and the Touch of Sound." In *Aural Cultures*, edited by Jim Drobnick. Toronto: YYZ Books, 2004.

McCauley, Jon. "Radio's Digital Future: Preserving Public Radio in the Age of New Media." In *Radio Reader: Essays in the Cultural History of Radio*, edited by Michele Hilmes and Jason Loviglio. London: Routledge, 2002.

McDowell, Linda. *Gender, Identity, and Place*. Minneapolis: University of Minnesota Press, 1999.

McGreevy, Patrick. *Imagining Niagara: The Meaning and Making of Niagara Falls*. Amherst: University of Massachusetts Press, 1994.

———. "The Wall of Mirrors: Nationalism and Perceptions of the Border at Niagara Falls." In *Borderlands Monograph Series*, no. 5. Orono, Maine: Borderlands Project, 1991.

McGregor, Gaile. *The Wacousta Syndrome: Explorations in the Canadian Landscape*. Toronto: University of Toronto Press, 1985.

McGuigan, Jim. *Culture and the Public Sphere*. London: Routledge, 1996.

McKegney, Sam. "Second-hand Shaman: Imag(in)ing Indigenity from Le Jeune to Pratt, Moore, and Beresford." *TOPIA: Canadian Journal of Cultural Studies* 12 (2004): 25–40.

McLuhan, Marshall. "Canada: The Borderline Case." In *The Canadian Imagination: Dimensions of a Literary Culture*, edited by David Staines. Cambridge, Mass.: Harvard University Press, 1976.

———. *Essential McLuhan*. Edited by Eric McLuhan and Frank Zingrone. Toronto: House of Anansi Press, 1995.

———. "The Relation of Environment to Anti-Environment." In *Esthetics Contemporary*, edited by Richard Kostelanetz. New York: Prometheus Books, 1978.

———. *Understanding Media: The Extensions of Man*. New York: Penguin Books, 1964.

McLuhan, Marshall, and Eric McLuhan. *Laws of Media: The New Science*. Toronto: University of Toronto Press, 1988.

McMichael, Anthony. J. *Planetary Overload: Global Environmental Change and the Health of the Human Species*. Cambridge: Cambridge University Press, 1993.

Medawar, Peter B. *The Future of Man*. London: Metheun, 1956.

Melody, William, Liora Salter, and Paul Heyer, eds. *Culture, Communication, and Dependency: The Tradition of Harold Adams Innis*. Norwood, N.J.: Ablex Publishing, 1981.

Menzies, Heather. *Fast Forward and Out of Control: How Technology is Changing Your Life*. Toronto: Lorimer, 1991.

Mercer, Colin. "Entertainment, or the Policing of Virtue." *New Formations* 4 (1988): 51–71.

Merrit, Chris. "Crossing the Border: The Canada–United States Boundary." In *Borderlands Monograph Series*, no. 5. Orono, Maine: Borderlands Project, 1991.

Midgley, Mary. *Evolution as Religion: Strange Hopes and Stranger Fears*. London: Story Press, 1985.

Millar, Melanie Stewart. *Cracking the Gender Code: Who Rules the Wired World?* Toronto: Second Story Press, 1998.

Miller, J. R. *Skyscrapers Hide the Heavens: A History of Indian-White Relations in Canada*. 3rd ed. Toronto: University of Toronto Press, 2000.

Miller, Toby. *The Well-Tempered Self*. Baltimore: Johns Hopkins University Press, 1993.

———. *Cultural Citizenship: Cosmpolitanism, Consumerism, and Television in a Neoliberal Age*. Temple University Press, 2007.

Minsky, Marvin. *The Society of Mind*. New York: Simon and Schuster, 1985.

Mitchell, Donald. *Cultural Geography: A Critical Introduction*. Oxford: Blackwell, 2000.

Mitchell, Timothy. *Colonizing Egypt*. Cambridge: Cambridge University Press, 1988.

Mokyr, Joel. *The Lever of Riches: Technological Creativity and Economic Progress*. New York: Oxford University Press, 1990.

Molson Canada. "'I AM Canadian' Rant." Cool Canuck Award website (visited July 20, 2007; printed-out pages on file with author).

Montgomery, Lucy Maud. *Anne of Green Gables*. Toronto: L. C. Page, 1908; New York: Signet Classics, 2003.

Moodie, Susannah. *Roughing It in the Bush* (1854). Edited by Carl Ballstadt. Montreal: McGill–Queen's Press, 1988.

———. *The History of Mary Prince, a West Indian Slave, Related by Herself* (1831). Edited by Moira Ferguson. Ann Arbor: University of Michigan Press, 1997.

Morantz, Alan. *Where is Here?: Canada's Maps and the Stories They Tell*. Toronto: Penguin Canada, 2002.

Morley, David, and Kevin Robins, eds. *Spaces of Identity: Global Media, Electronic Landscapes, and Cultural Boundaries*. London: Routledge, 1995.

Morris, Meaghan. *The Pirate's Fiancée: Feminism, Reading, Postmodernism*. London: Verso, 1988.

Morris, Peter. *Embattled Shadows: A History of Canadian Cinema, 1895–1939*. Montreal: McGill–Queen's University Press, 1978.

Morrison, Kathleen. *Canadians Are Not Americans: Myths and Literary Traditions*. Ann Arbor: University of Michigan Press / Second Story Press, 2003.

Morse, Margaret. *Virtualities: Television, Media Art, and Cyberculture*. Bloomington: Indiana University Press, 1998.

Mosco, Vincent. "Towards a Transnational World Information Order: The Canada-U.S. Free Trade Agreement." *Canadian Journal of Communications*, 15 (1990): 46–53.

Moser, Mary. A., ed. *Immersed in Technology: Art and Virtual Environments*. Banff Centre for the Arts. Cambridge, Mass.: MIT Press, 2000.

Moss, Laura, ed. *Is Canada Postcolonial? Unsettling Canadian Literature*. Waterloo, Ontario: Wilfrid Laurier University Press, 2003.

Mowatt, Farley. *Canada North Now: The Great Betrayal*. With Photographs by Shin Sugino. Toronto: McClelland and Stewart, 1976.

Mowitt, John. "The Sound of Music in the Era of Its Electronic Reproducibility." In *Music and Society: The Politics of Composition, Performance, and Reception,* edited by Richard Leppert and Susan McLary. New York: Cambridge University Press, 1987.

Mulvey, Laura. "Magnificent Obsession." *Parachute* 42 (1986): 6–12.

———. "Visual Pleasure and Narrative Cinema." *Screen* 16 (1975): 6–18.

Mumford, Lewis. *Technic and Civilization.* London: Routledge and Kegan Paul, 1962.

Murphie, Andrew. "The World as Clock: The Network Society and Experimental Ecologies." *TOPIA: Canadian Journal of Cultural Studies* 11 (2004): 117–39.

Murphie, Andrew, Larissa Hjorth, Gillian Fuller, and Sandra Buckley. "Mobility, New Social Intensities, and the Coordinates of Digital Networks." *Fibreculture* 6 (2005) (visited July 20, 2007; printed-out pages on file with author).

Murray, Janice L., ed. *Canadian Cultural Nationalism.* New York: New York University Press, 1977.

Myerson, George. *Heidegger, Habermas, and the Mobile Phone.* Duxford: Icon, 2001.

Negus, Keith. "Producing Pop." In *Production of Culture / Cultures of Production,* edited by Paul Du Gay. London: Sage, 1997.

———. "The Production of Culture." In *Production of Culture / Cultures of Production,* edited by Paul Du Gay. London: Sage, 1997.

Nelson, Joyce. *The Perfect Machine: TV in the Nuclear Age.* Toronto: Between the Lines, 1987.

New, William H. *Borderlands: How We Talk about Canada.* Vancouver: University of British Columbia Press, 1998.

———. *Grandchild of Empire: About Irony, Mainly in the Commonwealth.* Vancouver: Ronsdale Press, 2003.

———. *Land Sliding: Imagining Space, Presence, and Power in Canadian Writing.* Toronto: University of Toronto Press, 1997.

Noble, David. *The Religion of Technology: The Divinity of Man and the Spirit of Invention.* Toronto: Random House, 1997.

O'Hanlan, Michael. *Neither Star Wars nor Sanctuary: Constraining the Military Uses of Space.* Washington: Brookings Institute Press, 2004.

O'Neill, John. "Empire vs. Empire." *Theory, Culture, and Society* 19 (2002): 195–210.

———. *Plato's Cave: Television and Its Discontents.* Cresskill, N.J.: Hampton Press, 2002.

Ord-Hume, Arthur W. J. G. *Pianola: The History of the Self-Playing Piano.* London: George Allen & Unwin, 1984.

Osborne, Peter. *The Politics of Time: Modernity and the Avant-Garde.* New York: Verso, 1995.

———. "Whoever Speaks of Culture Speaks of Administration as Well: Disputing Pragmatism in Cultural Studies." *Cultural Studies* 20 (2006): 33–47.

Ostry, Bernard. *The Cultural Connection: An Essay on Government Policy in Canada.* Toronto: McClelland and Stewart, 1978.

Parker, Andrew, Mary Sommer, and Patricia Yaeger, eds. *Nationalisms and Sexualities.* New York: Routledge, 1992.

Patrick, Lanie. "Global Economy, Global Communication: The Canada-U.S. Free Trade Agreement." In *Communication: For and Against Democracy*, edited by Marc Raboy and Peter Bruck. Montreal: Black Rose Books, 1989.

Patterson, Graeme. *History and Communications: Harold Innis, Marshall McLuhan, and the Interpretation of History.* Toronto: University of Toronto Press, 1990.

Peers, Frank. *The Politics of Canadian Broadcasting, 1920–1951.* Toronto: University of Toronto Press, 1969.

Pennie, Donna Palmateer. "Looking Elsewhere for Answers to the Postcolonial Question." In *Is Canada Postcolonial? Unsettling Canadian Literature*, edited by Laura Moss. Waterloo, Ontario: Wilfrid Laurier University Press, 2003.

Penny, Simon. "The Darwin Machine: Artificial Life and Interactive Art." *New Formations* 29 (1996): 59–68.

Poster, Mark. *The Information Subject.* Amsterdam: G+B Arts, 2001.

Poulantzas, Nicos. *State, Power, Socialism.* London: Verso, 1980.

Purver, Ronald G. *Ballistic Missile Defence and Canada.* Ottawa: Canadian Centre for Arms Control and Disarmament, 1985.

Raboy, Mark. *Missed Opportunities: The Story of Canada's Broadcasting Policy.* Montreal: McGill–Queens University Press, 1990.

Radhakrishnan, Rajagopalan. "Nationalism, Gender, and the Narrative of Identity." In *Nationalisms and Sexualities*, edited by Andrew Parker, Mary Sommer, and Patricia Yaeger. New York: Routledge, 1992.

Razack, Sherene, ed. *Space, Race, and the Law: Unmapping a White Settler Society.* Toronto: Between The Lines, 2002.

Reid, Angus. *Shakedown: How the New Economy is Changing Our Lives.* Toronto: Doubleday Canada, 1996.

Resnick, Philip. *The Masks of Proteus: Canadian Reflections on the State.* Montreal: McGill–Queen's University Press, 1990.

———. *Thinking English Canada.* Toronto: Stoddart Publishing, 1994.

Rheingold, Howard. *The Virtual Community: Homesteading on the Electronic Frontier.* New York: Harper Collins, 1993.

Robbins, James. "What Can We Learn When They Sing, eh . . ." In *Canadian Music*, edited by Beverly Diamond and Robert Witmer. Toronto: Canadian Scholars' Press, 1995.

Robins, Kevin. *Into the Image: Culture and Politics in the Field of Vision.* London: Routledge, 1996.

Roell, Craig H. *The Piano in America, 1890–1940.* Chapel Hill: University of North Carolina Press, 1989.

Romanyshyn, Robert. *Technology as Symptom and Dream.* London: Routledge, 1990.

Ronell, Avital. "A Disappearance of Community" in *Reading Digital Culture*, edited by David Trend. Oxford: Blackwell, 2003.

Rose, Nicholas. "Governing 'Advanced' Liberal Democracies." In *Foucault and Political Reason: Liberalism, Neoliberalism, and Rationalities of Government*, edited by A. Barry, T. Osborne, and N. Rose. Chicago: University of Chicago Press, 1996.

Ross, Andrew. *The Chicago Gangster's Theory of Life: Nature's Debt to Society*. New York: Verso, 1994.

———. *Strange Weather: Culture, Science, and Technology in the Age of Limits*. New York: Verso, 1991.

———. *Universal Abandon?: The Politics of Postmodernism*. Minneapolis: University of Minnesota Press, 1988.

Rothenberg, David. *Wisdom in the Open Air: The Norwegian Roots of Deep Ecology*. Minneapolis: University of Minnesota Press, 1993.

Royal Commissions Studies: A Selection of Essays Prepared for the Royal Commission on National Development in the Arts, Letters, and Sciences. Ottawa: Edmund Cloutier, Printer to the King's Most Excellent Majesty, 1951.

Said, Edward. *Culture and Imperialism*. New York: Vintage Books / Random House, 1993.

———. *Orientalism*. New York: Vintage Books, 1979.

Santos, Boaventura de Sousa. "Towards a Multicultural Conception of Human Rights." In *Spaces of Culture: City, Nation, World*, edited by Mike Featherstone and Scott Lash. London: Sage, 1999.

Sassen, Saskia. *Globalization and Its Discontents: Essays on the Mobility of People and Money*. New York: New Press, 1998.

———. *Losing Control? Sovereignty in an Age of Globalization*. New York: Columbia University Press, 1996.

Saul, John Ralston. *Reflections of a Siamese Twin: Canada at the End of the Twentieth Century*. Toronto: Penguin, 1997.

Sauve, Roger. *Borderlines: What Canadians and Americans Should—But Don't—Know about Each Other ... A Witty, Punchy, and Personal Look*. Toronto: McGraw-Hill, 1994.

Schafer, Murray. *The Thinking Ear: Complete Writings on Music Education*. Toronto: Arcana Editions, 1986.

———. *The Tuning of the World: Toward a Theory of Soundscape Design*. Philadelphia: University of Pennsylvania Press, 1980.

Schecter, Stephen. *Zen and the Art of Postmodern Canada*. Montreal: Robert Davies Publishing, 1993.

Schiller, Herbert. *Culture, Inc.: The Corporate Takeover of Public Expression*. New York: Oxford University Press, 1989.

Schneider, Stephen. *Laboratory Earth: The Gamble We Can't Afford to Lose*. New York: Basic Books, 1997.

Sehdev, Robinder Kaur. "Unsettling the Settler State at Niagara Falls: Reading Colonial Culture through the Maid of the Mist." Ph.D. dissertation, York University, 2008.

———. "Vanishing at the Border." *Australian Critical Race and Whiteness Studies Association E-Journal* 3 (2007).

Seidler, Victor J. "Embodied Knowledge and Virtual Space." In *The Virtual Embodied: Presence/Practice/Technology*, edited by John Wood. London: Routledge, 1998.

Sekyi-Otu, Ato. *Fanon's Dialectic of Experience*. Cambridge, Mass.: Harvard University Press, 1996.

Seltzer, Mark. *Bodies and Machines*. New York: Routledge, 1992.

Semple, Ellen C. *Influences of Geographic Environment on the Basis of Ratzel's System of Anthropo-Geography*. New York: H. Holt, 1911.

Serres, Michel. *Angels: A Modern Myth*. Paris: Flammarion, 1995.

———. *The Parasite*. Translated by Lawrence R. Schehr, with a new introduction by Cary Wolfe. Minneapolis: University of Minnesota Press, 2007.

Shields, Rob. *Places at the Margins: Alternate Geographies or Modernity*. London: Routledge, 1991.

Shove, Elizabeth. *Comfort, Cleanliness, and Convenience: The Social Organization of Normality*. Oxford: Berg, 2003.

Siemerling, Winfried. *The New North American Studies: Culture, Writing, and the Politics of Re/cognition*. New York: Routledge, 2005.

Silverstone, Roger. *Why Study the Media?* London: Sage, 1999.

Sioui, Georges E. *For an Amerindian Autohistory: An Essay on the Foundations of a Social Ethic*. Translated by Sheila Fischman, with a foreword by Bruce G. Trigger. Kingston: McGill–Queen's Press, 1992.

Slade, Giles. *Made to Break: Technology and Obsolescence in America*. Cambridge, Mass.: Harvard University Press, 2006.

Slemon, Stephen. "Unsettling the Empire: Resistance Theory for the Second World." *World Literature Written in English* 30 (1990): 30–41. Excerpted in *Contemporary Postcolonial Theory: A Reader*, edited by Padmini Mongia. New Delhi: Oxford University Press, 1997; and *New Contexts of Canadian Criticism*, edited by Ajay Hable, Donna Palmateer Pennee, and J. R. (Tim) Struthers. Peterborough, Ontario: Broadview Press, 1997.

Small, Christopher. *Musicking: The Meaning of Performing and Listening*. Hanover, N.H.: University Press of New England for Wesleyan University Press, 1998.

Smith, Anthony. *The Geopolitics of Information: How Western Culture Dominates the World*. New York: Oxford University Press, 1980.

Smith, Karen A. "ICE Case Studies No. 39: The Canada–United States Border Dispute." *American University* website (visited July 15, 2008; printed-out pages on file with author).

Smith, Neil. *Uneven Development: Nature, Capital, and the Production of Space*. Oxford: Basil Blackwell, 1991.

Smythe, Dallas. *Dependency Road: Communications, Capitalism, Consciousness, and Canada*. Norwood, N.J.: Ablex, 1981.

Soja, Edward. *Postmodern Geographies: The Reassertion of Space in Critical Social Theory*. New York: Verso, 1989.

Sparke, Penny. *As Long as It's Pink: The Sexual Politics of Taste*. London: Pandora, 1995.

Spence, Martin. "Lost in Space." *Capital and Class* 52 (1994): 51–84.

Spengler, Oswald. *The Decline of the West: Form and Actuality*. Translation and Notes by Charles F. Atkinson. New York: Knopf, 1926.

Spigel, Lynn. "Installing the Television Set: Popular Discourses on Television and Domestic Space, 1948–1955." *Camera Obscura* 16(1988): 11–46.

Staines, David, ed. *The Canadian Imagination: Dimensions of a Literary Culture*. Cambridge, Mass.: Harvard University Press, 1976.

Stamps, Judith. *Unthinking Modernity: Innis, McLuhan, and the Frankfurt School*. Montreal: McGill–Queen's University Press, 1995.

Stares, Paul. *The Militarization of Space: U.S. Policy, 1945–1984*. Ithaca: Cornell University Press, 1985.

Stewart, Sandy. *From Coast to Coast: A Pictorial History of Radio in Canada*. Toronto: CBC, 1985.

Straw, Will. "In and Around Canadian Music." *Journal of Canadian Studies* 35 (2000): 173–84.

Straw, Will, Stacey Johnson, Rebecca Sullivan, and Paul Friedlander, eds. *Popular Music: Style and Identity*. Montreal: IASPM, 1995.

Straw, William. "The English Canadian Recording Industry since 1970." In *Rock and Popular Music: Politics, Policies, Institutions*, edited by Tony Bennet, Simon Frith, Larry Grossberg, John Shepard, and Graeme Turner. London: Routledge, 1993.

Swanson, Frank. "Canadian Cultural Nationalism and the U.S. Public Interest." In *Canadian Cultural Nationalism*, edited by Janice L. Murray. New York: New York University Press, 1977.

Talbott, Steve. "Technology, Alienation, and Freedom: On the Virtues of Abstraction." *Netfuture: Technology and Human Responsibility* 134 (visited October 14, 2003; printed-out pages on file with author).

Taussig, Michael. *Mimesis and Alterity: A Particular History of the Senses*. New York: Routledge, 1993.

Taylor, Charles. *Multiculturalism: Examining the Politics of Recognition*. Princeton: Princeton University Press, 1994.

Terranova, Tiziana. "Digital Darwin: Nature, Evolution and Control in the Rhetoric of Electronic Communication." *New Formations* 29 (1996): 69–83.

Theall, Donald. *The Medium Is the Rear View Window: Understanding McLuhan*. Montreal: McGill–Queen's University Press, 1971.

Theberge, Paul. *Any Sound You Can Imagine*. Hanover, N.H.: University Press of New England, 1997.

Theman, Diane Lynne. "Mental Treasure of the Land: The Idea of Literary Resource Development in Nineteenth-Century English Canada." Ph.D. dissertation, York University, 1996.

Thorner, Thomas, and Thor Frohn-Nielson. "A Country Nourished on Self-Doubt:" *Documents in Post-Confederation Canadian History*. 2nd ed. Peterborough, Ontario: Broadview Press, 2003.

Thwaites, Reuben Gold. *The Jesuit Relations and Allied Documents: Travels and Explorations of the Jesuit Missionaries in North America*. Toronto: McCellend & Stewart, 1925. Reprint. Vol. 7; New York: Pageant Book Company, 1979.

Todd, Jan. *Colonial Technology: Science and the Transfer of Innovation to Australia*. Cambridge: Cambridge University Press, 1995.

Tofts, Darren, Annemarie Jonson, and Alessio Cavellaro, eds. *Prefiguring Cyberculture: An Intellectual History*. Cambridge, Mass.: MIT Press, 1993.

Tomlinson, John. *Culture and Globalization*. Chicago: University of Chicago Press, 1999.

Turk, James L., ed. *The Corporate Campus: Commercialization and the Dangers to Canada's Colleges and Universities*. Toronto: James Lorimer, 2000.

Turner, Fredrick Jackson. *The Frontier in American History*. Reprint. New York: Courier Dover Publications, 1996.

Turner, Margaret. *Imagining Culture: New World Narrative and the Writing of Canada*. Montreal: McGill–Queen's University Press, 1995.

Turrow, Joseph. "A Mass Communication Perspective on Entertainment Industries." In *Mass Media and Society*, edited by James Curran and Michael Gurevitch. New York: Routledge, 1996.

United States of America. Government Accountability Office. Committee on Intergovernmental Affairs. "Bioterrorism: A Threat to Agriculture and the Food Supply." Government Accountability Office website (visited July 20, 2007; printed-out pages on file with author).

Van Wyck, Peter. "Telling Stories." *Semiotic Review of Books* 14 (2004): 3–7.

Virilio, Paul. *Speed and Politics*. Translated by Mark Polizzotti. New York: Semiotext(e), 1977.

———. "The Third Interval: A Critical Transition." In *Rethinking Technologies*, edited by Verena C. Andermatt. Minneapolis: University of Minnesota Press, 1993.

———. *War and Cinema: The Logistics of Perception*. London: Verso, 1989.

Walcott, Rinaldo. " 'Keep On Movin': Rap, Black Atlantic Identities, and the Problem of a Nation." *Black Like Who? Writing Black Canada*. London, Ontario: Insomniac Press, 2003.

Wark, McKenzie. "Third Nature." *Cultural Studies* 8 (1994): 115–32.

Warner, Remi. "Hiphop with a Northern Touch!? Diasporic Wanderings/Wonderings on Canadian Blackness." *TOPIA: Canadian Journal of Cultural Studies* 15 (2006): 45–68.

Washburn, Jennifer. *University, Inc.: The Corporate Corruption of Higher Education*. New York: Basic Books, 2006.

Weber, Max. *The Rational and Social Foundations of Music*. Translated by Gertrude Neuwirth. Carbondale: Southern Illinois University Press, 1958.

Wernick, Andrew. "American Popular Culture in Canada." In *The Beaver Bites Back? American Popular Culture in Canada*, edited by David H. Flaherty and Frank E. Manning. Montreal: McGill–Queen's University Press, 1993.

Wertheim, Margaret. *The Pearly Gates of Cyberspace: A History of Space from Dante to the Internet*. New York: W. W. Norton, 1999.

Whitehead, Mark. "Between the Marvelous and the Mundane: Everyday Life in the Socialist City and the Politics of the Environment." *Environment and Planning D: Society and Space* 23 (2005): 273–94.

Whiteside, Kerry. *Divided Natures: French Contributions to Political Ecology*. Cambridge, Mass.: MIT Press, 2002.

Whitlock, Gillian. "Exiles from Tradition: Women's Life Writing." In *Re-Siting Queen's English: Text and Tradition in Post-Colonial Literatures*, edited by Gillian Whitlock and Helen Tiffin. Amsterdam: Rodopi B. V., 1992.

Whitlock, Gillian, and Helen Tiffin, eds. *Re-Siting Queen's English: Text and Tradition in Post-Colonial Literatures*. Amsterdam: Editions Rodopi B. V., 1992.

Wilden, Anthony. *The Imaginary Canadian*. Vancouver: Pulp Press, 1990.

Williams, Raymond. *Marxism and Literature*. Oxford: Oxford University Press, 1977.

———. *The Politics of Modernism: Against the New Conformists*. London: Verso, 1989.

———. *Problems in Materialism and Culture: Selected Essays*. London: Verso Editions and NLB, 1980.

———. *Television: Technology and Cultural Form*. Glasgow: Fontanta, 1974.

———. *Toward 2000*. London: Chatto and Windus, 1983. Published in United States as *The Year 2000*. New York: Pantheon Books, 1983.

Willis, Anne Marie. *Illusions of Identity: The Art of Nation*. Sydney: Hale & Iremonger, 1993.

Wilson, Ann. "The Death of Princess Diana: Mourning a 'Very British Girl.'" In *Pop Can: Popular Culture in Canada*, edited by Lynne Van Luven and Priscilla L. Walton, Scarborough, Ontario: Prentice Hall Allyn and Bacon Canada, 1999.

Wilson, Peter Lamborn. *Angels*. New York: Pantheon Books, 1980.

Winner, Langdon. *Autonomous Technology: Technics Out-of-Control as a Theme in Political Thought*. Cambridge, Mass.: MIT Press, 1977.

———. *The Whale and the Reactor: A Search for Limits in an Age of High Technology*. Chicago: University of Chicago Press, 1986.

Winston, Brian. *Misunderstanding Media*. Cambridge, Mass.: Harvard University Press, 1986.

Wise, John M. "Intelligent Agency." *Cultural Studies* 12 (1998): 410–28.

Wolfe, Carey. *Animal Rites: American Culture, the Discourse of Species, and Posthumanist Theory*. Chicago: University of Chicago Press, 2003.

Wolin, Sheldon S. "Theory and Practice of Power." In *After Foucault: Humanistic Knowledge, Postmodern Challenges*, edited by Jonathan Arac. New Brunswick, N.J.: Rutgers University Press, 1998.

Wood, John, ed. *The Virtual Reader: Presence/Practice/Technology*. London: Routledge, 1998.

Woodward, Kathleen. "From Virtual Cyborgs to Biological Time Bombs: Techno-criticism and the Material Body." In *Culture on the Brink: Ideologies of Technology*, edited by Gretchen Bender and Timothy Druckrey. Seattle: Bay Press, 1994.

Yeffeth, Glen, ed. *Taking the Red Pill: Science, Philosophy, and Religion in "The Matrix."* Dallas: Benbella Books, 2003.

Yashinsky, Dan. "Eyes on the Street." *Spacing* (Winter–Spring 2007): 14–15.

Žižek, Slavoj. *For They Know Not What They Do: Enjoyment as a Political Factor*. London, New York: Verso, 2002.

Zuboff, Shoshana. *In the Age of the Smart Machine: The Future of Work and Power*. New York: Basic Books, 1988.

JODY BERLAND is an associate professor of humanities at York University. She co-edited *Capital Culture: A Reader on Modernist Legacies, State Institutions, and the Value(s) of Art* (2000) and *Theory Rules: Art as Theory / Theory as Art* (1996) and is the editor of TOPIA: *Canadian Journal of Cultural Studies*.

Library of Congress Cataloging-in-Publication Data

Berland, Jody.
North of empire : essays on the cultural technologies of space / Jody Berland.
p. cm.
Includes bibliographical references and index.
ISBN 978-0-8223-4288-5 (cloth : alk. paper)
ISBN 978-0-8223-4306-6 (pbk. : alk. paper)
1. Canada—Civilization. 2. Canada—Social conditions.
3. Mass media—Social aspects—Canada. 4. Canada—Relations—United States.
5. United States—Relations—Canada. I. Title.
F1021.2.B468 2009
303.48'27107309045—dc22
2009010568